Sir Bill Cash is the Member of P
educated at Stonyhurst College and L
he read History, and has since practised law as a solicitor. He has
been in Parliament for 33 years and was Shadow Attorney-General
and Shadow Secretary of State for Constitutional Affairs. He has
been elected as Chairman of the European Scrutiny Committee of
the House of Commons. *The Spectator* named him Parliamentary
Campaigner of the Year in 1991. As well as being the author of
several books on European affairs, Bill Cash writes regularly for
national newspapers, including *The Times* and the *Daily Telegraph*
and has made frequent appearances on radio and television. John
Bright was his great-grandfather's cousin.

'With this well-researched, well-written and sometimes deeply passionate book, Bill Cash has single-handedly saved one of Britain's greatest statesmen from an ill-deserved obscurity. Often using Bright's own fiery language, he has turned the once-forbidding Victorian granite statue back into a flesh-and-blood fighter for justice and human decency. John Bright was a key figure, perhaps even *the* key figure, in the struggle for democracy in Britain, yet his legacy was largely forgotten until this first-class, encapsulating biography.' — **Andrew Roberts, author of** *Salisbury: Victorian Titan*

'*John Bright* is a major biography about one of the towering politicians of the Victorian era. Bill Cash not only breathes new life into Bright but delivers an entirely fresh view of both the man himself and his stance as the professional scourge of the upper classes. Bright was always his country's greatest critic, and yet also its greatest parliamentarian. This and all the other contradictions that made up Bright's character receive their full due in Cash's nuanced portrait.' — **Amanda Foreman, author of** *A World on Fire* **and** *Georgiana, Duchess of Devonshire*

'Historians will enjoy this fine political portrait.' — **The** *Economist*

'...thoughtful and perceptive...[Bright] would surely have appreciated Cash's intellectually subtle and deftly written work. At last, his extraordinary life has the biography it deserves.' — **George Eaton,** *The New Statesman*

'Bright, a radical rooted in traditional social values, has found a fitting biographer. — *The Times*

'From the campaign for popular democracy to the fate of empire, the American Civil War to the roots of globalisation, John Bright was one of the most influential figures of the nineteenth century. Bill Cash's biography restores Bright not only to his rightful place at the heart of Victorian England but also as one of the creators of the modern age.' — **Graham Stewart, author of** *Burying Caesar: Churchill, Chamberlain and the Battle for the Tory Party*

'Cash's study is not only a useful addition to Bright's historiography but also a timely contribution to the current debate about the conduct and principles of elected politicians.' — *History Today*

JOHN BRIGHT

Statesman, Orator, Agitator

BILL CASH

I.B. TAURIS

LONDON · NEW YORK

For my children,
William, Sam and Laetitia,
and my grandchildren,
Tess, Arizona, Lucas and Frederick

New paperback edition published in 2017 by
I.B.Tauris & Co. Ltd
London • New York
www.ibtauris.com

First published in hardback in 2012 by I.B.Tauris & Co. Ltd

ISBN: 978 1 78453 975 7
eISBN: 978 0 85773 015 2
ePDF: 978 0 85772 083 2

A full CIP record for this book is available from the British Library
A full CIP record is available from the Library of Congress

Library of Congress Catalog Card Number: available

Typeset by 4word Ltd, Bristol, UK
Printed and bound by CPI Group (UK) Ltd, Croydon, CR0 4YY

MIX
Paper from
responsible sources
FSC   FSC® C013604
www.fsc.org

Contents

Illustrations

Text

Plates

Sir Robert Peel. (Carlton Club)

Earl of Derby. (Cash family collection)

Viscount Palmerston. (Cash family collection)

William Ewart Gladstone. (Cash family collection)

Earl Russell. (Cash family collection)

Benjamin Disraeli. (Carlton Club)

Abraham Lincoln. (Cash family collection)

Charles Sumner. (Library of Congress Prints)

Richard Cobden and John Bright. (Rochdale Library)

Gladstone's Cabinet of 1868. This painting is now in Committee Room 14 of the House of Commons. (National Portrait Gallery)

John Bright, Richard Cobden and Michel Chevalier following the signing of the French Commercial Treaty, 1860.
(Cash family collection)

Samuel Lucas. (Walkers Galleries Ltd)

Joseph Chamberlain. (Carlton Club)

Wedding of John Theodore Cash and Margaret Sophia Bright, 1881. John Bright stands next to his daughter, the bride. The author's great-grandparents, William and Rachel Maria Cash, are standing back row, 4th and 5th from left. (Cash family collection)

Acknowledgements

Over the many years of working on this book, I have had help and encouragement from a great number of people. Jo Godfrey and her colleagues at I.B.Tauris have been immensely constructive, perceptive and encouraging in bringing this book to its final form. In particular, I want to put on record my sincere thanks to Miles Taylor for his support, and to Stephen Roberts, Robert Saunders and Graham Stewart, whose specific observations led to a number of important corrections. I have also benefited greatly from conversations with many historians, including Keith Robbins, Amanda Foreman, Andrew Roberts, Alistair Cooke, and historically-minded Members of Parliament, in particular my good friend Richard Shepherd. I am also indebted to numerous former historians of the period, as the bibliography indicates. I would also like to put on record my gratitude for the interest in history and politics I derived from the late Geoffrey Holt, S. J. at Stonyhurst College, and my tutor, the late J. B. Owen of Lincoln College, Oxford.

Richard Clark, who is a direct descendent of John Bright and the custodian of the Bright papers, was immensely helpful at the Clark Archive at Street in Somerset, along with Charlotte Berry and Tim Crumplin, who painstakingly reproduced many of Bright's letters and papers, Duncan Darbishire and family, also descendants, have been most helpful. My thanks go also to Lady Aberconway and Michael McLaren, QC for permission to photograph the portraits of John Bright by Millais and Duval at Bodnant Hall, and to Isobel Crawford for photographing them. These portraits appear on the front and back covers of the book. My thanks also to Mike Wootton for digitizing photographs of Gladstone, Russell, Derby, Abraham Lincoln and Cobden, Bright and Chevalier from our family collection, to Fanny Rush for photographing the portraits of Disraeli, Chamberlain and Peel at the Carlton Club, and to the

Club Secretary, Jonathan Orr-Ewing, for permission to take the photographs.

Although written on an intermittent basis, this book has inevitably invaded parliamentary recesses and weekends and I have enjoyed continuous support and helpful criticism from my wife Biddy and my family, who have had more conversations about John Bright than they might otherwise have reasonably anticipated.

Finally, I owe a debt to my constituents, past and present, for reminding me on a daily basis of the value of the democracy we enjoy, and which John Bright so greatly influenced, with what should be, and must be, its firm foundations in the accountability of Government at Westminster.

Preface

My first engagement with politics of any kind, and the first political
book I ever read, was Benjamin Disraeli's *Sybil: A Tale of Two Nations*.
It was in the last summer of school at Stonyhurst before I went up to
Oxford and read History. There, I had the good fortune to be tutored
by one of the great Namierite historians, J. B. Owen, who taught us
about the development of parliamentary democracy in the mid-
eighteenth century. I discovered around this time that among the five
or so Members of Parliament in past generations of my family, that
John Bright, a Radical and by far the most prominent, was my great-
grandfather's cousin. His political career spanned nearly 50 years of
great historical change during the mid-nineteenth century. This led
to the beginning of my study of the historical development of democracy, not only in terms of Disraeli's Reform Act of 1867, but also of
Bright's part in the movement that led to its enactment, the reasons
for it and its relevance to the present time. Bright put conscience,
conviction, the working man and his country before party or any
personal interest. He was an independent Radical by principle, with a
persistent strain of innate conservatism. He was *in* the Liberal Party
as it evolved but not always *of*, or even *with*, the Liberal Party, especially when, as a prominent Liberal Unionist, he laid the foundations
for the new politics of the twentieth century.

I practised parliamentary and constitutional law for twenty years,
while taking part in local Conservative politics on the ground. In
1984, I was elected to Parliament itself in a by-election as the
Member for Stafford. Parliament has changed greatly since I first
took my seat, and even since I became the Member for Stone in
1997. My interest in Bright has increased since 1984 in inverse
proportion to the decline in the vibrancy, accountability and sovereignty of our Parliament.

When people were seeking the vote in the nineteenth century,
they, and the newspapers they read, took an intense and immediate

interest in the reporting of the daily workings of their own Parliament, for this is what it is. Today, in contrast, it is said that the best way to keep a secret is to make a speech in the House of Commons. MPs in Bright's day were also far less willing to be restricted by the whip system and by the restrictions imposed by procedural devices favouring the Government and the Establishment. There is no doubt that Parliament, in discharging its responsibilities on behalf of the electors, who vote for MPs as their representatives, and in keeping promises made in elections, has changed profoundly, and not for the better.

In part, therefore, this book has been prompted by the extraordinary efforts made by Bright and others in their time to achieve a proper reflection of the wishes of the electorate through household suffrage and parliamentary reform. As I examined his life, however, I became more interested in other aspects of his contribution to the freedoms we now take for granted, and how this can inform us today in a time of great change. I have been working on the outlines and content of the book since the early 1990s. The approaching bicentenary of Bright's birth encouraged me to complete it.

Bright said, 'My life is in my speeches.' This may be true, but his life is also in what he achieved and the legacy he left behind. This is still evident not only in our parliamentary system but also in Bright's contribution to free trade and to Britain's relationship with the USA, to the eradication of slavery, to Irish and foreign affairs, the principles of self-government in what is now the Commonwealth, and his espousal of Liberal Unionism with Joseph Chamberlain towards the end of his political life, having earlier rejected Disraeli's overtures of coalition.

The range of Bright's interests and the impact of his campaigns and political endeavours were recognized by his contemporaries, but later obscured and forgotten. The more I looked at his life, the clearer it became that his speeches and his campaigning deserved a renewed audience because of the combined relevance of all these characteristics to the present day and to show what can, yet, be done. The United Kingdom is now in a time of constitutional and political change, which reflect the challenges of modern society and the present-day media, including fundamental changes to the workings of Parliament itself. These include the unwise, voluntary subordination of Parliament's, and therefore the people's, democratic will (or sovereignty) to decision-making over their daily lives by the European Union, and even more recently to increasing assertions of judicial supremacy by members of the Supreme Court – unthinkable even 40 years ago, and of which Bright would have disapproved greatly.

These would have been impossible to justify against the principles and aspirations of those seeking reform in the earliest days of our modern democracy.[1] What John Bright did was to persuade and convince others that this modern democracy would improve the lot of the working man by engaging him in the political process. He did so by drawing on historical and personal convictions and political will, and translating these into campaigns with an energy and commitment, and on such a scale and range of matters, that has scarcely, if at all, been emulated by any other politician in recent times. He proved that it could be done from the backbenches, despite the Establishment and despite virulent opposition, illustrating that actions do indeed speak louder than words and that, however eloquent his oratory, his legacy was in changing the politics of his time. In today's world, he would have been greatly heartened by the apparently democratic aspirations of the Arab Spring, the election of a black president in the USA, and the formal reconciliation with the Queen's state visit to Ireland in 2011.

It will be for the reader to determine from this book, the extent to which, despite intermittent setbacks, frustration and disappointments, Bright succeeded. In 2009, I came across the marble statue of Bright sculpted for the City of Birmingham in 1888 by Albert Bruce Joy. It was in an iron cage and covered in some form of cement or plaster in a warehouse on the outskirts of Birmingham where superfluous historical artefacts were stored. To their great credit, the city fathers, led by Councillor Mike Whitby, agreed that he should be brought out of his obscurity, and renovated and restored to his rightful place. He now stands where he did originally, at the first-floor entrance of the Birmingham Museum and Art Gallery. A copy of this statue, commissioned by Andrew Carnegie, also stands in the Inner Lobby of the House of Commons. The restoration of the statue is a symbolic reflection of what I hope this book might provide – a reminder of the kinds of values needed today, which John Bright represented and for which he campaigned unstintingly throughout his political life. As his sister, Priscilla, said shortly after his death: 'Great has been the tribute of praise given my brother – but alas! How little do those who joined it follow his example. Where is the moral courage and fidelity to principle which was so much lauded – where do we see them? Not in the House of Commons...'.[2]

Clockwise from bottom left: Bright, Russell, Gladstone, Derby. Centre: Palmerston.

Introduction

He has lived to witness the triumph of almost every great
cause – perhaps I might say of every great cause – to which he had
especially devoted his heart and mind ... for him office had no
attraction ... extraordinary efforts [which] were required to induce
Mr. Bright under any circumstances to become a servant of the
Crown ... it was also his happy lot to teach us moral lessons, and
by the simplicity, by the consistency, and by the unfailing courage
and constancy of his life to present to us a combination of qualities
so moral in their nature as to carry us at once into a higher
atmosphere ... he lifted political life to a higher elevation and to
a loftier standard, and that he has thereby bequeathed to his
country the character of a statesman ... the triumphs of his life are
triumphs recorded in the advance of his country and in the
condition of his countrymen. His name remains indelibly written
in the annals of this Empire.
(W. E. Gladstone, House of Commons,
on the death of John Bright, 29 March 1889)

'Who is John Bright?' This may seem a reasonable question today, but any of the giants of the nineteenth century – Robert Peel, William Ewart Gladstone, Benjamin Disraeli, Lord Salisbury, and even Abraham Lincoln – would simply have been astonished that anyone might need to ask. The influence of John Bright on the politics of their time, both in Britain and abroad, was to them undeniable. Indeed, in 1878, *Punch* published a collection of cartoons of the three Britons whom they deemed to be the greatest statesmen of the age – Disraeli, Gladstone and Bright, and in the famous 'Statesmen' series in *Vanity Fair*, Bright was the third to be profiled.

Bright's political career spanned nearly fifty years during a time of massive industrial, commercial and democratic change. Though not exclusively responsible for the changes that occurred, he certainly acted as an anchor and a catalyst for those demanding reform, driving the arguments forward in line with his uncompromising motto, 'Be just and fear not'. In his alliance with Richard Cobden, and through the Anti-Corn Law League and the Manchester School, he was the most eloquent exponent of the campaign against the Corn Laws, which culminated in their repeal in 1846. To quote Asa Briggs,

> The accession of Bright to the movement brought to its service not only a great orator, who was scathingly effective both in social denunciation and in homely moralizing, but one of the key figures in the unfolding story of nineteenth-century English liberalism.[1]

This also has powerful messages for the twenty-first century. As a member of the Manchester School, Bright advocated restraint in public expenditure and military adventures. He was the foremost opponent of the Crimean War – an unpopular stance at the time, though later vindicated, which led in 1857 to the loss of his seat in Manchester. He soon became the MP for Birmingham, however, and devoted the next decade to his campaign for household suffrage – including improving access to information through the repeal of newspaper duties – which profoundly influenced the Reform Act of 1867. Throughout this period he also maintained a vigorous campaign against the oppression of the tenantry in Ireland, and devoted much of his energies to attacking the aristocratic privilege of the landed class, which made him deeply unpopular with them and with a significant section of Parliament itself, whose seats were dependent on that connection.

This innate belief in fairness, freedom and democracy was also expressed through his admiration for America and that country's political and social systems. As a profound opponent of slavery from his earliest years, and wishing to protect American democracy, he threw his weight behind the cause of the Northern states and Lincoln during the American Civil War – both inside and outside the British Parliament – and was credited with preventing Britain joining the conflict on the side of the South.

In relation to the British Empire, he was a firm advocate of the rights of the local population, and gave great support to the indigenous peoples of India and other colonies. Yet at the heart of this was a devotion to the Westminster Parliament. Indeed, it was Bright who coined the phrase 'England is the mother of Parliaments'. This ultimately led to his breaking with Gladstone and the Liberal Party over Home Rule for Ireland. His subsequent decision to espouse Liberal Unionism during the last phase of his political career, in alliance with Joseph Chamberlain, was in many ways the pathfinder for modern Conservatism.

However, today, Bright is almost forgotten. As has been said, in an analysis of Bright's letters held at the University of Rochester in New York,

> At his death, the *New York Times* and the *London Times* enshrined [John Bright] as one of the unquestionably great statesmen of the nineteenth century. Many contemporaries considered him a more moving and effective speaker than either of the leading Prime Ministers, Disraeli and Gladstone, and Walter Bagehot – one of the shrewdest Victorian political commentators and historians – speculated that Bright would be the one contemporary statesman whose fame and accomplishments transcended the age. Alas for John Bright, for his reputation has virtually disappeared, and he now turns up as one of those innumerable earnest Victorians whose attitudes and achievements we are vaguely conscious of, but whom we can scarcely separate from the mass of his fellows.[2]

This amnesia is mysterious, if not alarming, when one considers the events and the course of history that he influenced and drove, the effects of which are felt even today.

Bright himself did not personally seek adulation for his achievements. By contrast, Disraeli, as Robert Blake so brilliantly exposed in his biography, was preoccupied with the greasy pole. As noted by Bright in his diaries, Disraeli said to Bright, about the House of Commons, 'We come here for fame!'[3] The Irish MP, Justin McCarthy, recounted how

> Bright earnestly insisted that he came there for no purpose of the kind; but he assured me that it was impossible to convince Disraeli that he was serious in the disclaimer. Disraeli ceased to argue the point, and listened with a quiet half-sarcastic smile, evidently quite satisfied in his own mind that a man who could make great speeches must make them with the desire of obtaining fame.[4]

Bright was an outsider. He chose to operate for the most part as a backbencher outside Government, driving events and speaking for the great mass of people excluded and ignored by a parliamentary system still largely dominated by the aristocracy. In this, he was profoundly influenced by his Quaker history. He drew instinctively on the seventeenth century, during which one of his ancestors, John Gratton from Monyash in Derbyshire, had been imprisoned for several years for refusing to take an oath. He believed in liberty of the individual and of choice, and was deeply opposed to any interference with this by the use of privilege or aristocratic influence (in 1849 he called for the abolition of primogeniture and entail) or by religious or other discrimination.

Above all, despite its imperfections, which he sought to address, Bright believed implicitly in the British parliamentary system. In doing so, he rejected any manifestation of absolute power of the kind exercised by the Stuart monarchy in the seventeenth century or by the landed interest. Equally, he rejected any idea of violent revolution, using instead persuasion, argument and massive and sustained public campaigning to achieve his objectives through the very system he sought to reform.

The commercial success of Bright's fellow Quakers in banking and insurance in the City of London, in manufacture and in housing underpinned the nineteenth-century success of Great Britain. As with so many Quakers of his own time, Bright was a practical businessman – in the manufacture of cotton in Rochdale, Lancashire. His business, too, was driven by a simple belief in freedom of choice, and it was because of this that he was initially drawn into politics to combat the iniquities of the Corn Laws and to resist discrimination. In the late 1830s and the 1840s, as a leader of the Anti-Corn Law League with Cobden, he drove forward one of the greatest popular agitations seen in Britain up to that time. Gathering the support of the country through tireless campaigning, he and his fellow Leaguers took their arguments to Westminster – Bright himself being elected as MP for Durham in 1843, drawing attention to the unnecessary poverty and suffering caused by the protectionist policies of successive Governments. Bright and Cobden believed implicitly in freedom of the marketplace and trade as the best means of achieving growth and prosperity by the use of capital and business organization. Their efforts came to fruition in 1846, when Peel was converted to their cause and repealed the Corn Laws.

After this victory, the next logical step for Bright was freedom of choice in the democratic marketplace. He launched the second, and arguably the greatest, campaign of his career – for parliamentary reform – in October 1858, as the newly elected Member for Birmingham. Taking one step at a time, in line with his innate sense of practicality, he sought to enfranchise the working man and empower millions of new voters to elect their representatives to the Westminster Parliament, where decisions regarding the nation were made. Over the next ten years he would skilfully negotiate the tricky path towards reform, avoiding the revolutionary tendencies of those such as Karl Marx, and drawing out the common ground between such disparate groups as the Chartists, the Reform League and the Reform Union. As the spearhead of parliamentary reform, Bright raised the voice of the people to a pitch that could not be ignored through sustained campaigning and peaceful agitation. At the same time, he took on his stubborn, aristocratic opponents in the House of Commons in impassioned oratorical battles, driving forward the arguments for reform with a power that culminated in an intriguing and influential cross-party relationship with Disraeli. The full extent of this influence, which led to the passing of the Reform Act of 1867 and which was meted out quietly yet forcefully from the Liberal backbenches and in private correspondence, is explored in Chapter 4.

The repeal of the Corn Laws and the Reform Act of 1867 may have been the greatest triumphs of Bright's parliamentary career – and those to which the history books give most weight – but the effects of his fight for the freedom of men and nations can be seen throughout the nineteenth century and beyond. Living by the practical application of 'Be just and fear not', he battled oppression and monopoly wherever he found them, whether against slavery in the USA, the abuse of the tenantry in Ireland, the misuse of power by the creation of monopolies in trade, overly-centralized political power, or unreasonable public expenditure.

These battles were often fought at great personal cost. He lost his seat in Manchester in the 1857 general election because of his uncompromising opposition to Palmerston's policy in the Crimea. Not strictly speaking a pacifist, he repudiated what he saw as unnecessary wars, a stance that often proved unpopular in the heyday of the British Empire. While he considered some conflicts unavoidable – he strongly supported the North in the American Civil War, and the suppression of the Indian Mutiny – he believed that the expenditure of blood and treasure in unnecessary jingoistic engagements such as the Crimean War could never be justified. Whatever was done had not merely to be justified but had also to be just.

Bright's stance during the American Civil War would bring him hardship and praise in equal measure. His business all but ground to a halt because of his refusal to use slave-grown cotton in his mills. In this, he had the support of his workpeople, who willingly made great sacrifices on behalf of the beleaguered slaves, and many elsewhere.

His steadfast support for Lincoln, the North and the slaves was demonstrated in his speeches to the English people and in the House of Commons, often in the face of significant opposition, even by leading British statesmen such as Gladstone, who supported the Confederate cause. These speeches, and his public letters regarding the conflict, were reported widely in American newspapers.

Throughout the American Civil War, and for over a decade before it, Bright kept up an unwavering stream of correspondence with leading Americans, including those in Lincoln's inner circle and key diplomats. Bright's advice and support was deeply appreciated by his correspondents. Furthermore, in championing freedom for the slaves, the force of Bright's moral arguments won over his audience at home, thereby avoiding the prospect of England joining the war on the side of the Confederacy, and he influenced Lincoln significantly when he was considering the Emancipation Proclamation.

Bright's insistence on the principle of freedom was also reflected in his attitudes towards self-government in the Empire and in Ireland. Wherever he saw injustice – in Africa, Canada, India or Jamaica – he intervened in Parliament on behalf of native populations. Ireland raised in him the need to relieve the oppression of the Irish peasantry and tenantry, but his belief in the overriding virtues of the Westminster parliamentary system led to his insistence on the sovereignty of the United Kingdom in relation to that part of the realm. This in turn led him to resist Gladstone's Home Rule and gave rise to his alliance with Joseph Chamberlain, the creation of Liberal Unionism and his final departure from Gladstone's Liberal Party shortly before his death.

The Forgotten Legacy

Why was John Bright forgotten for so long? In the immediate aftermath of Bright's death in 1889, a spate of books and articles on his life were published, culminating in the then widely read biography by G. M. Trevelyan in 1913. During his lifetime, the tributes poured in. As Hermann Ausubel noted in his description of the fortieth anniversary in 1883 of Bright's entry into Parliament,

Bright was ... praised for his humanity, earnestness, consistency, trustworthiness, courage, independence, fidelity to principle, love of freedom and justice, and trust in the people. He was also thanked for what he had done to make Britain a better place in which to live. Indeed, he was assured that, as long as men studied the history of the Victorian age, they would dwell on his impressive achievements.[5]

The accolades came from individuals, from newspapers and journals such as the *Economist*, the *Annual Register*, and the *Pall Mall Gazette*, and from Liberal Associations up and down the land, who sent memorials to mark the occasion.

However, by the mid-twentieth century, Bright had been virtually wiped off the face of history, with the exception of a flurry of attention around the hundredth anniversary of the Reform Act in 1967. The reasons for this are unclear, but probably lie in the fact that his sense of purpose, conviction politics and accurate sense of certainty, even if eventually proved right, was unsettling and simply became unfashionable as people became cynical of moral and political certainties and Parliament lost centre stage. Indeed, from the 1920s onwards, with notable exceptions, there seems to have been a reluctance to face up to the reality that great figures with powerful political wills, such as Bright – and, later, Winston Churchill and Margaret Thatcher – can and do actually change the course of events. In Bright's case this was especially so, given that he refused to be part of the Establishment or to be at the whim or behest of the newspapers or, for most of his political life, to be a member of the Government.

Trevelyan himself appreciated that it was not necessary to eulogize Bright, but recognized his 'selfless motives and his rugged, fearless strength, a combination that made him a rare example of the hero as politician'.[6] This truth can easily be seen by referring back to the events as they unfolded, to the contemporary newspaper reportage and parliamentary debates, and by unearthing the views and reactions of his contemporaries.

Happily, today, around 200 years since Bright's birth on 16 November 1811, there are moves to restore his memory and to put his singular contribution to British democracy in its rightful place.

Bright among the Statesmen

One of the most remarkable characteristics of Bright's career was the extent to which his political contemporaries, powerful statesmen in their own right, recognized and became drawn almost involuntarily into his crusades, for that is what they were. With the possible exception of Palmerston, they recognized and appreciated Bright's involvement and tenacious effort. Even if they were wary or uncertain as to where he was leading, they were invariably driven to accept the direction and navigation which he set.

Peel, for example, experienced these driving forces even as Bright entered the House of Commons and embarked on his maiden speech on 7 August 1843. Bright must have taken the House of Commons somewhat by surprise, if not by storm, as will be seen in Chapter 1, by daring to instruct and cajole Peel, the prime minister himself, who, within three years, had resigned.

The opinion of Bright's political partner and friend, Cobden, is probably best encapsulated by his letter to Joseph Parkes in 1856:

> Perhaps there never were two men who lived in such transparent intimacy of mind as Bright and myself ... If you could take the opinion of the whole House, he would be pronounced by a large majority to combine more earnestness, courage, honesty and eloquence than any other man.[7]

In these qualities, Bright certainly outshone another great statesman he converted to his cause – Disraeli. The two men could not have been more different, but there were certain things Disraeli appreciated about Bright which, even if he could not bring himself to openly acknowledge, did surface from time to time, most notably in the run-up to the Reform Act of 1867, as discussed in Chapter 4. Among Disraeli's tactical political manoeuvrings, there is an unexpected degree of contact between the two men, sometimes verging on friendship, and certainly showing respect. This went beyond mere appearances. Disraeli's admiration for Bright even extended to attempts to bring Bright into his inner circle and into a kind of coalition – which Bright emphatically declined and even resented, as his diaries make absolutely clear. They did, however, fall out permanently after 1867, in part because Disraeli claimed Bright's legacy on the Reform Act for himself and the Conservative Party.

The measure of respect for Bright demonstrated by Peel and Disraeli, however, is to be weighed against the mutual virulence of his relationship with Palmerston. Bright regarded Palmerston, though prime minister of his own party, as the embodiment of the aristocratic Whig, deeply opposed to democratic reform. On almost every issue of any substance, except free trade, there existed a state of perpetual warfare between them. This reached its height in 1857, when, as noted earlier, Palmerston succeeded in getting Bright ejected from his Manchester seat over the latter's opposition to the Crimean War. Bright was later vindicated. If a clash of personalities leading to intense hatred may be a mark of respect between political opponents, the verbal jousting between these two, though ostensibly in the same party, permeated their careers.

The campaign Bright started in October 1858 for democratic reform also revealed another aristocratic and implacable enemy – Lord Salisbury. In 1860, Salisbury (at that time, Lord Robert Cecil) had an apocalyptic vision of what would happen if the working man, to quote Andrew Roberts, 'succeeded to uncontrolled power and then pursued his own self-interest'.[8]

Political Revolution: Bright and Marx

It was not only those directly engaged in British politics who recognized the force of Bright's energy. At the same time, one of the most powerful influences in modern history was lurking in the shadows of John Bright's campaigns – Karl Marx, whose co-existence with Bright has been significantly underestimated by commentators on the period.

The direct contact between Bright and Marx was minimal, yet, though Marx seems not to appear in Bright's life as much as might have been expected from the later influence he exerted, it is clear from Marx's own correspondence and that of his intimates, that he was watching and assessing the activities of Bright with great interest and concern.

At first, Marx was full of praise. Between 1852 and 1861, he wrote numerous reports of European news for the *New York Daily Tribune*. Two of these specifically concerned Bright. The first, published on 17 April 1857, analysed the defeat by Palmerston of Bright, Cobden and Thomas Milner Gibson in Manchester in the general election.[9] On 12 November 1858, following Bright's return as the Member for Birmingham, Marx opened his second report with the words,

> John Bright is not only one of the most gifted orators that England has ever produced; but he is at this moment the leader of the Radical members of the House of Commons, and holds the balance of power between the traditional parties of the Whigs and Tories.[10]

Marx also attended a meeting of London trade unionists in March 1863 and praised the keynote address of 'Father Bright'.[11] Marx's opinion changed, however, as Bright's campaign for parliamentary reform progressed. Nevertheless, he organized, in Jasper Ridley's words, 'public meetings at which Bright, whom he detested, was the main speaker'.[12]

In evaluating the degradation of English farm labourers in *Das Kapital*, Marx quoted Bright's Birmingham speech of 14 December 1865, calling for their enfranchisement and comparing their lot with that of the ruling class – but with the caveat that, if he did so, 'I shall be charged with communism.'[13]

Marx was clearly fully conscious of the role Bright was playing as part of what he described as the industrial bourgeoisie, though he could not understand why the industrial bourgeoisie in France in 1848–9 did not play the 'progressive part that they played in England'. He reasoned that the French manufacturers were petit bourgeois, unlike their English counterparts:

> We really find the manufacturers, a Cobden, a Bright, at the head of the crusade against the bank and stock exchange aristocracy. Why not in France? In England, industry predominates; in France, agriculture. In England, industry requires free trade; in France, protective tariffs ... the French industrialists therefore do not dominate the French bourgeoisie.

He argued that the French could not, like the English, 'take the lead of the movement and simultaneously push their class interests to the fore; they must follow in the train of the revolution.'[14] In this, Marx was correct, and it was Bright who led the workers along a peaceful path of democratic reform as revolutions erupted on the Continent, frustrating Marx's and Engels' own hopes for revolution in Britain. As Asa Briggs points out, but for Bright's responsible agitation and reforms, and the bringing together of disparate elements outside Parliament, 1867 'might have been one of bloodshed rather than reform'.[15]

Engels wrote to August Bebel in 1892 that

> The view that the Tories of today are more favourable to the workers than are the Liberals is the reverse of the truth. On the contrary, all the Manchesterian prejudices of the Liberals of 1850 are today articles of faith only to the Tories, while the Liberals know very well that if they are to survive as a party they

must capture the Labour vote. Because they are jackasses, the Tories can, from time to time, be induced by an outstanding man such as Disraeli to carry out a bold coup of which the Liberals would not be capable; but in the absence of an outstanding man it's the jackasses among them who rule the roost. The Tories are no longer simply the tail of the big landowners as they were up till 1850, for between 1855 and 1870 the sons of the Cobdens, Brights, etc., of the upper middle classes and the Anti-Corn Law men, have one and all gone over to the Tory camp, and the strength of the Liberals now lies in the dissenting middle and lower middle classes.[16]

The significance of all this – and the irony of Marx's early appreciation of Bright – was that, whereas Bright was seeking democracy from the bottom up in his campaign for parliamentary reform that began in October 1858, so Marx and Engels spent the rest of their lives campaigning for authoritarianism and the denial of the very democracy which Bright advocated and delivered. It was a strange irony that the culmination of this clash of titans, hidden for so long and buried in the sediment of time, should have re-emerged exactly a hundred years after Bright's death, as the Soviet Empire finally began to collapse and Mikhail Gorbachev engaged in his programme of democratization.[17] Marx would have turned in his grave.

Bright: A Beacon of Freedom

As will be seen in Chapter 5, Bright's American contemporaries regarded Bright with profound admiration. Bright never visited America, despite repeated invitations from leading Americans, including President Rutherford B. Hayes, but he maintained a steady stream of transatlantic correspondence throughout his life, including with Charles Sumner, the chairman of the United States Senate Committee on Foreign Relations from 1861 to 1871. It was through him that Bright's private counsel reached the ears of the President Lincoln. For reasons of protocol, Bright, being a back-bencher and not foreign secretary or prime minister, it would have been impossible for communication between him and the president to have been more direct. Yet, while the two men never met, their relationship was remarkable.

There was clear mutual admiration between Bright and Lincoln. The depth of the relationship was illustrated most clearly by the fact that, on the day Lincoln was assassinated, his pockets were found to contain few intimate possessions, but one of them was an article by Bright written the previous year calling for the re-election of Lincoln to the presidency, which Lincoln clearly greatly treasured.

American esteem for Bright did not end with Lincoln's assassination. The praise and invitations continued and there were also requests for likenesses of Bright. One, a portrait by the Italian-American artist, Giuseppe Fagnani, for whom Bright reluctantly sat in the summer of 1865, now hangs in the Morning Room of the Union Club in New York, having been subscribed to by members of the Club, including Theodore Roosevelt, Snr.

A statue of Bright was also commissioned after his death by one of the greatest of American philanthropists, Andrew Carnegie. This statue, by Albert Bruce Joy and an exact replica of the one recently restored to pride of place in Birmingham Museum and Art Gallery, was given to the House of Commons in 1902 as a replacement for an earlier work that had been removed at the request of Bright's family, who were dissatisfied with the likeness. The replacement stands in the Inner Lobby, the earlier statue's place in the Central Lobby having been taken in the interim by one of Gladstone. 'He had always been my favourite living hero in public life as he had been my father's,' Carnegie wrote of Bright in his autobiography.[18]

Bright's place in the history of India is again a good example of the esteem with which he was held by those who were striving for independence and freedom. Starting in 1911, the *Indian Review* in Madras published a series entitled 'The Friends of India', the first of which was a tribute to John Bright. As P. N. Raman Pillai wrote in that first article,

> John Bright was one of the most high-souled Englishmen of the nineteenth century ... He was dealing with the interests of large masses of mankind, and he strove to do justice to them irrespective of the consequences to himself as a politician ... His name will continue to shine, with ever-increasing lustre, in the pages of history, as that of an Englishman who fought against almost immeasurable odds for the introduction of the modern spirit in the Government of India.[19]

Professor Underhill pays specific tribute to Bright and his allies when he says

The truth is that the new British Commonwealth of nations …
bears a remarkable resemblance to the ideas of the Manchester
men in the 1860s … [They] have turned out to be much better
prophets of the future course of imperial development than
either Disraeli or Chamberlain.[20]

James Sturgis adds that 'Bright's example is no less relevant
today when questions of race threaten the very existence of the
organization.'[21]

Sturgis also asserts that 'John Bright's greatest triumph was that he
came to represent British Liberalism in its most appealing forms.'[22]
Indeed, on the website of the Indian National Congress, current at
the time of writing, under the heading 'British Friends of India', pre-
eminence is given to Bright under the pseudonym 'John Britain':
'Since the time of Edmund Burke scarcely a voice had been heard in
England in favour of the voiceless millions of India until John Britain
sounded his warning note against the injustices systematically being
done to the people of India.' From 1847 to 1880, the website states,
'He worked for India as none had worked before him.'[23]

In his special relationship with Ireland, Bright's words, deeds and
actions, discussed in Chapter 8, speak for themselves. Bright did not
approve of Charles Stewart Parnell and his tactics, but even the
Parnellites paid tribute to Bright at the end, and his reputation
cannot be better expressed than in the words of R. Barry O'Brien,
who said of Bright that 'Alone among leading English statesmen at
that time Bright fearlessly identified himself with the Irish popular
cause.'[24] As is so often the case, the most significant political tributes
to a statesman come from those who have the greatest reason to take
exception to what he has done. Voting for the Coercion Bill and
defeating Home Rule could be regarded as the worst of political
crimes to a man such as O'Brien, an Irish Catholic nationalist and
Parnell's unpaid secretary and biographer. Nevertheless, he paid
tribute to Bright, who had done both, in his monograph published
twenty years after Bright's death. O'Brien also quoted from Justin
McCarthy's tribute on Bright's death in 1889. McCarthy, the leading Parnellite (who had also served as the editor of Bright's newspaper, the *Morning Star*, in the early 1860s), was speaking in the
House of Commons in place of Parnell, whose absence was 'quite
unavoidable' and deeply regretted. He stated that

if we remained silent it might be thought that because of late years
we had not Mr. Bright's sympathy and support for our national

cause, we were unwilling to associate ourselves in the tribute all
other Parties are paying to his career and to his memory. Mr.
Speaker, the Irish Party is not so wanting in generosity, and the
memory of the Irish people is not so short ... Our memory goes
back to the time when he championed our Irish cause with an
eloquence and a sincerity never surpassed in the struggle for any
great purpose whatever ... We remember, too, we must remember, that some of the most superb, the most magnificent illustrations of his immortal eloquence were given to champion the
cause of the suffering Irish peasant, and to awaken in this country
a sympathy with the Irish cause.[25]

O'Brien concluded his book with the words, 'He will live in the
memory of his fellow countrymen as the greatest moral force which
appeared in English politics during his generation.'[26]

These were sentiments shared by one of the most celebrated
local influences in Birmingham, Robert William Dale, who knew
Birmingham intimately and was present at Bright's famous speech
in October 1858. In 1882, Dale wrote in a letter to Bright,

You have, I believe, inspired large numbers of men with the idea
that political action should be guided and sustained neither by
self-interest nor by ambition, but by loyalty to conscience. The
idea is a fruitful one, and will yield its harvests long after your
personal work is over; and so you will live in the lives of other
men.'[27]

CHAPTER 1

The Unquiet Quaker:
Battling Against the Corn Laws

I have nothing to gain by being the tool of any party.
(John Bright to the electors of Durham, 1843)

Bright the Man

'My life is in my speeches.'[1] This statement by John Bright in his later years, tinged as it was with exasperation at the stream of requests from would-be biographers, is only partly true. It may be that his speeches demonstrated his power of oratory, which by all contemporary accounts was remarkable, but they do not entirely convey the hidden and driven force which compelled Bright to deliver them. Nor do they show how Bright was a thoroughly rounded man, as well as being a political statesman.

Bright's ideas, which could not really be called a philosophy, were derived from practical experience – part social, part religious and part political. They intertwined in a strong conviction that he was right, a conviction that fascinated and repelled people in equal measure. He was also deeply honest and despised flattery, often speaking so plainly as to cause upset. As his sister, Priscilla, wrote to his clearly rattled sister-in-law in the 1840s,

> Thou must not mind all the fault John finds with thee, as he makes no scruple to say the *very* worst he can to our faces. But in justness to his character, I must say he says very little if anything against his friends, or enemies either, behind their backs; unless it be touching the aristocracy and the clergy. [2]

He certainly pulled no punches in the political arena, as Lord George Bentinck acknowledged when he said of Bright: 'If he hadn't been a Quaker, he would have been a prize fighter.'[3]

Bright's moral strength was also evident in his appearance. He wore plain Quaker dress, standing out from his more fashion-conscious colleagues at Westminster in his sombre black coat and cravat, but it was his bearing that was most imposing. As one American journalist, George W. Smalley who met John Bright in 1866, described him:

> His hair even then was gray [*sic*], though abundant, the complexion florid, and the rather irregular but powerful features gave you at first sight an impression of singular force and firmness of character. So did the whole man. The broad shoulders, the bulk of the figure, the solid massiveness of his masterful individuality, the immovable grasp of his feet upon the firm earth, his upright-ness of bearing, the body knit to the head as closely as capital to column – all together made the least careful observer feel that here was one in whose armour the flaws were few.[4]

Yet, despite these impressive, and occasionally unnerving, traits, Bright was a man of great sympathy and friendship. He adored, and was adored by, his family, and found great joy and comfort in children, most notably his own eight children and, later, his grandchildren. Twice widowed, Bright particularly enjoyed the company of women, and his diaries are peppered with compliments about the intelligent and attractive women he encountered. The editor of his diaries, R. A. J. Walling, records, for example, that on his travels in 1835, Bright 'studied female beauty on shore when it was available (and complained to his diary when it was not)'.[5] On one occasion he even described the wife of the MP for Glasgow, Mrs Dennistoun, as 'Magnificent! Perhaps the finest woman as animal I ever saw.'[6]

His powerful sense of humour was well recognized by those who met him. When it came to politics, however, no one underestimated his powerful and uncompromising sense of independence. Nevertheless, he invariably maintained courteous relations with his political opponents, reserving withering contempt only for those whom he loathed, such as Palmerston. It was his enemies who portrayed him as earnest and moralistic – as picked up by the histo-rian, Llewellyn Woodward, when he described Bright displaying at times a 'repellent religiosity';[7] others might call it courage of his moral convictions.

Religious belief was indeed central to Bright's being, but it was not overbearing. He stated clearly in the House of Commons on one occasion that 'This House is not the place for religious questions.'[8]

Even at home, where a pompous moralist might be expected to overwhelm family life with sermons and strictures, Bright was restrained. As his son, Philip, recalled, 'I never heard my father mention religious questions in our home, although he was a deeply religious man, as his speeches abundantly prove.'[9] Instead, the family shared a simple and enjoyable daily affirmation of their faith:

> My father when at Rochdale invariably read the Bible to our household before breakfast, and so greatly did we delight in his reading that we were always down in time to hear him. He had a remarkable gift for reading and reciting poetry, and often made use of it for our benefit.[10]

Bright's tastes included not only Milton and Tennyson but equally, and unexpectedly, the erotic Byron, and he had even visited the graves of Shelley and Keats.[11] He returned frequently to the *Meditations* of Marcus Aurelius.

Bright was immensely well read and a true man of culture, with a natural appreciation of fine art. He shared with Disraeli the common experience of visiting the Near East as a young man, but there is little doubt that there the comparison ended. Whereas Disraeli's visit with his friend James Clay could be described dissolute, Bright preferred culture, architecture and art. Indeed, when he travelled to Italy in 1857, he spent much of his time in art galleries, including the Vatican Museum, churches and ancient sites, and was fascinated by del Sarto, Michelangelo and Murillo, among many others.[12]

His company was much sought after at the best tables in London and around Westminster, where, despite the Quakers' temperance convictions, he would enjoy alcohol and fine cigars. He was also known to be an enthusiastic player of both cricket and billiards. He took particular pleasure in meeting poets and authors, including Longfellow and Dickens. But, while he was happy to play this role, his real need was for true friendship based on shared conviction and principles. This was to bring him both happiness and misery. When buttressed by friends allied to the same cause, most notably Richard Cobden, Bright's physical and mental capabilities could withstand any storm – as he proved during the days of the Anti-Corn Law League and the American Civil War. Disraeli himself acknowledged Bright's strength when he said in 1855,

> I have always thought Gladstone, Bright and myself the three most energetic men in the House. Bright is sometimes blunt, but

his eloquence is most powerful. He has not the subtleness of
Cobden, but he has far more energy and his talents are more
practically applied.[13]

Yet when Bright was forced to stand alone because of his opinions,
as during the Crimean War, he suffered the effects of the tempest
and his energy and health were depleted to the point of breakdown.
During such moments of personal crisis he would retreat to
Scotland, often for extended periods, to fish and rid himself of self-
doubt. Thus refreshed, he would return to the fray and to live by
the principles he set out in a speech to the working men of Rochdale
in 1847:

> There is only one way that is safe for any man, or any number of
> men, by which they can maintain their present position if it be a
> good one, or raise themselves above it if it be a bad one – that is,
> by the practice of the virtues of industry, frugality, temperance,
> and honesty.[14]

From his diaries, however, it is clear that Bright was unimpressed by
his own achievements. Above all, he was a humble man. At times, his
devoted family life inevitably had to give way to his formidable political timetables and commitments, but, as his personal correspondence clearly illustrates, he never lost sight of his personal affairs or
his commitment to the welfare of those who worked in the family
mill. It is highly significant that throughout his life, even when he
was one of the most revered and famous statesmen in Britain,
he maintained his position in the Society of Friends' meeting
houses he attended, in particular at Rochdale, where he served as
a doorkeeper.
    When it came to the many calls on him for likenesses and
biographies, therefore, Bright was understandably unenthusiastic.
'Obscurity better than this notoriety,' he grumbled while correcting
some proofs.[15] On one occasion, following a visit from Humphry
Ward, who was writing a biography of him for Cassell, he recorded,

> The proposition is not pleasant to me, for it involves trouble and
> lays me open to a charge or suspicion of vanity. I am against
> biographies and portraits and statues. They are troublesome and
> are soon forgotten, and of no influence in the future. I have been
> and am a victim of the habit of my time to commemorate the
> ordinary labours of ordinary lives.[16]

Nevertheless, albeit with great reluctance, he co-operated with his biographers and sat for a number of artists and sculptors, including the great Pre-Raphaelite, John Millais. Regarding one commission, he noted, 'I do not care for statues, and I have no wish to appear in marble in the Manchester Town Hall ... There have been only a few men worthy of statues, and to the memory of those so worthy, statues are not needed.'[17] In 1883, he even deprecated the making of the Birmingham statue by Albert Bruce Joy, though he recognized that 'The model seems very good.'[18] By January 1884, he was exasperated: 'I wish I had finished with photographers, artists, sculptors and interviewers and newspaper people. They have given me not a little trouble – and will not leave me "obscure".'[19]

As his colleague, Joseph Chamberlain, recalled after Bright's death, Bright had once told him 'that whenever he entered a strange house, if there were a dog or a cat in it, it always came to him directly and made friends with him'. Chamberlain concluded, 'I know – I am certain – that theirs was the only popularity that Mr. Bright ever courted.'[20]

Early Years

John Bright was born into a Quaker family in Rochdale, Lancashire, on 16 November 1811. His father, Jacob, was a book-keeper in the cotton industry who, when Bright was 12, established his own cotton-spinning firm. The eldest surviving child of 11, Bright had been born prematurely and was a delicate boy. His constitution dictated his schooling at a series of Friends' schools in various northern towns, culminating in 18 months at a boarding school in the idyllic Hodder Valley at Newton-in-Bowland. There, he grew strong as he joined his fellow pupils in hill-walking and bathing in the River Hodder, indulged his love of English literature and discovered a passion for the contemplative pursuit of fishing.

The Society of Friends had instilled in him the respect for humanity and unbreakable belief in people which would underpin his later career. His schooling, however, was patchy, as he himself later admitted: 'some Latin and a little French, with the common branches then taught in such schools as I had been placed in. Reading, writing, arithmetic, grammar and geography – no mathematics and no science.'[21] On leaving school at 15 to work at the family's Greenbank mill, he sought to fill these gaps in knowledge by reading in the early mornings before his working day began. He set up a small study above the counting house and there devoured books on all manner of subjects, from statistics to history.

Further lessons were learnt while working at the family's mill. Unlike the mills in larger towns such as Manchester, Greenbank, despite being the second-largest employer in Rochdale, did not suffer from a damaging gulf between rich and distant owners and struggling workers. While John Bright would later state that the purpose of his business activities was primarily 'to procure for myself and family a comfortable income',[22] the Bright family were by instinct benevolent employers. As G. M. Trevelyan describes it, they oversaw a 'half-democratic, half-patriarchal society'.[23] Jacob Bright lived with his family in a modest house next to the mill and knew all his workers by name. His own private funds were directed towards educating their children, many of whom were also employed at the mill, and he gave the workers' families both financial assistance and moral support during difficult times. As John Bright was to say in 1836, he

> envied neither the head nor the heart of that man who could live amongst the factory operatives of Lancashire without perceiving the injurious effects of the long hours and close confinement to which they were subjected and without feeling an ardent desire to assist in improving their condition.[24]

Starting in the warehouse, Bright became friendly with his fellow workers and learnt from them the radicalism that was sweeping the northern towns in the first quarter of the nineteenth century. His new friends taught Bright the realities of life in such an unequal society, and spoke of their desire for political enfranchisement. Some of them had witnessed the massacre at Peterloo in August 1819 at first hand. As Bright later wrote,

> I was, as I now am, a member of the Society of Friends. I know something of their history and of the persecutions they had endured, and of their principles of equality and justice. I knew that I came of the stock of the martyrs, that one of my ancestors … had been in prison for several years because he preferred to worship in the humble meeting-house of his own sect rather than in the church of the law-favoured sect by whom he and his friends were barbarously persecuted.[25]

In the summer of 1830, Bright's mother, Martha, died aged 41. She had been at the centre of the spirited and intellectually stimulating atmosphere of the Bright home, and the family were grief-stricken at her passing. As Bright recalled, it was 'a loss which never could be repaired. From it sprung many troubles and disappointments, which disturbed us in after years.' Bright and his surviving five brothers and four sisters, who had been raised to be independent in both mind and spirit, now sought a new focus for their intellectual and emotional energies. As Quakers, the obvious and most socially acceptable choices were religion and business but, as Trevelyan points out, 'the Brights of Greenbank were a law unto themselves'.[26] They chose politics, and radical politics at that, an arena frowned upon by the Quaker theologians, who spoke eloquently of the dangers of becoming entangled in the worldly diversions of public life. National politics was not for the Society of Friends.

Bright had his first taste of radical politics in action in December 1830, during the Preston by-election. His fellow warehouseman, Nicholas Nuttall, whom he described as 'a great politician of the radical type'[27] was a keen follower of Henry 'Orator' Hunt, one of the speakers at the meeting in August 1819 at St Peter's Field, Manchester, which led to the massacre. Hunt had put himself up against the latest in a line of untouchable and unchallenged Tories, the Stanleys, in Preston, and enthusiastically Nuttall kept Bright informed of the progress of the election. It lasted two weeks until 'The son of the great peer was defeated, and Hunt became member for Preston to the great joy of Nicholas and to my entire satisfaction.' As Bright said, 'Through him I became something of a politician.'[28]

In his room above the counting house, Bright had added the new radical publication, *The Spectator*, to his daily reading. Through its pages, he followed the progress of the agitation and parliamentary battles that led to the Reform Act of 1832. Many new seats were proposed for the new industrial towns, but Rochdale was not initially among their number. Bright threw himself into the issue, attending meetings and helping to raise a petition to Parliament. The local agitation and petition to Parliament met with success and the Whigs added Rochdale to the list of new boroughs. Further excitement came when Bright made his first trip to London. By chance, he was travelling by stagecoach on the morning after the second reading of the Reform Bill had been carried by a majority of nine. Bright and his fellow passengers 'met two post-chaises, with four horses each, coming at full gallop with the news for the

provinces. From the chaises handbills were thrown, giving particulars of the division in the Lords with a majority of nine in favour of
the Bill.'[29] Thus Bright learned of the victory. The first Member for
Rochdale, John Fenton, was elected in 1832. That year also saw the
first Quaker take his seat in the House of Commons, when Joseph
Pease was elected for South Durham.

One speaker in particular during the Reform Bill agitation stuck
in Bright's mind well into old age – a Dr Kay, who had quoted
Shelley's *The Mask of Anarchy* to rouse his listeners in Rochdale
marketplace. Bright had taken a few tentative steps into the art of
oratory himself in the preceding years, mainly on a temperance platform and not always with great success. On his first occasion, he had
muddled his notes and frozen, unable to continue, but with encouragement from the Revd John Aldis – and, crucially, the advice to
tear up his notes and speak extempore – his skills improved. In 1833,
he became a founding member of the Rochdale Literary and
Philosophical Society where he debated various topics including the
powers of the monarchy, education, the 'injurious' nature of public
amusements and, on one occasion, the motion that 'Laws for
restricting the importation of grain are impolitic'.[30] In time, this last
question would become pre-eminent in Bright's mind, with the
repeal of the Corn Laws as the most practical expression of the need
to alleviate the oppression of the working class from laws designed
to sustain the privilege of the aristocratic and landed interests which
increasingly he so despised.

The Corn Laws

While the Corn Laws hold a special place in the annals of Britain in
the early nineteenth century, the export of corn had in fact been
prohibited since the fifteenth-century reign of Henry VI. By the
1790s, the war with France and accompanying blockades in prod-
ucts of all kinds, including grain, had vastly increased the price of
bread, but there was little real control over the export of corn. Acts
were passed following the American War of Independence – in 1791,
in 1804 and, in particular in 1815 – which imposed taxes on the
import of corn.

Immediately after the second reading of the Corn Law Bill of
1815, there was a massive outcry in and around Westminster.
Attacks on the homes of Lord Liverpool, the prime minister, Lord
Castlereagh and other ministers were followed by the reading of the
Riot Act, with several protesters being shot. The situation became

extremely grave as the crowd became more violent, but the Bill became law in a mere two weeks. By this time, the working class, all too conscious of the French Revolution, was deeply enraged. In August 1819 in Manchester a mixture of taxes and the Corn Laws led to the reading of the Riot Act at St Peter's Fields. A peaceful demonstration calling for electoral reform was turned into a massacre, with 11 dead and many hundreds wounded. Feelings of injustice at the price of corn combined with resistance to the landowning class intensified the desire for political change.

In the 1820s, there were reasonably good harvests. Free trade was championed in the Cabinet in 1824 by William Huskisson, the Tory MP for Liverpool and president of the Board of Trade from 1823 to 1827. Huskisson used his position to liberalize Britain's commercial policies, and persuaded the prime minister, George Canning, that the Corn Laws needed to be reformed, proposing a sliding scale. His triumph was short-lived, however. He found himself out of the Cabinet in 1828, having been outmanoeuvred by the protectionist Duke of Wellington, and in 1830 he died, killed by Stephenson's Rocket, famously becoming the first casualty of the railway age.

None the less, in 1828 the Corn Laws were amended, with a sliding scale, as proposed by Canning. But, as Bright could see from his vantage point in Rochdale, this improvement did not prevent hardship over the next four years as bad harvests took their hold and pushed up bread prices. Privation and political discontent combined. Furthermore, having seen most of their own protective tariffs jettisoned in 1824, manufacturers no longer saw why landowners should enjoy such exclusive protection. Crucially, in turn, this discontent coincided with the demand for a widened franchise. In 1833, there was a resolution repudiating the Corn Laws in the House of Commons and Joseph Hume managed substantial support for their repeal, but it was not achieved. Charles Poulett Thomson, the Whig free trader, admitted, 'We hammered away with facts and figures and some arguments; but we could not evaluate the subject and excite the feelings of the people.'[31] Poulett Thomson became President of the Board of Trade but was ousted with the fall of the Whig Government in 1834, only to return when the Whigs regained power in February 1835.

The year 1835 also marked the entry into political life of Richard Cobden, through a series of pamphlets agitating for the repeal of the Corn Laws. In these early stages, the movement for the repeal of the Corn Laws was treated with disdain, but once the connection was made between the price of food, which was reaching critical levels, and the need to reform the House of Commons to achieve the change, together with mobilizing opinion outside Parliament, there was an irresistible confluence of circumstances which precipitated a new era in British politics that would see Cobden navigating its economic and Bright its political course.

Intensified Calls for Repeal

Meanwhile, Bright's involvement in politics had been somewhat curtailed. While continuing his interest in local affairs – by, for example, becoming a founding member with his father of the Rochdale Reform Association in 1834 (one of the first local electoral registration associations in the country) – he was also busy completing his self-education through travel. He had undertaken a tour of the Low Countries in 1833, a trip cut short by an epidemic of cholera in Rotterdam, but from which he came back 'speaking French with much greater facility'.[32] He had also visited Ireland, where he saw poverty on a scale he had never before encountered. From August 1835, he spent eight months travelling to Greece, and on through the Ottoman Empire, the Holy Land and Egypt, before returning via Italy and France.

On his return in January 1837, aged 25, he found the Lancashire cotton manufacturers much more organized in their opposition to the Corn Laws. Free trade and the abolition of the Corn Laws had increasingly become the central political issue in the northern manufacturing towns. Having traded without the shield of tariff walls since 1824, the manufacturers were increasingly blaming their mounting difficulties in penetrating markets abroad on the barriers foreign governments maintained as a quid pro quo for Britain's Corn Laws. They also felt that foreign industrialists had an unfair cost-base advantage, since the wages they paid could take into account the generally lower cost of food on the Continent. Bright shared the perception of his fellow industrialists that the sectional privileges and interests of the aristocracy were harming their own practical interests as manufacturers.

Bright joined this new movement with enthusiasm, both as a businessman and as a radical, as they led the return of free traders as MPs in the general election of 1837. In Rochdale, Bright appealed to the radical reformers in a written address calling for the re-election of the former MP, John Fenton, who had been ousted in 1835 by his Conservative rival. Fenton was in favour of the repeal of the Corn Laws and of church rates but, significantly, was also standing for household suffrage and the ballot. Fenton won by a narrow margin. Of the many other free traders who sought election to Parliament, mainly from the great provincial cities and supported by the manufacturers, as many as 38 were successful in obtaining seats that year.

It was during this period that Bright and Cobden first met. Cobden, who had just failed to obtain election at Stockport, was becoming increasingly well-known, and Bright travelled to Manchester to invite him to speak in Rochdale about education. Cobden accepted and during his subsequent visit stayed at Bright's father's home. Interestingly, Cobden's first calico business was in Clitheroe, in the Hodder Valley, where Bright went to school. Not only did they share interests, but also a similar environment, even before they met. Though it was some time before their friendship matured into the great alliance seeking the repeal of the Corn Laws, the seeds had been sown.

The iniquities of agricultural protection need not have come to dominate the waking hours of Bright. The course of his career appeared predetermined by his inheritance – developing the family business in Rochdale. What was more, the Corn Laws were an overtly political question, and one on which Parliament had made clear it was unlikely to change its mind for at least a generation. But most important, the disapprobation of the Society of Friends was ever-present. Bright was keen to marry, settle down and start a family, but his participation in local politics threatened to get in the way of his intentions. Indeed, his efforts to woo Elizabeth Priestman, a Newcastle Quaker, were frustrated initially by her family's concern that his growing political involvement was inconsistent with the simple godly concerns preached by their faith. Elizabeth's father put it bluntly, expressing his concern as to whether 'thy political engagements and the approbation which thou may have met with from thy friends may not interfere with the duties of a domestic and a quiet life'.[33]

There was much to keep him close to his home, however. He remained especially vexed by the privileges of the Church of England, especially in parishes such as Rochdale, where the dissenting spirit of Nonconformism had come to hold sway. He spent much energy denouncing the pretensions of Rochdale's new Anglican vicar and the continuing imposition of the church rate on Anglicans and non-Anglicans alike. At one stage, matters became so heated that he and the vicar mounted rival tombstones to shout condemnation at one another in the parish churchyard, while a great crowd gathered to cheer and jeer the rival pugilists of faith.

Bright's intellect could not ignore the clear moral link he saw between the unearned superiority of the Established Church, with its 'church rates' and expensive hierarchy, and the presumption of the political Establishment that cheerfully upheld self-serving tariffs on basic necessities regardless of the effects on the less fortunate. His defence of dissenting spiritual values, harking back to the seventeenth century, was intimately embedded with his defence of freedom of choice in both the marketplace and the ballot box.

Yet, even when the first of four years of bad harvests struck in 1838, it was all too apparent that no redress could be expected from the Palace of Westminster. In March of that year, Charles Pelham Villiers, the MP for Wolverhampton,[34] proposed the first of what became an annual ritual of parliamentary motions for an inquiry into the effects of the Corn Laws. This helped to identify a principled group of politicians who would act together on the issue – they had founded the London-based Anti-Corn Law Association in 1837 with a committee largely comprised of backbench MPs – but it also showed how few of them there were.

Instead, the decisive events pointing to where the natural constituency of opposition truly resided occurred in 1838. In August of that year, a young medical student, Abraham Paulton, fortuitously launched the beginnings of the Corn Law agitation with a mixture of argument, principle and dedicated determination in a speech in Bolton, where he was apprenticed as a surgeon. Paulton had been educated at Stonyhurst, the Jesuit School founded in France for young Catholic gentlemen from the time of the persecution of Catholics in the late sixteenth century, but was driven out of France by the revolutionaries in the late eighteenth century. It would hardly be surprising to anyone who knew the origins of the school and its type of education – a combination of discipline and principled fervour – that the iniquities of the Corn Laws would have generated an explosion of concern and action in equal measure.

With Paulton having pitched in at Bolton, others began to follow. John Bowring and Archibald Prentice called free traders together in Manchester in September 1838 at the York Hotel. Within two weeks another meeting at the same hotel saw the creation of the Manchester branch of the Anti-Corn Law Association. Soon, the membership was accelerating and within a month there was a provisional committee of 37, among whom was Bright, unable to resist the call. Cobden followed within a matter of days. Among others were Thomas Potter and J. B. Smith, both of whom were to become staunch allies of Cobden and Bright well into the 1860s in the campaign for parliamentary reform. The involvement of the Quakers, including Bright and his Friends, not to mention the wealthy anti-slaver, Joseph Sturge, from Birmingham, imbued the organization with a strong sense of moral purpose that gave them almost unbounded energy. In Manchester, the anti-Corn Law movement secured seats on the borough council, Potter becoming mayor and Cobden an alderman of the city. Paulton moved on from Manchester to Birmingham and then to Wolverhampton.

Bright delivered his first recorded speech against the Corn Laws in Rochdale in 1838, when he was only 27 years old. However, with his attention still focused primarily on business, and battling with the occasional vicar, it was Cobden who quickly became the guiding influence. By December 1838, under Cobden's guidance, Manchester was firmly in the saddle. Recently returned from a visit to Germany where he had been profoundly influenced by the liberalization of trade between the individual German nation states, he had persuaded the Manchester Chamber of Commerce to pledge its support.[35] There was another meeting in the York Hotel in January 1839 and the Anti-Corn Law Association got down to the serious business of organization with Cobden and Bright, Smith and Prentice, and the formation of a 12-man executive committee, headed by J. B. Smith. As the Association spread throughout the northern towns, including Liverpool, Glasgow, Leeds and Hull, the prime minister, Lord Melbourne, was becoming deeply concerned but could not decide what to do about it.

When the Anti-Corn Law Association was created, one of the key pledges was that party politics should be excluded. On 2 February 1839, Bright moved the first resolution at an anti-Corn Law meeting in Rochdale, arguing that it was not a question of party because men of all parties were united about it. He went on in a famous phrase to say it was not a party question, but 'a pantry question, a knife-and-fork question, a question between the working millions and the aristocracy'.[36] The meeting did not pass without an attempt by the chairman to interrupt Bright, saying that he was out of order, but the majority of the meeting prevailed in supporting him.

The Anti-Corn Law League

The Anti-Corn Law Association had entrenched itself as a representative voice of business opinion in the Manchester area. But how quickly could it, or should it, seek to expand beyond this regional base? It was the humiliating treatment meted out in Parliament to

Charles Villiers that provided the spur to expand into a national pressure group. On 12 March 1839, Villiers had tried again for an inquiry into the Corn Laws but was heavily defeated, losing by 342 votes to 195. Not only was the motion heavily defeated, Villiers himself was lucky to be heard at all above the uncouth babble that accompanied his speech: 'He was assailed from his outset with a volley of sounds, such as could have been heard in no other deliberative assembly in the world'[37] and his appeals to help the destitute and ill-fed being heard in silence only when most of the Members had retired for lunch. The aristocratic Whigs were no more disposed than the Tories to abolish the Corn Laws. To compound matters, the Whig prime minister, Lord Melbourne, dismissed the notion airily, 'To leave the whole agricultural interest without protection, I declare before God' – he was addressing the House of Lords – 'that I think it the wildest and maddest scheme, that has ever entered into the imagination of man to conceive.'[38] What this demonstrated was that Parliament, still riddled with the influence and vested interest of the landowners, had no real intention of repealing the Corn Laws, or even of inquiring seriously into their damaging results. Parliament was sticking its head in the sand and, dangerously, ignoring the political impetus.

Consequently, on 20 March 1839, the Anti-Corn Law League was instituted, with support from every corner of the land. Under the presidency of J. B. Smith, with the driving force of George Wilson as organizer, and Paulton, Cobden and Bright soon to go on the stump, its ambitions to win over hearts and minds were revealed from the first. In April, the League published 15,000 copies of its own news-sheet, the *Anti-Corn Law Circular*. Having only limited funds with which to pursue its agenda, it also set a massive target of £250,000 to back the campaign[39] – a sum equivalent to £17.5 million today.[40] This figure was a measure of their determination and practical awareness of what it would take to organize the campaign, and the necessity to reform not only the Corn Laws but also Parliament itself.

In November 1839, Bright married Elizabeth Priestman, having finally convinced her father that his spiritual integrity as a Quaker had not been compromised by his involvement in radical politics. But the new Mrs Bright shared her father's disapproval of getting caught up in national secular concerns, and it seemed likely that whatever he might privately be hankering after, Bright's political involvement would be confined to influencing only those within a reasonable walking distance. Nevertheless, he endeavoured to do all he could to further the League's cause despite these restricting circumstances. He spoke at Bolton on 6 November 1839, in honour of Paulton's determined advocacy for repeal over the previous twelve months. The gathering of 120 included Cobden and many Lancastrian members of Parliament, and Bright was commended for his speech, which 'gave evidence of his grasp of the subject, of his capacity soon to take a leading part in the great agitation', as the history of the Anti-Corn Law League put it.[41] In January 1840, he founded the Rochdale branch of the League and instigated a petition demanding the repeal of the 'accursed corn-laws' which gained 9,700 signatures, a figure almost equal to the entire male population of Rochdale. He also, crucially, became the League's treasurer. As a businessman, he understood only too well the importance of proper funding if they were to achieve their great objectives.

In October 1840, Elizabeth Bright gave birth to a daughter. Complications set in soon after the birth and Elizabeth contracted tuberculosis. Her health began to decline alarmingly and Bright moved with her to Leamington, believing the spa resort offered better prospects for recovery than the mill-towns of Lancashire. He none the less tried to honour his commitments to the Anti-Corn Law League and made at least one trip a week to Manchester, often staying afterwards to dine with Cobden. In early 1841, Cobden introduced Bright to Charles Villiers. Villiers was impressed by the young man and strongly urged Cobden to encourage him. As a result, Bright travelled from Rochdale to a League conference in Manchester on 14 April 1841, where he shared the platform with Cobden.

The Chartists

In campaigning for its objectives, the Anti-Corn Law League had to contend not only with opposition from Parliament but also from the Chartists, who believed that repealing the Corn Laws was a distraction from the struggle for manhood suffrage. The movement had come into formal existence with the publication of the People's Charter in May 1838. This document called for manhood suffrage, a secret ballot, annual parliaments, payment to Members of Parliament, and equal electoral districts. The Anti-Corn Law leaders, including Cobden and Bright, firmly believed it was necessary to achieve the repeal of the Corn Laws first, and this remained a point of division between the two campaigns. Bright understood the Chartists' objectives and had undoubted sympathy for extending the vote, as his interest in the Reform League illustrated later in the 1860s (see Chapter 4), but he was convinced that it was essential to take one step at a time.

What the Anti-Corn Law League and their allied middle-class reformers were seeking was a stable approach to a new, peaceful democracy. A natural and instinctive aversion to violent and unconstitutional change permeated the thinking of the dissenters such as Bright, and the Catholics such as Frederick Lucas.[42] In their campaign against aristocratic privilege, they linked freedom of trade and freedom from the Corn Laws with political freedom of choice. This became a salient feature on the political landscape throughout the mid-nineteenth century and was largely instrumental in formulating stability as a firm characteristic of British democracy.

Furthermore, there were class differences, the League leaders being mainly from the middle class and the Chartist leaders largely working-class. The engagement of the middle class was driven by their awareness that the repeal of the Corn Laws, the advantages of free trade and parliamentary reform were all interwoven. They were spurred on by the moral imperatives and principles no less than those who had been driving for the abolition of slavery and who, like Joseph Sturge and Samuel Lucas, showed a mutual and practical determination to achieve their objectives. The Chartists would go further. They believed in confrontation, and their rhetoric implied support for violence. Their slogan was 'Peaceably if we can, forcibly if we must.'

The confrontational tendencies of the Chartists also disrupted many a League meeting. In a letter to Samuel Smiles on 21 October 1841, Cobden referred to a meeting held in Manchester in 1837:

> Two years and a half ago we called a public meeting. The Chartist leaders attacked us on the platform at the head of their deluded followers. We were nearly the victims of physical force. I lost my hat, and all but had my head split open with the leg of a stool. In retaliation for this, we deluged the town with short tracts printed for the purpose. We called meetings of each trade and held conferences with them at their own lodges. We found ready listeners and many secret allies, even amongst the Chartists. We resolutely abstained from discussing the Charter or any other party question. We stuck to our subject and the right-minded amongst the working men gave us credit for being in earnest.[43]

Indeed, on 6 November 1841, Cobden continued, 'My opinion is every day strengthened that we must not seek official alliance with Chartists or any other party.' He went on to mention Chartists, such as O'Connor, who were verbally forceful and said, 'We must insist upon our right to carry on an independent agitation and if the hired knaves who interrupt our meetings persevere, we must harass them but in their own way.'[44]

It is clear that at this time, the situation was deteriorating and had the potential to become dangerous and socially disruptive. Hostile behaviour combined with some physical violence was a frequent characteristic of League meetings at this time. There was an Irish contingent of bouncers whom the League used to keep order but they were inclined to resort to physical means themselves. As Norman Longmate puts it,

> Those in Manchester were known as the "Irish Lambs" and their leader Michael Donohoe as "Big Mick". Unleashing Big Mick and his cohorts was a far cry from the reasoned exposition of economic truths for which the League had been formed, but there was probably no alternative.

The Irish working class were deeply involved and both sides meted out brute force in their pursuit of their version of the truth. As a participant wrote in respect of a meeting in May 1841, 'The Chartists were driven out of the hall four times. We regularly thrashed them and passed our own resolutions.'[45] By comparison, modern political meetings are like proverbial tea parties.

All this presented a bizarre picture of pacifist Quakers living in an island of internal tranquillity with ferocious storms – and a stream of projected missiles – raging around them, unleashed by tumultuous passions striving for truth and freedom but collapsing into occasional violent disorder. It was a political maelstrom, but no one could say that both sides were not in earnest.

Unrealistic comparisons with the French Revolution were beginning to emerge and, in correspondence in Cobden, Francis Place wrote with exaggeration:

> There I sat thinking of the terrible evils of the French Revolution in its earlier periods and sure I am that if the men who composed by far the greater portion of the audience were not restrained by their fellow subjects, the policemen and the soldiers, all the horrors of the worst scenes of the French Revolution, all its

monstrous cruelties and enormous evils of every kind, would be outdone.[46]

The violence spread to London and Leicester. No wonder the authorities were becoming concerned as to where all this would lead.

Cobden and Bright Enter the Fray

By this time, the convergence of the issue of free trade with that of the repeal of the Corn Laws had reached the cockpit of Westminster. It became a battle in the Budget of 1841, lasting for eight days and eight nights, with Palmerston converted to free trade and Peel dragging his heels. A confidence motion followed, with the Government winning a Pyrrhic victory of one, and then a summer General Election which turned on free trade. Perhaps alarmed by the riotous demonstrations associated with the repeal of the Corn Laws, the country voted against free trade, and Robert Peel became prime minister of a Conservative Government with a majority of 90 and a protectionist policy. In Lancashire, Cobden stood for the Anti-Corn Law League and entered Parliament as the Member for Stockport.

A new era began when Parliament assembled on 19 August 1841. Villiers himself said that Cobden had hesitated before seeking election and sought his advice. Villiers later recalled that he was, 'distinctly in favour of his doing so, if he could, for it is the House of Commons where our real opponents were in all their force, and where the fight had to really be carried on'.[47] Cobden knew what he was in for and had to endure ridicule, contempt and hostility from the Conservative majority whenever he mentioned free trade.

Speaking of his experiences on first entering Parliament, Cobden later wrote, 'The very first time I got up and spoke ... I declared I came there to do something – to repeal the Corn Laws, and I would know neither Whig nor Tory until that work was done.'[48] As with his future ally, Bright, Cobden trod a political path of being outside the control of the whips. To achieve great political change against the odds involves distance from the centre of gravity and the front bench.

Bright made a special visit to the House to listen to Cobden's maiden speech on 25 August 1841. Bright noted an absurd old Tory buffer by the name of Horace Twiss: 'When Mr Cobden sat down, he threw it off with a careless gesture and said, "Nothing in him; he is only a barker".' As Bright wrote, 'Well, this "barker" of Horace Twiss became a great power in the House of Commons and a great power in the country.'[49] So much for Mr Twiss and his kind, now as then.

Elizabeth Bright died on 10 September 1841. Bright tried to console himself by writing to Cobden the very same day: 'I know thou wilt sympathise with me in this very deep trial, and it is therefore I write to inform thee of it.'[50] Cobden replied the following day, asking if he might visit. Two days later, on 13 September, he arrived at the widower's home in Leamington. As Bright later recalled:

> I was in the depths of grief, I might almost say of despair, for the light and sunshine of my house had been extinguished ... Mr Cobden called upon me as his friend, and addressed me, as you might suppose with words of condolence. After a time he looked up and said, 'There are thousands of houses in England at this moment where wives, mothers, and children are dying of hunger. Now,' he said, 'when the first paroxysm of your grief is past, I would advise you to come with me, and we will never rest till the Corn Law is repealed.'[51]

In timing and execution, it was a shrewdly judged appeal, touching Bright's sense of duty and unlocking his pent-up energy and ambition at the very moment he felt fate compelling him to devote himself to the lives of others. Bright accepted. Cobden had come to recognize how rare a talent, how fine a character, Bright possessed. What was more, Cobden, an Anglican, realized Bright could better reach out to the Nonconformists whose support would be crucial if the Anti-Corn Law League was to build anything like a solid constituency. Bright wrote useful articles in the *Nonconformist*, but Cobden sensed it would be as an orator that Bright would really prove his worth. Hard work and a burning cause would indeed prove the antidote to personal grief. Between them, Cobden and Bright were about to bond together in a personal campaign, the like of which British politics had never seen before, or since, and which would affect Britain and the entire globe for generations to come.

1841–2

With his sister, Priscilla, caring for his daughter, and his presence not needed at the mill, Bright threw himself into the Anti-Corn Law League campaign. In December 1841, he drew attention to an independent report on the poor in Rochdale, and the high cost of food, high unemployment and extensive destitution:

We saw around us widespread distress. Misery was seen in the
house of every poor man ... Misery was to be seen on his very
threshold; haggard destitution and extreme poverty were the
most prominent things in his family. The consequence was that
discontent had so pervaded the country that scarcely any working man would lift a finger in defence of those institutions which
English men were wont to be proud of. Neither the monarch nor
the aristocracy were safe under such a state of things – a state of
things that would blast the fairest prospects and destroy the most
powerful nation that ever existed.[52]

Strong words, indeed. Bright moved a resolution at the Corn
Exchange, Manchester, on 16 December 1841, extending his cause to
the whole of Manchester. A report to the House of Commons demonstrated that since the sliding scale was introduced by Act of Parliament
in 1828, massive quantities of food had been deliberately thrown into
the Thames under the direction of customs officers because the value
of the food did not cover the cost of its warehousing.

In February 1842, Bright made his first speech in London at a
meeting at the Crown & Anchor in the Strand, chaired by Duncan
McLaren (soon to be his brother-in-law). Daniel O'Connell also
spoke. Bright told the meeting of the iniquities the people of
Rochdale were experiencing as a result of the Corn Laws, 'as
contrary to the most obvious requirements of morality and religion
and a wrong of so odious a nature as to make it imperatively necessary to insist on its total and immediate abolition'.[53] He said that
men in Rochdale were emigrating from England, but being so poor
they had to leave their families behind. Unemployment was accelerating and poverty was accompanied by starvation.

Peel's Free Trade Budget of 1842

The Corn Laws dominated parliamentary business in 1841 and
1842, but resolutions put forward by Lord John Russell and Villiers
were all defeated by substantial majorities. By March 1842, there
were 1.5 million signatures besieging Parliament via petitions organized by the Anti-Corn Law League. Indeed, what slender glimmer of
hope existed rested on the new prime minister, Sir Robert Peel, who
had been gradually edging away from his previous commitment to
protectionism. On the one hand, as the son of a cotton manufacturer
from Bury, Peel came from the sort of stock that was naturally align-
ing itself with the Anti-Corn Law League. But he had also been

moulded as a young man by two great bastions of the Anglican Establishment – Harrow School and Christ Church, Oxford (where he received a double first). His education, training and disposition divorced him from his commercial origins. An MP for Oxford University at the early age of 21, he had risen to become leader of a party of landowners and High Churchmen. As home secretary in the Duke of Wellington's Government in February 1829, and from his first election to Oxford, Peel had vigorously opposed Catholic emancipation, but had then come round to promoting it, even forcing a by-election in the University, because he recognized its necessity, not least because of the campaign of Daniel O'Connell, MP for County Clare in Ireland. Might the same sense of national emergency and national interest convince him of the need to face down his party's traditional wing a second time, this time over corn?

When Bright joined a 500-strong deputation of northern manufacturers from the League who travelled to London to see the new prime minister in person, Peel simply refused to clear his diary. Infuriated, the delegation decided on a display of protest – linking arms and walking along the Strand and down Whitehall. Reaching Palace Yard, their progress was blocked by 'Peelers' – as Sir Robert's policemen were widely known. Minor scuffles broke out, a chorus of 'Total Repeal!' and 'Cheap Food!' echoing around the entrance to Parliament. After a stand off, the delegation passed the entrance to Downing Street as Peel's carriage emerged on its way to the House of Commons. According to one eyewitness, 'He seemed to think at first that they were going to cheer him, but when he heard the angry shouts of "No Corn Law! Down with the Monopoly! Give Bread and Labour!" he leaned back in his carriage grave and pale.'[54] When he met one member of the deputation later, however, Peel found the arguments so persuasive that he thanked them and said that he believed the evidence was 'incontestable.'[55]

It would be surprising if this demonstration of hostility had caused Peel serious concern. He seemed very much in command of the situation. In April 1842 he introduced his Government's first budget and showed great mastery of the facts. Concentration on the Corn Laws should not divert attention from the importance of this and Peel's other Free Trade budgets which followed up on William Huskisson's initiatives in the 1820s and extended back to the economic theories of Adam Smith. It was one of the most significant budgets of the nineteenth century, representing a huge tilting of the economy towards free trade and, consequently, from indirect taxes on trade to direct taxes on income. In this,

Peel and his Treasury team showed advanced thinking beyond almost any other serious group – Whig, Radical or Tory – sitting in the Commons.

Even though, as part of his wider reforms, Peel did reduce the Corn Law rate at which foreign imports could be admitted from 64s to 56s per quarter, the problem for the prime minister was that, whereas reducing import duties on goods in general was looked on as understandable, as soon as the issue of corn arose, it became a matter of class, privilege and aristocratic landed vested interests. In other words, agriculture was politically off-limits for the Conservative Party as well as for the Whig landed interest, whose aristocratic friends dominated both parties in both Houses of Parliament.

Peel's practical approach to the stimulation of trade did not soothe the high emotions sweeping the country. The emotive issue of the Corn Laws made even Bright blind to the wider scope of Peel's budget, which included direct taxation instead of indirect taxes like the Corn Laws. The reintroduction of income tax left him apoplectic. 'No government,' he thundered to Cobden, 'can have a right to make me state the amount of my profits & it is a vile system of slavery to which Englishmen are about to be subjected.'[56] This view was shared by Cobden. Bright even envisaged helping to organize a civil disobedience campaign of non-payment against the income tax.

Agitation for Repeal

The agitation continued unabated. Bright spoke in Manchester in May and again in July 1842 in London. He reported on the campaign throughout the country and in Ireland. On 9 July 1842, after his earlier refusal, Peel agreed to meet a deputation from the north, among whom was Bright. As Bright himself later recalled,

> Sir Robert was sitting on a sofa. We made twelve speeches at him, and so impressively that he trembled like an aspen-leaf, and presently his nose began to bleed and he had to leave the room a while. That was a deputation to some purpose.[57]

As Peel listened, he was doubtless deeply conscious of his own family origins in Lancashire and, by contrast, the new prosperity and estates that he and others of his new class were now enjoying under the protection of the Corn Laws. Peel promised to bring the matters to the Cabinet.

At this time, Bright also first met W. E. Gladstone, then Conservative Member of Parliament for Newark. In later years, Gladstone recalled the meeting, saying, 'Mr Bright was, I think, almost the youngest among them. He is the only one of them all whom at this distance of time I recollect. I was much struck with the singular combination of business and energy in his countenance.'[58]

Bright was moving into his rhythm, the hallmark of which was a boundless energy when he was on the hoof. He spoke again in London at the end of July, alongside Joseph Hume, Villiers, Cobden and O'Connell. Bright was emerging as one of the Anti-Corn Law League's main weapons. Indeed, the League was nothing without oratory. As Norman Longmate points out, 'The early Victorian era was the golden age of the public speaker.'[59] Indeed, he quotes Sidney Smith as saying in 1840, 'Lecturing is truly the great engine of repeal.'[60] Longmate continues,

> The lecture was the classic means by which the ambitious sought self improvement; *Self-Help* itself, published in 1857, derived from the lectures delivered by Samuel Smiles, an active member of the League, to the Leeds Mechanics Institute in 1845. The League had been founded on lectures, first at Bolton and then in Manchester, and the earliest act of the Manchester Anti-Corn-Law Association was to offer the star of those occasions, A. W. Paulton, a regular appointment as peripatetic speaker.[61]

In consequence of Samuel Smiles' early lectures, which were heard by Newman Cash, the Quaker wool merchant who built Scarcroft Lodge on the outskirts of Leeds, Samuel Smiles was appointed as Secretary to the Leeds–Thirsk Railway, of which Newman Cash was founder and chairman. This was something of a sinecure to enable Smiles to continue his lecturing.[62] He then moved on to the National Provident Institution, of which William Cash was founder and chairman. There were many wheels within wheels in the radical reform movement, some of which overlapped with Quaker industrialists and entrepreneurs such as Joseph Sturge and the Birmingham circle, and the Lucas and Cash families.

The Campaign of the Chartists Continues

While Bright and his fellow orators appealed to great audiences, the campaign of the Chartists continued. Their leader, Feargus O'Connor, was himself embroiled in a monumental battle at a meeting in March 1842:

The result was a tremendous fight. All the furniture was smashed to atoms; forms, desks, chairs, gas pipes – were used as weapons and the result is something like as follows. 'The lion', the king of Chartism, F.O.'C knocked down three times; 'has,' he says, 'seven wounds, six he can tell the position of, the seventh was, I believe, inflicted as he was running away, which he did after fighting about two minutes.' Christopher Doyle very much hurt. Bailey: confined to his bed. Murray: ditto. Four others (Chartists) seriously hurt. Rev. Schofield: black eye, loose teeth, cut lips, contusions behind (got in following Feargus). Four of the 'lambs' are badly hurt, two with their skulls fractured. They, however, are used to it and will soon be well.[63]

Attempts to reconcile the antagonists were made, including by Smiles, who founded a Parliamentary Reform Association in Leeds. This was ridiculed as the 'Fox and Geese Club', indicating what would happen to those who sought reconciliation. By November 1841, Joseph Sturge, the Quaker pacifist and Bright's close friend, was advocating moderation in his paper, *Reconciliation Between the Middle and Lower Classes,* proposing that the middle class should seek the franchise. Out of all this emerged the Complete Suffrage Union. Bright had attended a meeting of this Union in Birmingham in April 1842 and written an optimistic report to Cobden. O'Connor, however, described it as 'a dodge of the League' and that 'Complete Suffrage was Complete Humbug'.[64] The Union lasted only three years. The middle class had no enthusiasm for an alliance with the Chartists.

In August 1842, the unrest arrived on Bright's own doorstep, with strikes across the north against wage cuts. In Rochdale, 6,000 people (a number that soon increased to 15,000), led by women, marched on mills in the neighbourhood. The Bright factory was besieged. The workers left the mill, the machinery stopped, and shortly afterwards, the Riot Act was read. The situation was becoming extremely dangerous. On 17 August, Bright himself spoke to the men of the town, saying,

You are suffering, you have long suffered, your wages for many years have declined and your position has gradually and steadily become worse ... You were urged to refuse to work until the Charter became the law. Many of you know full well that neither Act of Parliament nor act of multitude can keep up wages. You know that trade has long been bad and that with a bad trade, wages cannot rise.[65]

The issues were now directly confronting Bright's own business. He urged the strikers to return to work, which they soon did.

There were riots in other parts of Lancashire, with operatives pulling the plugs from boilers. Bright and Cobden by chance met O'Connor at a railway station on the London and Northwestern Railway, an encounter that resulted in strong exchanges.

In 1842, Bright wrote to Cobden, 'We must not touch the suffrage question.'[66] He explained how he had had a long discussion with a Chartist leader about the issue of wages. Bright wanted massive but constitutional meetings. The Chartists were in favour of confrontation, with strikes for higher wages. As Bright said, something had to be done in the light of the bad harvests and trade, and he argued against 'shutting our eyes and sticking our fingers in our ears, and railing at Chartists and Radicals.'[67]

Cobden and Bright

Cobden and Bright were in constant demand. Speaking to the working men of Rochdale in August 1842, Bright said, 'Moral force can only succeed through the electors, and these are not yet convinced.'[68] They addressed further meetings in Manchester and Coventry in November 1842, followed by meetings in Yorkshire, the North-West, the Midlands and Scotland. In January 1843, Bright demonstrated the impact of the Corn Laws in the following way:

> Perhaps you have seen a zoological garden, and you might have taken notice of the monkeys there. Monkeys generally have a can of porridge each to feed from; but I ask you, did ever you see a monkey begin with his own can? never; he commences with solemn grimace, and stealthily winds his long arms over the shoulder of his fellow-monkey, slipping his fingers into the can that belongs to his neighbour, and commences licking the produce of his mischief with delight – this is protection, or robbery – by which dignity is supported. But the evil does not cease with this simple abstraction. The monkey does not put into his mouth all that he has abstracted from his neighbour's can; no inconsiderable portion drops by the way, and is wasted. Every monkey follows the same practice and robs his neighbour, so that none receives a benefit; whilst a large portion of their food is spilt on the ground from their fingers in its conveyance to their mouths. So it is with the advocates of the Corn Laws.[69]

Bright's increasing role in the League was secondary to the economic influence of Cobden. However close the relationship, they were different in their approach, but not in the principles they were advocating. Less blunt and pugnacious than Bright, Cobden was never turned to anger or descended into personal attacks. As Longmate points out, he is said to have remarked, 'When I have done I leave off and sit down.' Indeed, Bright described Cobden as possessing 'A conversational eloquence, a persuasiveness which it is almost impossible to resist.'[70] Quoting Ebenezer Elliot, the poet to the Corn Law movement, Smiles wrote, 'To Cobden, he gave the praise of having popularized the cause and knocked it into the public mind by dint of sheer hard work and strong practical common sense.'[71] Bright and Cobden were a perfect match and devoted to one another from the moment they first met. The idea, somewhat put about by Donald Read, that Bright sought to upstage Cobden and even to exaggerate his own role, is unfair. As Bright himself stated when Cobden, faced with financial and personal difficulties, thought of resigning, 'Your retirement would be tantamount to a dissolution of the League. Its mainspring would be gone. I can in no degree take your place.'[72] Bright would invariably speak second when they were on the same platform, with Cobden seeking co-operation between all the classes, even the aristocracy, but Bright emphasising class war.

Many of these meetings aimed to raise the funds necessary to continue the campaign. In January 1843, Bright spoke at Lancaster, followed by Edinburgh, Dundee, Manchester and Ashton in rapid succession. The centre of gravity, however, remained in Manchester. By the end of 1839, it had been decided to build a dedicated League conference hall in the town to supplement the use of the Corn Exchange, which had been opened in 1838. The proposed site was on land owned by Cobden in St Peter's Field, coincidentally the site of the Peterloo Massacre. Unbelievably, this first building, The Pavilion, constructed mainly of wood, was put up in a mere eleven days. There were concerns about safety, but there were no mishaps. In 1842, its replacement, the brick-built Free Trade Hall, was constructed in just six weeks.[73]

The Anti-Corn Law League used the new building to hold fund-raising musical events, such as a performance of Haydn's *Creation* and so-called 'Grand Miscellaneous Concerts', and a wide variety of entertainments including ventriloquists, singing groups, dancing troupes and acrobatic displays. Black entertainers came from New Orleans. Not to be outdone, Mr Swaine, 'the Prince of Banjo

Players', played new solos and Master Ole Bull played Paganini on the violin, followed by burlesques from the Italian opera, all at the price of one shilling for a reserved seat, a gallery seat for sixpence and the promenade at threepence. Politics could be fun, but had to be organized.

A massive banquet for 4,000 people was held on 1 February 1843 to mark the opening of the Free Trade Hall. John Bright spoke of the unemployed,

> I hold myself in some degree the representative of them. And any man may, who has any capital by which he employs any of them. I hold that man, as the representative of those whom he employs, is bound to use his influence to save them from the ruin which the blind and slavish aristocracy of this country are very rapidly bringing upon them.[74]

Bright saw himself as their representative even before he entered the House of Commons. His commitment and representation transcended any formal public office. No one could accuse him of slacking. That first week of February 1843, during which Peel once again refused to amend the Corn Laws, Bright addressed the Leaguers convened in Manchester on five successive nights.

On 13 February, Viscount Howick (later the 3rd Earl Grey) moved a motion in the House of Commons on the national state of manufacturing. The debate raged for four days, set against the background of the murder of Peel's secretary, Edward Drummond, who had been shot in Whitehall a month before by a mentally deranged Scotsman who mistook him for the prime minister. Cobden uncharacteristically personalized his attack on Peel saying that the prime minister had taken the Corn Law into his own hands and passed the law, refusing to listen to the manufacturers, and was thereby responsible for the state of affairs. He went on, 'I must tell the right hon. Baronet that it is the duty of every honest and independent Member to hold him individually responsible for the present position of the country.'[75] Peel was outraged, and replied, 'Never will I be influenced by menaces either in this House or out of this House, to adopt a course which I consider ...' – at this point, his words were drowned out by shouts from various parts of the House.[76] Cobden denied that he had said that the prime minister was 'personally responsible', and Peel retorted, 'You did – you did!' Uproar ensued and the whole House was convulsed in fury.

In the meantime, outside Parliament, another massive meeting was held in the Free Trade Hall on 23 February. Bright said of Peel that he shrank from his responsibilities, adding that, 'I believe we shall be amply repaid in the marvellous change which, in a few years, will take place in the moral aspect of the country.'[77]

The League was brilliantly organized, distributing literally millions of pamphlets, tracts, souvenirs and stickers. In 1843, the League generated nine million items of literature, weighing 100 tons. They did not have the national press on their side, though *The Economist* – even today still true to its original principles – was created in September 1843 by George Wilson's brother, James, with their enthusiastic support of the League, but they did have organization. It is interesting to think what imaginative use they would have made of today's modern technology.

Bright spoke in Bristol in March, followed by the Drury Lane Theatre in London, then on to Tiverton, followed by Gloucester and Cheltenham, and then Nottingham, Taunton, Davenport, and Liskeard in Cornwall, before heading back up to Manchester, zigzagging about the country. He then moved on to Plymouth and Sheffield, and then back to the Drury Lane Theatre on 26 April, where he talked about not only the poverty in Leeds and Manchester but also in Ireland. Of the Irish, he said,

> Persons not more than twenty-five years or thirty years of age appeared poor decrepit creatures, as old as others at sixty or seventy. How could it be otherwise? They were born in the greatest possible degree of wretchedness; they had never had enough of good and substantial diet ... They had never been well-clothed or sheltered: they had no sunshine in their hearts, and grew up to be stunted and dwarfish and miserable. As to Sheffield, seven or eight years ago not one in a thousand of the population of Sheffield was a pauper, but now the proportion was one in nine.[78]

Between 1 and 19 May, Bright spoke in Macclesfield, High Wycombe, Weymouth, Lincoln and London – twice with Cobden and once alone – and in June travelled to Huntingdon and Norwich. The sheer intensity and exertion was simply extraordinary. He would frequently speak for many hours at a time, followed by questions and discussions with those from the audience. There was no time in those days for sound bites. Anyone observing this itinerary, given the measured tones and magnificence of his oratory, would know this could only be achieved by an inner conviction that drove him – and Cobden – on.

Much of Bright's travelling was by the newly created rail system, which became a vital ally in maintaining the momentum of his campaign. Throughout the nineteenth century, British society was very much based on locality, with villages and hamlets being owned by the local gentry and governed by the magistracy, itself under the control of landowners. The Chartist movement in particular was greatly stimulated by its use of meetings at central points which attracted very substantial numbers of people from outlying villages. O'Connor was the most remarkably active Chartist and managed 147 public meetings in 1838 and 1839 alone. Add to this the great meeting halls springing up in the industrial towns, and it was possible, with energy and determination, to reach out to the whole country on a scale of energy that makes present-day campaigners with modern means of communication seem lazy by comparison. Bright picked up on all this and moved forward the localist movements to a more national level.[79]

Election to Durham, 1843

It was an inevitable step from this campaign to Parliament itself. In the middle of all this activity and almost as an interval, in early April Bright fought an election in Durham against Lord Dungannon – a move clearly based on principle and national interest, not party. Bright's own principles were 'freedom of trade, justice to all classes of people, impartiality in the administration of the laws, a government to protect and not to oppress, and all those principles which were truly and really conservative of all that is worthy of conservation beneath the dominion of the British Crown.'[80] He stood also on the Corn Laws and Ireland. Having only a few hours to canvass before the hustings – compared to the many weeks his opponent had enjoyed, Bright lost the ballot, but only by 100 votes.

Defeated at Durham, he continued his tour of the country, but pursued his opponent on a petition for bribery. The petition began its procedure in the House of Commons at the beginning of July. It took two days, declaring Dungannon's election void, although they excused Dungannon personally of the actions of his agents. Villiers and Cobden consulted one another about Bright's prospects. Cobden believed that Bright would, 'From his peculiar and effective style of speaking at public meetings, do the cause more good by remaining out than by entering Parliament.'[81] Villiers disagreed, arguing that Bright's plain and hard-hitting way of speaking was as much required there as elsewhere. Villiers was right and Cobden unusually wrong.

On 4 July, the day after Dungannon's election was voided, Bright reissued his address to the Durham electors. Two days later he was in Winchester. There, he was heckled at an open air meeting of about 2,000 people. The heckler was the founder of modern socialism himself, Robert Owen, who had travelled to Winchester specifically to argue for his vision of the future and a new state of society. The following day, Bright appeared in Kelso in Scotland. On his way back, he spoke to farmers at a meeting hosted by the free traders of Alnwick. Bright then went to Newcastle, followed by North Shields and Sunderland. He spoke of Irishmen that he had recently met near Rochdale, saying of them that 'they were not men but skeletons walking abroad, exciting the pity of the people. It is a notorious fact that these men are old at thirty and thirty-five and such a population is not to be found in any country in Europe.'[82]

Returning to Durham on 17 July, he set his mind to fighting his new opponent, a barrister and Tory protectionist called Thomas Purvis. Hoarse from his activities of the previous two weeks, Bright addressed a meeting of 5,000 from the window of the City Tavern. He affirmed his working credentials and that his father had been as poor as any man in the crowd and what he had made was by his own industry and equally that Bright himself had achieved what he had from his own exertions. He then stated, as a hallmark of his future career,

> I have no interest in the extravagance of Government; I have no interest in receiving appointments under any Government; I have no interest in pandering to the views of any Government; I have nothing to gain by being the tool of any party. I come here before you as the friend of my own class and order, as one of the people; as one who would on all occasions, be the firm defender of all your rights, and asserter of all those privileges to which you are justly entitled.[83]

Following further meetings each day, Bright was nominated on 23 July and the hustings were erected in front of the Town Hall. Bright's nomination came amid a great palaver and some agitation and cheering. In the words of John Henderson, his proposer,

> We shall send Mr Bright to Parliament as the champion of Free
> Trade and when History records, as she will most assuredly do,
> the abolition of these wicked and unjust laws which have so long
> robbed you of your natural rights ... she will record at the same
> time that the men of the good old city of Durham came forward
> boldly, and set a glorious example to the other constituencies of
> the kingdom.[84]

Bright was to become not only a champion of free trade but also of
democracy. Both of these derived from Bright's acutely instinctive
awareness, from his Quaker background and concern for conscience
and internal reflection, that the troubles thrown up by the Corn
Laws by monopoly, privilege and aristocracy, were a denial to other
human beings by those who benefited from the advantages of being
of the landed gentry and the upper classes. The problems would
only be resolved by restoring to the individuals their human dignity,
their freedom of choice and the opportunity to better themselves by
self-help and personal industry. This was not a theory in a vacuum,
but a conscious awareness in practice that the destitute and the
starving, whether in England or Ireland, or in the case of the slaves
in the Southern states of America, would not be relieved of their
misery unless and until their own individual human spirit was
given the opportunity to break out of the chains of repression.
Bright's emphasis on the human spirit, freedom of choice and
individual will, based on moral purpose, principle and conviction,
led to a horizon of freedom and a new world that people could
inhabit with prosperity.

Bright then delivered a speech which extended over nearly five
columns in the newspapers, setting out why he proposed to go into
Parliament and outlining the path he would then follow. It contained
not only his immediate political and social objectives, but also a
depth of philosophical understanding of the benefits to be derived
from the repeal of the Corn Laws and the redress of grievances
in general:

> It must not be supposed, because I wish to represent the interest
> of the majority that I am hostile to the interest of the few. But is
> it not perfectly certain that if the foundation of the most magnif-
> icent building be destroyed and undermined, that the whole
> fabric itself is in danger? ... There never was a revolution in any
> country which destroyed the great body of the people.[85]

Purvis spoke next and a poll was demanded. The following day the
election took place, with Bright gaining the seat by 488 votes to 410.
Cobden was in Bristol when he heard of the result. He congratulated
the people of Durham, saying 'We complain of Parliament that it
does not do our work, but do we choose men likely to do it?'[86]
Cobden added that men were frequently elected 'who would shine
most in a horse race or an assembly, and who wear harlequin jackets
to ride a race,'[87] rather than those of substance and trust. When
Cobden met up with Bright in Manchester, he said to him, 'I've had
all the dirt thrown at me heretofore; now you, being younger, will
share it with me, and probably get the larger share. You'll have it in
style in the House of Commons.'[88] Never was a truer word said
in jest.

Making his way to London to enter Parliament, Bright demonstrated his personal, and rather un-Quakerlike, awareness of the
need to make a proper impression. He wrote to his sister, 'I want
thee to make up in a parcel my new coat and best greatcoat and send
them off immediately by the first train … as I must be decently
attired when I enter the House.'[89] By all accounts, he was always
very particular about his clothes, though throughout his life it was
always black and formal, in Quaker style, with a black cravat held
down by a black enamel pin and a simple gold watch chain.
How unlike Disraeli's entry into the House of Commons, with
clothes described as 'peculiar' and having 'much of a theatrical
aspect'.[90] Both men faced unfavourable comment about their dress,
but foolish were those who underestimated them.

Bright's entry to the House of Commons was, however, met
favourably and with great anticipation by the press, which is hardly
surprising, given the impact he had already made up and down the
country over the previous three years. The *Illustrated London News*
reported the occasion with the words:

> As a speaker, Mr Bright is far superior to many who are listened
> to in that assembly; but those who know the constitution of that
> House know also the great influence of station, name, and
> wealth, and how much dulness [*sic*] will be tolerated from one of
> a good family … Mr Bright is about the middle size, rather
> firmly and squarely built, with a fair, clear complexion and an
> intelligent and pleasing expression of countenance. His voice is
> good, his enunciation is distinct and his delivery free from any
> unpleasant peculiarity or mannerism. He is young, and has
> apparently a long career before him. His dress is rather more

recherché than that of the 'Friends' of a generation back, differing but slightly from the ordinary costume of the day.[91]

Even at this early stage his success was a matter of comment also in America, where it was written that

> Mr Bright is a man of great integrity, sound judgment, extensive information, pleasing address; an interesting and impressive speaker; frank, straightforward, persevering, and inflexible; a firm advocate for justice to Ireland, for universal suffrage and for the separation of Church and State; a friend of peace with all nations and of justice to all men; and the election of such a man to Parliament, under such unfavourable circumstances, is worthy to be recorded conspicuously amongst the signs of the times as the hope of England.[92]

Little did the author of this newspaper article appreciate, perhaps, how apposite his remarks were soon to be in respect of the history of America itself.

Bright took his seat on 28 July 1843. On 7 August, he delivered his maiden speech and, while it is said that he started somewhat nervously, he soon got into his stride. In typical fashion from the start, he turned his direct, personal attention to Prime Minister Peel and his policies. As a maiden speaker, to embark on such a controversial course would be regarded at least as daring and at the worst as dangerous. He attacked and challenged the prime minister on every front, as prime minister, as a minister of the Crown, as party leader and on principle:

> I am surprised at the course pursued by the right hon. Baronet. I should be glad to see him, not the Minister of the Queen merely, but the Minister of the people also. I should rejoice to see him disconnect himself from the party whose principles he declares to be unsound. I should be glad to see him bearing in mind the source from which he has sprung, the source of his power and wealth, as it is the source of much of the power and wealth, and greatness of this empire. He may have a laudable ambition – he may seek renown, but no man can be truly great who is content to serve an oligarchy, who regard no interest but their own; and whose legislation proves they have no sympathy with the wants of the great body of their countrymen. I live in the manufacturing districts, I am well acquainted with the wishes

and feelings of the population, and I do not hesitate to say, when
I view the utter disregard with which they are treated by this
House, that the dangers which impend are greater than those
which now surround us. I can assure the right hon. the President
of the Board of Trade, that his flimsy excuses will not avail him at
the bar of public opinion ... That this is not the time is an excuse
which is untrue as it is insulting. When will the time come? Will
monopoly resign its hold of the subsistence of the people?
Can the Ethiopian change his skin, or the leopard his spots?
The Government knows what is right – the people demand it to
be done, and the ministry who refuse to act incur a fearful
responsibility.[93]

Thus he began his political career as he continued throughout his
life: direct and to the point. It is hardly surprising that Peel subsequently said of Bright in a private conversation, 'Ah, here at last is
one of those terrible men of 1832.'[94]

CHAPTER 2

The Corn Laws in Parliament: Harrying Peel

*We have taught the people of this country
the value of a great principle.*
(John Bright, 2 July 1846)

The Agitation Continues

When Bright entered Parliament, Cobden was already an object of loathing in the House. Both were ridiculed. When they argued that women 'were crying for employment', 'making trousers at sixpence a pair', and that 'thousands were starving for food', there was a din of hilarious laughter from the Tory benches – the usual cackle of those found out.[1] In early August 1843, at a public meeting with Bright in Kent, Cobden had been prodded in the abdomen with a stick by an angry landowner. Undaunted, they went on to Reading, Liverpool, Bury, Oxford and Lancaster. Wherever they went they were joined by other like-minded MPs. Returning to London, the Anti-Corn Law League held its first monthly meeting at the Covent Garden Theatre on 28 September. Two weeks later, under the chairmanship of Villiers, they spoke again at the theatre, calling for 'the termination of the existence of the accursed Corn Laws'.[2] London was followed rapidly by Doncaster, Durham and Berwick-on-Tweed.

By early November, they had travelled 850 miles in nine days, delivering speech after speech. Henry Warburton was elected for free trade in Kendal against the Lonsdale family's candidate, but at Salisbury the free trade candidate went down. Within days they were back in Manchester, raising money for the campaign. Setting a new target of £100,000 (which today would be worth over £8 million) they raised £13,500 in a single day. In Rochdale, they raised a further £2,500. A torrent of pamphlets and newsletters was cascading from the League; in 1843 alone, five million copies of League material were issued to accompany the speaking tours.

Cobden and Bright both argued that poverty led to crime. Their own survey had demonstrated great poverty in Dorchester and Dorset, a constituency represented by Lord Ashley, who continuously criticized manufacturers and the conditions in the mills and workplaces. In response to Ashley's criticisms, Bright admitted that there were 'serious evils, and much distress' in the manufacturing towns, but pointed out that mill owners provided day schools and that his male workers received 16 shillings a week, compared to Dorset farmhands, who were paid less than eight shillings a week. He also maintained that the factories were safer than agricultural work, citing only five accidents at his own mills in the past 15 years.[3] Against this background, Cobden challenged Ashley to remedy his own constituency. This argument continued into the 1860s, with Ashley gaining more support as time went on, and manufacturing activity became further regulated. Bright's 'Observations' on the Factory Acts, however, did admit that employers were not blameless.[4]

The relentless provincial tour of 1843 was noted by *The Times* which, despite its editorial policy, admitted on 18 November that

> The League is a great fact. It would be foolish, nay rash, to deny its importance ... It demonstrates the hardy sense of purpose – the indomitable will – by which Englishmen, working together for a great object, are armed and animated ... These are facts important and worthy of consideration. No moralist can disregard them; no politician can sneer at them; no statesman can undervalue them ... A new power has arisen in the state.[5]

The Government really had nothing to offer against this barrage of articulate, passionate argument. As the *Gloucestershire Chronicle* put it, 'What are the Conservatives doing? Nothing. The contrast between the two parties is most striking. The Conservatives seem steeped in criminal apathy.'[6]

The speeches moved to Liverpool, raising £4,500, then Huddersfield, Manchester, Leeds, Holmfirth, Halifax and Warrington, until exhaustion took its toll in early 1844. With no means of communication other than personal appearance, they were driven by a relentless energy in pursuit of the cause, albeit with a freedom denied to modern MPs. They did not have to attend to constituency affairs and correspondence. They had more time to think and to adapt their message to different localities and, with minimal party discipline, their presence was not demanded in the House – no doubt to the relief of both Bright and Cobden. They had more important things to do than listen to the rantings of the landowners in the House of Commons.

In January 1844, Bright and Cobden made for Carlisle, Edinburgh and Ayr, followed by Kilmarnock and Dumfries, back down to Sunderland and Sheffield, York and Hull, Blackburn, Wakefield and Bradford. They finished at London's Covent Garden Theatre, where Bright stated,

> I am certain also that the world is looking on upon this great struggle ... and the time is not far distant when Britain shall add to all the other things of which she may boast, this greatest of all boasts – that she was the first of the great commercial nations of the earth who struck down a principle [protection] which has existed for centuries, and for centuries has been false.[7]

Peel remained unmoved. In the Queen's Speech in February, he stated that the Government 'have not contemplated, and do not contemplate any alteration of the law which at present regulates the importation of corn'.[8] Peel was not for repeal.

By the end of February, again at Covent Garden, Bright declared, 'We did not commence our agitation proposing always to use smooth phrases. Men do not use straws to cut down oaks.' On 7 March, the first free trade debate in Parliament saw Bright heckled and obstructed, with one member shouting 'Don't let that odious Leaguer talk of corn in connection with sugar!'[9] The free traders were soundly beaten. A few days later, on 12 March, Cobden moved a motion for a select committee to inquire into the effects of protection on tenant farmers and manual labourers. Yet again, the free trade argument was lost.

The tactics of the Anti-Corn Law League then took a significant change of direction. Concentrating on increasing the registration of electors to get more free traders into the House of Commons, they ensured registration of their eligible supporters while eliminating those disqualified who were likely to vote for protection. Another tactic was to buy land and, taking advantage of the property qualification, fill it with properties occupied by new voters sympathetic to free trade; £15,000 (£1.2 million today) was spent on all this in 1845 alone.

Another secret weapon the repealers employed to great effect in their cause was the enthusiasm, indeed total commitment, of

women. This had been emerging for several years, with massive
tea parties held under the banner of the Anti-Corn Law League.
In subsequent years, the Conservative Party would take its cue
from these in the creation of the Primrose League under Lord
Randolph Churchill (see Chapter 9). Cobden's wife took a very
active part and became President of the Manchester Ladies'
Committee, which highlighted the appalling conditions in which
women lived in poverty, and issued graphic descriptions of the inhu-
mane conditions in sweatshops in London and elsewhere. The
women Leaguers stepped up their level of activity, including a
massive bazaar run by 400 women on 8 May 1845 which included
manufactured produce from every corner of the land. In the words
of the *Morning Chronicle*,

> [This Free Trade bazaar] is by far the most decisive sign that the
> history of the Free Trade movement has yet shown, not only of
> the resources, zeal and sound judgement of the extraordinary
> association under whose auspices it is presented to the world, but
> of the extent and thoroughness with which Free Trade principles
> have leavened the public mind.[10]

The bazaar raised the massive sum of £25,000 in goods sold for the
cause – equal to no less than £2 million today.

In parallel, the menfolk of the League were increasing their determined efforts at public meetings. On 27 March 1844, Bright made
another powerful speech at the Covent Garden Theatre in London.
He said,

> The principles of free trade are so simple that the mind of
> no unbiased man who hears them will have any hesitation
> in receiving them as true ... We ask that the world should be our
> workshop, and the wide world our market.[11]

The case for global trade could not be better expressed today than in
those words.

On 19 July he returned to the House of Commons where he
launched a powerful attack against the landowning class, saying,

> The great and all-present evil of the rural districts is this – you
> have too many people for the work to be done, and you, the
> landed proprietors, are alone responsible for this state of things;
> and, to speak honestly, I believe many of you know it. I have been

charged with saying out of doors that this House is a club of landowners legislating for landowners.

He accused them of saying that

> the labourers did not understand political economy, or they would not apply to Parliament to raise wages; that Parliament could not raise wages; and yet the very next thing you did was to pass a law to raise the price of the produce of your own land at the expense of the very class whose wages you confessed your inability to increase.[12]

He launched into a condemnation of the Corn Laws and of the crime and rural agitation they had induced, including the murder of several gamekeepers in different counties.

In August 1844, Bright overcame Feargus O'Connor in a debate on free trade at Northampton. He visited Walsall in September and Manchester in late October, where he reminded his audience that they had been fighting the Corn Laws for seven years, and that Manchester had been the birthplace of the Anti-Corn Law movement. He added,

> I often wonder why it is that men are so willing to bow their necks to men who are ornamented with stars and garters and titles; for I am sure the more I come in contact with these characters, the more I come to the conclusion that it is something far beyond titles which constitutes true nobility of character ... And there is not any creature which crawls the earth, to my mind more despicable and more pitiable than the man who sacrifices the interests of his own class, of his own order, and of his own country, merely that he may toady to somebody who has a title to his name.[13]

Further meetings followed: Rochdale in November, Huddersfield at the beginning of December and Covent Garden again on 11 December. In London, Bright connected the issue of free trade with liberty itself, saying,

> Yes, freedom is Heaven's first gift to man. It is his heritage, he has it by charter from Heaven, and, although it has struggled so long, this principle is still living, breathing, growing, and every day increasing in strength ... Liberty is too precious and sacred a

thing ever to be entrusted to the keeping of another man. Be the
guardians of your own rights and liberties, if you be not, you will
have no protectors, but spoilers of all that you possess.[14]

His speech was infused with optimism:

The freedom from which you struggle, is the freedom to live; it
is the right to eat your bread by the sweat of your brow ... I think
I behold the dawn of a brighter day; all around are the elements
of a mighty movement.[15]

Bright went to Bradford the following day, followed by Wakefield, a
banquet in Farringdon Hall in London on 16 December, then on to
Keighley and Pontefract, with two days off for Christmas before
bringing the year and the procession of meetings to an end on
27 December at Cleckheaton and Batley in Yorkshire.

The next year – 1845 – opened with a meeting in Preston on
2 January, then Warrington and Chorley and back to Manchester
with Cobden on 8 January, followed by Wigan and Bramley. Around
1,300 people attended at Blackburn on 13 January, and Bright was
received enthusiastically when he returned to his constituency in
Durham two days later. On 22 January, the Anti-Corn Law League
held its annual meeting at the Free Trade Hall in Manchester. Bright
announced that between 1842 and that date, the League had raised
£240,000 (£19.3 million today) to support the cause by covering
the cost of its pamphlets and other literature, hire of meeting places,
and other expenses.[16]

Bright made a powerful attack on the Corn Laws in the debate on
the Queen's Speech in February 1845. He launched a new missile
on 27 February, calling for a select committee to inquire into the
Game Laws, another aspect of the growing battle between the landowning aristocracy and their working class tenants. This committee
was set up, but when Cobden moved a similar motion in mid-March
to look at agricultural distress, he was defeated.

The new strategies of the Anti-Corn Law League were having an
effect, as Bright wrote to Duncan McLaren, in 1845: the free trade
party 'have formed if not a numerous yet a somewhat valiant party
in a good cause'. In the same letter, referring to Lord John Russell
and his gradual but almost imperceptible movement towards them,
he wrote 'He is now for the extinction of protection and pleads only
for its gradual abolition' and that privately he was 'fully resolved now
on the principle'.[17]

Peel was also moving towards free trade. Famously, in March 1845, after a particularly withering attack from Cobden and Bright in the House of Commons, Peel turned to Sidney Herbert, his confidant, and said 'You must answer this, for I cannot.'[18] After adjourning for dinner, Peel confided in Herbert that within the year he would have to repeal the Corn Laws.

On 10 June 1845, when Villiers brought forward his annual call for repeal, the significant majority against him had shrunk. Evidence of poverty and the degradation of the agricultural workers was coming to light. One report from Herefordshire claimed that as many as 200 families were living like cattle. In August, Bright himself published statistics showing that there was a direct connection between the Corn Laws and emigration, crime and death, and that in the years when the price of corn was high, the situation rapidly became worse in each table of statistics.

A severe threat to the campaign arose that autumn, when Cobden decided to leave Parliament, his business interests having suffered profoundly as a result of incessant campaigning. Before doing so, however, he wrote to Bright, who immediately advised him not to make a sudden decision and that they should speak face to face before anything became public. His news, Bright wrote to Cobden, had 'made me more sad than I can express' and he swore that he would reveal nothing of this

> in the hope that some way of escape may be found. I am of the opinion that your retirement would be tantamount to a dissolution of the League; its mainspring would be gone. I can in no degree take your place. As a second I can fight, but there are incapacities about me, about which I am fully conscious, which prevent my being more than a second in such a work as we have laboured in.[19]

Bright made it clear that he would do everything possible to come to the rescue. This letter is the clearest evidence that, contrary to the impression given by Donald Read in his book, *Cobden and Bright*,[20] Bright had no desire to undermine his closest friend and colleague, or claim pre-eminence in their mutual struggles. Bright was true to his word and money was found to take care of Cobden's business difficulties, enabling his friend to continue their campaign.

Bright himself suffered business difficulties periodically. For example, between 1846 and 1848, John Bright & Co. had gone on short time and had lost £10,000.[21] As he later admitted, he was very

conscious of the debt he owed to his brother, Thomas, for managing
the firm while he was otherwise occupied: 'I have been permitted to
be free from the employments and engagements and embarrass-
ments of business by the constant and undeviating generosity and
kindness of my brother. These are things one ought not to forget.'[22]

On 2 October 1845, another great voice allied itself to the cause.
Thomas Babington Macaulay, the great historian, threw his weight
firmly behind the repeal of the Corn Laws as the Member for
Edinburgh, stating, 'I have always considered the principle of
protection to agriculture as a vicious principle. I thought that vicious
principles took, in the laws of 1815, of 1828, and of 1842, a pecu-
liarly vicious form.'[23] He had taken this view when standing for
Leeds in 1833, and again in 1839. Indeed, when invited by Lord
Melbourne in that year to join his Government he had told him to
his face that he would vote for the total repeal of the Corn Laws.
Macaulay said,

> No intermediate shades are now left. The light is divided from
> the darkness. There stand two parties, ranged against each other.
> There is the standard of monopoly and here is the standard of
> free trade; and as your representative, I pledge myself to be faith-
> ful to the standard of free trade.[24]

To great cheers and in language matching that of Bright himself,
Macaulay spoke at length and with great oratorical and literary
mastery. Condemning those who perpetuated the Corn Laws, and
drawing attention to the dreadful situation that was stalking
Parliament with the failure of the potato crop in Ireland, he added,
'You have the Irish population crying famine, while the index of
your Corn Law is pointed to plenty.'[25] He warned that the price of
corn and the famine together would lead to calamity, echoing the
repeated warnings of Cobden and Bright.

On 28 October, 8,000 people came to the Free Trade Hall, ten
days after yet another money-raising bazaar at the same venue,
and Cobden warned Peel in relation to the impending disaster in
Ireland that 'he would be a criminal and a poltroon'[26] if he did
not act immediately. Bright spoke after him, and he too accused
those perpetuating the Corn Laws of nothing less than criminal
behaviour. Even Lord Ashley in Dorset admitted that the
Government should find a way of repealing the laws, and Queen
Victoria herself wrote to Peel on 28 November saying that 'The
Queen thinks the time is come when a removal of the restrictions

upon the importation of food cannot be successfully resisted.'[27] She took the issue to heart.

There was a year of appalling weather affecting most of Europe in 1845, and the potato crop failed in Ireland, followed by immediate famine. Evidence emerged from across Ireland and Britain of destitution, starvation and death. In one report from Bicester in Oxfordshire, the local congregational minister reported,

> In one hovel I found only one bed for seven persons including husband, wife and children!! In another hovel, in Upper Arncott, I saw the corpse of a child laid out on a small table at the fireside. It was laid there because there was no room for it in the place in which the wretched family sleep.[28]

Sounding the Retreat

The pressure was building up on the Government, and Peel held as many as five Cabinet meetings in one week to try to find a solution. Lord John Russell wrote an open letter on 22 November to his constituents in the City of London, drawing attention to the urgency and dangers, but claimed that 'Government is no more subject to blame for the failure of the potato crop than it was entitled to credit for the plentiful corn harvest'.[29] But eventually he went on to blame the Corn Laws, stating that he had changed his views on these over the previous twenty years and urging his constituents to petition Parliament.

Under such pressure, Peel offered his resignation on 5 December 1845. Queen Victoria called on Russell, but he could not form a Cabinet. Peel resumed office knowing that 200 of his own Conservatives would vote against him on the repeal of the Corn Laws. He could only stay in office with the support of 90 Conservatives and 180 Radicals.

The League smelt blood and stepped up its efforts. On 4 December, Cobden wrote to his wife that 'Bright and I are almost off our legs.'[30] Meeting followed meeting: Gloucester, Stroud, Bath, Bristol, Nottingham, Derby, Stockport, one meeting after another, as the tempo and the pressure increased and the famine, death and political ferment fused together in Parliament and throughout the land. As Bright had pointed out in a speech at Bolton in November,

> If South Lancashire, the West Riding of Yorkshire, North Lancashire, North Cheshire, Middlesex, and South Staffordshire

> – if these counties and divisions of counties are ready to
> pronounce in favour of Free Trade by the return of men who
> are members and friends of the Anti-Corn Law League to
> Parliament at the next election – it is producing its effect now
> on the mind of Sir R. Peel. He is not the man to stop 'til the elec-
> tion comes. He knows that if the votes be on the register, the men
> will be in the House of Commons ... We have the weapon here;
> their hands are tied. Let us keep this weapon bright; let us use
> it bravely.[31]

The writing was on the wall.

On 23 December 1845, at an historic meeting with the Queen,
Peel committed himself to abolish the Corn Laws, in the certain
knowledge that this would split his party down the middle. The
punishing schedule that Bright and Cobden had pursued, and
the economic and political circumstances, had converged to burst
the dam. It was now only a matter of time. Vast sums of money
continued to pour in, with one Anti-Corn Law meeting in
Manchester raising £60,000 in a matter of hours.

The next year, 1846, began with uncertainty. The Government
was on the back foot. The Queen was in favour of repeal and Peel
was prime minister of a Government in which some Members were
refusing to comply and which was under siege from Cobden and
Bright, the reformers and repealers, mass agitation, and the spectre
of famine and death in Ireland.

It can scarcely be imagined these days, but every speech made by
Bright and Cobden, each adapted to its audience, resonated with
argument, statistics, principle and anecdote. They kept audiences
transfixed for hours at a time by a mixture of analysis, humour and
conviction of a kind simply unknown in the present day. In
Newcastle-upon-Tyne on 6 January, Bright drew attention to the
hatred that was now being heaped on Peel by the protectionists,
who sensed that the Government was staggering towards the abolition of the Corn Laws. The protectionists were, Bright said, stirring
up fears of war with America. Three days later, in Liverpool, he
argued that 'the great reduction of the American tariff must follow
the abolition of our Corn Laws; the abolition of our Corn Laws will
forever destroy all chance of war between this country and the
United States.'[32]

Bright piled on the pressure, driving Peel relentlessly into a
corner. The idea that Peel succumbed to the notion of repeal
overnight would be a myth; he was simply driven out on a limb by

principle, arguments, mass agitation and the sheer destitution of the people. It is as if, today, the Common Agricultural Policy were to be laid bare with an economic crisis in the Eurozone combining with high unemployment and debt throughout the European Union – and that this all came home to roost.

On 14 January 1846, Bright called on an audience at Leeds to rally 'under a flag upon which the term "No Surrender" is inscribed … The people of this country are to be hoodwinked no longer.'[33] He went on to list the sums of money recently raised: £60,000 at Manchester, £15,000 in Liverpool and now £33,000 in Leeds, where he was speaking. Referring to a meeting planned for later that week at the Free Trade Hall in Manchester, he said 10,000 people had applied for tickets and that, before returning to Parliament, he himself would be going to Manchester and then Oldham while Cobden went to Norwich.

At the Manchester meeting on 16 January, Bright reminded the audience of Peel's Lancashire background, stating that

> he sprang from cotton, was born in Lancashire, traces his origin to the mighty industry for which this district is distinguished and that he should be the statesman that should confer on industry that freedom and that entire emancipation that we now so unanimously ask at his hands. Let him do right by the people, and the people will do honestly by him.[34]

In the meantime, as *The Times* pointed out, at a meeting in Old Bond Street in London, the protectionists could barely muster a few hundred people plus the odd duke, 'all of the feeblest and stalest description'.[35] The Duke of Norfolk had even advised the destitute to take a pinch of curry powder in water to allay their craving for food, and reminded them that John Franklin and his team, on their expedition to the North Pole, had consumed a pair of leather breeches over several days. It was, however, pointed out that leather breeches would be too expensive for the people and if acquired might lead to a hankering 'for the nether garments of dukes and squires.'[36] No one can say that the whole of this episode was not punctuated by a sense of the absurd.

1846: Repeal of the Corn Laws

The impact of all these meetings and events converged on 22 January 1846 at the opening of Parliament, one of the most

momentous Parliaments in British history. Peel spoke on the
Queen's Speech for two hours, arguing that free trade did not
damage agriculture, and that the misery in Ireland required action
on the Corn Laws. At this, Disraeli launched an hour-long tirade
directed against Peel, his own leader, thus making him Peel's natural
successor and launching the Conservative Party into internal
convulsions.

As the House heard Peel's argument, the Opposition received his
conversion with enraptured cheering while the Conservative
benches sat despondent and sullen. Peel stated,

> I will not withhold the homage which is due to the progress of
> reason and to truth, by denying that my opinions on the subject
> of protection have undergone a change ... I will assert the privi-
> lege of yielding to the force of argument and conviction, and
> acting upon the results of enlarged experience. It may be
> supposed that there is something humiliating in making such
> admissions; Sir, I feel no such humiliation ... I should feel humil-
> iation, if, having modified or changed my opinions, I declined
> to acknowledge the change for fear of incurring the imputation
> of inconsistency. The question is whether the facts are sufficient
> to account for the change, and the motives for it are pure and
> disinterested.[37]

The case was made and the prime minister sounded the retreat.
The entire campaign for the previous seven years, driven by
Cobden's logic, Bright's energy, oratory and political skill, and
the work of the League, merged with popular discontent to change
the face of British politics.

Peel developed his arguments with a tour de force of technical and
statistical analysis, noting that he had tried to persuade the Cabinet
to no avail, but

> the lapse of time, the increase of agitation, and other circum-
> stances, had materially affected my position. I was overruled in
> the Cabinet ... I felt it to be my duty, not being supported by the
> unanimous voice of my Colleagues, humbly to tender to Her
> Majesty my resignation.

He then recited how he had returned to office when his proposed
successor could not form a Government, adding that

to conduct the Government of this country is a most arduous duty; I may say it without irreverence, that these ancient institutions, like our physical frames, are 'fearfully and wonderfully made'. It is no easy task to ensure the united action of an ancient monarchy, a proud aristocracy, and a reformed constituency ... These were my attempts, and I thought them not inconsistent with true and enlarged Conservative policy.[38]

His problem was that they were, and he knew it.

On 27 January, the House was packed for the unveiling of Peel's plans to repeal the Corn Laws. Even Prince Albert sat below the bar. The debate continued from 9 February for five days. When Peel spoke again on 16 February, it was to come clean and, in a sensitive and almost spiritual admission, to explain his U-turn. He exhorted the House that when addressing their constituents,

> may God grant that by your decision of this night you may have laid in store for yourselves the consolation of reflecting that such calamities are, in truth, the dispensations of Providence – that they have not been caused, they have not been aggravated by laws of man restricting, in the hour of scarcity, the supply of food![39]

A letter survives of Bright's appreciation of this speech, written to his sister Priscilla in glowing terms:

> Peel delivered the best speech I ever heard in Parliament. It was truly a magnificent speech, sustained throughout, thoroughly with us, and offering even to pass the immediate [repeal], if the House are willing. Villiers, Gibson, and myself cheered continually, and I never listened to any human being speaking in public with so much delight.[40]

With Cobden and the League, Bright had not only seized the initiative, but now in Parliament had also broken the back of the landed interest. Sadly, at the moment of triumph, though, Cobden was seriously ill with exhaustion and with an abscess on his head. On 17 February, Bright rose to speak on his behalf of the great cause to which they had been mutually committed for so long. It was one of his greatest speeches. Throughout this campaign, and indeed throughout his future political career, Bright never wavered in his consistency, his principles or his convictions, as one by one his opponents and antagonists fell by the wayside and, more to the point, fell into adopting his own opinions and policies – the test of real statesmanship.

At the moment of his triumph, the circumstances were described as follows:

> The singularity of his position ... seemed to animate him to an unwonted pitch of rhetorical excellence ... [His speech] alternately glittered with satire and burnt with energy and thrilled with a tone even occasionally pathetic.[41]

> Having dealt with the economic arguments and the objections to protectionism, Bright followed with his eulogy of Peel, during which Peel broke down in tears:

> You say the right hon. Baronet is a traitor. It would ill become me to attempt his defence after the speech which he delivered last night – a speech, I will venture to say, more powerful and more to be admired than any speech which has been delivered within the memory of any man in this House. I watched the right hon. Baronet as he went home last night, and, for the first time, I envied him his feelings. That speech has circulated by scores of thousands throughout the kingdom and throughout the world; and wherever a man is to be found who loves justice, and wherever there is a labourer whom you have trampled under foot, that speech will bring joy to the heart of the one, and hope to the breast of the other. You chose the right hon. Baronet – why? Because he was the ablest man of your party. You always said so, and you will not deny it now. Why was he the ablest? Because he had great experience, profound attainments, and an honest regard for the good of the country. You placed him in office. When a man is in office he is not the same man as when in opposition. The present generation, or posterity, does not deal as mildly with men in Government as with those in Opposition. There are such things as the responsibilities of office ... The right hon. Baronet took the only honourable course. He resigned. He told you by that act, 'I can't any longer do what you want – I can't defend your cause.'[42]

As one report of this speech said,

> There is something absolutely noble, there is something admirable, there is something great, in the pure and generous

eloquence with which the hon. member eulogised his former antagonist, the courageous, the large-spirited, and now popular Sir Robert Peel.[43]

Bright also wove his speech into his next objective of parliamentary reform, saying,

> If there be any Member of this House who fears that the incompleteness of the Reform Bill may give cause for agitation, it must be a matter of rejoicing to him that a mode has been discovered by which tens of thousands of honest, industrious, and meritorious artisans have brought themselves within the pale of the Constitution.

With this, Bright was moving his argument forward from free trade and economic reform to the enfranchisement of the working class.

Disraeli spoke on 20 February. Whatever his private thoughts might have been, he sought to elevate the tone of his previous invective against Peel. They were at daggers drawn – Disraeli armed with presentation and opportunism, Peel now with principle and the national interest. Disraeli said of his protectionist friends, 'I wish them to bear in mind that their cause must be sustained by great principles. I venture feebly and slightly to indicate those principles, principles of high policy, on which their system ought to be sustained.' This was the need to maintain an equal balance between the great branches of national industry for 'political considerations – social considerations, affecting the happiness, prosperity, and morality of the people, as well as the stability of the State.' He argued that this amounted to sustaining 'a territorial Constitution', which is why he supported 'the claims of agriculture' and that the free trade movement was not merely the repeal of the Corn Laws but the transfer of power from the landed interest to the manufacturers. It was rescued from the alleged power of one class only to sink under the avowed power of another. He attacked the 'thralldom of capital' and said he preferred an 'educated and enfranchised people'.[44]

Disraeli, in making his claim to be the exponent of the monarchy and stability through the landed aristocracy and agricultural protectionism, had resorted to a vague but hopefully comforting aspiration. It was enough to satisfy his supporters for the present. He had, however, let the cat out of the bag. It was the failure to catch the political tide and to unite for the right reasons behind Peel on the repeal of the Corn Laws that led the Conservative Party into the wilderness.

The party was redeemed only when Disraeli followed John Bright's lead into the new democracy of 1866/7 and against the prejudices of Lord Cranborne and the Conservative backwoodsmen.

Cobden, restored to health, spoke on 27 February. With great humour, he told the House of his thoughts as he had read 'speech after speech' at home. He argued that the free traders were 'the aristocracy of improvement and civilization. We have set an example to the world in all ages; we have given them the representative system.'[45]

Cobden, the Liberal, referred to Adam Smith, David Ricardo and Edmund Burke, all of whom would be regarded today as the epitome of Conservative economic and political philosophy, in a speech directed against the Conservative Party itself. This was as much to demonstrate the irrelevance of the rump of the Conservative Party, which Peel had abandoned and which continued to live in the past, as to demonstrate that changes, based on principles relevant to the time were the weapons of those who were prepared to get out among the people and develop policies based on such principles, untrammelled by party, and to provide practical answers to the circumstances the nation faced.

In March 1846, the second reading for repeal was carried by a majority of 88. Palmerston even managed to bring himself to refer to Cobden, whom he had previously described impersonally as 'The Honourable Member for Stockport', as his 'Honourable Friend', though this amity was not to last long. The third reading took place on 16 May as dawn broke, and the repeal of the Corn Laws was passed in the House of Commons with a majority of 98. Disraeli continued to protest, accusing Peel of trading on the intelligence of others and, in brilliant and witty invective, of being 'a burglar of others' intellect ... from the days of the Conqueror to the termination of the last reign, there is no statesman who has committed political petty larceny on so great a scale'.[46] He accused Peel of having bought his party on the cheapest and sold it on the dearest terms.

Peel turned the tables on Disraeli with the accusation that 'although you might for a time have relied on the fagot votes you created in a moment of excitement, yet the interval would not be long before that weapon would break short in your hands!' In language which Disraeli seems to have plagiarized in his later speeches, Peel stated,

> I have a strong belief that the greatest object which we or any other Government can contemplate should be to elevate the

social condition of that class of the people with whom we are
brought into no direct relationship by the exercise of the elective
franchise.[47]

Peel may have lost control of the Conservative Party, but his speech
left a legacy that Disraeli later adopted. Despite his attack on Peel,
Disraeli well understood that he would need to find a new narrative
for the Conservative Party – and that he would have to provide it
during a period in the wilderness he had helped to create. He wrote
of the events leading up to the repeal of the Corn Laws in his novel,
Coningsby, published in 1844. He identified the scale of the problem
facing the Conservative Party, with the words, 'There was indeed a
considerable shouting about what they called Conservative principles; but the awkward question naturally arose, what will you
conserve?'[48] Disraeli demonstrated equally in *Sybil; or the Tale of Two
Nations* that he did not fail to understand the obvious, of which
Bright and Cobden were deeply aware, that there were indeed two
nations, indeed two cultures, divided by class, wealth and poverty.
None of this was lost on Bright as their political careers evolved.
Indeed, Bright notes in his diary in December 1853 that he had read
Disraeli's *Vivian Grey* – 'Clever. His hero's principles seem to have
been those of the writer in his political life.'[49] He read *Sybil* the
following April – 'remarkable book in every way'[50] – and had
completed *Coningsby* by 18 May.[51] Bright was clearly trying to get
inside Disraeli's mind.

In the best tradition of self-preservation, prompted by the Duke
of Wellington, the House of Lords took one month to pass the
Repeal Bill. Bright stood at the bar in the House of Lords on 25 June
listening intently as the Lords concluded their debates. That same
day, Peel was turned out on the Irish Coercion Bill for Ireland, and
when the 'Act to Amend the Laws Relating to the Importation of
Corn' finally received Royal Assent on 26 June, a farmer in
Derbyshire marked the occasion by turning out to grass three fine
heifers named after Cobden, Bright and the Secretary of the Anti-
Corn Law League, George Wilson.

Bright wrote to Wilson, 'The assent is given. It was five o'clock
before the words were said, which completed our labours ... the
sensations were worth having. I wish you had been there.'[52]
However, he added an ominous warning of what was to come: 'We
have not seen the last of the barons, but have taught them which way
the world is turning ... My heart feels light now that our cause is
won.'[53] His obvious relief was shared by Cobden who, writing to his

wife, said, 'Hurrah! Hurrah! The Corn Bill is law and now my work is done ... I shall hope to be home in time for a late tea.'[54]

Peel gave his famous resignation speech on 29 June 1846. In deference to the scale of conviction, persuasion and political will in the national interest engendered by Bright and Cobden, he said,

> I shall leave a name execrated by every monopolist who, from less honourable motives, clamours for protection because it conduces to his own individual benefit; but it may be that I shall leave a name sometimes remembered with expressions of good will in the abodes of those whose lot it is to labour, and to earn their daily bread by the sweat of their brow, when they shall recruit their exhausted strength with abundant and untaxed food, the sweeter because it is no longer leavened by a sense of injustice.[55]

Peel had learned, as would Disraeli, Palmerston and Salisbury later, that when Bright was on the move nothing would stand in his way.

The following month, Bright recounted in his diary a meeting with Peel:

> In the lobby was alongside Sir R. Peel. Asked if he was recovered from his late accident, his foot having been cut by the breaking of a china basin.
>
> Sir R. inquired if I had been in Lancashire lately and what was doing. Said I had, and that the people were delighted with the results of the Session, and I wished personally to thank him for his great services to the cause of Free trade.
>
> Sir R. said he had had no conception of the depth of feeling which had possessed the public mind on the question, especially in Scotland, where he thought every town and village almost were unanimous on the question. He remarked how happy it was the question was settled, and what a condition we should have been in now when the blight in the potatoes was making so much progress. He hoped the use of Indian meal was extending and that suffering would be avoided.
>
> I told him it was greatly extending in Lancashire, at which he expressed his gratification, and said he felt great pleasure at the satisfaction evident among the working classes at what had been done. I told him I thought no Minister had ever retired from office more universally regretted. He added, 'or more execrated by the Monopolists', and laughed with the consciousness of the victory which had been won.[56]

Bright's relationship with Peel would continue in this affectionate vein until the latter's death in 1850. On 28 June of that year, Bright recorded in his diary that Peel 'made a most useful and excellent speech' on the issue of Palmerston's foreign policy: 'No party feeling in it, and no wish to inflict damage on the Government, but an honest and simple avowal of his real opinions on the question before us.'[57] This was Peel's last speech. The following day, he was thrown from his horse on Constitution Hill and died from his injuries four days later. On 3 July, Bright wrote, 'On reading the particulars in the daily news, I could not refrain from tears; I felt as if I had lost a dear friend, so great has been my admiration for the recent career of this great statesman.'[58] The next day, he wrote that Peel's 'labours and sacrifices on the Corn Law question have endeared him to the nation'. Referring again to Peel's speech earlier that week on foreign policy, he concluded, 'Would that his dying words might sink into the hearts of statesmen and people.'[59]

The intimacy that all this represents is proof of the mutual affection – borne out of political struggle and opposition, and crowned by respect and generosity on both sides – that the two men developed while grappling with the greatest issue of the day. Out of the crucible of this political battle, Bright, with Cobden, emerged victorious, and Peel's reputation was secured for posterity.

The End of the League

On 2 July 1846, the Anti-Corn Law League was wound up. They decided to call in only a proportion of the £250,000 already raised. In recognition of the sacrifice the Leaguers had made to open the door to a new era of free trade throughout the world, £10,000 was presented to George Wilson, the Secretary of the League, and each member of the Council received a silver tea and coffee service. Cobden received £75,000, which relieved him of the financial burden he had endured as a result of his efforts. Bright, for his part, was given at his own request a mere £5,000, which he used for the purchase of a library of 1,200 volumes in an oak bookcase engraved with representations of the battle they had successfully fought. The library was filled with books of history and biography, including a life of Thomas Jefferson, which he annotated copiously in his own hand, and his favourite poets such as Wordsworth and Milton.

Of course, for Bright, matters would not be allowed to rest there. The campaign for the repeal of the Corn Laws was not to be seen in

isolation, but was part of an ongoing exercise that required a cartog-
rapher, a navigator and a pilot at the political helm. Bright was to
fulfil each of these roles. His speech on the day the League ended
combined both instinct and calculation to move the argument
forward at this critical moment to the issue he was about to turn to –
parliamentary reform – encapsulating his innermost beliefs of freedom of choice for the individual and determination to translate them
into practice. He said,

> We have taught the people of this country the value of a great
> principle. They have learned that there is nothing that can be
> held out to the intelligent people of this kingdom so calculated to
> stimulate them to action, and to great and persevering action, as
> a great and sacred principle like that which the League has
> espoused. They have learned that there is in public opinion a
> power much greater than that residing in any particular form of
> government; and although you have in this kingdom a system
> of government which is called 'popular' and 'representative' – a
> system which is somewhat clumsily contrived, and which works
> with many jars and joltings – that still, under the impulse of a
> great principle, with great labour and with great sacrifices, all
> those obstacles are overcome, so that out of a machine especially
> contrived for the contrary, justice and freedom are at length
> achieved for the nation; and the people have learned something
> beyond this – that is, that the way to freedom is henceforward
> not through violence and bloodshed.[60]

Bright's motto, 'Be just and fear not', had been amply illustrated by
what had been achieved. With these words, he had demonstrated his
inner conviction and confidence that the whole of the British system
of government and parliamentary machinery was for a purpose –
and a moral purpose at that. It was possible to espouse democracy
without revolution, and thereby 'justice and freedom' for the nation.
Circumstances might have changed, but the underlying message of
what he had to say on that occasion is no less relevant to the present
day and provides a valuable and instructive template for the problems faced by politicians in the twenty-first century.

The Impact of Repeal

Parliament in the latter part of 1846 was somewhat bizarre. The
Opposition sat on the Government benches, with Conservative

ministers kept in power by the anti-Corn Law backbenchers led by Cobden and Bright, the Whigs and the part of the Conservative Party that came to be known as the Peelites. This latter group was prepared to support Peel so that the aristocratic Whigs could not take over, wanting him to stay in power in the hope that something would turn up. It did eventually appear in the shape of the campaign for parliamentary reform, with Bright at its helm against the aristocracy. But having won their victory, they were content for the present to allow events to unfold. Even more bizarrely, Disraeli's allies were campaigning in the Tory press for Bright, described by the future Earl of Derby in a backhanded compliment as 'a blaggard and a democrat'.[61]

The repeal of the Corn Laws took some of the sting out of the Chartists and, as Bright had foreseen, opened the door to a new movement for the franchise. Those like Thomas Cooper followed Bright's lead. As Peel noted when the French constitutional monarchy was overthrown and Louis-Philippe driven out of France during the Revolution in February 1848, 'This comes of trying to govern the country through a narrow representation in Parliament without regarding the wishes of the those outside. It is what this Party wanted me to do in the matter of the Corn Laws and I would not do it.'[62] This was his own epitaph on the fate of what had been his Conservative Party, and a good lesson for the future.

With protectionism having been effectively destroyed into the indefinite future, free trade became the principle that underpinned future budgets. Despite the massive move from the land to new urban areas and the corresponding increase in demand for corn, prices simply did not go up; they remained stable because of imported corn – assisted by the development of the railways, and intercontinental and transatlantic trade – which previously would not have been allowed to affect the domestic marketplace. This, together with an increased investment on the part of the farming community driven by competitiveness and new technologies, made up for the difference in demand created by the increase in population. Evidence of this can be seen across the countryside even today, where thousands of Victorian barns are testament to the capital investment in buildings that followed the repeal of the Corn Laws.

The principle of free trade may have been established but there was no let up, as had been feared by some, in the development of manufacturing and the search for new markets abroad. Indeed, as Cobden in particular had predicted, repeal was complemented by the export of manufactured goods. In 1842, British exports to the world at large and the growing Empire were worth a mere £47 million. By 1876, they were worth £200 million. The North West, the Midlands and the Black Country became the industrial power-house of the world, though both Germany and the USA gradually emerged as serious competitors and eventually caught up.

In Bright's own lifetime, however, the 1870s (no less than the 1970s and 2008) brought with it a commercial downturn and economic difficulties, leading to attempts to revive protectionism. This in no way affected Bright's conviction that free trade was essential to prosperity, as demonstrated by a continuing correspon-dence between Bright and others that extended for many years up to the end of his life, as his disciple Joseph Chamberlain moved from free trade to protectionism.

In 1879, Bright also took the Americans to task for their pursuit of a policy of protectionism that had certain characteristics in common with those that have become apparent in the USA in the early twenty-first century. As Bright wrote to Cyrus Field on 21 January 1879:

> It is strange that a people who put down slavery at an immense sacrifice are not able to suppress monopoly, which is but a milder form of the same evil. Under slavery the man was seized, and his labour was stolen from him, and the profit of it enjoyed by his master and owner. Under protection the man is appar-ently free, but he is denied the right to exchange the produce of his labour except with his countrymen, who offer him much less for it than the foreigner would give. Some portion of his labour is thus confiscated.[63]

CHAPTER 3

Parliamentary Reform: Manchester and Birmingham

Mr Bright was something more than the member for Birmingham – he was the member for Great Britain.
(Philip Henry Muntz[1])

The Commons League

The General Election in the summer of 1847 was dominated by the Whigs. Despite the fact that the Conservatives were still in a theoretical majority, they were divided between the Peelites and those who still hankered after protection. On 9 July, Bright was returned as one of the MPs for Manchester in an uncontested election, though there had been some unusual rivalry between himself and Cobden over who should be selected for the seat.[2] This was one month after he had remarried at the Friends Meeting House in Thornhill Street, Wakefield. His bride was 26-year-old (Margaret) Elizabeth Leatham, the daughter of a Quaker banker, 'serious-minded but of a cheerful and open disposition'.[3] Bright was clearly besotted with her from the first time they met whilst he was campaigning in Wakefield in November 1845, but she had reservations about his 'unQuakerlike' temperament and political activities. Nevertheless, he had wooed her doggedly, writing letters in which he declared his love openly and described the happiness that was to be had in Rochdale with him and his young daughter, Helen. Enlisting the support of his late wife's mother and his sister, Priscilla, in his campaign, he gradually overcame her misgivings – and those of her family. The union was to be happy and successful. The seven children they had together brought Bright great joy throughout his life and, perhaps most importantly for his political career, Elizabeth provided him with much needed support. As Walling records, 'He first wrote in July,

1846, and from that time onwards he sent her a letter almost every day he was away from her side, until her death thirty-two years afterwards.'[4]

When the new Parliament convened on 29 November 1847, it was preoccupied with troubles in Ireland. Bright opposed the Coercion Bill, which sought to suspend habeas corpus, and the Crime and Government Security Bill, which dealt with sedition and treason. He argued that the problems of Ireland were much deeper, partly because six out of seven men in Ireland were not allowed to vote, and because of the Irish land problem and discrimination against Catholics.

Trouble was also brewing again in mainland Britain, with renewed Chartist agitation. Bright wrote to his father-in-law, Jonathan Priestman, in March 1848: 'Liberty is on the march, and this year promises to be a great year in European history ... We must have another league of some kind and our aristocracy must be made to submit again.'[5] He also wrote along similar lines to George Wilson, warning that if Parliamentary changes were not made peacefully, they would be made violently and suggesting Manchester as the launch pad for the new League-style crusade for parliamentary reform.

Bright wanted a constitutional solution to the problem. As he said in the House of Commons in April 1848, there was a need to extend 'the pale of the constitution of which they boasted so much.' There were a mere 800,000 electors and yet five million should be included 'who, if admitted, would tend considerably to strengthen and support that constitution which was so highly prized not only in this but in other countries'. He referred to 'the excellence of the constitution; but it was only a mere theory to the great body of people in this country, for the benefits it admitted of were not enjoyed by them.'[6]

The same month, he wrote to his sister-in-law Margaret Priestman, 'In this country political agitation is not likely to be soon lulled.' He did not believe there would be violence except in Ireland, but

> we shall have and ought to have a powerful agitation in favour of real Parliamentary reform. We have deluded ourselves with the notion that we are a free people and have a good government and a representative system whilst in fact our representative system is for the most part a sham and the forms of representation are used to consolidate the supremacy of the titled and proprietary class. All this will break down by and by.[7]

As to the Chartists, he wrote to his wife on 10 June 1848,

> It is all well enough for rich and comfortably off people to complain that their quiet is disturbed by the growling of millions whom they tax to an enormous amount and yet shut out from all share in the power by which taxes are imposed. Things cannot go on as they now are. And who is to change them?[8]

As the Chartist agitation diminished, however, it became clear that Parliament would not reform itself. Indeed, the Chartists had frightened the horses. Bright wrote again to his wife in August 1848:

> The Government seem to make a great uproar about the Chartists. They have spies among these wretched fools, to stimulate them to conspiracy and to outrage ..., and then getting a lot of them together they pounce upon them, and imprison or transport them ... The aristocracy want to frighten the middle classes from the pursuit of Reform, and to do this they and their emissaries stimulate a portion of the least wise of the people to menace and violence, to damage the cause of Reform.[9]

Bright may have had some sympathy with what the Chartists wanted to achieve. He did not rule out manhood suffrage, but did not advocate it. In 'an unfortunate moment', as R. A. J. Walling put it, he even referred to that part of the population he did not include in his franchise proposals as 'the residuum'.[10] Bright certainly did not agree with the means by which the Chartists sought to achieve their aims. His was a constitutional approach; theirs was one of direct confrontation, which Bright knew would not engage the sympathies of those he wanted to direct towards parliamentary reform. Bright's enthusiasm for a new league increased as the year progressed. In December 1848, he wrote to Villiers, 'We can have a party out of doors more formidable than we had in the League and can work the Constitution so as to reform it through itself.'[11]

All this engendered a difference of opinion with Cobden, who was prepared to give Bright his head but cautioned against his enthusiasms for parliamentary reform. The disagreement had begun in the early years of the Corn Law agitation in 1842, when Cobden had insisted on 'keeping the agitation of the Corn Law apart from the suffrage'.[12] Following the repeal of the Corn Laws, Bright asked Cobden to join him in what he regarded as the logical extension of their campaign and to pursue the issue of the franchise, but Cobden refused. Cobden thought that the Manchester and anti-Corn Law groups were not the right leaders for reform agitation.

Bright, however, was keen to involve his friend. In late December 1848, he wrote to Cobden about the new movement: 'Now don't be alarmed at all this, for it will not involve our old sacrifices. I think it may be done without killing either of us or driving us from home as before.'[13] His entreaties worked to a certain extent. When Bright held a meeting in Manchester in January 1849 to inaugurate the new 'Commons League', which was aimed at the enfranchisement of the middle class and working men, the two men once again shared a platform. Cobden spoke on the issue of financial reform, and Bright on the extension of the franchise.

Unlike the campaign of the Anti-Corn Law League, which specifically addressed the bread-and-butter issues of food, starvation and famine, the appeal was now for institutional change. But it was difficult to create enthusiasm for parliamentary reform, lacking as it did the immediate resonance of food prices as with the Corn Laws. Furthermore, in 1848, because of the revolutions on the Continent, the very notion of enfranchisement evoked fears of revolution. Undeterred, Bright pressed on – 'working the constitution so as to reform it through itself', as he had written to Villiers[14] – while concentrating on the property qualifications for the middle and lower middle classes.

In June 1849, Joseph Hume proposed a Bill which for the first time included household suffrage, a ballot, triennial parliaments and the redistribution of seats. Bright and others supported this move, though more in hope than expectation. It was lost by 268 to 82. Referring to Hume's proposals, Bright said,

> We maintain that the constitution recognises another element – a popular, and, if you choose, a democratic, element – and we who stand here, and those we represent – the common people of England – have as great and as undoubted a right [sole and] absolute in this House, as the monarch on the throne, or the Peers in the other chamber of the Legislature. The system under which we sit in this House is by no means in accordance with the theory of the constitution, nor with the true interests of the nation.[15]

Bright was pitching his argument on the great principle of parliamentary reform, convinced that this was more important even than free trade. He had willingly espoused the repeal of the Corn Laws, not just as an economic venture, but as part of the enlargement of the control of affairs by Parliament through an extended franchise and a secret ballot. This was his distinctive contribution to democracy and, for him, it was a moral issue: 'I do most devoutly believe that the moral law was not written for men alone in their individual character, but that it was written as well for nations.'[16]

Bright had a clear understanding of the reasons for change, which he described as 'a peaceful, wise and enduring democracy'[17] with a Government recognizing the value of the five million men excluded from the political system. It was for him a matter of social justice based on a moral cause with immense practical implications and a basic human right. He clearly thought that both parliamentary reform and free trade were rooted in the question of freedom of choice but that, without parliamentary reform, the ultimate case for the democratic improvement of the working class from which economic improvement would flow would simply not take place. The entitlement of the working classes was a moral objective, but one with clearly identifiable practical advantages for the stability of the country during a time of great change, instability and uncertainty.

In contrast, though fighting for the same principle, Cobden was above all an economic reformer. Cobden's commitment to a 40-shilling freehold plan to increase the number of those eligible to vote also highlighted another fundamental difference between the two men: Bright was largely committed to the working class, Cobden to the middle class, though their thinking converged in what they termed 'the industrious classes'. In September 1849, Bright wrote to Cobden: 'Now you object to Parliamentary Reform as the thing to be worked for ... The case for Parliamentary Reform is more glaring and undeniable if possible than our Free Trade cause was.'[18] In December, he wrote again, saying, 'It would have been more above board and I think more effectual to have started for parliamentary reform, and *for this*, to have set in motion the 40 shilling freeholds.'[19]

For all this, Bright was not unaware of the relative significance of Cobden's proposal. Indeed, in 1851, Bright became President of the Rochdale Freehold Land Society, set up to enable the less well-off to buy an allotment of land sufficient to produce 40 shillings a year in rent, and through this to become a county voter. This was the beginning of the building society movement. In time, the National Freehold Land Society would merge with the Abbey Road, becoming the Abbey National Building Society, of which the Cashes were chairmen for several generations, complementing the acquisition through mutual societies of proper housing for the population as a whole.

Bright also spoke about the role of the MP in terms reminiscent of Edmund Burke's famous description. He said,

> When I speak of a vote in Parliament, I endeavour to shut out from my mind any idea of controlling influence down here or elsewhere. I am most happy, when I can, to agree with you but I think there is a higher, loftier, and purer standard for a representative than even the influence of those whom he may represent; and that standard is his own intelligent, conscientious conviction of duty on the question which is before him.[20]

He was strongly in favour of independent expression of opinion and certainly would never have gone along with present-day whipping arrangements.

The differences between Cobden and Bright did not stand in the way of their friendship, or of their shared vision of a fairer world. They were simply a matter of emphasis and judgement. Though undoubtedly difficult at the time, they were also to Bright's great advantage in the longer term, in that he was forced to find his own feet and his own territory, and was no longer led by Cobden on the great issues of the day.

'England does not love coalitions'

Throughout the late 1840s, the Whig prime minister, Lord John Russell, had been moving gradually towards the idea of a new Reform Bill, which he finally produced early in 1852. Bright was distinctly unenthusiastic and Russell's Government fell before the Bill had its second reading.

By this time, Disraeli had emerged as the accepted leader of the still divided Conservative Party. In March 1852, after much uncertainty caused by a balanced Parliament comprising many splits and factions, he led the new anti-Peelite Government in the Commons as chancellor of the exchequer, with Lord Derby as prime minister in the Lords. Bright repeatedly challenged Disraeli to declare the Government's stance on protectionism but the chancellor remained tight-lipped, fearful of upsetting the fine balance with which his party had gained power. Derby, in the meantime, tried to revise the tax system to benefit the landowners. This immediately stirred

Bright, with Cobden and Wilson, to revive the Anti-Corn Law League, with a call for subscriptions raising nearly £70,000.

Only once the General Election was over that summer, and the new House liberally supplied with free traders, would the Derby–Disraeli Government resolve to abandon protection. They were, however, extremely unwilling to say so. In his consistent and relentless pursuit of nailing down free trade as the fulcrum of political momentum, Bright seized every tactical and strategic opportunity, not only to drive the message home but to secure its political foundations. In September 1852, Bright and his fellow Manchester free traders drafted a Free Trade Resolution to which the Government would have to respond.

Bright's policy was approved and Villiers moved a motion that the repeal of the Corn Laws had been a measure 'just, wise and beneficial'.[21] Disraeli's description of this as 'three odious epithets'[22] would have led to the fall of the Government had not Palmerston immediately moved an amendment in favour of free trade, which the former protectionists found that they could accept. The Derby–Disraeli Government was living on borrowed time, however, and eventually fell when Disraeli's Budget was massacred by Gladstone and the Peelites in December 1852 – leading Disraeli to remark famously, 'England does not love coalitions.'[23]

In the midst of Gladstone's onslaught, a strange moment of affinity occurred between Bright and Disraeli. On the evening of 15 December, Disraeli asked Bright to call on him at his home in Grosvenor Gate in London. As Bright recorded:

> This was rather in consequence of a conversation I had with him yesterday in the lobby of the House. I waited upon him soon after 10 o'clock, found him near the top of the house, in his morning gown, surrounded by books, pictures, mirrors, etc. I told him I felt in a difficult situation, seeing how entirely opposed we had been in political life. He said he would speak without reserve, as he thought that, however opposed, there had been a good deal of free conversation and he thought even some sympathy between us. He then entered on the desperate condition of their affairs, and the almost certainty of their defeat on the following night, spoke of that infernal question, the question of Protection; said his difficulty had been his and their promises to the country party and farmers, local burdens and now Malt Tax ...

He spoke of his party, how well they had followed him, how faithfully they were prepared to support him. There was no jealousy – Cabinet friendly and disposed to act liberally – and he thought his party 'having stood so much already' would stand a good deal more if necessary. He then adverted to his wish to get rid of the old stagers and old 'redtapists' and said he could not see why we, that is Cobden, myself and Gibson – our section – should not some day be with him in a Cabinet; not within 24 hours, but before long: it was quite possible and not difficult.

I laughed at this as impossible and partly at the serious face he maintained as he explained his views. I objected that, putting aside the immorality of such changes, the constituencies would not permit it.

'Oh,' he said, 'a man of genius and power may do anything with a large constituency; I think I could represent Manchester, and be a very popular member.'

I assured him he was greatly mistaken in supposing the Manchester people would be trifled with, and I asked, 'How is it possible for you and us to work together?'

He said we much mistook them. I said they must change their name and repudiate all their antecedents before we could ever act with them. He said there was scarcely one member of their Cabinet who would not at once retire to make room for any gentleman who would be likely to give them strength.

He spoke of the new Administration, admitting that his defeat was certain, asked if I thought Cobden and myself were included in it, and said: 'If you are included in it, or are likely to be, if you see your own game in what is going to be done, then may God help you forward, my dear Bright, and no man will be more delighted than I shall be to witness your success.'

He said no man knew what he had struggled against and overcome; he had been a Minister and was now about to be beaten. He had always felt the insecurity of their position, and had not removed to Downing Street on that account. He would not keep office or try to cling to it if they could not have power, and it was clear they had not the numbers with them to enable them to go on, and it was doubtful if they could live till Easter if they now escaped.

I was with him from 10 to half-past 11 o'clock … This remarkable man is ambitious, most able, and without prejudices. He conceives it right to strive for a great career with such principles as are in vogue in his age and country – says the politics and principles to suit England must be of the 'English type', but having obtained power, would use it to found a great reputation on great services rendered to the country.

He seems unable to comprehend the morality of our political course, and on this ground was probably induced to seek the interview with me.[24]

The following day, as expected, the Government was defeated. Bright recorded his admiration for Disraeli's performance:

Disraeli rose at 10 and spoke till near 1 o'clock – he fought for his life, and never man fought more desperately or with more skill and power. The speech was his greatest speech; he was in earnest; argument, satire, sarcasm, invective, all were abundant and of the first class. His peroration was short, to the point, and forcible; but the 'numbers', as he said to me yesterday, were against him.[25]

This was not the last time Disraeli was to approach Bright, to whom he was invariably drawn whenever he was in the deepest trouble. He made approaches to many people, but it was as if he knew subconsciously that Bright would have an immediate suggestion as to what should be done, even though he would himself arrive later at the same conclusions, albeit for different, and largely opportune, reasons. By the same token, Bright's clear admiration for the courageous way in which Disraeli handled himself belies the premium Bright placed on personal and political bravery even against the greatest odds. This diary entry is as much a reflection of Bright's appreciation of the pressures of his own political life as it is of those of Disraeli. It is noteworthy, however, that while Disraeli would approach Bright privately to reinforce his own confidence and willpower when he most needed it, there is no evidence in his own private journals of a similar degree of empathetic admiration and understanding of the trials and tribulations that Bright himself endured. This was probably because Bright was interested in achieving objectives and principles, whereas the more opportunistic and less generous Disraeli was interested primarily, as Bright himself observed on Disraeli's death, in 'personal ambition'.[26]

The next Government was a Peelite–Whig coalition under Lord Aberdeen. Gladstone, having deserted the Conservatives as a prominent Peelite, became Disraeli's natural adversary when he assumed office as chancellor of the exchequer. Bright's diary records a meeting with Sir James Graham, the former Peelite home secretary, on 18 December, in which Graham said,

> I think your position in the House and the country, your popularity, the large party you influence, and your great public services, which I would be the first to recognise, all entitle you to a share in the Government, and I think no Government properly constituted in which you have no part. I think it a most unsound principle that men who so greatly influence opinion should not bear a portion of the responsibilities of the executive Government.[27]

Despite this view, shared by many, neither Bright nor Cobden was offered a Cabinet post. This was no loss to either of them, as Bright explained in his reply to an apologetic letter on the subject from Lord John Russell, the new Leader of the House of Commons: 'I told him what we want is not office for ourselves but for men and principles such as we value, that our future course would be like our past, clear and resolute, not factious, but pursuing our own objects.'[28]

At this time, there was also talk of an independent Radical party under Milner Gibson, with whom Disraeli had discussions, but Lord Malmesbury firmly rejected any such thought, comparing an alliance with Cobden and Bright as with a 'jack whore'.[29]

Bright preferred the independence of the backbenches, where he was free to pursue his own conscience, convictions and course, to the loss of freedom and principle involved in coalition – and the capacity to deliver them. This he did without hesitation, raising the issue of a new Reform Bill before the new Cabinet had had a chance to draw breath. It met with some resistance from within the Government, though Russell and the Whigs had agreed on some semblance of reform beforehand. As Bright explained to Cobden on 3 January 1853: 'I gather that there is a party in the Government that will not move on unless some pressure is applied, and that Lord John wishes the pressure not to be withheld.'[30] Russell's reforms were palliative rather than principled.

Cobden would not be drawn on the issue, however, preoccupied as he was with the peace movement fighting anti-French sentiment in the country. When he declined to attend a Reform meeting in Manchester, Bright wrote to him in strong terms: 'I think you have rarely been more clearly in the wrong ... Indeed I think your own arguments overthrow you.' Referring to press commentary that their influence had waned, he continued,

We have worked too hard, and are too much in earnest to be justified in giving up precisely when we seem to be most wanted. Depend upon it, our Parliamentary influence is not all gained in Parliament, nor is our influence in the country all gained in the country; the one acts upon the other ... Our meeting would show us armed at all points, it would bind our friends together, and excite a greater vigilance on the part of the public as to the events of the coming session.

In a final, somewhat tetchy, paragraph, he wrote,

Personally I would wish to have no meeting; but *personally* I would not be in public life. I would rather see more after my own interests and the interests of my children. But we are on the rails and must move on. We have work and must do it.[31]

However, to Bright's intense annoyance, Cobden still refused to attend the meeting. Bright therefore acted alone, addressing the meeting on the subject of the secret ballot as used in Massachusetts, and urging his listeners to petition the Government.

Russell introduced another Reform Bill in February 1854. Of this, Bright commented, 'I am unable to discover what should induce the towns of England to support it'[32] but conceded that it was a step in the right direction. His chief complaint, however, was that the real momentum for reform was being stymied by Palmerston – a supposed colleague in the administration and a fellow free trader, but also an aristocratic Whig. Palmerston had resigned briefly over the reform proposals in December 1853 and had no truck with Bright's conviction about giving the British electorate a real democracy and the working class a say in law-making. In this he was of a similar opinion to his fellow aristocrats, arguing that the lower classes were not fit to have the vote because they would be bribed and intimidated by Radical agitators, and that it could be observed 'daily in the United States the lowering effect of this dependence of members upon the lower orders of the community'.[33] As Bright wrote to Villiers in January 1854,

What a miserable policy it is to keep Palmerston on our side of the House. In his own place, on the other side, he would be no more capable of harm than any other clever fellow having a bad case and a party not supported by public opinion. Sitting with you [on the Treasury bench], he uses both sides for his purposes.[34]

The Reform Bill fell by the wayside as the Crimean War got under way. Bright was unimpressed with this turn of events, but not surprised. 'What a brainless lot they are,' he had written to Cobden in November of the previous year, referring to Palmerston and the war party, 'to run after everything but their own direct interests. Mrs Jellyby in *Bleak House* is their great original, putting everything right at "Borrioboola Gha" and neglecting everything at home.'[35]

Manchester Defeat, 1857

While Bright continued to press for reform whenever he could, over the next few years the country became increasingly preoccupied with the Crimean War. Bright was bitterly opposed to the conflict (see Chapter 6). His vocal opposition to the Government's position led to another curious meeting with Disraeli, who was as keen as Bright to see the back of Palmerston, if this would lead to power. On 20 February 1855, Bright recorded,

> Talk with Disraeli. Thought one or two speeches weekly like the one I made before Christmas would break up the Govt. in a month. I said I wanted peace, not to break up Govt.; but if they would not make peace, then I would make war upon them. He returned to an old topic, on my saying I thought they (Derby party) would come in soon: he could not see why I should not join Lord Derby's Cabinet! I smiled, and said I could never lift up my head after such an act – it would destroy me, etc. He thought Palmerston done: 'you may see the breed, but the action and power are gone', etc.[36]

Though Bright's stance on the war was subsequently vindicated, by the end of 1856, burnt out by the stress of conscientious objection, competing with the Establishment and his own party, his health completely broke down – but not for long. He was recuperating on the Continent when Palmerston was defeated in March 1857 following a breakdown of relations with China. Cobden had led the attack and called for a select committee into Britain's commercial relations with China. His motion against Palmerston's Government was carried by a majority of sixteen and Palmerston decided to dissolve Parliament. Bright was deeply sympathetic to Cobden's motion, as might have been expected, and this was well known in the House. They were mutually opposed to the Government's entire policy on the matter, which they regarded as extremely damaging to

B—T.   G—E.   D—I.

THE NEW COALITION.

☞ Messrs. Bright, Gladstone, and Disraeli were, at this time (though for different reasons) in accord in their opposition to Lord Palmerston's Government.—1855.

No. 6.

commercial relations between Britain and China, and contrary to
the amicable diplomacy that they saw as being necessary and which
Palmerston's Government had failed to deliver.

Bright's attitudes towards the Crimean War, to the Chinese question and to the bringing down of the leader of their party led to deep
resentments in Manchester, stirred up by those who favoured
Palmerston's policies. On 8 March 1857, while in Rome, Bright sent
a letter via George Wilson to his constituents offering to resign, but
the offer was declined. In January he had written from Rome about
his political motivation:

> I am no more able to tell the truth to my countrymen from the
> platform, I will not regret the effort then made, terrible as is the
> price it has cost me ... I can honestly say that a love of what I
> have believed to be the truth, a strong desire for the good and
> true greatness of my country, and an unchangeable hostility to
> the selfishness and fraud which distinguish the Government of
> the English oligarchy, have been the mainsprings of my public
> and political conduct. I have not sought that which is to be
> gained by submission to the ruling parties, and I have endeav-
> oured to act uninfluenced by the clamour or the momentary and
> impulsive applause of the people.[37]

At a meeting at the Manchester Free Trade Hall on 18 March 1857,
Cobden spoke on behalf of his friend. Among other matters, including those relating to foreign policy, Cobden referred to Palmerston's
intransigent opposition to reform. Regarding the opposition candidates, Bright noted in his diary,

> If they do succeed, it will only show that consistency to principle
> and fidelity of service are not sufficient to secure the confidence
> of the electors of Manchester. If I had bent the knee to power,
> and if I had sought and accepted (and if I had sought, I might
> have had) some office in the Govt., these crawling fellows that
> now combine against me would, I suppose, have been equally
> disposed to crawl to me. It is a melancholy thing to observe how
> slow a people are to discover their true friends. A member of
> the aristocracy, or anyone willing to act with the aristocracy and
> for them, is accepted by the people as if he were the friend of the
> people.[38]

Both Bright and Milner Gibson, the sitting Members for Manchester, were re-adopted by the Manchester Liberal Committee, but in the poll that followed both were turned out, as was Cobden from his Yorkshire seat. In place of Bright and Milner Gibson were elected Sir John Potter and a local merchant, James Aspinall Turner. Bright had lost on the astonishing grounds that he had been unpatriotic in his opposition to the Crimean War. As Sarah Bradford points out, the election turned on only one question, noted in Lord Shaftesbury's diary: 'Were you, or were not? Are you, or are you not, for Palmerston?'[39]

The defeat was widely lamented. As noted by the *Birmingham Journal*:

> The indecency of the ingratitude with which they are now treated would be bad enough; but the revolting hypocrisy of the grounds of that treatment is ten times worse. It is pretended that Cobden and Bright have changed. They have not changed. They are the same men they ever were and it is because they are that their memory will live. Their characters will be treasured as the most precious inheritance of an age barren indeed in public virtue.[40]

Even some of those newspapers that resented Bright's attitude towards the Crimean War expressed concern. *The Times* admitted,

> For ten years we have opposed these two gentlemen in well-nigh every act of their public lives, and yet now we must honestly say that we deeply regret to see erased from the roll-call of the House of Commons the names of Mr John Bright and Mr Richard Cobden.[41]

Similar remarks appeared in the *Morning Post*, the *Liverpool Daily Post*, the *Edinburgh Daily Express* and the *Daily News*. The *Saturday Review*, strongly opposed to the Manchester School, wrote,

> The Manchester men are eminently men of courage; and of all qualities, this – at least in the domain of politics – is the rarest in the present day ... Courage does not consist in swaggering where there is no danger and retreating before the first shadow of opposition ... Their bravery was of a less fashionable kind – they had opinions for which, right or wrong, they were ready to sacrifice their popularity.[42]

There were almost certainly two exceptions to this widespread dismay. First, Lord Palmerston himself clearly welcomed Bright being driven out of Manchester. Palmerston was in the ascendancy and one of his most vocal critics had been defeated. As A. J. P. Taylor pointed out, 'The general election of 1857 is unique in our history, the only election conducted as a simple plebiscite in favour of an individual.'[43] A portion of the Manchester commercial class – which was divided over cotton – would also have rejoiced.

Bright took the news calmly. At the time of the poll, he was travelling in Italy. 'The news scarcely affected me in the least,' he wrote to his wife from Florence on 31 March 1857. 'I was partly prepared for it by the delay in receiving it. And the simple fact of my being out of Parliament, I need hardly tell thee, does not cost me a thought.'[44] That same day he wrote his farewell address to the electors of Manchester, which was an explanation of his political career, in his own words, up to that point in time:

> Gentlemen, I have received a telegraph despatch informing me of the result of the election contest in which you have been engaged. That result has not greatly surprised me, and so far as I am personally concerned – inasmuch as it liberates me from public life in a manner which involves on my part no shrinking from any duty – I cannot seriously regret it. I lament it on public grounds, because it tells the world that many amongst you have abandoned the opinions you professed to hold in the year 1847, and even so recently as the year 1852 ... The charge against me has rather been that I have too warmly and too faithfully defended the political views which found so much favour with you at the two previous elections. If the change in the opinion of me has arisen from my course on the question of the war with Russia, I can only say that on calm review of all the circumstances of the case – and during the past twelve months I have had ample time for such a review – I would not unsay or retract any one of the speeches I have spoken, or erase from the records of Parliament any one of the votes I have given upon it ... I am free, and will remain free, from any share in the needless and guilty bloodshed of that melancholy chapter in the annals of my country.[45]

On 16 April, from Venice, Bright sent a commentary to Cobden on their mutual efforts over the past years, demonstrating his statesmanlike grasp of the importance of principle in the big landscape of the how and why of government:

During the comparatively short period since we entered public life, see what has been done. Through our labours, mainly the whole creed of millions of people, and of the statesmen of our day, has been totally changed on all the questions which affect commerce and customs duties and taxation. They now agree to repudiate as folly what twenty years ago they accepted as wisdom.[46]

What he did not know was that he was about to receive an invitation that would set him on course towards even greater achievements on behalf of the disenfranchised and the oppressed.

The Member for Birmingham

On 30 July 1857, the radical MP George Muntz died, leaving a vacancy in one of the two parliamentary seats for Birmingham. Two days later, the city's Liberals held a meeting to discuss who might be invited to stand. They were seeking a prominent figure to demonstrate their radical heritage. When Alderman Lloyd proposed Bright, it was agreed to call a public meeting on Tuesday, 4 August to decide the question. Bright had no previous connection with Birmingham and neither he nor his associates had approached the city's movers and shakers with any suggestion that he might represent them. Indeed, the nervous exhaustion brought on by the events of the previous few years still plagued him and he had been entirely absent from the House of Commons since January 1856. Nevertheless, the public meeting attracted 8,000 people of all parties, and the proposal was agreed.

Bright was convalescing in Scotland at the time, walking the glens and unaware of the events unfolding in Birmingham. The invitation reached him by telegram sent via his brother-in-law, Duncan McLaren.

Bright did not answer immediately, but first met his Quaker friend Joseph Sturge in Edinburgh, who told him that the Birmingham Liberals 'promised to return me without opposition, and, perhaps foolishly, I consented to sit if elected'.[47] He travelled to Tamworth where, on 8 August 1857, he and McLaren met a deputation of Birmingham Liberals at the Castle Inn. Bright agreed to their proposal, He wrote in an address that day,

After fourteen years' service in the House of Commons, having spoken and voted on almost every great question which has been

discussed during that period, I feel it unnecessary to write at
length in detail as to my political opinions and my public course.
You will not require to be told that I am a warm supporter of
such measures as shall render the representation of the nation
more real and complete in the House of Commons.

This was in the midst of the Indian Mutiny, so he also dealt with the
question of the 'revolt', which was a matter of grave concern to the
country, and, in particular, to the deputation that had met him:

I am not prepared to defend the steps by which England has
obtained dominion in the East, but, looking to the interests of
India, and England, I cannot oppose such measures as may be
necessary to suppress the existing disorder. To restore order to
India is mercy to India, but heavy will be the guilt of our countrymen should we neglect hereafter any measures which would
contribute to the welfare of its hundred millions of population.[48]

Though Bright did not feel well enough to go to Birmingham at that
time, word of his adoption spread, and the Conservative and other
candidates withdrew their names from the ballot. On 10 August, just
two days later, Bright was returned to Parliament unopposed as the
Member for Birmingham.

His health was not to be fully restored for many months, but
Bright's personal crusade for political reform had at last found its
natural home. Birmingham, a city populated with small-scale
commercial enterprises and disenfranchised workers, offered him a
true democratic home from which he could begin his mission to
instil real democracy into the British Parliament. Indeed, as Cobden
wrote,

The honest and independent course taken by the people at
Birmingham, their exemption from aristocratic snobbery, and
their fair appreciation of a democratic son of the people, confirm
me in the opinion I have always had that the social and political
state of that town is far more healthy than that of Manchester ...
in my opinion Birmingham will be a better home for him than
Manchester.[49]

Bright took his seat in the House of Commons on 9 January 1858.
In his diary on 15 January he noted that he attended the House
after an eight-mile walk. His health was restored and he seemed

galvanized by his return to Westminster. On the same day, in conversation with Sir James Graham on the loss of Graham's wife, they exchanged thoughts about political vanity, Graham saying 'How little is Fame worth striving for! Look at Peel – sympathy and feeling on his death, and now little thought of; even the Duke of Wellington, dead and buried – a nine-days' wonder and the world passes on.' Bright himself said that he thought that Peel 'was unfortunately too sensitive and Disraeli found this out and attacked him accordingly, without hating Peel, but as a way to his own elevation'.[50]

As though he had been waiting for his moment, Bright's mind became fully and immediately focused on the issue of parliamentary reform. On 2 February, 5,000 people assembled in Birmingham to hear a letter from Bright read out in which he stated flatly that Birmingham deserved more than two MPs, as did other metropolitan boroughs of the great cities. Bright presented a petition to the House of Commons to this effect, which included vote by ballot, triennial parliaments and the abolition of the property qualification of MPs. He had re-entered the fray.

With Bright now enjoying the backing of Birmingham and Milner Gibson representing Ashton-under-Lyme, the pair made their move when Palmerston's Conspiracy to Murder Bill was up for its second reading on 18 February 1858. Its intention was to punish conspiracies for the murder of foreign leaders in Great Britain, but in reality it was a bill to protect the Emperor Napoleon III, whom Palmerston was keen to impress, following an assassination attempt in Paris by Felice Orsini using bombs manufactured in Birmingham. The very idea of changing English law at the direction of France had led Lord John Russell to put down an amendment. This was moved by Milner Gibson and seconded by Bright. Significantly, they were both tellers against the Government. The debate became very fractious, and Palmerston, losing his temper, launched a bitter attack on Milner Gibson, effectively accusing him of past collaboration with the enemy. As the debate progressed, Palmerston became increasingly enraged and at one point shook his fist at Bright and Milner Gibson.[51]

On 20 February, Palmerston and his Cabinet resigned, and Derby and Disraeli took over. Within the space of a month, Bright had marked his man and watched Palmerston fall like a stone. As Cobden wrote to an acquaintance,

> There was surely something more than chance in bringing back these two men [Bright and Milner Gibson] to inflict summary punishment on the man who flattered himself a few months ago

that he had put his heel on their political necks? For the first
time, I have felt regret at not being there to witness that scene of
retributive justice.[52]

This crushing blow to Palmerston, who sat in the Commons with his
face hidden and in great distress, cannot be underestimated. The
poignancy of the removal of the prime minister through the agency
of a backbencher whose political demise Palmerston had seemingly
accomplished, yet who had revived and returned to the fray, was not
lost on the House, nor on the country at large.

With the defeat of Palmerston, a new era was born. Bright could
now turn his attention to the battles for parliamentary reform that lay
ahead, though his focus was diverted briefly by the India question in
the spring and summer of 1858, with a series of bills that moved
towards the fulfilment of Bright's campaign against the East India
Company and the transfer of its powers to the Crown (see Chapter
6). In June, he reaffirmed his commitment to the national interest in
the wake of rumours of a potential French invasion. Asked why
Bright supported the Conservative Government on European armaments at this time, William Robertson records that Bright replied,

> the question was not one of Conservatism nor one of aristocracy
> but of the obvious interests of a country and of humanity;
> and that a Government with a foreign policy of moderation
> and justice was the Government he should select, rather than a
> Government that pretended to give an exhibition of power for all
> parts of the world.[53]

He would support the Conservative Party in power on the grounds
of principle and morality, but not on the grounds of convenience or
opportunism merely because he preferred it to a Government under
Palmerston.

There were some skirmishes with the issue of parliamentary
reform at this time, including Peter Locke King's bill for the abolition of the property qualification for representatives of English and
Irish constituencies. Berkeley's annual motion in favour of vote by
ballot was supported vigorously by Bright, who insisted that a
Reform Bill was necessary and asserted that no such bill should be
passed without the great principle of the ballot.

The scene was set for Bright's great movement for parliamentary
reform to begin in earnest. He believed that the secret ballot was an
integral part of these reforms. In 1854, he had argued for such a

measure so that the voter should 'give his vote by a certain machinery which will protect him against the influence of his landlord, his creditor, or his customer'.[54] Palmerston had rejected this on the specious grounds that a person's morality would be undermined if he violated an open promise with a secret vote. It was this kind of Palmerstonian hypocrisy to which Bright objected the most:

> The noble Lord appears not to be aware of the fact that if a man is made to promise contrary to his conscience, he by that promise is equally guilty of immorality; and if he votes in accordance with that promise, he doubly violates the rule which the noble Lord professes to support.[55]

Bright's commitment to the idea of the ballot was well developed by this time. As early as 1853, he was looking in this respect to North America, where, as he recorded in his diary, the

> ballot has recently been established in the municipal elections in Canada. Formerly riot and intimidation, now tranquil as possible. The question is growing there and it is expected it will before long be applied to parliamentary elections also ... Englishmen are everywhere more rational than in their own country.[56]

Similarly, in reply to a resolution at a public meeting in Ardwick, Manchester, in May 1857, he had urged secrecy of the ballot as being the only antidote to

> the aristocratic influence in Parliament ... To give votes without giving representation in some fair degree in proportion to the votes is to cheat the people; to give a large number of votes without security of the ballot will subject the increased numbers of our countrymen to the degrading influence which wealth and power now exercise so unscrupulously upon the existing electoral body.[57]

By 1858, Bright was giving equal importance to the redistribution of seats as to extension of the franchise, because he wanted to give greater political influence to the large new manufacturing and commercial towns. Connected with this was his advocacy of a peaceful foreign policy and a reduction in public expenditure, and he applied similar principles to his campaigns in respect of India and Ireland.

On the evening of 27 October 1858, he addressed his Birmingham constituents for the first time since his election the previous year. The Town Hall was transformed, with all seating removed apart from that in the great gallery and on the platform, and around 5,000 people crammed into a building designed for half that number. The atmosphere was electric. Newspapers from every corner of the land sent reporters. As Bright noted in his diary – the only note he made during this period, 'Attended meeting and dinner at Birmingham. Speeches. Reporters more numerous than at any meeting ever held before in the country. Telegraph and special trains – as if some very important person here to utter words of great import!'[58] He also wrote to his wife, '*The Times* reporter called this morning to ask when I thought the meeting would be over, that he might arrange for their special engine! Other men, I mean our public men, must be very little if I am so great.'[59] His self-deprecating humour belied the significance of the event.

'I shall take this opportunity,' he stated to the crowd, 'of discussing and as far as I am able with brevity and distinctness what I think we ought to aim at now, when the great question of parliamentary reform is before the country.' He traced the minimalist measures of former Governments, and to loud laughter turned to the present:

> We now have a Government under the chiefdomship of Lord Derby, who, during his short term of office in 1852, stated, if I remember right, that one of the chief objects of his government would be to stem the tide of democracy ... Now, it may be that Lord Derby has entirely changed his mind, that he is as much converted to parliamentary reform, as Sir Robert Peel in 1846 was converted to Corn Law repeal,

as Bright knew only too well.

The journalists who had scurried to hear Bright speak in the flesh reported the occasion vividly. As Trevelyan poetically described the historic occasion:

> This night for the first time, and on many a night to come, that great audience swayed, like a cornfield beneath the wind, under the gusts of cheering a laughter that shook them as he spoke. Although, when he began, they seemed packed as tightly as human beings can stand and breathe, yet more than once, in some storm of emotion, the front of the mass swung forward and the rear backward, leaving a broad strip of floor bare to view, like

an island of sea-sand revealed for a moment when the waves are sucked down by the tide. And the magic that swayed them was not some hard appeal to the lower part of their nature, but drew its compelling virtue from the simplest invocation of moral principles, in words which survive the speaker as part of the wealth of our mother tongue.[60]

This description was based on the recollections of the Reverend Robert Dale, the celebrated congregational minister in Birmingham. In his words,

The hush which had fallen on the vast and excited assembly as soon as he began to speak deepened into awe. We had expected a fierce assault on the 'obstinacy' and 'iniquity' of the defenders of what the orator afterwards described as 'the fabric of privilege', but the storms of political passion were for a moment stilled; we suddenly found ourselves in the presence of the Eternal, and some of us, perhaps, rebuked ourselves in the words of the patriarch, 'Surely, the Lord is in this place, and I knew it not.'[61]

The next day, Bright met with the Reform Union and in the evening spoke again at Birmingham Town Hall on the issue of foreign policy, which he linked to the issue of democracy.

Following his success in Birmingham, Bright embarked on another exhaustive speaking tour, in which he developed the themes he had initiated in Birmingham. In Manchester on 10 December, he spoke at the Free Trade Hall with Milner Gibson and received a great reception, almost as though the people of Manchester had not rejected him the year before. Pointing out that more than half the members of the House of Commons were returned by less than a sixth of those who were eligible to vote, he argued that every householder in the land should have a vote – including any who had property out of which they contributed to the support of the poor – and that, the cause of reform being just, it was necessary to agitate to achieve that justice, 'The Government is at a dead-lock without parliamentary reform,' he stated.[62]

At Bradford, 4,000 gathered to hear Bright speak. In Edinburgh, he spoke to an audience of 2,000 and in Glasgow a few days later he re-emphasized the importance of the ballot to an equally large crowd.

However, all was not plain sailing. Despite his growing popularity, Bright was set on a collision course with the Establishment and the

MR. BRIGHT OFFERS TO GIVE SATISFACTION TO THE LIBERAL PARTY.

☞ Mr. Bright rejected the timid Reform proposals of the Whigs, and demanded the widest extension of the franchise.—1858.

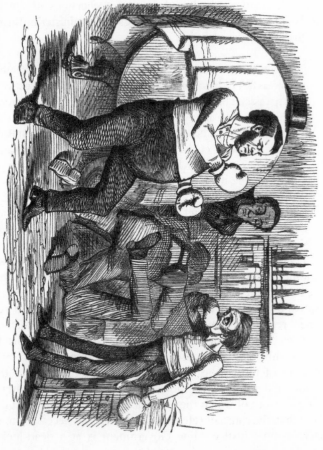

No. 10.

aristocracy. Moreover, he also received criticism from that element of the working class that wanted him to go even further than his judgement suggested was prudent. Despite his private intentions – 'Personally, I have not the smallest objection to the widest possible suffrage that the ingenuity of man can devise'[63] – Bright clearly felt that to go further at this stage would produce a backlash that would be counter-productive.

He also received criticism from *The Times*, the *Illustrated London News*, the *Manchester Guardian*, *The Economist* and *Punch*, who particularly feared his enthusiasm for American democracy. Nevertheless, he was being both noticed and reported.

Derby Reform Bill, 1859

The Queen opened Parliament on 3 February 1859, and in her Speech recommended the introduction of a Reform Bill. Reform was in the air. Bright had developed his own draft bill for parliamentary reform, supported by a petition to the House of Commons which had been endorsed at a meeting in Birmingham on 1 February. This proposed the franchise for those rated to the relief of the poor and all lodgers paying a rent of £10, with the county franchise reduced to £10 rent, as well as votes taken by ballot. He proposed disenfranchising 56 English, 9 Irish and 21 Scottish boroughs and one MP from each of the remaining 34 boroughs, redistributing these seats according to population throughout the larger towns and counties.

The Reform Bill brought in by the Derby–Disraeli Government on 28 February, however, was neither fish nor fowl. Indeed, Bright described it in his diary as 'an insult to the country'. It would, he believed, 'disturb everything, irritate vast masses of the people and settle nothing'.[64] On 9 March, a resolution passed by 7,000 people in Birmingham also dismissed the bill as 'an insult to the people'.[65] Bright condemned the bill: 'It indicates not only that your rulers distrust you, but that they despise you.' If it were to be passed, he said, 'I should abandon all hope of the future of this country. Not one single week longer would I take my seat in the House of Commons as your representative.'[66]

On 24 March, during the second reading, Bright warned Disraeli that the Bill was 'framed to satisfy the prejudices, scruples, convictions, and fears of the 150 county gentlemen who sit behind him'. He warned that by excluding the working class, the bill threatened their future and condemned them 'as dangerous and ignorant as they were twenty-seven years ago', in 1832. He gave a number of hilarious examples of the ways in which rotten boroughs still persisted, including one where the election had turned on 'free traders' imprisoned for smuggling and a parson who had not left his residence for two years but who, 'by the aid of cordials, stimulants and a sedan chair' was brought out to vote.[67]

At the same time, Bright continued to prepare the ground with popular opinion, stirred up in huge meetings and petitions endorsing his views before he presented them to the House of Commons. Bright states in his diary, 'I presented a petition from Birmingham signed by more than 40,000 persons. A petition from Manchester had 53,000 names to it.'[68] The synchrony of this strategy was not lost on Disraeli as the campaign for reform, pre-endorsed by the people, moved inexorably forward and gradually whittled down or cowed the vehemence of those opposed to democracy.

Bright's opposition to the bill demonstrated his political will and his great skill in the use of language. Measures contained in the bill, such as the idea of giving the vote as a reward for education, he described as, in an expression which shot the bill to pieces, 'fancy franchises'.[69] Disraeli's curt response was that 'Alliteration tickles the ear and is a very popular form of language among savages. It is, I believe, the characteristic of rude and barbarous poetry; but it is not an argument in legislation.'[70]

The second reading of the Reform Bill at the end of March lasted seven nights and excited passions throughout the land. On the political substance of the issue, Bright made one of his greatest ironic speeches, adopting real conservatism as a principle in the national interest and yet turning Conservative principles against the Conservative Members of the House:

> Let me assure the House then that resistance is not always Conservative ... I profess to be in intention as Conservative as you are. I believe that in reality I am infinitely more Conservative, if you will cast your eyes twenty or thirty years forward. Was not free trade Conservative? and yet you resisted it to the last ... Is economy in finance a Conservative principle? Is peace Conservative? ... I believe that a real and substantial measure of Reform, which the people of this country would accept as such ... would elevate and strengthen the character of your population. I believe that, in the language of that beautiful prayer which is read here every day, it would tend to 'knit together the hearts of all persons and estates within this realm'.[71]

On another occasion, Bright would even declare himself to be 'the perfect Conservative. I should like to know what there would have been left of Conservatism for Conservatives to conserve at this hour but for me.'[72] Indeed, in the heat of the debate on the Reform Bill, Bright drew almost unconsciously on his future path towards Liberal Unionism (see Chapter 8), politically opposed as he was to Disraeli and those who represented the Conservative Party at the time. He also touched upon, almost by instinct, what bound them together in the national interest, which became evident in the run-up to the 1867 Act itself.

Finally, on 1 April 1859, the bill fell, with a majority of 39 against the Government. Derby resigned. Bright had at last moved popular opinion to the floor of the House of Commons itself and won his first battle on parliamentary reform in the very theatre he sought to change. However, any hopes of an immediate follow-up to this victory were dashed when the Conservative Government decided to dissolve Parliament, which was prorogued on 19 April. As Bright wrote to Samuel Morley,

> I regret very much that I have been unable to introduce my Bill to the House of Commons ... But on the very evening when I intended to give notice of the introduction of my Bill, we were informed of the impending dissolution of Parliament and thus all chance of proceeding with any important business was at an end.[73]

On the hustings in the ensuing General Election of 1859, Bright, to great acclaim, was said to be more than the Member for Birmingham, he was 'the member for Great Britain'.[74] Bright gave compliments as well as received them. On 13 April, he spoke on behalf of Cobden, who was in America, in support of his candidature for Rochdale, Bright's home town.

In the run-up to the election, Bright addressed three meetings in his own constituency of Birmingham, including one in the Town Hall on 25 April with 7,000 people present, pressing vigorously for parliamentary reform. Three days later, he returned to the Town Hall, which was bursting at the seams with 9,000 people, and said they had 'come to the time when no institution, however deeply rooted in tradition or sentiment, could dare with impunity and safety to stand against the opinion of the people of this great nation'. He went on, 'If I am anything in political life, I strive to be at least a servant of the people and of truth.'[75]

Bright was not universally welcomed in Birmingham, however. Some Liberals thought him too radical and put up Sir Thomas Dyke Acland, a moderate Liberal who had not entirely abandoned his earlier Conservative principles, to contest the election. Sir Thomas put up a good fight but nevertheless, on 29 April, Bright and his colleague William Scholefield defeated their opponents in Birmingham by around 3,000 votes. In Rochdale, Cobden was returned unopposed.

Parliament met on 31 May, but within a fortnight the new Conservative Government, still under Lord Derby but with a diminished majority of 48 seats, had come under siege during the debate on the Address. Bright spoke against the Government on the question of foreign policy, distinctly unenthusiastic as he was about proposals for an alliance with the Emperor of France and doubting the Government's commitment to neutrality. The Marquess of Hartington, a strong supporter of Bright, called for a vote of confidence. In the division, the Government lost by 13 votes and Bright effectively won the day. Derby's Government resigned on 11 June 1859.

Bright had again helped to defeat the Government with popular support from the country. Yet, on 12 June 1859, Bright's political enemy within his own party, Lord Palmerston, became prime minister for the second time. On this occasion, the uncomfortable strife was to last for more than six years. Russell was appointed foreign secretary, and Gladstone chancellor of the exchequer.

That day, Bright recorded in his diary a chance meeting the previous week in the City of London with Lord Stanley, Derby's son, who, anticipating the fall of the Conservative Government, had urged him to accept office if offered 'on the grounds that the more peace men in the Government, the more peace was likely to be kept'. For his own part, Bright wrote, 'I am in a great dilemma. It may not be offered, but if it be offered, I am, or shall be, sorely puzzled.' After discussions with his brother-in-law, he came to the conclusion that 'it is better to bide our time, and to form opinion outside, than to enter a Government without satisfactory conditions ... I do not think I can ever consent to hold any office in the Government of this country.'[76]

On 13 June, Bright recorded that while, according to Milner Gibson, neither Russell nor Palmerston had any objection to his joining the Government, if he had been asked directly, he would have refused. He said, clearly indicating his preference for independence of action,

> In truth, I do not see how I could join Palmerston for whom
> I have felt so much contempt, and against whom I have spoken
> so freely, and in whom I can have no confidence; and I suspect
> I should be miserable in a Court dress, and in official fetters.

He continued, 'Better teach the people something good for the
future than resign oneself to work institutions already in existence.'[77]

The following day, Bright advised Milner Gibson to decline office
to 'retain our freedom and our power'. He then wrote 'a severe
leader', as he put it, for the *Morning Star*.[78] On 15 June, he heard
from Lord John Russell that while Gibson and Cobden were to be
offered Cabinet posts:

> Palmerston would not offer me office, not on account on my
> views on Reform, but owing to my opinion or sayings with
> regard to institutions 'which are considered essential by a major-
> ity of Englishmen' … This is amusing, and I suppose the excuse
> will serve its purpose. Palmerston would not have raised himself
> in my opinion by offering me office, and I could not have
> accepted it or anything else at his hands.[79]

Palmerston later said of Bright, 'It is not personalities that are
complained of; a public man is right in attacking persons. But it is
his attacks on *classes* that have given offence to powerful bodies who
can make their resentment felt.'[80] Having already dished Palmerston
once, and Palmerston having had his revenge with Bright's ejection
from Manchester, none of this is very surprising, but what it does
demonstrate is that independence and principle were fundamental
to Bright's course of political action. As Bright himself asked in his
diary, 'Surely they don't dream of purchasing my silence in the
questions on which I have been accustomed to speak and act freely
before the public?'[81]

A few weeks later, after the new Cabinet had been formed,
Palmerston suggested offering Bright a Privy Councillorship, but
the Queen refused:

> it would be impossible to allege any service Mr Bright has
> rendered, and if the honour were looked upon as a reward for his
> systematic attacks upon the institution of this country, a very erro-
> neous impression might be produced as to the feeling which the
> Queen or her Government entertain towards these institutions.[82]

She later greatly changed her mind about him.

While all this was going on, Cobden had been travelling back from America, where he had been received with much acclaim. It was only when his boat docked in Liverpool on 29 June that he discovered the Derby Government had fallen, and that Palmerston wished to offer him the Board of Trade. Lord John Russell was wheeled in to urge him to accept. Palmerston tried to bribe Bright by claiming that he was framing his administration so that 'it should contain representatives of all sections of the Liberal Party'.[83] Milner Gibson had agreed to become a member of the new Cabinet, but he did not reckon on Cobden's integrity. The object clearly was to split Cobden and Bright.

Cobden had a meeting with Palmerston on his arrival in London, and the prime minister could hardly have expected the tongue-lashing he received in return for his munificent attempt to break Cobden's political trust with Bright. Cobden ranted,

> For the last twelve years, I have been the systematic and constant assailant of the principle on which your foreign policy has been carried on. I believed you to be warlike, intermeddling, and quarrelsome, and that your policy was calculated to embroil us with foreign nations. At the same time, I have expressed a general want of confidence in your domestic politics. Now, I may have been altogether wrong in my views; it is possible I may have been; but I put it candidly to you whether it ought to be in your Cabinet, whilst holding a post of high honour and emolument derived from you, that I should make the first avowal of a change of opinion respecting your public policy? Should I not expose myself to severe suspicions, and deservedly so, if I were, under these circumstances, to step from an Atlantic steamer into your Cabinet?[84]

It would take more than the minor trappings of office to disturb the consistency and principle on which Cobden and Bright had conducted their alliance over the previous 23 years.

French Commercial Treaty

On 21 July 1859, Disraeli – for the Opposition – proposed a foreign policy of peace and neutrality combined with prudence in public finances. Gladstone, the new Chancellor of the Exchequer, agreed. Bright took the opportunity to thank Disraeli 'with great satisfaction', taunting him with the words, 'Sir Robert Peel on one occasion made a speech of very much the same tenor and the Honourable Gentleman opposite [Disraeli] charged him with being a convert to our views.'[85]

As part of the proposals, Gladstone had suggested that an income tax should be imposed for one year. Bright, complaining bitterly that the annual burden of taxation was already well over £50 million, attacked the idea, describing it as 'odious beyond all others that I know of, and odious beyond all others, because it is unjust beyond all others; and I will never consent that in its present shape it should be made a permanent tax'. Bright analysed in great detail the way in which public finances were regrettably employed in the pursuit of war – a pursuit he knew his leader, Palmerston, was not afraid to take up – and spoke of 'acres of bloody and mangled human bodies over which guns have been dragged and cavalry have galloped'.[86]

He then made an original, if optimistic, call for a commercial treaty with France to remove duties and barriers of trade between the two countries. Bright had visited France in 1853 and had concluded that it would be no bad thing if the British were, at least, to desist from criticising the French, despite old antagonisms. In turn, this would reduce the tensions that led the French to fortify Cherbourg against a potential British invasion. As Bright wrote to George Wilson, 'What a glorious revolution for England and France when we scan our mutual imports and exports, instead of counting up the number of ships of war!'[87]

In his speech in July 1859, Bright complained that 'the trade between us is nothing like what it ought to be, considering the population of the two countries, their vast increase of productive power and their great wealth'. Ordinary French people, he said, were 'as anxious for perpetual peace with England as the most intelligent and Christian Englishmen can be for a perpetual peace with France'.[88]

Michel Chevalier, the French economist, read Bright's speech. He was impressed, given the antipathy to the French by Palmerston and the free trader, Villiers. Chevalier wrote to Cobden and arranged for him to meet the Comte de Persigny, the French ambassador, and leaders of the French Government. The idea of a commercial treaty with France was objected to deeply from a number of quarters, including many in Parliament, the press and the British commercial world. Fortunately, Gladstone, increasingly influential in the Cabinet, was strongly committed to the idea. Cobden spoke to Gladstone and, while he could not immediately obtain Palmerston's agreement, travelled to Paris in October 1859 to negotiate. He met the Emperor personally and drew his attention to the higher standard of living of British workers compared to the French, referring to the work of Peel in advancing free trade. Bright was sworn to secrecy and, despite the ups and downs, kept Cobden's spirits up by reminding him that encouraging commerce would avoid war with France. The negotiations were ultimately concluded in January 1860. As Gladstone's biographer, John Morley, wrote: 'Bright had opened it, Chevalier had followed it up, Persigny agreed, Cobden made an opportunity, Gladstone seized it.'[89]

Bright's journal records on 25 January 1860:

> The Commercial Treaty with France signed yesterday by Cobden on behalf of this Government – a wonderful event, and may have great and blessed results… [Cobden's] judgment, patience, intelligence, and tact has brought about a treaty, invaluable, as I hope and believe, to both countries and to Europe … Cobden, a simple citizen, unpaid, unofficial – but earnest and disinterested – has done all. If our statesmen were such as he, what would England not become! … Such events are compensations for the disappointments and wearisome labours of public life.[90]

While being committed to the principle of free trade in the national interests of Britain and of the world at large, one of Bright's prime motives for free trade was international peace, which he believed profoundly would come from commercial intercourse between countries previously at war. Between them, Cobden, Bright and Gladstone achieved not only the peace and stability the Treaty offered, but also instigated an abrupt turn in foreign policy. Indeed, the treaty remains an international benchmark for free trade up to the present day. Attempts to hide the prime minister's warmongering occurred even at the time. As Trevelyan records, in 1863 an amused Bright came across a painting, now in Committee Room 12 of the House of Commons, created for Speaker Denison, which depicted the treaty lying open in front of a triumphant Palmerston, with the Cabinet – and Cobden and Bright – apparently unified behind him on the Government benches.[91]

A Free Press

In the meantime, on 17 August 1859, Cobden and Bright had come together on the issue of parliamentary reform at a meeting in

Rochdale. Bright clearly enjoyed the moment, and the fact that Cobden was now his own MP:

> I have had the privilege of being his political associate, his politi-
> cal brother, his personal friend for nearly 20 years. If there be
> one man in England whom I wish to call my representative more
> than another, I have the gratification tonight of being repre-
> sented by that man.[92]

The next day, the pair made speeches on the vote and the ballot to an audience of 8,000.

When Parliament returned in 1860, Bright's campaign received a boost when Gladstone revealed plans, against Palmerston's inclina-
tions, to repeal the paper duties in his budget on 10 February in response to agitation driven by Bright, Milner Gibson and Bright's brother-in-law and the founder of the Society for the Repeal of Taxes on Knowledge, Samuel Lucas.[93] The significance of this for the reformers cannot be overestimated. For Bright, it was a matter of principle and practical necessity. As John Vincent clearly demonstrates, Bright was well aware of the necessity of using the provincial press as a means of communicating with the middle and working classes.[94] It was a deliberate, calculated and effective campaign.

Bright certainly understood the power of the press. In the early 1850s, *The Times* – with a readership three times as large as all the other national newspapers combined – had been vehemently opposed to Bright's policy on the Crimean War, and had thus contributed to his ejection from Manchester. On the other hand, the deluge of reporters from all over the country who descended on Birmingham on the evening of 27 October 1858 had been a significant contribution to Bright's campaign for reform, as was the wide, verbatim reporting of his other speeches, both in Parliament and at public meetings. In this, the clarity and articulation of Bright's argu-
ments helped, by ensuring easy work for the reporters.[95]

The repeal of the paper duties had its origins in the early 1850s with the abolition of 'taxes on knowledge', which had imposed three taxes on daily papers, making them luxuries for the ordinary reader. Indeed, for lack of competition, *The Times*, the *Daily News* and the *Morning Post* could be priced at fivepence. Cobden and Bright, for reasons of freedom of trade and their aversion to monopoly, but also wanting direct contact with the masses, had campaigned in the spring and summer of 1853 for the repeal of the advertisement duty. They succeeded ultimately, and belatedly, with the help of

Disraeli. The abolition of the advertisement duty was followed in 1855 by that of the newspaper stamp.

As a result, on 17 March 1856, the one-penny *Morning Star* began publication. Promoting non-intervention, arbitration, free trade and parliamentary reform, it was edited by Samuel Lucas. Bright and Lucas worked closely together on matters of policy, with Bright writing leaders into the bargain. The paper had the backing of Joseph Sturge,[96] who was also influential with the *Birmingham Daily Post*, part owned by an early protégée of his, John Feeney, and whose support was vital to Bright's unopposed return in 1858 as the Member for Birmingham.

The passage of Gladstone's Paper Duty Repeal Bill through Parliament in 1860 was not without difficulties. After a bruising parliamentary tussle with the House of Lords, the duty was eventually repealed the following year. All the financial measures were consolidated into the Finance Bill 1861. Gladstone, with Bright's strong support (and with even Palmerston saying that Bright was 'our real budget maker and Chancellor of the Exchequer'[97]), brought matters to a head as to whether the House of Lords would dare to confront the House of Commons by rejecting the whole Budget. The Lords backed down. Those opposed to the repeal no longer had the stomach for the fight, given the constitutional brinkmanship of the previous year, and Royal Assent was given on 12 July. Ultimately, however, the Lords did confront the House of Commons again, in 1909, which led to the removal of the Lords' veto, as proposed by Bright in 1883, through the Parliament Act 1911. This put a stop to their audacity in seeking to influence or control taxation when they had no mandate from the people.

The true significance, therefore, of the repeal of the paper duties was not only in relation to the freedom of the press (at that time genuinely concerned with the flow of essential information in the public interest rather than merely of what is of interest to the public), but also to the behaviour of Lord Palmerston and his cronies, and their continuing resistance to parliamentary reform. Reform and press freedom were mutually dependent, and the nation's press seized the opportunity. *The Times* had long been the unchallenged, pre-eminent newspaper of the day and was the only journal that had its own parliamentary reporter in the House of Commons. By the late 1860s, others, including provincial newspapers, took seats in the press gallery in the House of Commons. Indeed, in 1864, Edward Baines of the *Leeds Mercury* proclaimed that, of a total annual newspaper circulation of 546 million, 340 million were provincial – embracing the general population.[98] This was followed in 1869 by the foundation of the Press Association. Reports of parliamentary debates were now widely available throughout the country – a crucial step in Bright's campaign for reform.

Reform 1860–4: Ups and Downs

Against this background, and in parallel with the negotiations on the French Commercial Treaty, Bright continued his persistent quest for reform based on the policy of his proposed legislation. He accepted Russell's Reform Bill of March 1860 purely as a gesture in the right direction, but without the enthusiastic support of Palmerston, as Prime Minister, it was withdrawn. As William Monypenny and George Buckle record,

> Bright complained bitterly, and with perfect justice, that the failure to proceed with Reform was a breach of the most explicit pledges, public and private, given by the Government in order to obtain office; but he received scant sympathy, as neither warning nor experience had deterred him from trusting the promises of the Whigs and placing them in power.[99]

According to Palmerston, Bright had even gone so far as to propose to Disraeli that the Radicals and Conservatives join together

> for the purpose of turning out the present Government and especially to get rid of Viscount Palmerston and Lord John Russell. Mr Bright said he would in that case give the Conservative Government two years' existence and by the end of that time the country, it might be hoped, would be prepared for a good, real Reform Bill, and then a proper Government might be formed.[100]

This proposal, said Palmerston, had been declined.

Bright's commitment to the ballot and redistribution was supported by Cobden, though their joint enthusiasm was dampened somewhat by Cobden having come to the conclusion that parliamentary reform had lost its immediate appeal both inside and outside Parliament. At the beginning of the new session on 5 February 1861, Russell announced to the House that it would be better to leave the question of reform alone for the present rather than bring forward a Bill that would disappoint its supporters. Bright was deeply angered. He told the House of Commons,

> You won't poll the nation; you won't refer the question to the people of the country and let them decide it; you confine the franchise to the million, whom you hocus pocus until their votes are of no value even to themselves, and then say, 'Why don't these six millions show they want it?'

He warned that there were dangers ahead, 'even though they be in some degree distant', in doing next to nothing and merely coming forward with a compromise measure for reform.[101]

That same day, an amendment on the Address was defeated by 124 to 46, further demonstrating a lack of interest for reform in the House, whatever quiet undercurrents were building up in the population at large. Bright recorded in his diary that evening that Russell

> threw over the reform question in a speech of offensive tone and language ... Had great difficulty in restraining my indignation at his conduct. I shall keep no terms with this Government for the future. It is base, as was the former government of Lord Palmerston. How long Mr Gladstone and Mr Gibson will go through the mire, I know not.[102]

That Bright put Russell in the same category as Palmerston speaks for itself. Indeed, Bright was so furious that he did not speak to Russell for many years. Russell's acceptance of an earldom in 1861 for his services to the nation added insult to injury. The fact that Russell had conducted the Reform Act of 1832 made his offence of not carrying reform through in the 1860s worse for Bright. Their relationship had always been somewhat uneasy. Russell's antagonism towards Bright was evident as early as March 1849, when he had told the Queen, fearing that his Navigation Bill would fail, that there would be 'dissolution, agitation, Bright and chaos'.[103] In March 1864, Bright noted, after receiving a dinner invitation from Russell, which he declined, that 'since his abandonment of the cause of the reform, have not had any intercourse with him, and since his acceptance of a peerage, have not even seen him except once or twice in the House of Lords'.[104] A year later, he declined further invitations and noted, 'Have not spoken to him for about five years.'[105]

Bright did, however, temporarily step back his nationwide agitation. While he agreed to make a speech at the inaugural meeting of the Leeds Working Men's Parliamentary Reform Association in December 1860, by January 1861 he was refusing all invitations to address political meetings 'for I cannot undertake the weight of an agitation which does not seem able to sustain itself'.[106]

The climate was calm and quiet. Despite the crucial victory of the repeal of paper duties in 1861, establishing the primacy of the House of Commons and putting the House of Lords in its place, Bright was becoming increasingly disheartened. The pusillanimous attitude of Russell and the obstructionism of Palmerston had taken their toll. It was around this time, as Asa Briggs notes, that Bright told an equally disheartened Gladstone,

> your *chief* and your *foreign minister* will still cling to the past ... a new policy and a wiser and a higher morality are sighed for by the best of the people, and there is a prevalent feeling that *you* are destined to guide that wise policy and to teach that higher morality.[107]

In January, Bright had discussions with Disraeli about ousting Palmerston, but was rebuffed.[108] He even went so far as to wonder whether he should give up politics and return to his business and his family. He was resigned to the fact that reform was condemned to the backwaters as long as Palmerston, whom he referred to as 'the hoary imposter',[109] remained in charge.

Instead, Bright concentrated on reform of a different kind through his absorption in the Civil War raging on the other side of the Atlantic (see Chapter 5). The American Republic, with its democracy so much admired by Bright, was in crisis. Described by *Punch* as the 'Untied States', it was now seen by many to be dangerous and unstable. During this period, Bright's Quaker instincts engaged his full attention. For Bright, slavery was another aspect of the denial of human freedom, greater in its implications because it specifically denied freedom of every kind to the slave.

Supporting the States of the North now subsumed all his energies. At the same time, it acted as a catalyst to his belief in the American Constitution and the democracy epitomized by his hero, Thomas Jefferson, and the other great founding fathers. Bright's opposition to slavery and his dedication to democracy stemmed from the same deep well of freedom from which he derived his political convictions. In Bright's mind, the American Civil War was the testing ground for the future of British parliamentary reform.

Despite writing to his wife in 1863 that he could not give himself to any other issue until the war was over,[110] Bright returned to the issue of parliamentary reform at a meeting in Rochdale on 24 November. Sharing the platform was Cobden, who referred to the 1832 Reform Act and pointed out that, since that time, the British colonies such as Australia and New Zealand had received representative institutions 'much freer in their representative system than we are in England'. He added that, on the Continent, there were wide extensions of political franchises. Bright, in his own speech, said,

> Look at the power which the United States have developed ... Look at the order which has prevailed. Their elections, at which as you see by the papers 50,000 or 100,000 or a quarter of a million persons vote in a given State, are conducted with less disorder than you have seen lately in three of the smallest boroughs in England.'

He continued,

> When this mortal strife is over, when peace is restored, when slavery is destroyed, when the Union is cemented afresh ... then Europe and England may learn that an instructed democracy is the surest foundation of government, and that education and freedom are the only sources of true greatness and true happiness among any people.[111]

This speech had an electric effect, and *The Times* accused Cobden and Bright of inciting discontent.

But the strain of events in America and attitudes at home were again taking their toll. In March, Bright wrote, 'I keep in Parlt because I do not seem able to give a good reason for leaving it'.[112] Despite still wanting to see the franchise extended and the secret ballot introduced, he was pessimistic about the prospects of success, and indicated that he was once again withdrawing from public meetings.

He did, however, venture out in April 1864 to meet the Italian patriot, General Giuseppe Garibaldi, who was visiting Britain. The pair first met at a reception given by the Duke and Duchess of Sutherland at Stafford House on 13 April. Bright wrote in his diary,

> It was a singular spectacle to see the most renowned living soldier of democracy cared for, as by a loving daughter, by a lady

who is a countess and duchess at the head of the aristocracy of England ... Lord Stanley said to me a day or two ago 'I wonder if it ever occurs to the Duke that if Garibaldi had his way there would be no Dukes of Sutherland?'[113]

Six days later, they met again:

Garibaldi said to me 'I am of your principles for if I am a soldier, I am a soldier of peace' ... There is a singular kindness and gentleness and dreamy enthusiasm in his face and in his eye, and a charming simplicity about him ... It is said, and doubtless truly, that the Government wants him out of the country. They fear he may excite political feeling in the provinces.[114]

At the Stafford House reception, Bright also spent much time in deep conversation with Gladstone. According to Trevelyan, that evening was the catalyst for the political relationship between Bright and Gladstone, which itself was the beginnings of the then great Liberal Party. Indeed, in the House of Commons, with Palmerston rumoured to be severely ill, events suddenly turned on 11 May towards reform, less than a month after Bright and Gladstone had talked at length at Stafford House. In response to a motion for a £6 franchise proposed by Edward Baines, MP, Gladstone unexpectedly stated, 'I venture to say that every man who is not presumably incapacitated by some consideration of personal unfitness or of political danger, is morally entitled to come within the pale of the constitution.'[115] As Bright wrote in his diary: '[Gladstone's] speech caused great sensation, and is considered as marking out his line in the future.'[116]

Gladstone was accused of dangerous lunacy and Disraeli wrote to him in dismay, saying that it was 'more like the sort of speech with which Bright would have introduced the Reform Bill which he would like to propose than the sort of speech which might have been expected from the Treasury bench in the present state of things'.[117] Bright wrote to his wife,

Gladstone made a memorable speech yesterday. It makes a new era in the reform question and shows what he is looking towards in the future. *The Times* is wroth with him this morning and he will be more than ever the dread of the aristocratic mob of the West End of London. I was silent, wishing others to come in. I think the political prospect is Brighter than for some time. Palmerston in truth only stops the way for a time.[118]

In the debate, the political ructions, party divisions and thunderous rumblings of a renewed battle for parliamentary reform were illustrated by a speech of great oratory by Robert Lowe, a Liberal, in which he inveighed against giving the vote to the masses. Drawing on his interpretation of his own experiences in Australia, he warned that reform would ruin the Liberal Party. Disraeli even went so far as to accuse Gladstone of having revived the doctrine of the revolutionary, Tom Paine.

For his part, Gladstone appears to have felt that he went too far, and clearly sensed the astonishment of Palmerston, who was lying at home, ill with gout. He told a friend that 'he had unwarily set the Thames on fire'[119] before adding, 'but I have great hopes that the Thames will, on reflection, perceive that he had no business or title to catch the flame and will revert to his ordinary temperature accordingly'.[120] But the genie was out of the bottle and the battle lines were being drawn for the revival of reform. Despite Edward Baines' proposal being defeated by 74 votes, and the Liberals enjoying a substantial majority in the House, Gladstone had drawn a line in the sand.

The Mother of Parliaments

In his annual address to his constituents at Birmingham Town Hall on 18 January 1865, Bright pitched into the issue of parliamentary reform and made the famous remark, often misquoted, that 'England is the mother of Parliaments':

> We are proud of our country ... We may be proud of this: that England is the ancient country of Parliaments. We have had here, with scarcely an intermission, Parliaments meeting constantly for six hundred years ... England is the mother of Parliaments.

Echoing Cobden's Rochdale speech of November 1863, Bright questioned why fair representation was afforded to Englishmen in 35 different states, from the Cape to the New World, when

> It is only in his own country, on his own soil, where he was born, the very soil which he has enriched with his labour and with the sweat of his brow, that he is denied this right ... [England] has long been famous for the enjoyment of personal freedom by her people. They are free to think, they are free to speak, they are free to write; and England has been famed of late years, and is

famed now the world over, for the freedom of her industry and the freedom and greatness of her commerce. I want to know, then, why it is that her people should not be free to vote?

Not until the representatives of the millions of the disenfranchised were admitted to Parliament, he argued, could it be 'truly said that England, the august mother of free nations, herself is free'.[121]

The fact that Bright was able to campaign and agitate for reform was itself an established freedom, which had grown through the eighteenth century and survived the repressive years of the Napoleonic Wars. To that extent, the tradition of John Wilkes and liberty dovetailed with Bright's own campaigns from the Corn Laws to parliamentary reform itself. Still, the Establishment did not give up trying to diminish his impact by attempting to drive a wedge into his partnership with Cobden. In February, Cobden was offered the post of chairman of the Board of Audit, worth £2,000 a year, knowing as they did that his finances were in bad shape. Cobden gave them short shrift:

> Believing as I do that while the income of the Government is derived in a greater proportion than in any other country from the taxation of the humblest classes, its expenditure is to the last degree wasteful and indefensible. It would be almost a penal appointment to consign me for the remainder of my life to the task of passively auditing our finance accounts. I fear my health would sicken and my days be shortened by the nauseous ordeal.

As so often today, the Establishment neither understood nor cared what it was that really motivated and drove men such as Cobden and Bright. They simply could not appreciate how it was possible for men to pursue their goals without regard for themselves or their personal circumstances, or that they genuinely believed in a higher purpose, not on pompous moral grounds, but on the basis of conviction and principle.

Cobden informed Bright on 5 March of the failed attempt to buy him off. From Bright's diary, it appears that they had not discussed it beforehand, with each operating on his own terms. Indeed, Bright had noted three days earlier that he had declined an offer from Gladstone to 'place me on the Railway Commission about to be appointed. I cannot afford to give more time and labour to the public.'[122] They both had better things to do.

Cobden's End: 'My friend and as my brother'

On 5 March, Bright visited Cobden at home in Midhurst, Sussex. Cobden had been ill with asthma and bronchial problems for some months, but Bright 'found him pretty well in health, but looking older. Intelligent and agreeable as ever ... Much talk on America and Canada and politics generally'.[123] When he visited his friend on 22 March in London, however, he 'Found him in bed - ill since coming to town.'[124] On 25 March, he notes again, 'He is very ill and I am very anxious about him.'[125]

Bright knew that his enduring and historic relationship with his closest friend and ally was nearing its end, and the trauma for him was palpable. On 2 April, Bright wrote, 'I heard the bell ring and sprang up to dress, conscious of the ill tidings that were coming ... my poor friend was worse and sinking. I was with him soon after 8 o'clock. I found him insensible and dying.' In typical Quaker fashion, wishing to recall the vivid details for posterity, Bright recorded Cobden's last moments in great detail. Just after 11 a.m., 'the breathing ceased ... and the manly and gentle spirit of one of the noblest of men passed away to the rewards which surely wait upon a life passed in works of good to mankind, a life of unselfish benevolence and of unspotted honour'. Bright's vivid observations, suffused with emotion at this tragic time, evoked in him some of his most graphic and eloquent language:

> It was a scene never to be forgotten ...We stood, and looked, and wept with almost breaking hearts and then came away with a burden of grief hard to bear. I pressed his hand for the last time, and kissed his forehead, and left him with a sense of the loss I have suffered.[126]

On Monday 3 April, Palmerston entered the House as Big Ben struck four. As Robertson records, there was complete silence:

> Every eye seemed to be in search of one familiar figure as the assembly rapidly increased; and at last there was seen approaching, with sorrowful countenance and bowed head, the friend of one whose vacant seat by his side would never be filled again.[127]

Palmerston and Disraeli made eloquent tributes. When it was Bright's turn to speak, it was clearly more than he could bear. He stood in silence and then tried twice to speak, but his emotions and voice failed him. As he recorded in his diary,

House. Great sorrow manifested on all sides. Palmerston and
Disraeli spoke in fitting language of the loss the House has
sustained. I wish his eulogy could have been spoken by men
more in harmony with his own great and good character. I
thought the House expected something from me. I was bowed
down with grief. My eyes were filled with tears. I stood up trembling and with my heart bursting and my head on fire. I pressed
my forehead with my right hand to steady my brain. I said 'It
may be expected that I should say something on this sad event,
but I feel that I cannot speak … He has been my friend and as
my brother for more than twenty years, and I did now [*sic*] know
how much I loved him til I found that I had lost him.'[128]

When eventually he managed to utter his words, the House
applauded his fortitude: 'I sat down sobbing with grief and trembling with excitement and passionate sorrow. There were many
members present whose eyes were filled with tears. Such a time has
probably never been known before in the House of Commons.'[129]
This undoubtedly is true. Enemies, opponents, friends and
colleagues alike would all have sensed a page of British history turning and the end of era built on a relationship they had witnessed day
in, day out for the best part of 30 years.

It could be said that their relationship was unique in modern
political times. Individual men have claims to greatness – such as
William Pitt, Charles James Fox or Winston Churchill – but it is very
rare to find achievements on the scale that were brought about by
a combination of skills, determination and purpose, with each partner playing to the other's strengths in perfect harmony. Their battle
for what they believed in not only succeeded against all the odds and
at tremendous personal cost, both financial and emotional, but – and
perhaps this is what would have given them the greatest satisfaction
– it produced results that have stood the test of time. It is difficult to
exaggerate how much Cobden and Bright, in their partnership of
public service and principle, achieved for Great Britain, or for the
well-being of future generations throughout the world. Indeed, as
Bright himself stated when unveiling a statue of Cobden many
years later,

There is not a homestead in the country in which there is not
added comfort from his labours – not a cottage the dwellers in
which have not steadier employment, higher wages, and a more
solid independence. This is his enduring monument.[130]

Though many urged that Cobden should be buried in Westminster Abbey, he had already stated that 'My spirit could not rest in peace among these men of war. No, no; cathedrals are not meant to contain the remains of such men as Bright and me.'[131] He preferred to be buried in a simple grave in his home town, as was Bright many years later in Rochdale.

The funeral took place in Midhurst on 7 April 1865. Bright wrote:

> There were many hundreds of persons present ... I was one of the pallbearers, Mr Gladstone and I walking foremost, Mr Villiers and Mr Gibson next ... When the coffin was being placed in the vault, I could hold out no longer and my anguish found some vent in passionate sobs and tears. I think I am becoming weaker that I am thus affected. Generally, men seem to become harder and less given to tears as they grow older. In me, it is not so.[132]

Death of Palmerston

No sooner had Cobden been buried than Bright's brother-in-law, editorial mentor and partner in the *Morning Star*, Samuel Lucas, died on 16 April. As Bright stated in his diary, 'How soon this loss and shock succeed the other and how unstable everything seems.'[133] Given the importance at this time of the *Morning Star*, Bright had to find a new editor to carry on the work of campaigning for parliamentary reform. This was to be the Irish journalist, Justin McCarthy, who had been a regular contributor to the paper under Lucas and would later become one of Parnell's right-hand men.[134]

One shaft of light that lit up Bright's life at this tragic time was the news of Robert E. Lee's surrender to General Grant at Appomattox, so bringing an end to the American Civil War, which Bright received on 23 April. Within a matter of days, however, he was struck again by the wheel of fortune, with the news of assassination of President Lincoln (see Chapter 5). Thus the tide of history was carried along on the massive convulsion of events that took place within a matter of a few days, as Bright faced the future with both sorrow and eager anticipation for democracy and freedom.

Parliament was dissolved on 6 July 1865 and a General Election called. In his election address, Bright vehemently condemned the broken promises for parliamentary reform, complaining that the previous Parliament, led by Palmerston, had neglected its first duty; the Administration which in 1859 climbed into office under the pretence of its devotion to the question of Parliamentary Reform has violated its solemn pledges. Its chiefs have purposefully betrayed the cause they undertook to defend, and its less eminent members have tamely acquiesced in that betrayal.[135]

When Palmerston returned as prime minister later that month, he remained firmly against reform, admonishing his Chief Whip, who had changed his view on these matters, in August: 'My dear Brand, you are almost equal to Bright in your zeal for reform.' But Bright had no equal when it came to pushing for reform. Addressing his constituents in Birmingham, he referred to the Derby/Disraeli failed Reform Bill of 1859 with its 'fancy franchises' and expressed his fear that these notions were still in the minds of those responsible, before launching into what remains one of the most memorable descriptions of a political opponent:

Mr Disraeli is a man who does what may be called the conjuring for his party. He is what, amongst a tribe of Red Indians, would be called 'the mystery man'. He invents phrases for them; and one of the phrases, the last and the newest, is this lateral extension of the franchise. Now, Mr Disraeli is a man of brains, of genius, of great capacity for action, of a wonderful tenacity of purpose, and of a rare courage. He would have been a statesman if his powers had been directed by any noble principle or idea. But, unhappily, he prefers a temporary and worthless distinction as the head of a decaying party, fighting for impossible ends ...

To the electors of the middle classes ... I would just address one observation. I would ask them, whence comes the freedom we now enjoy? It does not come from the monarch, it does not come from the peerage; it comes from the House of Commons.

It came, he said, neither from his political opponents, nor even from his own party – and certainly not from its leadership – but 'from that section which sits chiefly below the gangway rather than from that which sits close to the Ministers of the day'.[136] In other words, it came from himself and his backbench friends who acted on principle in the national interest, irrespective of party. He had thrown down the gauntlet that the battle for parliamentary reform was again under way and would be conducted against all comers of whatever party persuasion.

One major obstacle in Bright's path was removed when Palmerston died on 19 October 1865. There is no doubt that Bright, while not saying so publicly, was thoroughly relieved that Palmerston had gone to his Maker. On hearing the news, he wrote to Charles Sturge in a damning and ungenerous epitaph,

> The old Minister is gone at last. I wish there were more to be said in his praise. We are breaking with the old generation and I hope we will see new and better principles and policy in the ascendant. I think the present Cabinet with merely a new chief cannot go on doing nothing. It cannot be provided with another chief who can keep so many people quiet as Lord Palmerston was able to do.[137]

Bright loathed Palmerston. In return, Lord Shaftesbury, who was devoted to Palmerston, declared that the prime minister had only had two real enemies 'of whom he used strong language'.[138] – one was Bright and the other Gladstone. What made the position worse for Bright, and certainly ironic, was that in the broad political spectrum of the time, Bright and Palmerston were generically of the same party. Yet, on so many issues they were as chalk to cheese – Bright the Liberal commoner, Palmerston the aristocratic Whig – as their speeches and the division lists show. Indeed, the loose associations of those early days of party politics found Bright frequently having more in common with his political opponents on the other side of the House. But, while he might work with, for example, Peel or Disraeli if their interests coincided, these alliances were always tempered by Bright's bedrock of conviction and principle. He could not ally himself with the bulk of their supporters that made up the Conservative Party. In contrast, he could agree with the bulk of the political party led by Palmerston and Russell but could not agree with their insufficient dedication to reform nor their attitude to war. Thus Bright's relationship with Palmerston illustrates his own assessment when he described himself as 'an "outsider" and a "pariah" among politicians'.[139]

In the meantime, Russell became prime minister. Bright still despised Russell. He told Villiers that he did not believe him to be a bad man, but one who was 'often capricious and sometimes feeble', adding, 'He is now in power and we must do the best we can.'[140] Bright's aversion to Russell was clearly reciprocated. When Robert Lowe, who was passionately against reform, refused Russell's approach to join his administration, Gladstone suggested asking Bright. Russell refused on the grounds that, with Lowe having refused as an opponent of reform, he was certainly not going to go 180 degrees in inviting its most vigorous supporter. He had his own 'moderate' reform agenda without Bright. Irrespective of this, as the *Punch* cartoon accurately states of the 'wall-flower' Bright, 'Nobody asks me and if they did, I should certainly decline.'[141]

For his part, Bright made his position clear. He was adamant that the Government would only get his support if they took the correct position on reform – and this was household suffrage. As he wrote in October 1865, 'I have never said anything in favour of universal suffrage and am not of the opinion that it is or would be the best suffrage.' Household suffrage, on the other hand, was 'the ancient franchise of this country' and he had no fears about its consequences. 'There is no reason whatever to believe,' he said, 'and indeed the contrary is certain, that the working classes would act together and that all power would be vested in them.'[142] A month later, he wrote to Charles Sturge,

> The Suffrage is the only thing possible or probable now, and I have advised the Government for ten years past to do the Suffrage alone in their first measure. And I am prepared to defend this course before all the radicals in England. It is the only way ever to get anything until the Revolution of violence comes, which I do not wish to see.[143]

His optimism was again evident at the beginning of January 1866, when he stated,

> In all the nations of the world at this day, I believe, the powers of good are gaining steadily on the powers of evil ... Let us take courage then. We are endeavouring by constitutional means to pass a great constitutional measure; to make the Parliament not only the organ of the will, but the honest and faithful guardian of the interests of all the classes in this country. It is a great and noble purpose which we have set ourselves to do and it is a purpose which cannot fail if we are true to it and ourselves.[144]

Bright was in a powerful position. The *Saturday Review*, though firmly anti-Bright, said in January 1866, 'Mr Bright governs although he does not reign. When at this critical time, he declares his views on reform, a Cabinet cannot avoid being to some extent guided by his views.'[145] Yet Russell's parliamentary reform programme was driven less by principle and more by timing and his deteriorating health. By the end of January 1866, Bright had become thoroughly infuriated, not only with Russell, but even with Gladstone, whose proposals for a £6 rating franchise he described as 'fraud of the worst character'.[146] His exasperation at the Government's delay in presenting a Reform Bill was expressed in a letter he wrote to Gladstone on 10 February. Though reform legislation was complex, he complained, 'You have had 3 months in which to frame a Bill, which any man knowing anything of the subject could have done in a week.' He went on to lament the delays, 'as if a question like this were to be decided in a huckstering spirit, & as if a few thousands of electors more or less were of the smallest consequence'.[147] Unsurprisingly, he once again declined dinner with Russell who, if nothing else could be said of him, was certainly anxious to keep Bright on side.

In the midst of the turmoil of the Government's slowly emerging Reform Bill, a great fear of insurrection had been caused by the return of large numbers of Irishmen who had fought with the North in the American Civil War and arrived home with deep disaffection for the British Government. Violence had erupted in Ireland, leading to the Habeas Corpus Suspension (Ireland) Bill, which was condemned by Bright (see Chapter 7) and analogous to the control treatment of alleged radical terrorists today. Habeas corpus had been the basis on which Britain had taken over the Government of Ireland in 1800, the circumstances of which Bright claimed 'were disgraceful and corrupt to the last degree'. Promises made to the Irish had been broken and he attacked the circumstances that had led to the present situation, including the refusal to listen to the complaints of the Irish people, stating that 'there is no statesmanship merely in acts of force and acts of repression'.[148] He believed fervently that the suspension of habeas corpus had been brought about by a failure of both justice and policy.

The Bill was rushed through with a massive majority of 354 to 6 on 17 February 1866. Gladstone, along with Milner Gibson and Villiers, voted for the suspension. Bright abstained, thereby avoiding any accusations of support for the atrocities taking place, or for those who were alleged to have committed them, while clearly defending the principles of freedom and protection from mistreatment. The essential question for him was whether an individual should have the continuing right to habeas corpus.

Bright wrote to his wife the day after the Habeas Corpus Suspension Bill vote, 'I am the great terror of the squires – they seem to be seized with a sort of bucolic mania in dealing with me.'[149] Shortly before his death, Cobden had warned Bright not to alienate the middle classes in his pursuit of the rights of the working class, and Bright's unpopularity with the landowners who still ran the House of Commons remained undiminished. But Bright, however loathed by those who feared his cause, was undeterred. By remaining separate from the Government, Bright had managed to retain both his principles and his popularity outside the parliamentary and governmental processes, a position that had already been greatly enhanced by his support for the North in the American Civil War.

Gladstone's Reform Bill, 1866

Gladstone finally introduced his Reform Bill on 12 March 1866. Bright, without endorsing the Bill enthusiastically, recognized that it represented a move in the right direction. In a public letter on 25 March, Bright wrote,

> It will, if it becomes law, give votes extensively to the middle classes, both in counties and boroughs, and it will overthrow the principle of working class exclusion which was established by the Reform Bill of 1832. It will admit to the franchise so many of the working men in all important and populous boroughs, that they, as a class, will no longer feel themselves intentionally excluded and insulted by the law. I say the Bill is an honest Bill; and if it is the least the Government could offer, it may be that it is the greatest which the Government could carry through Parliament.[150]

He urged the Conservative Party to support it, but they were alarmed by the impact the county clauses would have on their own vote. This was Disraeli's great mistake. By rejecting the Gladstone–Russell compromise at this stage, Disraeli paved the way for Bright's great campaign, which ultimately forced his hand to adopt in 1867 a measure even more to Bright's liking. Indeed, Bright said of the 1866 Bill that it was 'distinct, clear and without any trickery, but was not adequate to the occasion and its concessions were not sufficient'.[151]

Bright wrote in his public letter,

> The Tory Party and those from the Liberal ranks who join it ...
> regard the workmen here as the southern planter regards
> the negroes who were so lately his slaves. They can no longer be
> bought and sold; so far they are free men. They may work and
> pay taxes; but they must not vote. They must obey the laws, but
> must have no share in selecting the men who are to make them.
> The future position of the millions of working men in the United
> Kingdom is now determined, if the opposition of the Tory party
> is to prevail – it is precisely that fixed by the southern planter for
> the negro.[152]

By drawing a clear analogy with slavery, Bright at once brought the
campaign for parliamentary reform to the immediate attention and
minds of the people who had seen the fight in America as being
about freedom and democracy. The battle lines were drawn and the
greatest backbench protagonists – John Bright and Robert Lowe –
emerged, both Liberals and both from the Government backbenches, each equally convinced that they were battling for the
national interest. If ever there was a case of demonstrating that
governments may govern but backbenchers may drive the issues,
this was such an occasion.

The campaign was also a test of the British temperament. To what
extent could the campaign be conducted through agitation while
falling short of revolution, despite the passions it aroused? The
Reform Act of 1832 had been based on the aristocratic assumption
that ownership of property was the basis of the right to vote, and
proper government needed to be protected from too much democracy and from the violence of the masses. Bright rejected the views
of those such as Lowe and Cranborne (later Lord Salisbury) who,
looking back to the French Revolution, and the continental disturbances of the 1840s, believed that the working class were depraved
and had to be kept in order by the Government in the interests of
public order. Instead, he believed that reform would draw on the
good sense of the working man, who would behave responsibly
and avoid civil insurrection. The issue was therefore by no means
theoretical, but practical: it was about who governed, and how.

Though the Reform Bill had been introduced on 12 March 1866,
it was not until 16 March that the Conservative Party was given its
instructions by Disraeli's statement, as recalled by Lord Northcote,
that it was 'obviously our duty unanimously to oppose the Bill'.[153]
On the surface, much of the argument turned on the complexities
of rating and rental, and a bewildering array of qualifications and

criteria, but, at the heart 'of it all, the issues on which Bright concentrated came through. It fell to Lowe – a brilliant, if reactionary, orator and intellectual – to lead the assault. On 13 March, he set about attacking the argument in favour of the 'moral right' of the working man by denying that he was morally or intellectually entitled to vote. He argued that the balance of the classes already achieved was perfect, and that the prosperity of British farming and the development of manufacture, the greater harmony among the classes and the growth of British influence abroad all demonstrated the freedom of enterprise that existed under the rule of enlightened men. He argued that this recent equilibrium would be disturbed by giving the vote to the lower classes, who would inevitably dominate and undermine British greatness.

What can at least be said of the debate that ensued was that it aspired to intellectual heights – if not rational ones – rarely scaled. At one point, Lowe even compared himself to Callimachus at Marathon, with the artisans as the embodiment of the Persians who were put to flight. But he went far too far in his indictment of what he saw as the immorality of the working man when he said,

> If you want venality, if you want ignorance, if you want drunkenness, and facility for being intimidated; or if … you want impulsive, unreflecting, and violent people, where do you look for them in the constituencies? Do you go to the top or to the bottom?[154]

Lowe would expand on this the following year, when he stated his patronising belief that, 'It is the order of Providence that men should be unequal, and it is, in my opinion, the wisdom of a State to make its institutions conform to that order.'[155]

All this played straight into John Bright's hands, which he relished. In the words of Trevelyan, 'Nothing but the gangway separated Bright and Lowe, the two champions who represented the forces of democracy and aristocracy.' Gladstone and Disraeli sat opposite each other on their respective front benches, John Stuart Mill sat behind Bright 'in constant communication'[156] and Cranborne sat with the Conservatives, egging on Lowe across the floor of the House. The House of Commons reverberated with the thrills and spills of political excitement, invective and moral and political force.

Bright moved into the attack. Lowe's monumental diatribe against the working man had drawn heavily on a distorted picture he painted of his experiences in Australia. Indeed, Lowe had made some money during his time in Australia, as had the Member for Salisbury, Matthew Henry Marsh, who strongly endorsed Lowe's bigoted analysis. Bright responded by saying that their 'Botany Bay view of the character of the great bulk of their countrymen' and their attack on the working man did far more than he had ever done – and of which he had been much accused – 'to set class against class'.

In one of the greatest and most destructive passages ever printed in *Hansard*, Bright famously compared Lowe and his supporters to the malcontents who hid with David in the biblical Cave of Adullam. Bright tore into the political stance of Lowe and his fellow traveller, Edward Horsman:

> The right hon. Gentleman is the first of the new party who has expressed his great grief by his actions – who has retired into what may be called his political Cave of Adullam – and he has called about him every one that was in distress and every one that was discontented. The right hon. Gentleman has been long anxious to form a party in this House ... and lastly, the right hon. Gentleman has succeeded in hooking the right hon. Gentleman the Member for Calne [Lowe]. I know there was an opinion expressed many years ago by a Member of the Treasury Bench and of the Cabinet, that two men would make a party ... But there is one difficulty which it is impossible to remove. This party of two is like the Scotch terrier that was so covered with hair that you could not tell which was the head and which was the tail.[157]

The House collapsed in laughter. Bright had suborned the Opposition into laughing down their own allies on the Government backbenches, often the greatest measure of political success in the House of Commons. As the *Scotsman* described it,

> It was all done so easily! No effort, no haste, no anger! The broad, comely Saxon features were lit up by a genial and good-humoured smile; but otherwise, while the House roared, and every other sentence was the signal for a burst of laughter prolonged beyond all usual limits of duration, the orator stood bland, calm, and unmoved. A gentle but expressive gesture of the right hand seemed to send forth winged words – banter, pleas-antry, sarcasm – in one arrowy shower. Mr Lowe could not help laughing. The grimmest Derbyites laughed as heartily as the youngest country squires.

Even the Deputy Speaker 'bit his lip and in vain attempted to assume a look of unnatural and transcendent gravity' but 'was obliged to give way and laugh like the rest'. Gladstone's face 'was lit up as if by forty smiles transmuted and condensed into one', while Disraeli was 'content to smile faintly and laugh with his eyes'. The target of Bright's censure, Horsman, on the other hand, 'wore a look of agony as of a man sitting in a dentist's chair'.[158]

This incomparable description by a political columnist encapsulates the brilliance of the invective combined with the exquisite derision which Bright was able to produce while he at the same time both destroyed and divided his opponents and their arguments. It is occasions of this kind that the House of Commons most relishes, particularly when it is on a matter of such important national interest. No doubt more people today would find Parliament worth watching and listening to if debates of this kind were more available.

The division on 27 April gave the Government a majority of only five, which they regarded as encouragement to continue. In the meantime, Bright's campaign continued. The abusive sentiments Lowe had expressed in the House of Commons became a weapon in the hands of those who printed leaflets, bringing the insults to the attention of the working man in every street of every town and city in the land. The intellectual Lowe had failed to see the obvious. The Conservatives, against their own convictions and interests, had laughed with Bright in the greatest debating chamber of the land, but now the floodgates of change streamed open in mass meetings of those demanding the right to be represented in that very place.

Inside the House of Commons, Disraeli, having decided to pitch his camp with the Adullamites, was adroitly organising a coalition of opposition to reform. As time would tell, he could not hold this position indefinitely – those who are against democracy can manipulate the Establishment and the elite but cannot face down the convictions, principles and justice of the case for reform when allied to the expression of popular will – but for a time it proved to be effective.

Russell was almost saved from this growing loss of support by a financial crisis on 10 May when the bank, Overend & Gurney, collapsed. Gladstone suspended the Bank Charter Act and the bank rate shot up to 10 per cent. The Liberal connection with the Whig peers led many of them, in alarm, to promote the interests of their friends in Government. The Earl Grosvenor, in panic, began to shift his ground by temporarily suspending his campaign against the Bill, throwing Disraeli's alliance into jeopardy. However, by a process of carefully contrived coalitions and appeals to prejudice, Disraeli manoeuvred his way towards a defeat of the Government. At last, on 18 June, he triumphed, by 21 votes.

Russell decided to go, but the Queen, worried about the Prussian–Austrian War and its effect on the United Kingdom, refused to accept the Government's resignation and kept the Cabinet reluctantly in office for a further week. Gladstone wrote to Russell on 20 June that

> the history of the question of Reform from 1850 to 1866 is the one discreditable and dishonouring chapter in the history of the Reformed Parliament. All other battles have been honourably fought ... The two objects which ought to outweigh the doubtful considerations of party convenience are 1. To keep faith with the people. 2. To redeem the honour of Parliament ... It is through Dissolution that they are to be pursued.[159]

Nothing could have better summed up Bright's own desire for a dissolution to draw the people back into the debate. The whole saga, with its labyrinthine procedures, amendments, political manoeuvrings, alliances, counter-alliances, divisions, betrayals, oratory, conviction, principle and agitation had drawn ever closer to the great object that Bright had consistently persevered to achieve. What he needed now was the combination of a weak Conservative Government in power, striving to maintain office by manoeuvrings and opportunism, and preying on the divisions of Russell's Government and the prejudices of those on either side, and coincidental pressure from the great bulk of the British people, who were only too ready to express their feelings and opinions on reform through public meetings that he and his supporters would arrange.

The following week generated outpourings of resentment from the country at the behaviour of Disraeli, the Conservative Party and the Liberal traitors. Bright was in full flow, and Gladstone was besieged by letters calling for a dissolution. Bright himself wrote to Gladstone on 24 June that 'A General Election for Reform & for a Reform Govt would bring an immense force of popular feeling into the field & I do not believe in your being beaten.'[160] Bright reminded Gladstone of Earl Grey's dissolution in 1831, saying that he remained

> confirmed in my opinion that the true policy is to have a new Parliament. Resignation I only dread, or dread chiefly, in the fear that the Tory Government if formed might conspire with the

'40 thieves' to force a Reform Bill which would be worse than nothing ... Besides, there is something far worse than a defeat, namely, to carry on your Government with a party poisoned and enfeebled by the baseness of the 40 traitors.[161]

The Cabinet dithered. Brand, the Chief Whip, even went so far as to say in a letter on 24 June that he would refuse to manage the election if Gladstone forced it on him with the party divided. In the meantime, Disraeli and Derby, no doubt thinking of what had happened to Peel over the Corn Laws when faced with similar demands from Bright and Cobden, began to wonder what the price of victory would be if a General Election was on the terms demanded by Bright, and increasingly Gladstone, in the cause of parliamentary reform.

But Russell was worn out and could take it no longer. He resigned on 26 June. The Queen tried again to stay the Cabinet's hand, without success. She wrote that evening to Derby to ask him to form a Government, which he did on 6 July, with Disraeli as chancellor of the exchequer.

The Conservatives had internal party problems, but Disraeli certainly understood what was happening. He wrote to Derby in terms that Bright would understand: 'The question is not Adullamite; it is national. You *must* take the Government; the honour of your house and the necessity of the country alike require it.'[162] The indigenous Tories, led by the Marquess of Bath, who did not trust Disraeli in the slightest, were approached but to no avail. All these manoeuvrings and scramblings for office, permeated by competing claims to represent the national interest, had all the characteristics of a death wish, but eventually Disraeli prevailed.

Yet Disraeli, the mastermind and 'mystery man', was not perhaps quite as mysterious as all that. He was a brilliant manipulator of men and occasions, but he was seeking power rather than navigating a moral path of conviction. Disraeli's victory, if that is what it was, was a victory of intrigue and of what he had described in 1845, speaking of the Conservative Party, as 'an organised hypocrisy'.[163] It was soon to catch up with him when he was bound to accept the force of public opinion and the political will of Bright and his allies in the struggles and pitfalls of the Reform Bill of 1867.

CHAPTER 4

The New Democracy: Converting Disraeli

If the Conservative Party has determined to capitulate on this Question, it should act with the foresight and the breadth which are inseparable from a true Statesmanship ... These suggestions are made with an honest purpose; to assist in the settlement of a great question, and with no hostile feeling to the existing Administration.
(John Bright's confidential advice to Disraeli on the Reform Bill, 12 March 1867)

The League, the Union and the Internationale

In 1866, Bright was engaged in his own campaign for peaceful agitation throughout the country. Irrespective of the internecine warfare within both his own party and the Conservative Party, Bright fell back on his rock-like determination to remain above party and to address the issues and the country on his own terms. He knew, however, that he needed help from the kind of campaign that had delivered the repeal of the Corn Laws. At the end of June 1866, he wrote to his friend, and the new MP for Rochdale, Thomas Bayley Potter, urging 'an attempt at better organisation'. Holding conferences, issuing petitions and having meetings was all very useful, but what was needed was a 'formidable organisation or movement'.[1] Bright was entirely conscious that whatever efforts he himself might make – and whatever advantages he might have from the divisions in the parliamentary parties – there was no substitute for the creation of a real, nationwide movement attaching popular sentiment to a businesslike structure, well-funded and driven by conviction and charisma. He had been the treasurer of the Anti-Corn Law League, and knew the value of organization.

This time, however, there were already organizations in place that could take the agitation forward. The Reform League, aimed at the working class, had been inaugurated in London on 23 February 1865 under the presidency of Edmond Beales, a barrister from Lincoln's Inn described by Bright as 'an honorable man and very sincere'.[2] Parallel to this, was the Manchester-based Reform Union, which modelled itself on the Anti-Corn Law League but identified more with the middle class. Bright's connection with the Chartist movement also remained important, though the old tensions remained. Many key Chartists – including Ernest Jones and Arthur O'Neill – were embedded in the movement for parliamentary reform throughout this period. Bright sympathized with the eventual aim of manhood suffrage promoted by the Chartists – and the new Reform League – but he regarded household suffrage, on his own terms, as the first and vital step. In this, he had the support of the Reform Union.

During the summer of 1866, O'Neill took part in Reform League meetings in Birmingham and, when Gladstone's Reform Bill fell, O'Neill called for 'the Queen and a reform Cabinet'.[3] While O'Neill kept his distance at first from Bright, believing that household suffrage fell short, he did speak at a meeting on 22 August in Birmingham, headed by Bright, where he argued to great applause that the Conservatives were 'unkind, unbrotherly and even cruel to the people'.[4] Over the next months, the Reform League is reckoned to have held 600 meetings in the Midlands, many attended by O'Neill, who by now saw Bright as the fulcrum for change. Nothing could better illustrate Bright's credentials than his alliance with O'Neill as the wedge to drive through the vote for the working man. Bright's own attack on the unreformed House of Commons in March 1866 must have helped this alliance:

> Parliament is never hearty for reform, or for any good measures. It hated the Reform Bill of 1831 and 1832. It does not like the Franchise Bill now upon its table. It is to a large extent the offspring of landed power in the counties and of tumult and corruption in the boroughs ... But notwithstanding such a Parliament, this Bill will pass if Birmingham and the other towns do their duty.[5]

Of course, there were parallel and more revolutionary undercurrents swirling in the political mists. George Howell, a prominent trade unionist and founding member and Secretary of the Reform

League, had been in contact with continental radicals such as Giuseppe Mazzini and Lajos Kossuth in the 1850s and, notably, with Karl Marx in the 1860s. He subsequently participated in the International Workingmen's Association, or First Internationale, the inaugural meeting of which was held in London on 28 September 1864 with representatives of workers from all over Europe. Howell was on its council and the address and provisional rules – including the objectives of 'the protection, advancement, and complete emancipation of the working classes'[6] – had been drawn up by Marx. Howell and his associates from the London Trades Council, in pursuit of trade unionism, had in mind the promotion of international co-operation, but also wanted to prevent the importation of workers from Europe undercutting the British workforce.

At this point, Bright was ambivalent about trade unionism, but by 1876 he disapproved of 'combinations' on wages as being likely to induce menace and warfare.[7] In relation to the Internationale, however, it was Howell's opinion that, 'A Gladstone or a Bright could have accepted it with a good conscience.'[8] In fact, the closest that Marx and Bright came to one another in seeking change for the working class was only a matter of physical proximity at St James' Hall on 26 March 1863, when Marx attended a meeting convened by London trade unionists to support the American North and oppose slavery. Howell never really grasped Marx's philosophy or his denial of capitalism, nor his ideological loathing for the ideas of self help, belief in the individual and the virtues of the middle class as promoted by Samuel Smiles in his 1859 book, *Self Help*. Together with Smiles' other books, such as *Thrift* and *Character*, this represented the belief, shared by Bright, that men could change the future direction of their own lives through attendance at working men's institutes and educational classes, however deprived they had been in childhood. It is said that *Self Help* sold more copies than any one of Charles Dickens' immensely popular books, and was read throughout the world. Nevertheless, it was a philosophy diametrically opposed to Marx. Marx believed in top-down solutions, whereas Bright sought change from the bottom up by encouraging human aspirations within the framework of democratic freedom of choice. Each was aiming for the opposite in terms of social and political ideas – and, of the two, Bright's insistence on democracy and constitutional reform succeeded.

For his part, George Howell shifted his interest from the Internationale to the Reform League which, after its committee met Bright on 11 March 1865, soon committed itself to a policy of agitation by peaceful means despite a difference of opinion with Bright over manhood suffrage. This was a turning point in both British and world history. The cause of parliamentary reform in British politics had turned its face away from the ideology of Marx's Internationale and placed itself firmly on the path of democracy and constitutional reform that permeated much of the globe and largely remains today.

At the Manchester Conference of 22 May 1865 – where the Reform League, the Reform Union and the Internationale were all represented – the Reform League, in another moment of importance for modern democracy, agreed not to fight the Reform Union, which supported Bright's 'one step at a time' strategy.[9] The Reform League further scaled down its demands by accepting household rather than manhood suffrage following the verbal abuse against the working class meted out by Robert Lowe. Unity was created in line with Bright's own policy.

Both the Reform Union and the Reform League needed Bright as their spokesman and their spearhead, but they had an interdependence based on mutual strengths. Bright's political pre-eminence enabled him to hold the ring because, while he believed in the objectives of the Reform Union, he understood the necessity for agitation by the Reform League. It was this crucial role, combined with his own political will, oratory and popular support, that enabled Bright to take the argument through the swirling currents of peaceful and popular agitation, which he himself both fostered and contained, into the House of Commons.

Howell had been appointed as the supervisor of a Reform League demonstration planned for 2 July 1866 in Trafalgar Square and invited Bright to take part. On 2 July, Edmond Beales, President of the Reform League, challenged the Metropolitan Police, who had denied the legal right of public meetings in Trafalgar Square. According to Ausubel, there was also a stream of correspondence between Bright and his old friend George Wilson around this time.[10] Bright was delighted with the meeting organized by the Reform League and expressed the hope that this would be followed by bigger and better ones. When the Reform League tried to gain permission to hold another massive meeting on 23 July in Hyde Park, the Home Secretary, Walpole, was minded to allow it but the Cabinet clamped down and refused. Bright himself was in Rochdale and 'unable' to attend, but he wrote on 19 July to Howell,

I see that the chief of the metropolitan police force has announced his intention to prevent the holding of the meeting. It appears from this that the people may meet in the parks for every purpose but that which ought to be most important and most dear to them ... If a public meeting in a public park is denied you, and if millions of intelligent and honest men are denied the franchise, on what foundation does our liberty rest, or is there in the country any liberty but the toleration of the ruling class?[11]

Bright sent a telegram and a letter the next day asking Howell not to publish this letter, 'as it so strongly condemns the Tory Govt for that which Sir Geo. Grey had already asked to be done'.[12] But the League did so in *The Times* the following day, clearly at Howell's instigation.

The critical meeting went ahead on 23 July. Beales led a peaceful procession to Marble Arch and was formally refused entry to the park. Proceeding to Trafalgar Square, they held their meeting there, passing votes of confidence in Bright and Gladstone. The meeting had been well advertised, and many Londoners and others had turned up to view the spectacle. Inevitably, matters got somewhat out of hand. The park railings and flowerbeds were disturbed, but the trespass, such as it was, was portrayed as a violent event. The Government made the most of it. Fortunately, it was not possible to accuse Bright of having fomented violence, but members of the Reform League and others were arrested. Bright made a useful contribution to their defence fund.

Bright remained determined that political change would come by peaceful argument and popular demonstration, but he did accept that there were dangers. As he acknowledged in a private letter, revolution 'might fail & in any case will involve a great ruin and much evil every way. Accident may force on this violence & I am not sure that the aristocratic class will shrink from it – but I prefer to leave it to accident rather than to undertake to stimulate or recommend it.'[13]

Bright's standing as a peaceful agitator was essential. The physical presence of enormous masses of people needed to be conducted in a peaceful and orderly manner, unlike the situation on the Continent in the 1840s, if the words that were spoken at these meetings were to convey the full force of Bright's arguments without providing an excuse to claim that he was creating instability and disorder. Bright was a realistic tactician and strategist. He knew where his line was, but he also knew that it must be drawn in the right place. The boundary between a lawful demonstration and unlawful behaviour was crucially important and he never stepped over the boundary in his public meetings or calls for agitation. If he had, all would have been lost.

The Leaguers had become more practical and less extreme. Yet, without Bright leading the way, the situation could have been very different indeed. Watching the outcome of the so-called Hyde Park riots, Marx wrote to Friedrich Engels that they were engaged in a movement of 'immense and irresistible dimensions'. He noted, 'the Englishman first needs a revolutionary education, and two weeks would be enough for this if Sir Richard Mayne [the Commissioner of Police] had absolute control'.[14] It was precisely because Sir Richard and the Home Secretary, Spencer Walpole, were outflanked by Bright's insistence on peaceful, democratic methods that such revolutionary ambitions were frustrated in Britain.

It has been argued that Bright was against manhood suffrage because of his repudiation of the Chartists and his concerns about the 'residuum'. This is clearly disproved by his expressed sympathies for the Chartists' ultimate objectives, and that he wished for 'the widest possible suffrage'. The real question is whether he knew that by taking one stage at a time and consolidating it, he could move to the point where their aspirations would eventually be fulfilled. What is certain is that Bright's practical and measured approach ensured that his proposals for household suffrage were pitched at a level and at a point in time when the convergence of public opinion, the dismay with the lack of practical results from Russell and the Liberals, and the opportunism of Disraeli made possible the coming Reform Act of 1867 and, later, manhood suffrage. As Asa Briggs points out, the *English Leader* remarked that after the 1866 Hyde Park demonstration the reform question had been reduced 'to one simply of date and extent'.[15]

With the Trafalgar Square and Hyde Park meetings, a precedent had been established and vast meetings then began to take place, with Bright leading the charge. His energy, determination and political will rode the crest of a wave and, in what must have been an exhausting programme, between July and December 1866 he gave speech after speech at meetings that dwarf anything seen in Britain in modern times. According to Trevelyan and other historians, Bright, the greatest orator of his time, could attract audiences of up to 200,000 people to open air meetings, even in bad weather. One of the great tributes not only to Bright and the organizers of the events but also to the British people was that these meetings of unparalleled size never gave rise to any severe violence. This served to confound those against reform, who could no longer plead the case of Robert Lowe and the Adullamites.

When Bright arrived in Birmingham to speak on 22 August, such was his popularity in the city that his carriage could not get through the crowds and was forced to stop while he acknowledged their applause.[16] On 27 August, as Angus Hawkins notes, as many as 150,000 people attended another meeting in the city addressed by Bright.[17] On 24 September at the Free Trade Hall in Manchester, his old stamping ground, he was greeted by the strains of Auld Lang Syne. There, he turned the arguments of the anti-reformers against themselves. Reversing the accusation that he was dividing the nation, he stated that it was those opposed to reform who were setting 'class against class', and that both the middle class and the working class were being defrauded by those who claimed that 'the middle classes are in possession of power'.[18] Bright was pressing every button in sight and managing to bridge the gap between the classes.

W. Robertson records that Bright addressed 150,000 people gathered at Woodhouse Moor in Leeds on 8 October, before appearing again that evening at Victoria Hall, where he was greeted by a five-minute standing ovation before he even uttered a word. On 16 October in Glasgow, he moved his argument forward, expanding his call to the middle and working classes to the greater theme of the democratic rights of the nation as a whole. He called for just laws and an enlightened administration of them that would 'change the face of the country'.[19] He said, 'The class which has hitherto ruled in this country has failed miserably', then, in words that were later adopted by Lord Randolph Churchill, Bright added, 'If a class has failed, let us try the nation. That is our faith, that is our purpose, that is our cry – Let us try the nation.'[20] Churchill's version of this, 'Trust the people' – often wrongly ascribed to Disraeli and which was also employed by Gladstone as 'Trust the nation' or 'Trust in the people' – later became the rallying call of the Fourth Party in Churchill's celebrated battle with the Marquess of Salisbury, during which he contested Bright's own seat in 1885.

The physical tiredness which these meetings caused Bright was expressed to his wife alone. 'I wish it were not necessary to leave home,' he wrote in October 1866. 'I seem to long very much for quiet. I suppose it is my advancing age which causes this and my love for my family.'[21] For the remainder of the year and into early 1867, however, Bright was constantly mindful of maintaining good relations with the Reform League and the Reform Union. For their part, they did not raise manhood suffrage.

Throughout this time, Bright was under severe attack from all quarters of those who were against parliamentary reform. Indeed, on 7 February 1867, he recorded in his diary: 'Received note warning me of plot to assassinate me on Tuesday next! My letters contain many that are curious, and some that are insulting and offensive.'[22]

Parliament, 1867: Reform Achieved

Bright had addressed the failures of the Tory Party at St James's Hall on 4 December 1866, saying, 'Let me tell them that this question will not sleep ... Unfinished questions have no pity for the repose of nations.'[23] While pressure grew from the great mass meetings throughout the country, Derby and Disraeli were weighing up the situation for a Reform Bill in the certain knowledge that Cabinet members such as Cranborne would oppose any such move. The largely peaceful nature of the reform demonstrations and public meetings had served to convince Disraeli that he could be associated with genuine reform, not to mention with Bright, without being embroiled in accusations of revolutionary activity. Yet, even as late as December, he wrote to Cranborne saying that he had 'throughout been against legislation, and continue so'.[24] One thing he was sure about was that, if there was to be reform, he would manoeuvre himself to the front. Conviction was low on his agenda and he cleverly weaved this way and that.

Indeed, on 24 September 1866, Disraeli had warned against a Reform Bill.[25] In late October, he proposed that the Queen's Speech should bypass the issue of reform, but Derby was set on reform resolutions. He drafted these on 1 November, including the concept of household suffrage, and foisted them on his uneasy Cabinet on 8 November. Disraeli wrote to Derby on 18 November, 'We are entirely unpledged upon the subject.' His calculation was that this would push Gladstone into an amendment to the Queen's Speech for an immediate Bill that could lead to a break-up in the Liberal Party, thereby strengthening the Government. On the other hand, if Gladstone succeeded on the vote, he believed that 'It will probably be by a narrow majority, and the dissolution [of Parliament] will then take place on an issue between Bright's policy and our programme.'[26] Disraeli well understood that it was Bright's campaign and the principles of reform he pursued that would be the ultimate test of public opinion and would therefore determine the route of democratic reform. Derby, on the other hand, misread Bright's real effectiveness, when he recorded in his diary on 1 November that 'no person of importance has joined Bright. Many say he is doing his cause more harm than good'.[27] Disraeli's nervousness was justified and Derby's attempt to trump Bright was seriously at risk.

Despite Derby's assessment, Bright dominated the political landscape. But Gladstone was by no means supportive of him. Henry Brand, the Liberal Whip, would not even attend a Reform Union dinner in Manchester and refused to commit the Liberal Party until the Derby Government's intentions were clear. The fact that Bright's views and speeches were reported in virtually every national and provincial newspaper worried Gladstone, who wrote to Brand, 'I do not like what I see of Bright's speeches. We have no claim upon him, more than the Government have on us; and I imagine he will part company the moment he sees his way to more than we would give him.'[28] By the time he wrote his memoirs 30 years later, however, he acknowledged that 'perhaps we ought to have recognised that the idea of household suffrage ... was irresistible.'[29]

Ironically, it was Bright's personal stature among the people themselves that provided Gladstone with the political platform he later developed as prime minister in four administrations. At the time, however, Bright could only wonder on Gladstone's return from a visit to Italy with Russell, 'we shall see whether they are willing to *lead* or not'.[30]

Trevelyan gives a perceptive summary of Bright's position at this time:

> If we consider Bright's long career as an independent force in the House and country and his immense popularity at that moment with the great majority of Englishmen, his ready consent to serve under Gladstone's banner will appear as creditable to him as it was certainly useful to his cause. The greatest guerrilla warrior of our parliamentary history, he had contracted none of the indiscipline characteristic of irregular troops.[31]

Bright had gone out on a limb on his own convictions and principles for parliamentary reform, but knew there were times and occasions for working together, for those ends, with the party as a whole. Despite Bright vigorously denouncing Palmerston in the previous decade and even being prepared to bring down his Government, he now adopted a different approach in the knowledge that he could rely ultimately on Gladstone's natural sympathy and statesmanship – at any rate, until Home Rule.

As John Vincent indicates, without Bright, reform would have had very different consequences for the Liberal Party. Vincent adds that the reform

> would have been inadequate without the work done by Bright, as Gladstone's bulldog, in holding together the centrifugal, confessional and working class interests outside Parliament in a broad-bottomed Radicalism. Bright, the great destroyer by nature, made the work of his prime the turning of discord into harmony and it was he, not Gladstone, who first greatly extended and deepened the range of meanings that could be read into support of a party.[32]

The Conservatives remained divided, though Disraeli's closest friend, Montagu Corry (later Lord Rowton), Disraeli's confidant and literary executor, who wrote to Disraeli that he had 'been rather surprised at the unanimity with which all classes in the provinces where I have been desire a Reform Bill – from Lord Shaftesbury to the Shropshire rustic'.[33] As Disraeli began to hatch his plot, playing one side of his party off against the other, the Conservatives reluctantly but realistically began to converge on the necessity to have their own Bill.

When Parliament returned on 5 February 1867, reform was mentioned in the Queen's Speech, but in as vague a way as possible. That day, Bright noted in his diary,

> Tory Government 'all in a row' on the Treasury bench. The Party puzzled at its position on reform question. Gladstone spoke with dignity and discretion; Disraeli excited and nervous. Monday next will disclose schemes of the Tory leaders on Reform.[34]

The Mystery Man had taken to conjuring, but Bright sensed the smoke and mirrors ahead.

On 11 February 1867, after visiting Gladstone with a Reform League deputation organized by Howell, Bright attended the House in the evening to hear Disraeli's speech on the Government's plans for reform. As he recorded in his diary, 'Speech very bad in every respect; much unfavourable comment and nothing satisfactory as to reform.'[35] Gladstone pointed out that Disraeli's halfway house was not a basis for reform, and that the Government's resolutions provided no answer. The following day, Bright recorded, 'House: nothing new: general opinion much against Government resolutions on reform. A meeting of the Liberal Party intended for next week to determine course when resolutions moved on the 25th.'[36]

The resolutions – drafted by Derby in November 1866 and revised with Disraeli on 27 December – were a means of avoiding, if they could, an actual Bill in Parliament, which could become law, and were more a statement of intent than actual legislation. Nevertheless, on 25 February, Cranborne and Lord Carnarvon struck, threatening to resign with the secretary of state for war, Jonathan Peel (Sir Robert Peel's younger brother), and calling for an immediate Cabinet meeting. In panic, Derby wrote to Disraeli, who was still asleep in bed, 'The enclosed just received is utter ruin. What on earth are we to do?' Disraeli replied, 'This is stabbing in the back!' Making the excuse that he was indisposed, he added 'But I shall rally immediately in such dangers. It seems like treachery.'[37] Following a massive row at Derby's house at midday about the inclusion of household suffrage, Disraeli went down to the House knowing that the threats of resignation were real. As Bright noted in his diary, 'Disraeli explained Tory reform, a wretched proposition ... The whole discussion greatly injurious to the administration.'[38] Disraeli waffled about and tried to dodge the issue of introducing a Bill, which played straight into Bright's hands.

The Liberals moved into the attack. Lowe spoke first, before Bright weighed in saying that Disraeli's proposals were

> ludicrously crude ... Why, under this Bill, a ratcatcher who keeps four dogs would pay a direct tax to the amount of 20s., and, of course, would come into that new constituency, which the right hon. Gentleman says is to save this country from destruction.[39]

Disraeli was slaughtered and abandoned his immediate proposals on the spot.

The following day, Bright's diary read:

> Meeting of Liberal members at Mr Gladstone's house: very large, and Party more united than for a year past. I spoke briefly, urging more active policy against the Government and its sham Reform measures. House: Disraeli withdrew resolutions. I spoke, urging the proceeding with the Franchise Bill by itself.[40]

Disraeli knew that his cover was blown and he had to outflank
Gladstone, whose party was also split and under pressure from
Bright. A bill was the only way out, a policy settled on in a flurry of
correspondence on 26 and 27 February between Disraeli and
Derby. The Conservative Party, however, remained deeply divided.
A meeting of 150 backbenchers was held at the Carlton Club on
28 February to support a bill. Colonel Hogg bridled at the thought
of household suffrage in Bath, saying it would destroy him, and
another backbencher urged that 'we *must* make a stand against
"Democracy"',[41] but the general view seemed to be that a Bill was
needed – and it should be based on the Government's proposals to
give the impression at least that it was not based on Bright's
campaign.

At this absolutely crucial time, as they watched one another while
events swirled around them, Disraeli and Bright had a remarkable
conversation in the lobby of the House of Commons on 1 March,
calling to mind their earlier meeting in December 1852 (see Chapter
3). Disraeli, as usual, was talking to others as well, and household
suffrage was being discussed in various forms in many quarters. But
it was on Bright and his external campaigns that the issue ultimately
turned. In Bright's own words:

> Conversation with Disraeli in the Lobby. Asked him what was to
> be done, and could he do it? He said he 'would do it if he could;
> was doing all he could.' I said, 'You ought to have taken me into
> your counsels.' He said, 'I offered you that in 1852, you remem-
> ber.' I said, 'Yes, but I do not mean officially.' He said, 'The
> Whigs have only betrayed you: I told you they would do nothing
> for you.' I replied, 'I want nothing. I am satisfied with my posi-
> tion, and office would be intolerable to me.' He said, 'Well, I have
> had enough of it. I have had 30 years, and 20 years as leader of a
> party. I am sick of it, and if I can get this thing done, then I shall
> (or can) go away.'
>
> I told him of a conversation with three of his party in the
> smoking-room – how far they were willing to go, and that, at the
> pace they were moving, I should soon have to hold them back.
> He thought they were fair specimens of a considerable section of
> the party. I advised him to advance his offers so far in regard to
> the suffrage that he would not be driven to accept defeat on
> every proposition – that £5 rating franchise, or household
> suffrage, would save him in the boroughs, and that £10 or £12
> would do for the counties.

He said he did not care much for the counties: the Working Class Question was the real question, and that was the thing that demanded to be settled. He had once proposed a £10 franchise for the counties. He said, 'You will attack me whatever I propose.' I said, 'No, I will not; I will do all I can fairly to help a Bill through, if you will do the right thing. I am against faction, and if our leaders do as you did last year I shall openly denounce them.' I told him that people said he and I always fought with gloves on, but sometimes I had been tempted to take them off. He said, 'there had always been something of sympathy between us,' which I suppose is true – tho' our course and aims have seemed so different.

I spoke to him about passing only a 'Franchise Bill' as the only thing possible for the session – and urged it strongly upon him to give up the 'Distribution of Seats' portion of the measure, should we ever reach it. He made no reply, but the argument on that point may affect his opinion, and I hope may induce further consideration of it.

As we were talking, Mr. Brand, the Opposition 'Whip', went by, and Disraeli said, 'He will think it is a Coalition' – that he and I should be seen in conversation at such a crisis as this.

At parting, he pressed my hand with an apparent earnestness of feeling, saying, 'Well, whatever happens, you and I will always be friends.'

Disraeli has been possessed by a devouring ambition – not to preach and act the truth, but to distinguish himself. 'We come here for fame!' he said to me many years ago. And he has distinguished himself, but on a low field, and with no results which can be looked back upon with satisfaction.[42]

The next day, the Cabinet met amid a furious row. Cranborne led the revolt and Derby brought the meeting to a close with the momentous words, 'This is the end of the Conservative Party.' When Cranborne stalked out of the room, Derby added, 'The Tory Party is ruined!' Disraeli summed it all up with the words, 'Poor Tory Party.'[43] But he had got his way, albeit on Bright's terms, and with the approbation of the Queen who, though not fully conscious of the problems creating disunity in her Government, had been constantly moving towards reform.

Cranborne, who loathed Disraeli, found his own style and influence waning. Disraeli, for his part, wanted to maintain as civilized a relationship with Cranborne as possible, but Cranborne remained as

obdurate as he had been since 1858, when he wrote his essay
condemning reform,[44] knowing even then that Bright's campaign
meant business. He was now profoundly suspicious that Disraeli
and Derby had entered into a secret agreement in 1866 to bring
forward reform. His subsequent resignation on 3 March – along
with Jonathan Peel and Carnarvon – had been coming for some
time. As Bright noted after the event, 'Derby Government in a crisis
... Excitement in political circles. I seem to feel it less than others,
but am deeply concerned in the evident progress the Reform question is making.'[45]

On 4 March, Bright recorded, 'Government will attempt to go on.
Derby and Disraeli intend to propose and carry a Reform Bill. Great
interest excited: wonderful conversion to household suffrage on
every side. I begin to be an authority with the Tory Party! What
next?'[46] He could sense the movement towards his original proposals of 1858–9, and was now bridging the political divide not only
with reformers outside Parliament, but also within it. Seizing upon
the weakness that the resignations had caused the Government,
and having already spoken to Disraeli in the lobby, Bright then got
down to the crucial question of how to follow this up in earnest
and in detail, in terms of amendments to the legislation itself.

Robert Blake states of the furore that, 'Strange though these
numerous changes may appear they were the result of muddle,
confusion, lack of forethought, inadequate statistics and Cabinet
dissensions, rather than of a Machiavellian plan prepared by Derby
and Disraeli.'[47] What Blake did not perhaps really appreciate is that,
while Disraeli may have turned around, this was because he had
been driven into a whirlpool by Bright's campaigning in the country,
and consistency of purpose. One thing was certain, Disraeli was
determined to position himself so as to ensure that Gladstone and
his party were routed and that he himself not only climbed up the
greasy pole, but also stayed there.

Bright was indeed now 'an authority with the Tory Party', his
fundamental principle of household suffrage having been adopted
by the Conservative Party as a whole. Ironically, he had helped the
Tory Party to move from turmoil to unity. This was more accurate
than anyone at the time could know. On 9 March, he had drafted a
confidential letter to Disraeli, setting out clear advice on how to
prepare a Bill that would stop the agitation (that is, to satisfy Bright
himself and his followers) and pass the divisions in the House. It was
not only advice, but an historic ultimatum. Bright's own draft (set
out below with his own deletions as to redistribution of seats) reads:

Suggestions on the Coming Reform Bill
3rd month, 9, 1867

What is wanted is (1) a Bill on which the Cabinet can be agreed, (2) one which the House will accept, & (3) one which will so far content the people as to extinguish the associations now agitating the question.

If it fail on the points 2 & 3, the agreement of the Cabinet is useless, and if it meet only the points 1 & 2, it will be of no real ~~use~~ value. It must meet ~~three~~ the points 2 & 3, or it should not be attempted.

I believe a Bill may be proposed which the House will accept, & which will put an end to suffrage agitation. If the Govt cannot propose such a Bill, it has no right to meddle with the question. What should the Bill be?

The oldest & wisest basis for the Boro' franchise is Household suffrage. Probably only a minority of the House is in favor of it, tho' proposed by the present Govt, it would be carried. This would end the agitation.

The next thing to the wisest is a rental franchise of £6, or a rating franchise of £5. For either of these there would be a large majority in the House. If proposed by the Govt it would pass probably without a division – if proposed against the Govt as an amendment on any higher qualification, it would be carried by a considerable majority. Either of these would terminate the agitation.

The Household suffrage would be better than the £6 or £5, but would be less acceptable than either if accompanied by any novel propositions, in themselves evil or undesirable, ~~except as~~ & proposed only as restrictions ~~of a~~ on or compensations for Household suffrage. The proposal of such restrictions & compensations will be unfavourably viewed by the House, & by Reformers outside, & will tend to create the opinion that the Govt is insincere. If they should be rejected by the House, which is all but certain, then the question may be involved in fresh difficulty, & the Govt may fail to carry any Bill. In the Counties, the franchise most in favour is that proposed in 1859 & 1860 – the £10 occupation. If the Boro' franchise is fixed at £5 or £6 as above mentioned, then £10 or £12 in the Counties would probably be acceptable. Such a proposal made by the Govt would pass by a large majority, & probably without a division.

For London a lodger franchise is absolutely necessary, & the clause in the Bill of last year seemed to meet the views of the friends of Reform, & it would be wise to adopt it now.

The Ratepaying clauses should be abolished to simplify the Boro' franchise; but if the Govt did not propose this, it might leave it to the decision of the House after a fresh discussion of it. A Bill framed as above sketched would pass without difficulty, & there would be an end of all agitation on the Suffrage question for an indefinite, but, I believe, for a <u>very long period</u>. If the Govt ~~are~~ is in earnest about doing anything, it should do the right thing, with simplicity and courage. If the Conservative Party has determined to capitulate on this question, it should act with the foresight & the breadth which are inseparable from a true states-manship. It will be more honourable to the Govt to propose the right clauses than to have them forced upon it by the Opposition.

~~As to the redistribution of seats—~~
~~The difficulty of doing what is needed is much greater than in the case of the Franchise. The Bill of last year was bad, the sketched Bill of the Govt but trifles with the question.~~

~~If there is no disfranchisement, the new Franchise Bill will only make the existence of Calne & Arundel & many other Boros the more ludicrous & intolerable. The large Boros will have much larger Constituencies, & the small Boros will look the smaller & more odious, & the Bill will not have come fairly into operation before new efforts will be made to obtain a better adjustment of seats. The question will be reopened, indeed it will not have been closed even for a single Parlt.~~

~~The wise course is to leave the question of the 'seats' for another a future Parlt, or for the time when opinion shall be more ripe, & when all both sides in the House will accept a larger & better measure. It can hardly be dealt with this session, & if it is it will be only to disturb, & not to settle it. Besides, to persist in it may risk the Franchise Bill, the necessity for which is urgent.~~

~~The work of this session is to reconcile the working classes to the Parlt. It is a great work, & yet not a difficult one. It is enough for one session. What remains of the Reform question can be hereafter discussed in a calmer time; it will be a question for Parlt & the constituencies, & will not invite an angry & turbulent agitation.~~

> I am not a minister, or a partisan of the present Govt; but I
> have some responsibility ~~as~~ in regard to this subject of Reform. If
> I were a minister or a partisan of the present Govt, I should say
> precisely what I say now.
>
> The Govt may propose a Franchise Bill which will pass the
> House without difficulty, & will extinguish all the existing &
> growing agitation. If the ministers cannot agree among them-
> selves, or if their Party will not allow them to do what is right &
> needful to be done, – then the Govt should abandon the attempt
> & leave Reform to be dealt with by the friends of Reform.
>
> These suggestions are made with an honest purpose; to assist in
> the settlement of a great question, & with no hostile feeling to the
> existing Administration.[48]

While Bright dated and clearly wrote this memorandum on
9 March, his diary records that he did not send it until 12 March:
'This morning I have sent a Memorandum on the Reform question
to Mr Disraeli to point out what seems to me to be the duty of the
Government in the present crisis.'[49] It was discovered among
Disraeli's papers after his death by Montagu Corry, later Lord
Rowton, who told Bright in 1887 that it 'would be historical'.[50] As
Monypenny and Buckle state, the proposals in this memorandum
'corresponded with the Bill as finally passed in more detail'.[51] Yet,
though Bright's own copy, written in his own hand and with some
significant deletions about the issue of redistribution of seats, is now
in the Clark company archive,[52] deposited there by Bright's daughter Helen Bright Clark, the current whereabouts of the actual
'historical' letter received by Disraeli is itself a mystery.

The contents of the memorandum, however, are clear. Bright
claimed the high ground of the national interest, reminding Disraeli
that he was and remained the driver of reform, and focused on the
absolute necessity of gaining the support not only of the House of
Commons but also of the people. He knew that whatever front was
put on it, Disraeli was deeply worried, as were many others, about
the agitation. He also knew that Disraeli appreciated that Bright
himself was not only the author of it, but also had the means to
persuade the agitators to calm down. Bright made it clear that if the
Conservative Party itself proposed household suffrage, the agitation
would end. This, and his prediction that a bill drafted along the lines
he proposed would pass without difficulty, turning what was a
minority in the House into a majority, is indeed what eventually
happened.

Bright's insistence that Disraeli himself should be the one to carry through reform is no surprise, considering how badly scarred he himself had been by the Liberal Party, particularly under Palmerston and Russell, reneging on its promise to bring in substantial reform in 1860/1. Yet Bright was no doubt appealing to Disraeli's vanity and tactical sense when he drove home the point that, when capitulating, Disraeli and the Conservative Party should be statesmanlike, and that it would be better for the Government to devise the right legislation than to be driven into it by the Opposition. None of this was lost on Disraeli. With one fell swoop, Bright had offered his own plan calling for Disraeli's capitulation but with the tempting prospect that it would be the Conservative Party itself that delivered the plan in the national interest – and this is just what Disraeli later claimed.

This strange interaction between Bright and Disraeli, one man driven by principle and the other by expediency, changed the face of British politics. As Disraeli said later, 'The Tory party, unless it is a national party, is nothing.'[53] What he omitted to mention was that it often got there only reluctantly, under the influence of external forces, and almost too late.

Disraeli's Reform Bill

Against this background, Disraeli introduced his Representation of the People Bill to the House on 18 March. In the words of one back-bencher, 'It was the most wonderful piece of acting & the most extraordinary exhibition of talent I have ever heard. He pitched into everybody, he abandoned all his principles & all through he delighted and amused the House.'[54] However, while the Bill did include the expression 'household suffrage', it was riddled with so many qualifications that its value was undermined. The issues themselves were clouded by Disraeli's determination to gain credit while not admitting credit to others and the necessary attempt to satisfy both the House and public opinion. As it stood, the Bill was obscure and complex, and really satisfied no one. 'Reform Bill a failure; the debate much against the Government,' Bright noted in his diary.[55]

The following day, Bright had a meeting with Gladstone:

> He strong in condemnation of Bill, and wishful to oppose the 2nd reading ... I agree with him as to the proper course, but doubt if our side will take it. Much jealousy; some fear of dissolution, however absurd this may be, and much ignorance of Parliamentary tactics.[56]

John Bright, 1843.

Richard Cobden, 1855.

Richard Cobden addressing the Council of the Anti-Corn Law League, 1846. John Bright sits to his right, holding a document towards which Charles Villiers is pointing.

Sir Robert Peel.

Earl of Derby.

Viscount Palmerston.

William Ewart Gladstone.

Earl Russell.

Benjamin Disraeli.

Abraham Lincoln.

Charles Sumner.

Richard Cobden and John Bright.

Gladstone's Cabinet of 1868. This painting is now in Committee Room 14 of the House of Commons.

John Bright, Richard Cobden and Michel Chevalier following the signing of the French Commercial Treaty, 1860.

Samuel Lucas.

Joseph Chamberlain.

Wedding of John Theodore Cash and Margaret Sophia Bright, 1881. John Bright stands next to his daughter, the bride. The author's great-grandparents, William and Rachel Maria Cash, are standing back row, 4th and 5th from left.

The Govt. may propose a Franchise Bile which will pass the House without difficulty, & will extinguish all the existing & growing agitation. If the ministers cannot agree among themselves, or if their Party will not allow them to do what is right & needful to be done, — then the Govt. should abandon the attempt, & leave Reform to be dealt with by the friends of Reform.

Ultimatum to Disraeli from Bright's confidential memorandum, 12 March 1867.

CARTOON.—MARCH 23, 1867.

BLIND MAN'S BUFF.
"*Turn round three times, and catch whom you may.*"

☞ The scheme of Mr. Disraeli's Reform Bill was largely altered by amendments in its passage through the House.—1867.

The Bill fell so far short of Bright's scheme that, no doubt thinking that Disraeli had declined his advice, he was against it going forward. On 21 March, however, Bright agreed at a meeting of the Liberal Party not to oppose the second reading, 'owing to differences of opinion in the Party. I consented to the policy adopted tho' expressing my entire dissent from it.'[57] Bright understood from past experience how unpredictable the Liberal Party could be.

The net result was that Disraeli obtained his second reading on 27 March without a division of the House and with hardly anybody satisfied with the Bill. The Bill was thrown on to the mercy of the Committee.

The following day, Bright had another meeting with Gladstone and they discussed at length the next steps they should take. Gladstone proposed moving resolutions for a £5 borough rating franchise, which Bright had advocated as a second option to his overall preference in his memorandum to Disraeli – and 'to which I assented as the best thing that could be carried'.[58] On 2 April, Gladstone told Bright he intended to give an instruction to the Committee to bind them to certain principles. This was agreed at the meeting of the party on 5 April in advance of an expected debate on 8 April, for which Bright prepared. On the day, however, the debate was abandoned following a Tearoom revolt. As Bright recorded,

> Some malcontents on our side met this afternoon; conspired to defeat measures of Mr. Gladstone; urged him to withdraw 'Instruction' to the Committee, to which he consented. They have done their utmost to humiliate him and the Liberal Party ... Disraeli in great spirits at the failure of the effort which was to have been made against him. The corruption of the House is something extraordinary. Men fear a dissolution and will descend to any meanness to escape it. They are destroying the unity and power of the Liberal Party, and are making its leader an object of commiseration. They are more willing to express want of confidence in Mr. Gladstone than in Disraeli![59]

The House moved on to an amendment by Gladstone to enfranchise householders who paid their rates through landlords as well as those who paid directly – 'the question being critical ... establishing equality among all classes of voters', Bright wrote.[60] On 13 April, however, this was defeated by 21 votes. Gladstone's amendment had been sidelined by another amendment put forward by John Hibbert, part of the Tearoom revolt, which Disraeli, seeking to divide the Liberals, indicated he would accept. Bright noted with disgust, 'We are destroyed by deserters from our Party, some honest and misled, some far from honest.'[61]

Gladstone noted the extent of his humiliation and even thought of resigning. 'A smash, perhaps, without example,' he wrote.[62] Disraeli, on the other hand, was on a high. He was cheered at the Carlton Club, where Sir Matthew Ridley proposed a toast: 'Here's to the man who rode the race, who took the time, who kept the time, and who did the trick!' On returning home in the early hours of the morning, he famously ate half a pie from Fortnum & Mason and drank a whole bottle of champagne, saying to his wife, Mary Ann, as he swigged it down, 'Why, my dear, you are more like a mistress than a wife.'[63]

Bright's anger at the rebels and the trickery of the Government was evident when he spoke on 22 April at a reform meeting in Birmingham: 'This House of Commons, I undertake to say, is by far the most corrupt House that has been elected and assembled since the Reform Bill.' Calling on the Liberal Party to unite under Gladstone, he asked,

> Who equals him in earnestness? Who equals him in eloquence? Who equals him in courage and fidelity to his conviction? If these gentlemen who say they will not follow him have any one who is his equal, let them show him.[64]

On 2 May, Bright had a meeting with the home secretary, Walpole – 'always kind and moderate'[65] – regarding a Reform League meeting planned for 6 May in Hyde Park. Walpole had ordered a ban the previous day – with good reason, for the possibility of violence was very real – and the situation was critical. There was also unease about Gladstone's commitment to household suffrage, so much so that the alliance between the Reform Union and the Reform League was tested to breaking point, only to be saved by the agreement to hold the rally in Hyde Park. Even Howell was against the proposal, but, as he wrote on 5 May, 'there is less danger of disturbance by our being present tomorrow, than by our staying away'.[66] In the event, the Government backed down on Derby's own instruction, though they organized 5,000 police, and the military were brought in from Aldershot. On the day itself, Bright was busy in the House, but recorded, undoubtedly with some relief, 'Great meeting in Hyde Park perfectly peaceful; Government in discredit and humiliated by their foolish conduct on this question.'[67]

The connection between this meeting and Disraeli's actions a few days later in the House of Commons is tangible. The masses had made it clear that Disraeli's Bill did not meet their requirements. Surprisingly, however, Blake does not refer to this crucial Hyde Park meeting in his biography of Disraeli, and even Bright's own biographer, Trevelyan, seems to have slightly underplayed the full significance of the Government climb-down on the matter. Whatever Disraeli's motives, or wherever his opportunism might have led him, without the pressure exerted by these reform organizations under the influence and aegis of Bright, he would never have been driven to make the changes that now ensued.

The peaceful manner of the Hyde Park meeting also buttressed the case for household suffrage, lessening the chances of concessions by the Government being impugned successfully by Cranborne and his friends.

Hodgkinson's Amendment

On Saturday, 11 May, Bright went to see Gladstone with a 360-strong Reform Union deputation. Bright had written out for Gladstone's consideration a scheme to address the issue of compounding for rates, thereby bringing every householder within the household franchise. Bright thought it would have no chance as an amendment, suggesting that it would be more acceptable as a separate Bill. The deputation urged, however, that it should be introduced as an amendment.

This was six days before the famous Hodgkinson Amendment was moved, which changed the face of the Reform Act of 1867 and of British democracy, yet around which there is so much mystery. Why Grosvenor Hodgkinson? And how and from what was his amendment derived? It too sought to ban the practice of compounding and override the myriad of public and private enactments that allowed different rating systems to operate in different parts of the country, a system so complex and overwhelming that it was barely understood even by MPs at the time. F. B. Smith describes Hodgkinson's amendment as 'a crude variant of Bright's scheme' and infers that Hodgkinson had participated in a secret meeting of freebooters, from which 'it seems certain that Hodgkinson's motion was the outcome'.[68] John Simpson Penman goes so far as to state that 'This important amendment was decided on [by Bright through Gladstone] and Mr Hodgkinson was delegated to propose it.'[69] Smith also states that the outcome of the deputation to Gladstone was a separate amendment moved by Hugh Childers – 'a faithful, moderate colleague of Gladstone's and much more in the counsel of the Liberal leadership than Hodgkinson, who was a non-entity and, moreover, a freebooter who had previous voted against Gladstone's and Hibbert's amendments'.[70] In fact, Childers' amendment was not an alternative to Hodgkinson's at all. It was a rider, as can be seen in the Notice of Motions for Friday, 17 May, where it states clearly under Childers' name that 'If Mr Hodgkinson's amendment to Clause 3 is adopted to add the following words.'

Under the Parliamentary timetable, Hodgkinson's amendment had to be tabled by Wednesday, 15 May at the latest to be selected for debate as it was on 17 May. There seems little doubt that Hodgkinson became party to a deal. In turn, Childers, at Gladstone's behest, also became party to achieving Bright's scheme and objectives. All this was almost certainly a game of political chess to throw Disraeli off guard, as far as that was ever possible. Indeed, a close reading of the proceedings indicates that when the amendment came up for debate on 17 May, Disraeli, far from being on his way to a carefully orchestrated victory, as he so often later portrayed it, was in fact being outflanked by Gladstone and Bright and had to put as good a face upon it as possible.

In moving his amendment, Hodgkinson stated, in language strikingly similar to that used by Bright himself in his memorandum of 9/12 March, that it was 'conceived in no hostile spirit to the Bill of the Government'. He launched an attack on the principle of compounding and the inequity in the way in which the system functioned. He explained why the compounding Acts, including the Small Tenements Act, should be overridden, saying that he had received communications since his amendment had appeared on the order paper that 'there was anything but a unanimous feeling in their favour'. He ended his speech by calling for 'the total abolition of the compounding system'[71] and warned that if the Bill was not amended in such a way it would lead to renewed agitation. He then conceded that his proposals required some further provisions, adding that some had already been suggested by Childers. In other words, he realized that his amendment needed improvement and that Childers, who had been in discussion with Gladstone, had remedied the deficiency.

Gladstone spoke second in the debate. In Gladstone's recollections, written 30 years later, he referred to the sequence of events in the following terms:

> [Hodgkinson] went there to support it, but without an idea that it
> could be carried, and anticipating its defeat by a majority of a
> hundred. Never have I undergone a stranger emotion of surprise
> than when, as I was entering the House, our Whip met me and
> stated that Disraeli was about to support Hodgkinson's motion.[72]

Perhaps he and Hodgkinson would not have been so surprised had
they known about Bright's confidential memorandum to Disraeli of
9/12 March.

The absence of Bright's direct and open engagement at this stage
was evidently tactical. Having already put forward his scheme,
which had been accepted and acted upon, it was clearly appropriate
that Gladstone, as Leader, should now step to the front. Gladstone
would later tell a deputation at his own house, with reference to the
abolition of compounding, 'I have deprecated it all along and have
assented to it as I would assent to cut off my leg rather than lose my
life on the principle of choosing the lesser evil.'[73] But he knew what
was up on this amendment, otherwise he would not have taken such
a forward position, and had no intention of allowing Disraeli to
outdo him again, as he had in April. Indeed, while he may have been
manoeuvred by Bright, Gladstone's contribution to the debate was
utterly crucial to its outcome, and it is surprising that his speech,
demonstrating such quickly summoned and brilliant intellectual
command, was in the past either ignored or played down.

Noting that Disraeli was in his place on the other side of the
House, and having been tipped off by his Whip about Disraeli's
intentions, Gladstone pushed himself to the fore of the debate. He
began by making it clear that he had already entered into consultations on the matter. He said he might have preferred Childers' rider
as an improvement to Hodgkinson's amendment but he did not
want to draw any vital distinction. Believing that the restrictions
hedging household suffrage in the Government's Bill would lead to
prolonged agitation, he put it to the House whether Hodgkinson's
amendment would or would not mitigate the evil. Getting ahead of
Disraeli, Gladstone asserted that the Government could have no
objection to accepting the amendment, adding,

> For myself, I am ready to accept the proposal of my hon. Friend.
> In so doing I do not accept it in preference to the basis on which
> we desired to act. I accept it simply as the best proposal of which
> the circumstances will admit.

Indicating his wariness about external popular movements, and perhaps Bright's own campaigning, Gladstone added,

> I am not a lover of circumstances by which the business of governing this country is taken from within the walls of this House and transferred to places beyond them. I foresee ... that that is the state of things at which we are likely to arrive, unless some measures be adopted to prevent it.[74]

At this point, Disraeli must have realized that Gladstone had got there before him in the nick of time. He reacted by claiming that the Government would have recommended such a policy long ago if they had been masters of the situation. 'Months ago,' he said, 'It is possible I might in vain have proposed a policy which is now generally accepted as of the wisest character. But it is proposed now by the House of Commons.'

In his final words, Disraeli claimed that he accepted Hodgkinson's amendment not as a result of pressure from inside the House of Commons or outside, but out of principle: 'I can assure the House that Her Majesty's Government, in the course they are taking, are not influenced by the terrors which have been depicted, and the agitation with which we have been threatened'[75] – no doubt recalling Bright's advice in the 9/12 March memorandum.

Hodgkinson's Amendment may not have been perfect, but Disraeli got his way, though the amendment had to be rectified the following week. Cranborne attacked Disraeli for announcing

> a change of startling magnitude, a change which involves the certain admission, instead of the contingent and doubtful admission, of some 500,000 people to the franchise. Of this policy I express no opinion; but I say it is entirely an abnegation of all the principles of his party.[76]

But Hodgkinson's amendment had been accepted by the Government and that was that.

Further revelations about the various manoeuvres that led to this historic event were provided in a letter written the following day by Disraeli to his colleague, Gathorne Hardy. He explained how, on the morning of the debate, he had managed to persuade Robert Dalgleish of the Tearoom revolt to withdraw a motion on compounding. Dalgleish had told him that, in return, 'He and all his friends and many of ours, as we knew, must support Hodgkinson's amendment for repeal of the Small Tenements Act.' Disraeli had also been 'secretly informed' of Gladstone's decision to 'reorganise on the principle of repeal of Local Acts'.

Disraeli wrote,

> In this state of doubt and difficulty I went down to the House and about 9 o'clock, being quite alone on our bench, and only forty-five men on our side, some of whom were going to vote for Hodgkinson, the amendment was moved ... Having revolved everything in my mind, I felt that the critical moment had arrived.

He saw he was completely trapped and would have to support the amendment, whether or not that was his original intention. Certainly, as Bright had advised in his confidential memorandum, he knew that it would be opportune for a Conservative Government to pass the legislation. Nevertheless, Disraeli's account of his decision was somewhat disingenuous. 'Without in the slightest degree receding from our principle and position of a rating and residential franchise,' he wrote, 'we might take a step which would destroy the present agitation and extinguish Gladstone and Co. I therefore accepted the spirit of H's amendment.'[77] When he spoke on the Reform Bill in Edinburgh in October of that year, Disraeli went so far as to say,

> When you try to settle any great question, there are two considerations which statesmen ought not to forget ... let your plan be founded upon some principle ... Let it also be a principle that is in harmony with the manners and customs of the people you are attempting to legislate for.[78]

Following what must have been a good deal of discussion over the weekend, Disraeli was the first person on his feet on Monday 20 May. He urged Hodgkinson to withdraw his amendment. Hodgkinson agreed, leaving the Government with a free hand. As if he had discharged the role expected of him, Hodgkinson did not speak again throughout the remaining passage of the Bill.

All this, despite the machinations, manoeuvrings and complications, is by no means untypical of the way in which the House conducts itself on matters of great controversy when the battle has been fought to a standstill. None the less, Lowe launched a massive attack on the way it had all come about, filling no less than nineteen columns in *Hansard* with withering invective, ending with the words,

> I took upon myself two years ago – only two years – to make a prophecy. I said that if we embarked on the course of democracy we should either ruin our party or our country. Sir, I was wrong, as prophets very often are. It is not a question of alternatives; we are going to ruin both.[79]

But the political scene had been set and, while there was a stream of drafts and redrafts with accompanying argument, no one was prepared or able to upset the apple-cart, despite Cranborne's and Lowe's continuing best efforts.

Bright's long campaign had been vindicated. As he had noted on 28 May, 'The Bill adopted the precise franchise I recommended in 1858/59.' In a footnote to this diary entry, Walling notes that Cranborne said the Bill in its final shape was 'the result of the adoption of the principles of Bright at the dictation of Gladstone'.[80] It was more a matter of Gladstone and Disraeli being manoeuvred by Bright and his external strategy, supported by the Reform organizations and the people as a whole.

Bright's contributions during the remaining passage of the Bill were minimal, though he spoke powerfully for the ballot on 19 June – a clause subsequently defeated – and in the debate on 1 July, which gave an additional MP to Liverpool, Manchester, Leeds and his own Birmingham. On 15 July, on the third reading, Bright recorded in his diary, 'Amusing recriminations between Lowe and Disraeli' and a 'severe speech from Lord Cranborne'. He concluded with the simple words, 'Bill passed with cheers from our side.'[81]

Cranborne's speech on that occasion drew an unfavourable comparison of Disraeli's behaviour with that of Peel in 1846 over the Corn Laws, when he had accepted Cobden's and Bright's argument for repeal (at a time, of course, when Disraeli had been for their retention). He tried to make Disraeli feel as uncomfortable as possible, saying,

> I have heard that this Bill is a Conservative triumph. If it be a Conservative triumph to have adopted the principles of your most determined adversary ... the hon. Member for Birmingham; if it be a Conservative triumph to have introduced a Bill guarded with precautions and securities, and to have abandoned every one of those precautions and securities at the

bidding of your opponents, then in the whole course of your annals I will venture to say the Conservative party has won no triumph so signal as this.[82]

Little did he, or any of the other players in the House, know that Disraeli had in fact received counsel from that 'most determined adversary' as early as March.

Of course, it was not the Conservative Party, but the aristocratic influence, embodied by Cranborne and so much despised by Bright, that was the real loser in all of this. Indeed, the House of Lords capitulated rapidly after the Bill had passed the Commons, no doubt relieved to have preserved its status for the present, given that its privileges and those of its membership were always in Bright's sights.

The historic Representation of the People Act 1867 made its way on to the Statute Book on 15 August 1867. According to Homersham Cox, writing in 1868, the number of unenfranchised men given the right to vote was about 427,000, a figure that did not include lodgers, whose numbers could not be estimated, with Hodgkinson's amendment adding 'almost four times as much as was originally contemplated'.[83] F. B. Smith, drawing on the figures of the statistician, Robert Dudley Baxter, reckoned that the increase was far above this and gave a figure of almost 1,120,000, a total increase of 82.5 per cent between 1866 and 1868.[84]

The Reform Act was followed by a redistribution Bill to bolster the Conservative vote in the rural counties, and constituency boundaries were redrawn so that 700,000 people were transferred from the counties to the boroughs. In the event, Hodgkinson's amendment, even as redrafted, disintegrated some time later in the welter of landlord and tenant law. What mattered, however, was that the enfranchisement of the working class, Bright's overall objective, had succeeded – and without revolution. In the closing words of his essay, *John Bright and the Creed of Reform*, Asa Briggs quotes Bright himself:

> It is discovered in the year 1867 that my principles all along have been entirely constitutional and my course perfectly patriotic. The invective and vituperation that have been poured upon me have now been proved to be entirely a mistake.[85]

Amen.

Reform after 1867

The Reform Act of 1867 was a great victory for Bright. However, given the limitations of what Parliament and the circumstances of the time would accept, more reforms were needed. Just three days after the Reform Bill was enacted, he wrote to Edmond Beales regarding what he described as 'the next great question' – the secret ballot. 'The more wide the suffrage, the more there are of men in humble circumstances who are admitted to the exercise of political rights, the more clearly is it necessary that the shelter of the ballot should be granted,' he wrote. This would greatly diminish corruption and 'destroy the odious system of intimidation which now so extensively prevails', thereby making the House of Commons 'a more complete representation of the opinions and wishes of the electoral body'. He urged the Reform League and Reform Union to take on this cause, adding, 'I need not tell you that I shall heartily join in their labours for this great end.'[86] As ever, Bright believed in one step at a time, at the right time, and for the right reasons. His hopes were realized five years later by the Ballot Act 1872.

Women's suffrage, however, was not on his agenda. In common with most of his contemporaries, Bright was reluctant to include any such proposals in his own schemes. Though he had voted for John Stuart Mill's failed amendment to the 1867 Reform Bill to admit women to the vote, this was perhaps partly out of admiration for Mill himself, and he later confessed that he was unsure whether he had done the right thing.[87] Bright certainly knew the arguments. His sisters, Priscilla McLaren and Margaret Lucas, and daughter, Helen Bright Clark, were all pre-eminent and early suffragists. His brother, Jacob Bright, MP, presented the Women's Disabilities Removal Bill, drafted by Dr Richard Pankhurst, in 1870. This was defeated but, in the words of Melanie Phillips, 'began nearly half a century of parliamentary struggle',[88] the campaign for which largely modelled itself on that of the Anti-Corn Law League.

Bright, however, did not himself consider the question a priority. In 1858, he had written to Agnes Pochin, who wanted him to include women's suffrage in his draft reform bill, saying he knew 'no valid argument against your proposal' but feared 'it would do harm to the cause of improved representation, without doing any good to the object you have in view'. He added, 'Your question is somewhat too far in advance, I fear.'[89] In 1871, Bright told Eliza Sturge, wavering, 'I hope this view of the question may be a mistaken one, because it does not seem to me very unlikely that the suffrage will be granted to women.'[90] In 1876, he was actually to vote *against* women's suffrage: 'Some of my relations will be angry, but I could not but speak my own convictions on the question.'[91] He simply didn't believe the time was right.

In 1884, however, Bright did witness the number of male electors growing from three million to over five million. Gladstone's Franchise Bill, introduced on 28 February, extended the household and lodger franchises from the towns to the counties, a substantial measure that strongly endorsed Bright's strategy for the extension of the franchise by degrees through household suffrage. 'Bill large and complete and satisfactory,'[92] he noted in his diary. He spoke for an hour during the second reading on 24 March, stating that the Bill had been 'drawn up with statesmanlike sagacity and wisdom, and I believe that that is the general opinion of it throughout the country'.[93] The second reading was passed by a significant majority and, on 26 June, the Bill was passed without a division. Bright's diary simply records 'A memorable evening.'[94]

However, on 8 July, the House of Lords rejected the Bill, refusing to accept the franchise without redistribution. Gladstone called a crisis meeting of the Liberal Party on 10 July. Bright noted, 'I was called on and forced to speak quite unprepared.'[95] His opinions, however, were fully formed. In 1863, he had explained to an American friend,

> In the House of Commons, a large proportion of the members, more than one third of them, I think, are directly connected with the House of Lords and thus the whole thing is so interwoven that it makes a fabric so strong that probably only some great convulsion will ever break through it.[96]

The political parties were dominated by the aristocracy and he regarded the British Parliament as a 'sham' for this reason. His aversion to the aristocracy and, by default, the House of Lords, stretched back to his Anti-Corn Law days and had been cemented by parliamentary battles with the peers over reform and other issues such as the paper duties. Just nine months earlier he had delivered his most historic speech on the subject at a reform conference in Leeds. There, on 18 October 1883, he set out his ideas for House of Lords reform, including the policy of the limited veto. Just as the Crown could no longer reject a Bill sent to it, he argued, why should not the power of the Lords be limited in the same way? He asked:

Why not enact that if the Peers have rejected a Bill once, and it has been reconsidered in a subsequent session by the Commons, and after due deliberation has been again sent up to the Peers, that then the Peers shall pass it on, and it will receive the Royal assent, and it will become law?[97]

This in essence is what became embodied in the Parliament Act 1911 and remains the basis for the limitation of the power of the House of Lords today.

At the crisis meeting in July 1884, Bright stated, 'A hereditary House of Parliament is not and cannot be perpetual in a free country' – strangely, Bright never proposed an elected House of Lords – and called again for a limit on the House of Lords' power of veto.[98] Later that month, in the light of the peers' behaviour and the importance of the Bill, there was a massive march in London. 'Great Reform procession passed my windows', Bright noted on 21 July. 'Crowd enormous. Stood 3 hours at the window. Cheering extraordinary and continuous, which I recd. with such courtesy as I could show the multitude.'[99]

In the wake of the row and the stalemate between the Commons and Lords, a deal was made between the Government and the Opposition, and a new Franchise Bill was introduced. This swept through the House of Commons and on 14 November received a third reading without a division. A Bill for the redistribution of seats was brought in on 1 December and Bright noted, 'Singular sight. After months of contest, all calm and all apparently agreed. 3 months of agitation has had its effect. The Opposition no longer opposes.'[100]

CHAPTER 5

Lincoln and Bright:
Fighting against Slavery and
for America

The friend of my country because the friend of mankind.
(Horace Greeley, dedicating his book *The American Conflict:
A History of the Great Rebellion* to John Bright)[1]

When, on 14 April 1865, Abraham Lincoln was assassinated by John
Wilkes Booth, his pockets were found to contain a number of items
of intimate and personal value which the president clearly treasured
and carried with him as mementoes of his enormous struggles over
the previous year. These included not only a symbolic Confederate
five-dollar bill, a news clipping on unrest within the Confederate
army, a record of emancipation in Missouri and the Union election
address of 1864, but notably a testimonial for the president by John
Bright, calling for him to be re-elected. This had been printed by
Horace Greeley, anti-slaver and peace campaigner, in the *New York
Tribune* as well as being widely published in *The Times* and other
newspapers. On 29 April 1865, having just learned of Lincoln's
death, Bright independently recalled having written this very letter,
but without, of course, knowing that Lincoln had been carrying it on
his person at that fatal moment.[2]

There is no doubt that Lincoln admired Bright. Indeed, as early as
December 1861, the president had presented Bright with two copies
of a portrait of himself. The Republican senator, Charles Sumner,
later wrote to Bright, 'Your full length photograph is on the mantle
in his office, where the only other portrait is one of his predecessors,
Andrew Jackson.'[3] A month after the assassination, Mrs Lincoln
gave this photograph to Sumner, describing it as 'a likeness of
Mr Bright, as having belonged to my beloved husband, and which

he prized as representing a noble and good friend of our cause in this unholy rebellion'.[4] This poignantly sums up the depth of Abraham Lincoln's admiration and personal esteem for the man whom many believed had saved America from war with England when powerful commercial interests, MPs with constituencies involved in confederate contracts and many in the House of Commons, not to mention some pre-eminent Cabinet members, were supporting the South. Bright was also part of the influential coalition that had convinced Lincoln to issue the proclamation against slavery in the autumn of 1862.

Bright's commitment to America stretched back well before the Civil War itself and was deeply connected with his concepts of free trade, parliamentary reform, democracy and sense of freedom. Just as Abraham Lincoln's bust was placed in the White House by President Obama on his own inauguration, so also there is a bust of John Bright by John Wood. This was commissioned as a gift for Abraham Lincoln, but it did not reach Washington until after the president's assassination.[5] It was moved from the State Department to the White House in June 1866 and 'placed in one of the alcoves of the lower Hall'.[6] It was rediscovered by Jackie Kennedy and placed by her near the public entrance. It remains in the White House despite the recent return of the bust of Winston Churchill that was loaned by the British Government when George W. Bush was president.

In Lincoln's inner circle, Bright's reputation and commitment were legendary, and his letters were passed to Lincoln and read out in Cabinet meetings. In 1861, William H. Seward, then secretary of state, wrote to Charles Sumner, then chairman of the Senate Foreign Relations Committee, with whom Bright regularly corresponded,

> Many thanks my dear Sumner for the perusal of the noble letter from John Bright. How sad for the cause of humanity, yet how honourable to John Bright, that he is the only Englishman having public position or character, who has written one word of favour to or desire for the preservation of the American Union. Tell him that I appreciate his honesty, his manliness, his virtue.[7]

Lincoln himself showed his admiration for Bright by granting a presidential pardon to one of his constituents in October 1863:

> Whereas one Alfred Rubery was convicted on or about the twelfth day of October 1863 ... of engaging in, and giving aid

and comfort to the existing rebellion against the Government of this country and sentenced to ten years' imprisonment, and to pay a fine of ten thousand dollars;

...

And whereas, the said Alfred Rubery is a subject of Great Britain, and his pardon is desired by John Bright of England;

Now, therefore, be it known that I, Abraham Lincoln, President of the United States of America ... especially as a public mark of the esteem held by the United States of America for the high character and steady friendship of the said John Bright, do hereby grant a pardon to the said Alfred Rubery[8]

Bright was an intimate of William Lloyd Garrison, one of the greatest of the abolitionists, and his speech at a breakfast for Garrison in June 1867 is among Bright's most memorable orations. He was also a close friend of one of the most renowned former slaves, Frederick Douglass, who stayed with Bright in Rochdale on his visit to England as early as 1847. In the biography of Douglass by Booker Washington it says, 'from no one could Douglass have received a more gracious welcome and friendly benediction than from the great commoner'.[9] Bright himself was to write the introduction to the English edition of another Douglass biography in 1882.

Thomas Dudley, the American consul at Liverpool, presented Bright with a banner from Philadelphia and wrote of him that

he was opposed to human slavery and opposed to war, but among his countrymen at that time, he stood almost alone ... Bright stood alone in England when he arose to make this speech [at Rochdale on 4 December 1861], but when he sat down there were hundreds ... who were ready to gather around and stand by him. These men did come forward and raise their voices for the right in the mighty struggle with slavery.[10]

John Bigelow, who was the American representative in Paris, said of one of John Bright's speeches supporting America, 'I do not know how to express my gratitude sufficiently to Mr Bright for his Rochdale speech ... It was worthy the heart and the head of Chas. J. Fox. He will live to bless the day that he was inspired to make it.'[11] Charles Francis Adams, the American ambassador to England in the 1860s, said that if the North should win, Bright, by virtue of his support of their cause, 'would become the most powerful man in the country'.[12] When Bright spoke in St James's Hall in London

on 26 March 1863 against the abomination of slavery, even Karl
Marx, who was at the meeting, praised 'Father Bright' for his
views.[13] In 1869, Bigelow suggested that Bright should visit the
USA, saying, 'I do not doubt that he would be more successful
here than anyone else ... For he is at present by far the most popular
European with the Yankees.'[14]

Writing a lengthy letter to Seward on 21 October 1865, Bright
summarized his thoughts on the state of affairs at that time, asking
'What shall be done to secure the rights of the innocent – of the
negro who has been made free by so profuse an expenditure of
blood?' The solution, he said, was for him to be given the vote:

> He may not be hereafter bought & sold – but he may be
> subjected to almost infinite damage & injustice by the
> Legislatures in which, shut out from the franchise, he has no
> influence. He may be, & I suppose he will be, under State laws
> only; & these laws may be framed, as hitherto they have been
> framed, with a total disregard of his rights & interests.[15]

Thus, Bright anticipated the civil rights movement, led a hundred
years later by Martin Luther King.

In that same letter, Bright specifically criticized Lord Russell for
his attitude towards the Alabama claims, and proposed to Secretary
of State Seward that there should be arbitration by selected jurists
from different countries. He set out his ideas on this in detail. On the
death of Lord Palmerston, he wrote that his old enemy 'Did much
evil, perhaps without a clear perception that it was evil,' and that
Gladstone 'has been deplorably wrong on your great question – but
he is a man of high motives – more conscientious than many statesmen have been, & much more anxious to do right than willing to do
wrong.'[16] He was less condemnatory of motives than some allege,
though he was always candid.

Bright later wrote to Lloyd Garrison's son, Francis Jackson
Garrison, on receiving his father's biography in February 1886, that

> the great slavery question is settled but it remains as a lesson to
> all future generations of men in all countries of the danger of the
> commission of great crimes by governments and nations and of
> the certainty that punishment will follow and that compensation
> must be paid. Had your people been just and courageous in
> defence of justice, how much of treasure and of blood might
> have been saved? But nations learn slowly and they purchase

their experience and their wisdom at a fearful price. So long as freedom is valued on earth and so long as your language and ours is spoken and written, so long will the name of your father be held in remembrance – so long will he be reverenced as among the most illustrious friends of freedom.[17]

In the Introduction to the *Speeches of John Bright MP on the American Question*, published in Boston, Mass. by Little, Brown in June 1865, Frank Moore, the editor of the *Rebellion Record*, stated that 'Mr Bright ... was largely instrumental in presenting the Union cause in its true light to the Government and the people of Great Britain' – being 'the death-struggle between freedom and slavery'.[18]

As discussed in the Introduction, and as is clear from the above, Bright in his own time was widely recognized at home and abroad by politicians, the press, commentators and historians as one of the greatest statesmen and orators of his age. However, from the 1920s onwards, with a few exceptions, acknowledgment of Bright's achievements evaporated and diminished for reasons that are not entirely clear. This is equally true of his role in relation to the USA, which was fully acknowledged by Lincoln and his closest friends and associates.

A perceptive acknowledgement comes from Elton Trueblood, a scholar who studied and taught at Harvard, Stanford and Johns Hopkins Universities, who wrote in his book, *Abraham Lincoln: Theologian of American Anguish* (1973),

> John Bright is remembered for his influence upon American history, both in the way he helped to avoid armed conflict between Britain and America, and also in the way he prevented the recognition of the Confederacy by Great Britain and France. But many who are familiar with the work of Bright as a states-man are not equally familiar with him as a thinker who influenced the mind of Abraham Lincoln. The fact that most of the connection was through Charles Sumner, as an intermediary, does not lessen the importance of the impact.[19]

What Bright thought, said and achieved in the course of his political career in relation to this great American question was decisive, and he acted on the basis of an interest in the country that stretched back decades. Indeed, among the volumes that Bright chose for the personal library he created in 1846 to mark the successful repeal of the Corn Laws, was a biography of Thomas Jefferson, which he marked up copiously in his own hand. He was also greatly influenced by his intimate knowledge of the country drawn from his Quaker Friends and their anti-slavery campaigns, including most particularly his close friend and supporter, Joseph Sturge. For the Quaker, anti-slavery was an article of faith. Even as early as 1657, George Fox, the founder of the Society of Friends, wrote 'to Friends beyond the sea that have blacks or Indian slaves' to remind them that 'God made of one blood all nations of the world, and that the Gospel was glad tidings to every captivated creature'.[20] By the end of the eighteenth century, there were no Quaker slave owners in America.

British Feeling towards the USA, 1861

On 18 February 1861, two weeks before Abraham Lincoln took up office as president of the United States, the Southern States of America, fearful of the implications of a Republican Government, proclaimed their independence under President Jefferson Davis. In his inaugural address, President Lincoln spoke strongly against secession, but stated, 'I have no purpose, directly or indirectly, to interfere with the institution of slavery in the States where it exists. I believe I have no lawful right to do so, and I have no inclination to do so.'[21] Within two months, Lincoln's determination to restore the Union, and the Confederacy's determination to break away, led to the first battle of the American Civil War at Fort Sumter. When, in response, Lincoln ordered a blockade of the Southern ports, the conflict developed international implications, restricting as it did the supply of raw cotton from America to the world's mills, including those in Lancashire.

Up to this point, the level of knowledge in Britain of the diversity of culture in America was fairly basic. The people had no real understanding, nor a compelling reason to understand, the differences between the 'Yankee' North and the slave-owning South. Furthermore, many took at face value President Lincoln's statements that the conflict was purely about maintaining the Union. At a time when Bright's campaign for democracy in Britain was threatening the status quo, for many the Southern States were reassuringly anti-democratic and, by supporting their cause, conservative Britons could stop, or at the very least delay, the spread of democracy through the Western world. As the American historian, John Lothrop Motley, wrote after the first Southern victory in battle, 'The real secret of the exultation which manifests itself in *The Times* and other organs over our troubles and disasters, is their hatred, not to America so much as to democracy in England.'[22]

The British Government's first reaction was to acknowledge the belligerent rights of the South. After taking hasty legal advice, Lord John Russell gave a statement to this effect in the House of Commons on 8 May 1861. Despite a quick reversal of position a few days later, this was an unfortunate beginning to the relations between Britain and the USA during the Civil War. On 13 May, the British Government issued a Proclamation of Neutrality, forbidding all British subjects from aiding either side in the American conflict, directly or indirectly. Initially, Bright approved of this, and in a speech in the House of Commons on 28 May, he added a request that, to assist the Government in maintaining its neutral position, the House should refrain from discussions on matters over which Britain had no influence, regardless of which side of the conflict they involved. But feelings ran deep, and a state of benevolent neutrality was impossible to maintain in the country at large. Favour in the British press, with a few notable exceptions, was firmly directed towards the South, with epithets such as 'gallant' and 'heroic' being added to the reputation of the plucky Southerners as the conflict escalated during the summer of 1861.

However, a conservative sympathy and a fear of democracy were not the only reasons that the Confederate cause found favour in Britain. Many of Bright's fellow free traders supported the South because it advocated freedom of trade, in contrast to the protectionist policies of the North. Bright would not tolerate this simplistic argument, which relied on turning a blind eye to the fact that the economy of the Southern states could not exist without slave labour, and he found himself in conflict with many of his natural allies, including, for a time, even Richard Cobden.

In the hierarchy of Bright's thinking, the degradation of human beings in the form of slavery, followed by the degradation of countries in war, both took precedence over free trade as motive forces. For Bright, free trade was a realization of the emancipation of freedom of choice in the economic marketplace, which in turn was subordinated to the freedom of the individual and that person's political and democratic choice, and to Bright's commitment to peace, both for nations and the individual – a Quaker sense of priorities. Free trade had to serve a purpose. However, during the early months of the American Civil War, Cobden for a time had certain reservations about denying support to the South, though at no point, it must be stressed, did he in any way condone slavery. These reservations, voiced on free trade grounds, arose chiefly from his objections to British intervention and were soon dismissed.[23] As much cannot be said of Gladstone, also a free trader and the arch proponent of Peel's budgets in the early 1840s, whose family fortunes were partly derived from the slave trade, and who later apologized for his support of the South during the Civil War.

Even among those for whom slavery was the key issue, there were supporters of the secession of the Southern States. Cobden, for example, certainly felt sympathy for the Confederacy's legal right to secede, and in a letter written in June 1861, he cited Alexis de Tocqueville and questioned whether the Southern States were indeed 'rebels'.[24] Others supported secession if only to see the North freed from the contamination of the slave economy. While this position was also an anti-war stance, Bright could not agree with it. As he wrote to Cobden in February 1861,

> I agree with you as to the grandeur of the free States, free from political brotherhood with the South. Still, it was a noble prospect to see a great continent under one central Republican Government, and I cannot help hoping it might be realised.[25]

Later that year, Bright recalled a conversation that demonstrated another aspect of British feeling and which added to the unofficial support for the Confederacy – that of a fear of the USA itself. Speaking at Rochdale on 4 December 1861, Bright said,

> It has been said, 'How much better it would be' – not for the United States, but – 'for us, that these States should be divided.' I recollect meeting a gentleman in Bond Street one day … and he said to me, 'After all, this is a sad business about the United States; but still I think it very much better that they should be split up. In twenty years' – or in fifty years, I forget which it was – 'they will be so powerful that they will bully all Europe'.

In contrast, Bright saw a properly united America as an expression of the highest ideals of man, and shared his vision with the crowds at Rochdale of a day when

> the whole of that vast continent might become one great confederation of States – without a great army, and without a great navy – not mixing itself up with the entanglements of European politics – without a custom-house inside, through the whole length

and breadth of its territory – and with freedom everywhere, equality everywhere, law everywhere, peace everywhere.[26]

This view of a benevolent USA was shared by his sometime unlikely ally, Disraeli, whom Bright later recalled, 'with a thoughtfulness and statesmanship which you do not all acknowledge, did not say a word from that Bench likely to create difficulty with the United States. I think his chief and his followers might learn something from his example.'[27]

While these arguments were being debated in the clubs of London and on the floor of the House of Commons, equally strong opinions were to be found on both sides within the unenfranchised working class. Many took the opposite view to those supporting the South and the anti-democracy lobby – that in America lay the future of the democracy they craved – and, after decades of emigration, many had family ties with those fighting in the Union army. Their voice, however, was largely drowned out by the monopoly of the press. While some newspapers did promote the Northern cause, *The Times* remained firmly pro-South and, as President Lincoln himself acknowledged when he met *The Times* journalist, William Howard Russell, in March 1861, 'The London 'Times' is one of the greatest powers in the world – in fact, I don't know anything which has much more power – except perhaps the Mississippi.'[28] However, Bright, engaged as he was in the middle of his long campaign for parliamentary reform, saw a potentially equal power in elements of the working class. As Trevelyan, writing in 1913, pointed out:

> If England had in 1770 possessed institutions as representative as those in 1861, there would have been no American Revolution. If in 1861 she had possessed institutions as democratic as those of our own day, there would have been no ... effective 'Southern sympathy'.[29]

Though enfranchisement was some way off, the working classes when brought together were still capable of influencing decision-making at Westminster by dint of their great mass and the Establishment's memory of recent revolutions on the Continent.

Bright's campaign to mobilize people on this issue began on 1 August 1861 at Rochdale, with his first public speech on the war. To loud cheers, he compared the USA favourably with the British Government, over whose decisions the majority of his audience had no control:

[The Americans] have never fought 'for the balance of power' in
Europe. They have never fought to keep a decaying Empire.
They have never squandered the money of their people in such a
phantom expedition as we have been engaged in. And now, at
this moment, when you are told that they are going to be ruined
by their vast expenditure, why, the sum that they are going to
raise in the great emergency of this grievous war is not greater
than what we raise every year during a time of peace.[30]

In this speech, Bright also outlined his belief in the inevitability of
the war:

No man is more in favour of peace than I am; no man has
denounced war more than I have, probably, in this country; few
men in their public life suffer more obloquy – I had almost said
more indignity – in consequence of it. But I cannot for the life of
me see upon any of those principles upon which States are
governed now ... how the state of affairs in America, with regard
to the United States Government, could have been different
from what it is at this moment.[31]

After the First Battle of Bull Run in July 1861 – the first major battle
of the war and a victory for the Confederate army – many believed,
regardless of where their sympathies lay, that the North had picked a
fight it could not win, and that the obvious solution to the conflict
was for the North to let the Southern states go. As the summer
fighting continued, even Bright wondered briefly if this might be
true. Outwardly, he displayed a confidence in the North, while also
heeding his own advice to the House of Commons of 28 May not to
comment unduly on matters that he could not influence, but
inwardly he was extremely anxious about the situation. Throughout
the war he took a great and detailed interest in the military strategies
employed by both sides, visiting the offices of the *Morning Star*
for any news while acknowledging to his wife that it was 'sad to
feel so much interest in transactions which have in them so much
to condemn'.[32]

   After studying the reports of Bull Run, he wrote to Cobden,
saying,

I think the accounts from the States indicate that the North will
have to submit to some recognition of the South ... The disasters
caused by the war, and the hopelessness of a real union after

what has passed, must turn the minds of all sensible men in the North to some mode of extrication other than that of conquest.[33]

On 4 September 1861 he wrote to James Henderson of New York that

> without a regular army, without skilled and experienced commanders, with the population of the Border States against you or divided in opinion & interests, & with so vast a territory in insurrection against you, there is little chance of anything like a conquest of the insurgent states.[34]

At the same time, however, Bright never lost faith in the ideal of American democracy, writing to Charles Sumner on 6 September 1861 that

> Whatever is done and whatsoever comes I need not tell you that I am for the Government which was founded by your great men of eighty years ago, and that all my sympathies and hopes are with those who are for freedom. If you are ever again one nation I shall rejoice in your greatness; if your Northern States are henceforth to form your nation, I shall still have faith in your greatness and rejoice in your renown.[35]

The *Trent* Affair, November 1861 to January 1862

Bright's uncharacteristic pessimism and sense of impotence, however, did not last long. In November 1861, an emergency arose in which he was to play an active role when the journey of two Confederate envoys – one bound for Britain, the other for France – was interrupted off the coast of Cuba. The envoys, James M. Mason and John Slidell, were travelling to Europe to promote the recognition of the Southern States' independence when their ship was stopped and they were seized by a Northern sloop of war and taken to Boston, Mass. Crucially for Britain, the pair were travelling on an English mail steamer, the *Trent*, under the British flag. When news reached England of this violation of a British ship in international waters, the reaction was largely one of indignation and outrage. The press portrayed the incident as a deliberate attempt to pick a fight with England, as summed up by the *Morning Chronicle*:

Abraham Lincoln, whose accession to power was generally
welcomed on this side of the Atlantic, has proved himself a
feeble, confused and little-minded mediocrity. Mr Seward, the
firebrand at his elbow, is exerting himself to provoke a quarrel
with all Europe.[36]

Palmerston and Russell's initial reaction could have plunged the
country straight into war, but this was tempered by the intervention
of Queen Victoria and Prince Albert, the latter virtually from his
deathbed. The resulting letters to William H. Seward, the American
Secretary of State, demanded the prisoners' release but also
requested clarification about whether the actions of the sloop of
war's Captain Wilkes had been a result of a Government order or if
he had been acting on his own initiative. If it was the former, then
war was unavoidable and, in preparation, 8,000 British troops set
sail for Canada.

The warmongering attitude in Britain worried Bright. While he
had, in Amanda Foreman's words, 'lost his appetite for being a
national hate-figure' following his experiences during the Crimean
War,[37] his speech on 4 December 1861 in Rochdale was an attempt
to ease the situation. After reiterating the arguments for supporting
the North and for remaining 'neutral as far as regards mingling in
the strife' although 'not neutral in opinion or sympathy', he ended
his rousing speech by saying that, within a short space of time, the
Northern states would have a population

> equal to or exceeding that of this kingdom. When that time
> comes, I pray that it may not be said amongst them, that, in the
> darkest hour of their country's trials, England, the land of their
> fathers, looked on with icy coldness and saw unmoved the perils
> and calamities of their children … if all other tongues are silent,
> mine shall speak for that policy which gives hope to the bonds-
> men of the South, and which tends to generous thoughts, and
> generous words, and generous deeds, between the two great
> nations who speak the English language, and from their origin
> are alike entitled to the English name.[38]

The power of his oratory fulfilled its purpose. Bright's speech was
met with much gratitude by his American friends. The ill-feeling
between Britain and the USA had been as evident in the Union
press and public opinion as it was in Britain. John Bigelow wrote
from Paris to thank Bright, saying,

God bless you for your noble speech at Rochdale. If the time should come, as to many here seems probable, when my countrymen will be provoked to call every Englishman his enemy, I shall turn to these records to guard me from the guilt of such injustice ... I trust my government may prove worthy of such a defender.[39]

The same month, Bright received the two copies of Lincoln's portrait sent by the president himself. On the back of one of these, R. Barry O'Brien records, Bright inscribed, 'And if there be on Earth and among men any right Divine to govern, surely it rests with the Ruler so chosen and so appointed – December 4th, 1861' – the date of his Rochdale speech.[40]

While Lincoln and his Cabinet were deliberating over which course of action to take regarding the *Trent* Affair, Bright was also busy behind the scenes, writing to his friends in Government urging peace and offering counsel to his friend, Charles Sumner, one of Lincoln's chief advisers. Sumner was a firm anti-slaver and foreign affairs specialist with a particular regard for Europe. His passions for peace, freedom and democracy echoed those of Bright and, as Sumner's biographer, Edward L. Pierce, states, 'Next to the freedom of the African race, no political object was ever so constant with him as perpetual peace between England and the United States.'[41] Sumner had met Bright's brother, Jacob, in Washington in 1851, but did not meet Bright until November 1857 during a visit to Britain when Sumner was recovering from a brutal attempt on his life by the representative for South Carolina the previous year. During 24 hours in Llandudno, where Bright frequently stayed on holiday, Bright and Sumner struck up a friendship that was to last until Sumner's death in 1874.

Sumner and Bright corresponded frequently – Sumner addressing Bright as 'my master – maestro mio'[42] – and by the time of the Civil War, Sumner regularly shared Bright's letters with Lincoln and his Cabinet. At a time of dwindling support in England, these letters were much appreciated. As Cobden, also a frequent correspondent of Charles Sumner, wrote on 12 February 1862, 'I hardly know anybody, except our courageous friend Bright (who rather likes to battle with the long odds against him), that thinks you can put down the rebellion.'[43]

In a letter to Sumner dated 5 December 1861, Bright wrote, 'If I were Minister or President in your country, I would write the most complete answer the case is capable of, and in a friendly and courteous tone, send it to this country.' Bright advised him to ask for arbitration by a European tribunal regarding international law, a course he had advocated previously. However, he believed that 'Any moderate course you may take will meet with great support here, and in the English Cabinet there are, as I certainly know, some who will gladly accept any fair proposition for friendly arrangement from your side.'[44] On 7 December, he warned,

> At all hazards you must not let this matter grow to a war with England, even if you are right and we are wrong. War will be fatal to your idea of restoring the Union, and we know not what may survive its evil influences.[45]

On December 14, Bright wrote again, acknowledging the difficulty of backing down but remaining firm on the course that needed to be taken:

> If you are resolved to succeed against the South, have no war with England; make every concession that can be made; don't even hesitate to tell the world that you will even concede what two years ago no Power would have asked of you, rather than give another nation a pretence for assisting in the breaking up of your country. The time will probably come when you can safely disregard the menaces of the English oligarchy; now it is your interest to baffle it, even by any concession which is not disgraceful.[46]

Sumner showed these letters to Lincoln, along with those from Cobden and others, and wrote to Bright that 'The President is much moved and astonished by the English intelligence. He is essentially honest and pacific in disposition, with a natural slowness. Yesterday, he said to me, "There will be no war unless England is bent on having one."'[47]

As it happened, President Lincoln had not authorized the action of Captain Wilkes, and had despaired when he heard of it. But he felt bitter about the British reaction, saying,

> This is the very thing the British captains used to do. They claimed the right of searching American ships and carrying men out of them. That was the cause of war in 1812. Now, we cannot abandon our own principles. We shall have to give these men up and apologise for what we have done.[48]

In the last week of December 1861, Seward wrote to Russell, agreeing to the release of the prisoners. This diplomatic move belied Lincoln's true feelings about the affair, as he later recorded:

> It was a pretty bitter pill to swallow, but I contented myself with believing that England's triumph in the matter would be short-lived, and that after ending our war successfully we would be so powerful that we could call her to account for all the embarrassments she had inflicted on us.[49]

This did happen in 1867 and, as will be seen, Bright's intervention prevented a new source of conflict.

Bright, too, had found the whole business a bitter and tiring experience. During the crisis, he had confided in friends more than once that, if war broke out with America, he would retire from public life. As he wrote to Cobden on 9 December 1861, 'I will look for a retirement from Parliament if war actually takes place. I will not kill myself with proving it wicked, as I nearly did seven years ago [during the Crimean War].'[50] Cobden was of a similar mind, having written to Bright on 6 December, 'Might we not be justified in turning hermits, letting our beards grow, and returning to our caves?'[51]

After Mason and Slidell had been released and the crisis was over, Bright attacked the British Government for its conduct on 17 February 1862:

> It is not customary in ordinary life for a person to send a polite messenger with a polite message to a friend, or neighbour, or acquaintance, and at the same time to send a man of portentous strength, handling a gigantic club, making every kind of ferocious gesticulation, and, at the same time, to profess that all this is done in the most friendly and courteous manner. Now, that seems to me precisely what has been done by Her Majesty's Government in this particular case.[52]

As Bright noted in his diary that evening, 'Palmerston replied civilly, and well from his point of view: he believes in force and in force only.'[53]

The Proclamation of Emancipation

As tensions between Britain and the USA continued in 1862, the slavery question became ever more important. Bright saw that once

President Lincoln had stated explicitly that the Union was fighting for the abolition of slavery, many supporters of the Confederacy in Britain would have to change their position or face censure. Thus, the likelihood of Britain recognising the Confederacy – and effectively declaring war – would be greatly lessened. However, at the same time, he was measured in his approach, fully aware that by urging war on behalf of the slaves he would also be urging Britain to drop its policy of peaceful neutrality and declare itself as a wartime ally of the Northern states.

On 28 July 1862, the *Alabama*, a cruiser built for the Confederate States, set sail down the Mersey from Birkenhead, leaving British–US relations scattered in its wake. Practically every aspect of the affair caused outrage in America as well as with those in Britain who favoured the North. The ship had been built by Messrs Laird and Co., the family shipbuilding firm of the Conservative MP for Birkenhead, John Laird, and even before the ship set sail it was widely known that it was being built as a war vessel for Confederate forces. There were others in the pipeline, including some for the Royal Navy. The American ambassador to London, Charles Francis Adams, had written to the foreign secretary, Lord Russell, requesting that the ship be detained. The Government had plenty of time to act under the Foreign Enlistment Act, but Lord Russell dithered, asking for proof, legal advice, further proof and a second legal opinion. By the time he was content that the case for detaining the ship was sound and had telegraphed the Custom House at Liverpool on 29 July, it was too late. The ship had sailed the previous day. Once safely at sea, the *Alabama* raised the Confederate flag and the Captain appeared on deck in full Confederate uniform. To make matters worse, most of the crew were English, some even being members of the Royal Naval Reserve and, as such, received pay from the British Government.

In August, Lincoln reiterated to Horace Greeley that

> My paramount objective in this struggle is to save the Union, and is not either to save or destroy slavery. If I could save the Union without freeing any slave, I would do it; and if I could save it by freeing all the slaves, I would do it; and if I could do it by freeing some and leaving others alone, I would also do that. What I do about Slavery, and the colored race, I do because I believe it helps to save the Union; and what I forbear, I forbear because I do not believe it would help to save the Union.

He added that this was his 'official duty; and I intend no modification of my oft-expressed personal wish that all men every where could be free'.[54]

Lincoln was showing some willingness to set aside his valid doubts about the legality of banning slavery without the support of a united House of Representatives and make a stand using his vague 'war powers'. Yet, as Sumner reported to Bright,

> He is hard to move ... I urged him on the 4th of July to put forth an edict of emancipation, telling him he could make the day more sacred and historic than ever. He replied, 'I would do it if I were not afraid that half the officers would fling down their arms and three more States would rise.'[55]

On 22 July 1862, Lincoln had told his Cabinet that

> I felt we ... must change our tactics, or lose the game. I now determined upon the adoption of the emancipation policy ... I prepared the original draft of the proclamation, and ... I said to the Cabinet that I ... had not called them together to ask their advice, but to lay the subject matter of a proclamation before them, suggestions as to which would be in order, after they had heard it read.[56]

Whatever his instincts, Lincoln at this time was teetering on the edge of political uncertainty in what were clearly difficult circumstances, and was in need not only of external advice, but also moral support. This he gained from a number of his closest friends and associates, but also from Bright, whose influence in English Government and Parliament and popular opinion, based on his moral repudiation of slavery, would soon be decisive in international relations.

That a proclamation was of dubious legality and unenforceable, affecting as it did only those parts of the country over which Lincoln could not at that time assert his authority, was beside the point. It was a statement of principle necessary to fire up the Union troops and to silence any neutral powers wavering in the direction of the Confederacy. To ensure its effectiveness, and on Seward's advice, Lincoln was now waiting for a Northern victory, sensing that a declaration made during times of defeat could be construed as a sign of desperation rather than a strong statement of principle. The victory that Lincoln had been waiting for came on 17 September 1862 at the Battle of Antietam, and five days later he issued his famous Emancipation Proclamation.

Post-Proclamation to the End of the Civil War

In England, Bright was proved right in his earlier hopes of increased support following the proclamation. However, the effect was far from universal. One notable figure among those whose loyalties remained unaffected was Gladstone, emerging as the most forceful of the Whigs on the issue, being more pro-South than even the Conservative Party leadership. Gladstone's moral earnestness was attenuated by an atavistic sympathy for the South. In October 1862, he gave a speech at Newcastle in which he stated that, 'There is no doubt that Jefferson Davis and other leaders of the South have made an Army. They are making, it appears, a Navy; and they have made – what is more than either – they have made a Nation.'[57] Bright was incensed. He could accept that his bitter enemy, Palmerston, would wish to see the Union fragmented, and therefore weakened, but for Gladstone to join him was unbearable. He could not accept that Gladstone could allow his Christian and Liberal morals to be subsumed by what Bright no doubt presumed was a subconscious toleration of slavery linked to the fact that the Gladstone family fortune derived from it. As Bright wrote to Sumner, 'He is unstable as water in some things; he is for union and freedom in Italy, and for disunion and bondage in America.'[58]

For his part, Gladstone later said that his support for the South was 'an undoubted error, the most singular and palpable, I may add the least excusable of them all.'[59] As to the constitutional issue of 'State Rights' and the rights of secession, these were swept aside, and perhaps never fully grasped in their historical implications. It was loyalty to the individual State that ranged men such as General Robert E Lee[60] on the side of the South. But in the dissension that led to the war, the constitutional question was inextricably mixed with the maintenance and extension of the Slave States. Bright viewed the Southern politicians as rebels within an organized State, in the same way as he later considered the Irish Nationalists of the Home Rule agitation as rebels when they resorted to violence and crime. Tellingly, as Travis Mills points out, 'nearly all the leading Liberals who afterwards adopted Gladstone's Irish Home Rule policy were at this time in favour of the South'.[61]

At Birmingham on 18 December 1862, Bright responded to Gladstone's assertion that the Confederacy would succeed, quoting Gray's *Elegy* to describe the South's supporters as those 'who seek to "wade through slaughter to a throne, and shut the gates of mercy on mankind'. He then reiterated his own vision for America:

I see one vast confederation, stretching from the frozen north to the glowing south, and from the wild billows of the Atlantic westward to the calmer waters of the Pacific main; and I see one people, and one language, and one law, and one faith, and over all that wide continent the home of freedom and a refuge for the oppressed of every race and of every clime.[62]

For Bright, being able to witness the first black President of the USA addressing the joint Houses of Parliament in ancient Westminster Hall in 2011 would have been a dream come true.

Sumner wrote to Bright on 28 October, thanking him for his support:

I wish I were at Llandudno, where for a day I could talk on our affairs and enjoy a little repose ... I have from the beginning seen that our only chance against the rebellion was by striking slavery; and it seemed to me that these mighty armaments on both sides, and their terrible shock, were intended to ensure its destruction. It is time for it to come to an end. I am grateful to you that you have kept your faith in us, and I pray you to persevere.[63]

Bright certainly did persevere. His clarion call of support across the Atlantic was joined at this critical time by others from Britain who were actively engaged on their own account and in concert with his campaign. For example, in November 1862, in response to the ambivalent attitudes within the British Government and the conflict between those who wanted to suppress the slave trade and those who did not – further complicated by the fact that Palmerston, Russell and Gladstone favoured the South – the London Emancipation Committee, founded in 1859 by Frederick Chesson and George Thompson, stepped up its activities and changed its name to the London Emancipation Society. With offices at 65 Fleet Street, its members included Bright himself and a host of other distinguished names including John Stuart Mill, Richard Cobden, Justin McCarthy, Samuel Lucas and Francis Newman (the brother of Cardinal Newman). As a mark of its faith in Lincoln, the Society passed a resolution on 15 January 1863 offering President Lincoln and his Cabinet 'its warmest congratulations on the auspicious aspect they have given to this new year, and joins with the President in invoking for these acts for freedom, justice and mercy, "the considerate judgement of mankind and the gracious favour of Almighty God".'[64]

Another group particularly heartened by the Emancipation Proclamation were many of the mill workers of northern England. As the supply of American cotton to the mills had dwindled as a result of the Union blockade of Confederate ports, they had been forced to accept shorter and shorter hours until the mills stopped production completely. Their basic needs were met by charity and relief work organized by benevolent industrialists and supporters of the North, but their goodwill relied on the belief that their sacrifice was worthwhile. Bright's own mill at Rochdale was forced to close its doors. As Bright wrote to his sister, Priscilla, in December 1861, 'We have no trade. Everything is in suspense. Buying and selling must soon be classed among the obsolete or forgotten arts.'[65] None the less, he continued to pay his workers two-thirds of their normal wages. Soup kitchens were set up to feed the town's starving workers. In such a situation, it might be expected that self-interest would prevail. Indeed, some Confederate cotton farmers attempted to hasten this expected result by burning their own cotton. Yet, as Trevelyan notes,

> Every one behaved in a manner worthy of the citizens of a great and free nation. Through all the prolonged distress there was no rioting, because the mill hands had the wit to perceive that they were not the victims of injustice. The moral and intellectual qualities of Lancashire were displayed to the world, and had their effect on opinion in both hemispheres.[66]

The South had its working-class supporters, often connected with the commercial interests of their employers in the building of ironclads and related activities.

Bright's speeches played a large part in educating a divided popular English opinion on the importance of the slavery question, even in their own reduced circumstances. Lincoln, with the issuing of the Emancipation Proclamation, reassured them that their sacrifice would be welcome and effective. In the meantime, those unemployed in Rochdale in Bright's own works had access to a newly established adult school. Elsewhere, mill hands were employed by the Government in an early form of job creation scheme, using an emergency fund of £200,000 (£14 million today) set up by Villiers, then president of the Poor Law Board, to carry out public works such as road repairs.

The cotton famine ended after 18 months of hardship, when supplies started to arrive from India, a solution that could have been achieved sooner had Bright's opponents listened to him in 1847, when he foresaw the destruction of the American slave system and the knock-on effect on English mills, and called for the increased planting of cotton in India. This was clearly on his mind when he wrote to his wife on 19 July 1862,

> It is a sort of retribution on these Manchester people who are now howling for cotton, that they are now represented by a man who crawled on his belly in the mud before the East India Directors, and refused out of pure flunkeyism and spite of me, to do the only thing that could have averted the terrible disaster which is overtaking the great Manchester interest. If I did not grieve for the ignorant and powerless workers, I could almost be content to see the sufferings of those who, when time permitted it, refused to help provide for their own safety.[67]

In December 1862, Bright had also ensured that a tangible connection with the North was felt by the workers, by suggesting to Sumner that a gift be sent: He wrote:

> I see that some one in the States has proposed to send something to our aid ... If a few cargoes of flour could come, say 50,000 barrels, as a gift from persons in your Northern States to the Lancashire working men, it would have a prodigious effect in your favor here. Our working class is with you, and against the South, but such a token of your good will would cover with confusion all who talk against you.[68]

Early the next year, three ships loaded with American flour docked in Liverpool and their contents were distributed throughout the affected areas.

All this combined to create a true sense of purpose and a fierce loyalty to the anti-slavery cause. As Bright's daughter later recalled:

> We used to live for the transatlantic steamers that twice a week brought the anxiously expected news. America and its history, past and in the making, was the breath of our nostrils. It was a great time in Rochdale, with all its cotton workers in enforced idleness and so alive to the reason: a meeting was called in the town by a Liverpool Association of Southern sympathies, formed to promote the breaking up of the blockade. The lecturer delivered his address, and the meeting passed a Resolution censuring him for endeavouring to mislead them.[69]

On 6 December 1862, Bright wrote to Sumner that

> The anti-slavery sentiment here has been more called forth of late, especially since the Proclamation was issued, and I am confident that every day the supporters of the South among us find themselves in greater difficulty, owing to the course taken by your Government in reference to the Negro question ... The Proclamation, like everything else you have done, has been misrepresented – but it has had a large effect here, and men are looking with great interest to the 1st January [when the slaves were to be considered free] and hoping the President may be firm.[70]

Less than two months later, he was able to report that

> You will see what meetings are being held here in favour of your emancipation policy and of the North in general. I think in every town in the kingdom a public meeting would go by an overwhelming majority in favour of President Lincoln and of the North.[71]

On 26 March 1863, Bright gave a rousing speech at a meeting of trade unionists at St James's Hall in London, witnessed approvingly by Karl Marx, which had been convened to enable working men to express their support for the North. Rising to the occasion, Bright played heavily on class consciousness and linked his speech to the working-class vote, saying,

> Impartial history will tell that, when your statesmen were hostile or coldly neutral, when many of your rich men were corrupt, when your press – which ought to have instructed and defended – was mainly written to betray, the fate of a Continent and of its vast population being in peril, you clung to freedom with an unfaltering trust that God in His infinite mercy will yet make it the heritage of all His children.[72]

Lincoln further encouraged this upsurge of support in England when he sent a resolution to Bright through Sumner in April 1863. As Sumner wrote,

> Two days ago the President sent for me to come to him at once. When I arrived, he said that he had been thinking of a matter on which we had often spoken, the way in which English opinion

should be directed, and that he had drawn up a resolution embodying the ideas which he should hope to see adopted by public meetings in England. I enclose the resolution, in his autograph, as he gave it to me. He thought it might serve to suggest the point which he regarded as important.[73]

Lincoln's resolution read:

> Whereas, while heretofore States and nations have tolerated slavery, recently, for the first [time] in the world, an attempt has been made to construct a new nation, upon the basis of, and with the primary and fundamental object to maintain, enlarge and perpetuate human slavery; therefore, Resolved, That no such embryo State should ever be recognized by, or admitted into, the family of Christian and civilized nations; and that all Christian and civilized men everywhere should, by all lawful means, resist to the utmost such recognition and admission.[74]

With such a personal endorsement, and news of the increasing success of the Northern forces in battle, Bright's passion was equally reignited and he continued his campaign in England with gusto as challenges arose.

Throughout this time, the British-built *Alabama* had continued to sail the seas, destroying Union merchant ships by using the British flag as bait. The ship became a symbol of pro-Southern support in Britain, to both its supporters and detractors. For his part, Bright made it clear that he sympathized fully with the North in their fury over his country's part in the *Alabama* affair. The bitterness felt by the North was understandable, and Bright did not hold back in his condemnation of the situation, nor in his efforts to preserve the peace. As he had explained to his constituents in Birmingham in December 1862,

> She hoists the English flag when she wants to come alongside a ship; she sets a ship on fire in the night, and when, seeing fire, another ship bears down to lend help, she seizes it, and pillages and burns it. I think that, if we were citizens of New York, it would require a little more calmness than is shown in this country to look at all this as if it was a matter with which we had no concern.[75]

The lasting animosity between America and Britain over this matter, not to mention the protectionist Morrill Tariff imposed by the

Northern States, was exacerbated when it became known in 1863 that the family firm of John Laird, MP, was building further lucrative ironclads for the Confederate navy funded by speculators in both the South and the City of London. Once again, the prospect of war between England and America loomed large. As Sumner wrote to Bright on 30 March 1863:

> my chief anxiety now is on account of the ships said to be building for the rebels in England. If half of what is reported be true, then is the future dark; I do not like to penetrate it. If those ships get to sea our commerce is annihilated; but this would be the most trivial of the terrible consequences. Mr. Canning said once in the House of Commons: 'If a war must come, let it come in the shape of satisfaction to be demanded for injuries, etc. But, in God's name, let it not come in the paltry, pettifogging way of fitting out ships in our harbors to cruise for gain! At all events, let the country disdain to be sneaked into a war. If I wished for a guide in a system of neutrality, I should take that laid down by America,' etc. Pray avert this result.[76]

But Bright had already started fighting this latest threat three days earlier, when the issue had been raised in the House of Commons. Laird had stated that he would

> rather be handed down to posterity as the builder of a dozen Alabamas than as the man [Bright] who applies himself deliberately to set class against class, and to cry up the institutions of another country which, when they come to be tested, are of no value whatever, and which reduce the very name of liberty to an utter absurdity.[77]

Bright tried to calm the situation by emphasising to his American contacts that the British Government had never condoned the activities of Messrs Laird and Co., and that Russell's belated order to arrest the ship had in fact been confounded by those at the dockyard who had 'as it were, smuggled [the *Alabama*] out to sea before she was ready and before she was expected to go'.[78] Indeed, the stateside reaction to the *Alabama* incident prompted the Government to be more proactive in dealing with Laird this time. Yet Bright was sceptical about the Government's sincerity in clamping down on his activity, writing to John Bigelow at Paris in April 1863 that

You will have heard that our Government have seized a ship building in Liverpool for the Southern conspirators, and that they are manifesting some activity in regard to other vessels building for the same respectable concern. I hope they are in earnest; but I never trust them in anything – there is much more baseness than of magnanimity in the policy of our ruling class. But I hear that Mr Adams observes a sensible change in the tone and conduct of our Foreign Office towards his Government, and I hope this is true and that the change is sincere. I am sure that if the news from the States becomes more and more favourable to your Government, then our Government will become more and more civil to yours. There will be plenty of dirt for our people (our Government) to eat if you should succeed in restoring the Union, and I shall not make a wry face if they have to eat it.[79]

Anti-Northern feeling, however, continued in many quarters in Britain. Confederate victories were on the rise and a Northern defeat seemed imminent. In three days in April 1863, £9 million in subscriptions was raised in London to support a Confederate loan, which later grew to £16 million[80] – an amount equal to £1.16 billion today. Then, on 30 June 1863, a resolution was proposed in the House of Commons by John Roebuck, the radical MP who represented the steel-making town of Sheffield, that Britain should make an alliance with Napoleon III to support the Confederacy. Bright launched a fierce attack on Roebuck, shaking him 'as a terrier shakes a rat' as one observer noted,[81] before cleverly appealing to the various positions taken by those in the House. Aware that many Members were increasingly unable to justify their support for the South now that they had been forced to admit that the conflict was about more than the Union, and having routed his enemies, Bright called upon their humanity. He asked,

How many Members are there who can say with me that the most innocent, the most pure, the most holy joy, which in their past years they have felt, or in their future years they have hoped for, has not arisen from contact and association with our precious children?

before pointing out that 150,000 such children were born into slavery every year in the Southern States 'amongst these "gentlemen", amongst this chivalry, amongst these men that we can make our friends?'[82]

However, while Roebuck's resolution was under debate in the House of Commons, the war suddenly turned in favour of the North. The crucial Union victories at Gettysburg and Vicksburg in the first week of July forced Confederate supporters in Britain to rethink their position. The debate was adjourned, never to be resumed. At the end of July, Bright reported to Sumner:

> I need not tell you with what feelings of gratification and relief I have received the news of your recent successes. The debate on the foolish Roebuck proposition took place when there was much gloom over your prospects, and the friends of Secesh here were rejoicing in the belief that your last hour had come. How soon are the clouds cleared away; and how great is now the despondency of those who have dishonoured themselves by their hatred of your people and Government. The [Confederate] loan is down near 20 per cent in a little more than a week and is now, I suspect, unsaleable, and people are rubbing their eyes, and wondering where the invincible South is gone to. Our Pro-slavery newspapers are desperately puzzled and the whole mass of opinion is in confusion.[83]

Bright did not wish for too hasty an end to the conflict, however. As he wrote to Villiers in August, in a very unpacifistic mood, 'I want no end of the war, and no compromise, and no re-union till the negro is made free beyond all chance of failure.'[84]

Throughout this period, furious negotiations had also been taking place over the Laird ironclads. Bright spent many hours discussing Laird's ships with Charles Francis Adams, who was also in contact with Lord Russell, and by the time Adams belatedly wrote to Russell formally requesting the ships' detention on 5 September 1863 with the words 'It would be superfluous of me to point out to your lordship that this is an act of war,'[85] the Government's support was secure. Russell issued instructions to detain the ships. Later that week, Bright wrote to Sumner, noting the change in attitude of the Government:

> You will hear by the mail that the iron-clad steam rams are detained by the Government ... I suppose the changed position of your affairs has helped our Foreign Office to the decision they have come to! Lord Russell has just made a short speech at Dundee, and he has said nothing foolish, which shows that there is an opening of the eyes among our statesmen, as to the prospects of your war.

At the same time, he reaffirmed that 'The Union is only good and great when a Union of Freedom, and any compromise which gives up the Proclamation will be the most deplorable event in history. It will be a curse on your reputation which no time can remove.'[86]

By 1864, the Northern forces were firmly on the offensive and more Britons – including even Palmerston and Russell – became reconciled by events to the Union cause. While Bright welcomed this increase in support, he bemoaned the fact that it appeared to be based on factors other than issues of right and wrong. Writing to Sumner in February 1864, he said,

> But what a miserable thing to see our friendliness and our justice depending on your strength! When you seemed weak and staggering under the weight of the insurrection, the Prime Minister and his law officer continued to insult you; when you are strong and the revolt is staggering under your blows, they speak gently and pay you compliments. This statesmanship is a very low morality, and I despise it from my heart.[87]

Bright's work for America was done. For the remainder of the war, he would watch events unfold as the Northern armies claimed victory after victory. He kept up his correspondence with his American friends and in June 1864 twice met Levi Coffin, a leading American Quaker from Indiana and in the Underground Railroad. He recorded in his diary that, 'L.C. is a quiet "back country" Friend, who has devoted himself to the assistance of the fugitive slaves. Not less than 3,000 of them have passed through his hands during the last 30 years ... L.C. comes here to try to interest us in the condition of the Freedmen, and I hope he may succeed'[88] – the Schindler or Winton of his time.

Five days later, the infamous *Alabama* was sunk off Cherbourg. Bright found the wait for news of the progress of the war difficult. As he wrote to Sumner in September 1864,

> There is great uncertainty of opinion. It fluctuates with the varying news from week to week, and men become puzzled with the long-continued strife. For myself I am rendered unhappy very often by your disasters, and all my efforts to harden myself against the anxiety which oppresses me are unsuccessful.[89]

Tragically, however, when the Confederate forces finally surrendered at Appomattox on 9 April 1865, Bright was in no mood to celebrate.

By the time the news of the Confederate surrender reached Britain, he was immersed in a fresh grief, having buried his dear friend Richard Cobden on 7 April (see Chapter 3). As he wrote to Sumner, 'Cobden is taken from us. It seemed that half my life were buried with him in that grave.'[90] Cobden's passing had compounded Bright's grief over the death of his third son, five-year-old Leonard, the previous year. Just over a week later, on 16 April, Bright lost his brother-in law, close friend and colleague, Samuel Lucas, to a sudden illness. Lucas's interest in the American Civil War is recorded in the rare inscription on his tombstone at Highgate Cemetery, which was listed as being of special historic interest in 2007:

> Here rest the remains of Samuel Lucas aged 54. He died on the 16th April, 1865, a few hours after hearing the tidings of the destruction of the slave power in the United States, by the fall of Richmond; an object which he had unceasingly laboured to promote as managing proprietor of the Morning Star.

Despite his massive grief, Bright's sense of triumph at the surrender is clear from his diary entry for 23 April:

> News received of the surrender of Lee and his army to General Grant. This may be taken to be the end of the great and wicked rebellion. Slavery has measured itself with Freedom, and Slavery has perished in the struggle. How often have I longed and prayed for this result, and how much have I suffered from anxiety while it has been slowly working out, I only know! This great triumph of the Republic is the event of our age, and future ages will confess it, for they will be better able than this is to estimate the gain to freedom and humanity which will spring from it. I have had an almost unfaltering faith from the beginning, and I now rejoice more than I can tell that the cause of personal freedom and free government has triumphed. The friends of freedom everywhere should thank God and take courage. They may believe that the world is not forsaken by Him who made and rules it.[91]

In a letter to his wife on the same day, emphasizing his own personal moral convictions, Bright exclaimed, 'What a grand result! White and black are henceforth alike free on the American continent! I seem to have more reason to rejoice than most others, for I have had more anxiety and more faith. It is another proof that He who made the world still rules it, and will not forsake it.'[92]

Four days after hearing of the surrender of Robert E. Lee came the dreadful news of Lincoln's assassination. Bright's next diary entry reads,

> For an hour or near it, I felt stunned and ill. It is a terrible event, but it will not affect the issue of the great struggle, tho' it may change some of its details. I will not write an eulogy on the character of President Lincoln. There will be many to do that now he is dead ... In him I have observed a singular resolution honestly to do his duty, a great courage, shown in the fact that in his speeches and writings no word of passion or of panic, or of ill-will, has ever escaped him; a great gentleness of temper and nobleness of soul proved by the absence of irritation and menace under circumstances of the most desperate provocation, and a pity and mercifulness to his enemies which seemed drawn as from the very fount of Christian charity and love. His simplicity for a time did much to hide his greatness, but all good men everywhere will mourn for him, and history will place him high among the best and noblest of men.[93]

He wrote to Sumner on the same day:

> For fifty years, I think, no other event has created such a sensation in this country as the great crime which has robbed you of your President ... In times of great excitement, dangerous men become more dangerous, partly vicious, and partly mad, and men of great mark become the objects of their hate and passion. The deed is done, and it is now too late to take precautions.

He ended with the simple words, 'It is easy to kill a President, but it is not easy to destroy a nation.'[94]

Despite this concentrated period of personal tragedy, triumph and sadness, Bright's mind was still focused on the moral course. He was alarmed at the cries for vengeance coming from the victorious North, where Sumner had reported that 'public opinion insists upon executions'.[95] On 16 May 1865, he wrote a long and detailed letter to Sumner on the issue, appealing for mercy in the Government's dealings with the captured rebel leaders. Stating that he believed capital punishments to be 'barbarous and needless', he argued that 'a "Bloody Assize" in every Southern State' would be a tactical as well as a moral mistake:

One of the great objects of your Government now should be to
change the character of the South, to root out the brutality and
cruelty which have sprung from Slavery, to create a reverence for
human life, and to prove the mercy no less than the justice of
your Federal Government. To hang any of these men will exas-
perate multitudes. You must remember that in the rebellion
millions have been involved, and have regarded their leaders with
confidence, and often with admiration ... They will therefore
look upon their execution ... as an act of vengeance, savage,
needless and unjustifiable.

His letter ended with the words,

To me this appears the wise course and the great course ... It will
add incalculably to the force of your example if now in the hour
of triumph you can show the same moral grandeur that you have
displayed during your mortal conflict.[96]

After the War

One final Anglo-American conflict in which Bright's intervention
was needed occurred after the war had ended, when the US
Government demanded reparation from Britain for the damages
inflicted by the *Alabama* on American commerce. Lincoln had previously made clear his determination to call Britain to account. When
the claim was first made in May 1865, the British Government
was willing for this to be pursued. However, the prospect of an
amicable agreement was ruined in 1867 when President Johnson's
Government escalated the claim to include thousands of millions of
dollars for 'indirect damages' resulting from Britain's actions, which
they claimed had prolonged the war. Bright, who had been corresponding amicably with Charles Sumner for some time on the question of reparation, was astounded to discover that his friend shared
this view. In his diary on 9 May 1869 he records: 'Charles Sumner's
speech, so hostile and vindictive, has caused me much pain and
disappointment.'[97] Yet, as Travis Mills notes, his subsequent letter was
'pervaded from the first word to the last by justice and moderation':[98]

I have always condemned the act of our Government in regard
to the question of belligerent rights I thought it unnecessary at
the time, ungracious and unfriendly, and calculated to irritate
and to injure you, and I have said this in Parliament and out of it;

but I have never seen any conclusive argument to show that it was a breach of international law, or a course which our Government was not entitled legally to take under the circumstances. It was a foolish act, an unfriendly act, at the moment an unnecessary act, and it was done at a bad time and in a bad manner, and for all this you had reason to feel irritated and aggrieved; but to me it seems a matter wholly different from the Alabama question, in which I fear and believe there was a distinct breach of a well-known international law, and one which is capable of proof, and where the damage inflicted can be fairly valued ... I condemn the act as strongly as you do, but I cannot believe that any existing Government in the world would consent that its conduct in such a matter should be put to reference, or that it would consent to pay money, or to make an apology for having done what it had a legal right to do ... I have said nothing of this question in public and probably shall say nothing, but I am compelled to say to you that I think you will put yourselves in the wrong before the world in refusing an agreement based upon a reference on the question as to the damages done by the ships which were fitted out in this country. Beyond this I think our Government will not go, and in their decision I believe they will be sustained by the whole public opinion of the nation.[99]

Ever practical, Bright also devised an arbitration scheme, not unlike his proposals for arbitration during the *Trent* Affair as far back as 1861. Gladstone and the foreign secretary approved. It was set out in a letter to J. C. Hamilton of New York and shown to President Johnson and his Cabinet. His proposals subsequently formed the essentials of a treaty made in Geneva in 1872. Writing on this successful conclusion of a long dispute, Bright said,

> The great virtue of the treaty, beyond the settlement of a dangerous dispute, is the exhibition and adoption by two great nations of a principle of fairness and reason in its settlement, and, as we may trust, in the adjustment of any future question that may arise between them. I believe if the English Government had shown the same wise and just disposition in times past, almost all wars with European powers since the days of William III might have been avoided.[100]

Many accounts of John Bright's relations with America end with the conclusion of the Civil War. However, his compassionate interest in the wellbeing of its institutions and people never ceased. As previously noted, on 29 June 1867, Bright presided over a breakfast at St James's Hall in London in honour of the visiting American abolitionist, William Lloyd Garrison. He praised the clemency of the victors in the Civil War, with the words,

> An ancient and renowned poet has said 'Unholy is the voice of loud thanksgiving over slaughtered men.' It becomes us not to rejoice but to be humbled that a chastisement so terrible should have fallen on any of our race; but we may be thankful for this – that this chastisement was at least not sent in vain.[101]

His diary entries during his later years show that he continued his friendships with influential American public figures such as Charles Adams, Cyrus Field and the editor of Sumner's papers, E. L. Pierce. With these and others, he spent many evenings discussing stateside affairs, while keeping up a transatlantic correspondence with many more. In November 1872, he welcomed Charles Sumner as an overnight guest and had a 'Long and pleasant talk with him'.[102]

The appreciation of Americans for Bright's support during the war also came in the form of gifts. O'Brien recounts how, after Bright's death, he saw at One Ash, the Bright family home, a gold-headed cane which bore the inscriptions 'J. A. McClernand to the Hon A. Lincoln, June 1857' and

> Presented to the Rev Jas Smith, D.D., late pastor of First Presbyterian Church, Springfield Ills, by the family of the late President Lincoln in memoriam of the high esteem in which he was held by him and them as their pastor and dear friend, 27th April, 1868.

When Reverend Smith died in 1871, he in turn bequeathed the cane ('the very cane which the chivalrous Stephen Douglas held in his hand on the steps of the Capitol while his rival delivered his great Inaugural', Travis Mills reports)[103] to John Bright 'because of his unwearied zeal and defence of the United States in suppressing the civil rebellion of the Southern States'.[104] The cane was treasured at One Ash, as was one of the portraits of Lincoln given to Bright in 1861 by the president himself, which hung in the library. Another gift came from the 'National Association for the Relief of Destitute Colored Women and Children' in Washington, D.C., who sent to

Bright in 1867 an afghan blanket that had also previously belonged to President Lincoln.[105]

However, despite being informed that he was 'the most popular man in America'[106] and receiving a stream of invitations, Bright never visited these friends in their home country. His dislike of travelling, particularly by sea, no doubt played a significant part in this decision, but in the early years following the Civil War, an equally important factor was his natural humility. As Trevelyan notes, he was 'a democrat who sympathised with the masses without desiring their applause'.[107] Bright himself wrote to one friend,

> I fear I am getting too far on in life to cross the ocean, unless I saw some prospect of being useful, and had some duty clearly before me … Mr Walker and many others alarm me by telling me I should have a reception that would astonish me. What they promise me would be a great affliction, for I am not ambitious of demonstrations on my behalf.[108]

Not even an invitation to the White House by President Hayes would change his mind. The president made the invitation in a letter written on 14 July 1879, assuring the recently widowed Bright (Elizabeth having died in May 1878) that

> It will give Mrs Hayes and myself the greatest pleasure to receive you as our guest at Washington, at such time and as long as may comport with your own comfort and convenience; and you will find in all parts of the country a disposition to make your stay with us in all respects agreeable to your own wishes in respect to the measure and the modes of our hospitality.[109]

The following month, Bright recorded in his diary:

> Wrote to the President of the United States thanking him for his invitation to be his guest if I would visit America; also to Mr. Evarts, Secretary of State, in answer to his kind letter. Explained why I cannot cross the Atlantic. I shrink from the excitement.[110]

In this letter, he also wrote,

> You refer to the course I took during the great trial through which your country passed from 1860 to 1865. I was anxious that your continent should be the home of freedom, and that, as respects

your country and my own, although we are two nations, we should only be one people. Hence I rejoice now in your union, your freedom, and your growing influence and prosperity.[111]

Nevertheless, even in his last years, Bright greatly appreciated the affection in which he was held by Americans. In one of the last entries of his diary, he recorded a dinner with the American ambassador in July 1887:

I sat between the U.S. Minister at Madrid and one of his countrymen ... I recd. many compliments and expressions of kindness from Americans present. They said no other man in Europe would be received with so much enthusiasm of welcome as I should if I crossed the Atlantic.[112]

It was never to be, but his legacy lives on.

CHAPTER 6

A Just Foreign Policy for India and the Empire

Bright had a hand in the making of modern India. His services to her were so vast and of such a character that his memory will ever be green in the minds of the Indian people.
(P. N. Raman Pillai, *Indian Review*, August 1911)

The historian, Romesh Chunder Dutt, wrote in 1904 in his trenchant book *India in the Victorian Age*, before memories had faded and just as Gandhi was beginning his campaigns,

> It may be said without exaggeration that John Bright filled the same place in the House of Commons in the middle of the nineteenth century that Edmund Burke had done in the last decades of the eighteenth. Their endeavours to render justice to a vast Eastern Dependency will lie in the memory of mankind when England's empire shall have passed away. And their published utterances will be read as among the finest specimens of English prose, possibly when the present English language shall have ceased to be a spoken tongue.[1]

Bright's involvement in the countries of the Empire was characteristic of his moral sense and practical administrative approach. The Empire was militarily and economically controlled from Whitehall and Westminster. As with Ireland, Bright tackled the abuses with vigour. He encouraged freedom of trade and compassion for the local populations under the Crown, but with moral principle and mutual respect. Bright harked back to the conservatism of Edmund Burke and his instruction, which insisted on the universality of the moral law and trust as the basis for governance in India. Bright

extended this to other parts of the British Empire. Freedom of trade
was the touchstone for Bright and Cobden. Both were profoundly
influenced by Adam Smith's *Wealth of Nations* and his criticisms of
the East India Company, shared by Burke, that it was impossible
simultaneously to run a country on moral principles and exploit it
commercially. Indeed, Smith's notions were inimical to the Empire
because, for him, expenditure on overseas possessions was a burden
on the taxpayer. Free trade was the mainspring for Bright and
Cobden but, unlike Smith and David Ricardo, Bright applied a
more modern criteria, the morality of 'fair trade', because of his
respect for the governed as well as the governors. Bright believed in
the universality of free trade, but not unfair global trading conditions, and would have disapproved of unfair European Union (EU)
dumping or the idea of arms sales. He would surely also have
campaigned against the injustice of Third-World debt. Bright
upheld imperial free trade in June 1848 when he moved an amendment to repeal sugar duties, despite the hardship this would place on
West Indian plantations when beet sugar came to Europe. For him,
sugar duties were on a par with the Corn Laws and promoted agricultural inefficiency in the colonies. With both the protectionists and
anti-slavery lobby against him, Bright's amendment was defeated by
302 to 36 votes.[2]

The nineteenth-century Empire raised complex questions. As
H. T. Manning pointed out, doubts about the value of the Empire
followed the American Revolution, when it was proved that the
benefits of trade did not depend on control of the countries abroad.[3]
Others, such as James Stephen,[4] emphasized the costs and burdens
of responsibility of the Empire. Stephen, like Bright, believed in
temporary British rule geared to the interests of the governed. As
James Sturgis points out, these views were at odds with the traditional British approach, which aimed 'to strengthen as much as
possible the ties with the mother country' and grant constitutions
'designed to reproduce the conditions of the more stratified British
society'.[5]

This traditional model of Empire was to Bright a magnification of
aristocratic privilege, against which he railed throughout his life, and
his remedy for the unjust treatment of the British colonies ran on
similar lines to those for the working classes of England. Britain's
primary responsibility was to prepare its colonies for self-government by creating solid economic conditions in which the people
could thrive, removing stifling economic obligations and creating
democratic institutions.

It was all very well to talk about 'this great empire' but, for his
own part, he could not help thinking that unless the colonies and
dependencies which were united to England were inhabited by a
free, happy, contented, and prosperous population, it would be
infinitely better for the English Crown and the English people to
abandon the thought of dependencies, altogether, and to be
content with this tight little island of their own.[6]

Bright did not call for the dissolution of the Empire but believed in
the gradual reversal of direct control, the development of the colonies
and the eventual end of British rule. However, as Sturgis points out,
'neither did he favour [the Empire's] dismemberment except under
circumstances where a particular colony desired independence'.[7] His
views were not unlike those in the Durham Report of 1839, nudging
towards self-government where possible. Even if he did desire the
breaking up of the Empire, he did not see how it could be achieved:
'give up all the colonies and dependencies of the Empire? Can any
Statesman do this, or can any country do this? I doubt it.'[8]

Bright believed that each colony was different and that the
Empire, which covered much of North America, the West Indies,
Australasia, South Asia and the Cape of Good Hope, housed a spec-
trum of societies in varying stages of democratic development.

'John Britain'

Bright had a particular interest in India. He believed that Parliament
could influence the government of India for the good, and that
Britain had a duty to govern the country properly, with the practical
co-operation of the people and with moral purpose.

Bright's first speech of any significance about India was in
Rochdale in 1832, in a vote of thanks to James Silk Buckingham, the
founder of the Athenaeum, who had given a lecture on India. 'We
have had bad Government in Ireland,' he said. 'It has often been said
and with some show of truth that India is about twenty Irelands put
together.'[9] He confided to Cobden in 1850, however, that because
India was so vast, he worried that he might be wasting his time, not
because he thought the object should not be pursued, but because it
was such an enormous task.[10]

This early interest in India refutes the later accusations during
the American Civil War of a conflict of interest in promoting
Indian cotton, as opposed to cotton from the American South.
Bright's refusal of Southern cotton was based on his antipathy to slave

labour and damaged his own business. His interest in Indian cotton was accompanied by seeking the practical improvement of Indian cotton operations, supplies, transport and navigation as well as improving the governance of India to provide greater self-government and commercial benefit to the Indian population rather than to the primary benefit of the East India Company and its shareholders.

In May 1847, Bright pressed for an inquiry into alternatives to slave cotton from the Deep South. As early as 1846 he had pointed out that the price of raw cotton had gone up by 40 per cent during a seven-month period that year[11] and there was growing aspiration in the 1840s, with the repeal of the Corn Laws and the pressure for free trade combined with the growth of English manufacturing, particularly in Lancashire and the North, for a reliable and available alternative source of cotton.

A Select Committee chaired by Lord George Bentinck in 1848 looked into the question of sugar and coffee in the West Indies. John Bagshawe, MP, noted the disadvantages experienced by India in competition with other British dependencies and demonstrated that the East India Company was lining its pockets without benefiting either India or Britain, and the cotton industry was being severely neglected.

A new Select Committee was appointed in 1848 to look into the growing of cotton in India, with John Bright, then representing Manchester, in the chair. Evidence from the Manchester Chamber of Commerce showed that, of all the cotton imported into England, less than 15 per cent came from India in the period 1837 to 1846, the bulk coming from the USA.[12] Bright's report of the Select Committee on Indian Cotton was published on 17 July 1848, and stated it was satisfied that India could produce improved cotton, but that the cultivators of Indian cotton, particularly in Madras and Bombay, were 'in the most abject condition'[13] – the consequence of Government rent and tax policy, bad administration, appalling roads and a lack of railways.

Bright criticized the 'double government' of the East India Company on the one hand and the Board of Control on the other, with the former interested in dividends rather than in running India properly. He insisted that the complex legislation and the Charter left Parliament 'deluded and baffled whenever it attempted to lay hold of anything connected with India'.[14] He complained that 'divided responsibility, of concealed responsibility, and of no responsibility whatever; that was the real pith of the matter'.[15]

The following year, at the request of the Manchester Chamber of Commerce, Bright called for a Royal Commission to be sent to

India, a proposal that had been supported by Sir Robert Peel before his death in 1846, but the Government refused.

Calls for Reform, 1850

In 1850, Bright turned his attention to Ceylon (Sri Lanka), where the Governor, Lord Torrington, had been forced to resign following a disastrous period of martial law in the Kandy province. The ensuing insurrection had been bloody and Torrington had been accused of using unnecessarily severe measures to put it down. The matter was investigated by a Select Committee, the evidence of which Bright and Joseph Hume considered to be inadequate.

By this time, Bright was promoting self-government as the way forward for the colonies, linking this to the struggle for parliamentary reform at home. At reform meetings, he alluded to the similarities between the unenfranchised masses in Britain and the colonies under direct British rule. In Manchester on 29 January, 1850 he asked,

> How is it that our colonial government remains unreformed, when it is notorious that wherever there is a British colony there is constant discontent and dissatisfaction with the Colonial Office and threats (not uttered in whispered tones) that they will throw off their allegiance as soon as they are able? And why is it that the glorious Empire over which, by fraud and force, this country has obtained a mastery, with its hundred millions of inhabitants, is left to drag on its decaying and miserable existence in ignorance and cruelty under the rule of Leadenhall-street?[16]

He criticized individual governors – whom he thought were either military types or men with 'a bad banking account, but had at the same time some claim upon a political party'[17] – if they proved themselves unworthy, on the basis that

> almost the only tie which connects our Colonies with the mother country is the tie of the colonial government, and probably nothing in the whole colonial system is more important than the appointment of the individuals who in those Colonies shall represent the Crown.[18]

In 1851, he criticized the Governor of the Cape, Sir Harry Smith, for his bellicose and racist attitude towards native inhabitants and said, 'If he were a colonist at the Cape, he would say, "Give us a Government of our own, let us carry on our own affairs, and we shall go on without entering into these barbarous and horrible wars."' He pointed out that Britons 'by the exercise of mercy and justice' co-existed peacefully with native populations elsewhere and, if such a policy were extended to the Africans, 'we should not be involved in these cruel and sanguinary struggles'.[19]

Bright had been concerned about such clashes between the British and native tribes for some time. In 1848, he suggested that the conflicts between New Zealand settlers and the Maoris might be diminished if the colony had self-government and had to fund its own wars, rather than relying on British coffers with little consideration of the alternatives to violence.[20]

Government of India Bill, 1853

Despite Bright's proposals for a Royal Commission on India being rejected, his 1848 Select Committee Report on Indian Cotton was followed by an assessment of the East India Company's Charter, which was coming up for renewal. This led to further Select Committees of both Houses in 1852 and 1853 on the East India Company, and on the system created by William Pitt the Younger in 1784 of double government through the Company and the Board of Control, with patronage under the control of the Company. This had generated serious corruption and exploitation of India, made worse by the fact that many members of the East India Company sat in the House of Commons, lining their pockets, a situation severely criticized by Bright in 1853.

Bright took an intense interest in a new body, the India Reform Society, created in March 1853 to press for reform of the Company Charter. It was much influenced by John Dickinson, the son of a paper manufacturer whose family ties and knowledge of India had inspired him to found the Society with two MPs, Henry Danby Seymour and John Blackett. According to Dickinson, Bright 'was the backbone of our committee and he brought with him into our ranks about thirty MPs'.[21] These included close acquaintances of Bright, such as his cousin, Frederick Lucas, and Milner Gibson.

Sir Charles Wood's Government of India Bill in June 1853 sought to reform the East India Company, reducing the number of directors and introducing competition for appointments, but did not provide for the termination of the new Charter. Bright was gravely concerned and, in correspondence with Joseph Sturge shortly before the Bill, stated his intention 'to overthrow the East India Compy, & to establish a Govt. here responsible to Parlt. & to public opinion'.[22]

He argued for the removal of the double government, and that 'India should be governed in the manner most consistent with the true dignity of this country and with the true interests of India herself.'[23] He argued that Britain should do

> justice to the people ... by a wise and judicious administration, which would convince the educated Natives of India, that although there was some humiliation in being governed by a foreign country ... she derived enormous advantages from her connexion with this Empire, where Government was based upon experience, civilisation, and justice.[24]

He criticized the government of India bitterly, saying that, despite being eligible since 1833 to hold office in the East India Company, 'No native had, in the twenty years which had since elapsed, been appointed to any office in pursuance of that clause.'[25] Bright complained that he was refused answers to his questions relating to education in India. Out of a population of 100 million, there were only 25,000 children being educated and, out of a gross revenue of £29 million, only £66,000 was spent on education. He argued that the people of India were 'in a state of poverty, and of decay, unexampled in the annals of the country under their native rulers'.[26]

Bright predicted that with a free press and with more Indians studying English there would be greater unrest unless there was justice for the Indian people. He further argued that, from 1835 to 1851, British taxation of India produced £340 million, which was less than the cost of administration. A mere £5 million was spent on public works, but the dividends paid out to owners of East India stock totalled £10 million, while the Company had raised loans of £16 million. 'This seems to me to be a formidable, an alarming state of things,' Bright remarked. India, he said, was being exploited and undermined. 'Educate the people of India, and govern them wisely, and gradually the distinctions of caste would disappear, and they would look upon us rather as benefactors than as conquerors.'[27]

India, 1854–7

In 1854, the House of Commons agreed on proper financial accounts for India. Bright criticized the extortionate methods of

taxation and argued strongly that there should be a greater employment of Indians in their own government. The East India Company
had prevented the creation of a university in Calcutta, he said, and
that the way things were going could lead to rebellion. He criticized
severely the way in which Indian judges were paid so little and
strongly endorsed the Torture Commission's conclusions that
Indians were sometimes tortured to raise taxes. In particular, he criticized Sir James Hogg, an MP with strong East India Company
connections, saying, 'It was part of the system of the Government to
which the hon. Baronet belonged to suppress all such impertinent
exposures by dogmatic assertion and arrogant abuse.'[28]

Bright also argued continuously for better communications and
roads, and irrigation. The same year, he put a plan devised by Sir
Arthur Cotton to improve the irrigation on rivers in India to
the Manchester Chamber of Commerce. This was turned down
because they took the view that American cotton was both available
and reliable, a view soon to be disproved by the American Civil War.
None the less, Bright's Select Committee report and active promotion of the improvement of communications in India did bear fruit,
and Lord Aberdeen's Government backed investment in Indian
infrastructure.

The Times, after initial misgivings, strongly supported Bright's
policy on India. The newspaper had even gone so far as to say
in 1853 that if he were to get his way in relation to India, 'Mr
Bright will be made the greatest man of his day.'[29] He was also
strongly supported by the *Manchester Examiner and Times*. Samuel
Lucas took a special interest in Indian matters, influenced in
part by his brother, Frederick Lucas, who had been an early
member of the India Reform Society before his death in 1855. By
1857, the *Morning Star* was publishing as many as 30,000 copies
a day, and Lucas, assisted by Bright, had persuaded experts
on Indian affairs, such as A. H. Layard, H. Meade and John
Hamilton, to contribute articles regularly to the paper. The newspaper shared Bright's deep commitment to the idea of decentralization in India and that the country's future was dependent on reform
in the House of Commons, and gave Bright the space to promote
these views.

In August 1857, when the Birmingham Liberals offered Bright
a seat following his ejection from Manchester, it was on the
understanding that he would not oppose the putting down of the
Indian Mutiny; indeed, that he would support it. Bright had long
been deeply opposed to war in India and Burma, saying of the

conflict in February 1853, 'of all the atrocious and unjustifiable wars which have been carried on by this country in India, I believe there is not one of a blacker character'.[30] He took a different view, however, of the Indian Mutiny. Despite efforts by General Napier in the early 1850s to improve the conditions of the Bengal army, nothing had been done. The lack of any relationship between the British officers and the Indian soldiers made the situation combustible, particularly as there were only half a million men under arms in a territory inhabited by 180 million people, and rebellion broke out in the spring of 1857. In May, a British force arrived from England and the mutiny was put down, with Bright's support.

In general, Bright was feeling buoyant about the progress he had made in turning British Government opinion on matters of foreign and colonial policy. 'During the comparatively short period since we entered public life, see what has been done,' he had written to Cobden in April:

> Through our labours mainly the whole creed of millions of people, and of the statesmen of our day, has been totally changed … They now agree to repudiate as folly, what, twenty years ago, they accepted as wisdom … now men actually abhor the notion of undertaking the government of the Colonies; on the contrary, they give to every Colony that asks for it, a Constitution as democratic as that which exists in the United States.[31]

However, despite the praise he received from influential quarters and newspapers such as *The Times*, Bright's influence over India affairs waned in the late 1850s as a result of his unpopularity over the Crimea and his vigorous opposition to Palmerston. The India Reform Society, of which Bright had become chairman in 1855 and which had proved to be at its most effective during the Indian Mutiny, also lost impetus. After Bright resigned the chair in 1861, John Dickinson took his place and remained involved until the 1870s. Bright continued to receive advice and support on India from Dickinson and his old friend J. B. Smith, the MP for Stockport and former chairman of the Anti-Corn Law League, and Sir William Molesworth, a supporter of colonial self-government and a member of Lord Aberdeen's Cabinet. Disraeli and other Tories were also prepared to challenge the East India Company, but the cross-party alliance faltered and an air of despondency settled around those who had taken up the Indian cause.

India, 1858–60

On 20 February 1858, Derby and Disraeli took over the
Government after Palmerston was ousted over Ireland. In his first
six months of power in 1858, Disraeli introduced three successive
Government of India Bills to abolish the power of the East India
Company. The first of these was introduced on 26 March. Bright
had his reservations, but, as he wrote to Joseph Sturge in August,

> the whole Indian question is a swamp to which there seems
> neither bottom nor firm shore – England cannot govern distant
> nations – our statesmen have no time and no principles ... The
> thing is a dream. Nevertheless, we may try to do something.[32]

In May, he pleaded for the people of India: 'I am in favour of justice
and conciliation – of the law of justice and of kindness.' He said,
'The history of our connection with this country ... is of a nature
that ought to make us pause before we consent to any measure that
shall fill up the cup of injury which we have offered to the lips of that
people.' He criticized the deposition of the sovereign of Oudh and
the seizure of his revenues, and argued that there needed to be a fair
and just solution without factionalism to resolve the Indian question
– 'I am terrified for the future of India when I look at the indiscriminate slaughter which is now going on there ... I believe the whole of
India is now trembling under the action of volcanic fires.' If the present policy continued, 'we shall be guilty of the greatest recklessness,
and I say of great crime to the Monarchy of England'.[33] Bright
insisted on judges being professionally trained and sent to promote
the Indian legal process and greater opportunities for Indians to take
on public service. Bright not only influenced the future government
of the people of India, but set benchmarks for fairness, toleration
and recognition of their rights, including a system of competitive
examinations in the Indian Civil Service.

On 24 June, Bright set out the way he believed India could and
should be governed, drawing on his past experience as chairman of
the Select Committee on Indian Cotton. He attacked the East India
Company and the exorbitant pay given to its civil service. He was
not happy with the proposed great powers of the Governor-General
and set out his own proposals for reform which would, in his own
words, 'render it unnecessary for any man in India to cross the
ocean to seek for that justice which he would then be able to get in
his own country without corruption or secret bargain'.[34]

His speech struck a balance between recognition of the oppression that the East India Company had inflicted on the Indian people – bringing with it hatred and revolt – and a plea for proper government of the country. He proposed the abolition of the post of Governor-General. In its place, he argued for a Secretary of State for India, directly responsible to Parliament, and a decentralized system of government. This was much in keeping with the times. As Theodore Hoppen points out, there was a great movement against centralization in English domestic politics. As early as 1847, Disraeli had spoken against 'the elevating system of centralisation which if left unchecked will prove fatal to the national character'.[35] Both Disraeli and Bright argued for localism.

Bright's specific proposals were that each of five presidencies in India – at Calcutta, Madras, Bombay, Agra and Lahore – would operate on its own terms as a dependency of England. He argued for each of these councils to be open and transparent, with full involvement of Indians in Indian affairs. He asked:

> But how long does England propose to govern India? Nobody answers that question, and nobody can answer it … does any man with the smallest glimmering of common sense believe that that great country, with its twenty different nations and its twenty languages, can ever be bound up and consolidated into one compact and enduring empire?

He called for an entirely new policy, adding, 'You may govern India, if you like, for the good of England, but the good of England must come through the channel of the good of India.' He argued that England should trade with India rather than plunder the country. India would only become rich through the honest administration of justice and through security of life and property.

'The people of India do not like us, but they scarcely know where to turn if we left them,' Bright said. He accepted that Britain was in possession of India, but he wanted a proclamation promising the Indians security and title for their property, and a proper Court of Appeal based in India. He admitted that his policy was original and unusual, but that this was needed to allay the anxieties of the Indian people. He ended the speech setting out his proposals with the words,

> I invite you to something better, and higher, and holier … I invite you to a glory not 'fanned by conquest's crimson wing', but based upon the solid and lasting benefits which I believe the

Parliament of England can, if it will, confer upon the countless populations of India.[36]

In essence, his proposals for India, as for Ireland, were to give people self-respect through their own land tenure and ownership, and to accentuate their proper and fair treatment by the governing British class.

The Government of India Bill was passed with amendments and became law. Despite falling short of Bright's wishes, the Act did bring an end of the 'double government' of India, with the territories, duties and power of the East India Company transferred to the Crown. The eventual Royal Proclamation to the people of India drew upon Bright's principles, disclaiming 'the right and the desire to impose our convictions on any of our subjects' and that 'none be molested or disquieted by reason of their religious faith or observances but that all shall enjoy alike the equal and impartial protection of the law'. The proclamation went further, to command that all in authority 'abstain from all interference with the religious belief or worship of any of our subjects' and that 'those of whatever race or creed be freely and impartially admitted to offices in our service, the duties of which they may be qualified by their education, ability, and integrity, duly to discharge'.[37]

Within a year, Bright had moved his arguments into the economic field. He called for Indian officials to be paid more, and a reduction in the pay of the Indian civil service. He took grave exception to the fact that the Indian taxpayer, and not the British taxpayer, was bearing the cost of the Afghan War. He reiterated his views that there should be better communications and irrigation works, and called for proper financial accounts to be reported to Parliament.

In 1860, Bright defended Sir Charles Edward Trevelyan, who had been dismissed as Governor of Madras after opposing the idea of increased direct taxation in India. Bright was particularly enthusiastic about Trevelyan's preference for decentralized government, and for his treatment of the Indian people. In a speech in August 1859 on the finances of India, Bright had argued that Trevelyan found that 'at Madras he is like a man who is manacled, as all the Governors are. He is able to do almost nothing.' He laid into his superior Governor-General, stating that he 'goes out knowing little or nothing' of the country other than what he might discover from Mill's *History of India*.[38] By contrast, he pointed out that Trevelyan had tried to conciliate the Indians by abolishing ceremonies that were supposed to degrade them, he showed personal courtesy to them, rewarded those who had rendered public service, attempted to improve land tenure, and reduce the paperwork of the public servants. In the light of these reforms, Bright said, Trevelyan had 'raised a hornets' nest about him'.

Despite the problems besetting the India Reform Society and Bright's own preoccupation with parliamentary reform in the late 1850s, Bright insisted in 1859 that 'If this matter of India were settled so that we could feel satisfied about it, it would afford me greater pleasure than any change connected with the institutions or the Government of England which could take place.'[39]

British North America

Unsatisfactory governors, one of Bright's main bugbears, could be found throughout the Empire. In 1854, the British Government had granted the colony of Newfoundland 'responsible government', under which the Governor would officiate the appointment of elected representatives to administer the colony. The Liberal Party in Newfoundland won the General Election which followed, and in 1855 its leader, Philip F. Little, was elected as the colony's first premier. His appointment, however, was delayed by the Governor, Baillie Hamilton. Little travelled to England, where he approached Bright to lodge a complaint about the Governor, during which visit Bright also presented memorials from Gibraltarians complaining about their Governor.[40] Bright suggested that the Assembly of Newfoundland, along with other colonies, should appoint the Governor, rather than the other way round, and that all this gave the colonists 'good cause to wish to get rid of the Home Government altogether'.[41]

Bright's commitment to self-government in the Empire, however, was tested briefly in 1858 and 1859, when the Legislative Assembly of Canada undertook a thorough reform of tariffs and adopted a semi-protectionist policy. This was an anathema to Bright, but he placed the right of the Canadian Government to take such decisions firmly above his own views on free trade. When it was suggested that the British Government could veto the Canadian legislation, as was its right under the Union Act of 1840, Bright argued that such a move could endanger the young Canadian democracy and lead to a premature separation from Britain.[42] While he wasn't against the idea of separation in principle, should the Canadians themselves decide to become independent, he was adamant that Canada should not be driven to do so by foolish government policy.

Bright considered the Canadian legislature to be a particular success in the just development of British colonial policy. Furthermore, he saw a common purpose in the democratic development of all English-speaking nations, and linked the success of democracy in Canada to his ongoing campaign for an extension of the vote in Britain. He would later state firmly that 'English nations are brought together and they must march on together'.[43] Speaking at a banquet in Birmingham on 29 October 1858, Bright used the example of Canada to bat away fears that an extension of the franchise in Britain would lead to widespread disorder, or even revolution:

> Twenty years ago the government of our colonies was a huge job …We had then discontent, and, now and then, insurrection, especially in Canada. The result was that we have given up the colonial policy which had hitherto been held sacred, and since that time not only had they gone on progressing in wealth and material resources, but no parts of the empire are more tranquil and loyal.[44]

The American Civil War highlighted a number of questions about the future of Canada. Bright's hope was that it would become part of the 'one great confederation of States'[45] that he envisaged for the North American continent, a vision shared and epitomized in the idea of Manifest Destiny that was increasingly prevalent in the USA itself. The inhabitants of Canada, however, did not generally share this view. Bright's enthusiasm for American democracy as a whole overtook his usual enthusiasm for self-government and led him to believe for a time that Canada would eventually become part of a greater united American continent, in line with Secretary of State Seward's own hopes.

The interaction between Britain, the Canadian territory and the USA was complex. Canadian–American relations had an uneasy history following the American War of Independence in the late eighteenth century and the war of 1812, during the course of which conflicts the USA attempted to overrun Canada, and Canada was used by Britain as a base from which to launch John Burgoyne's retaliation against the American rebels. Border disputes were numerous. When the American Civil War broke out, Canadians feared that their frontier would again come under attack. On the other hand, the North was justifiably angered by the ease with which Confederate raiders found shelter in Canada, adding to the uneasy relations between America and Britain. Trade relations between Canada and America were strained.

In March 1865, there was much debate regarding the defence of Canada against America. Some favoured fortification, while others argued for granting Canada independence to protect her from actions based on anti-British feeling. The notion that America would invade Canada was repudiated by Bright. While he admitted that there was, thanks to the failure of British government in Ireland, a deep resentment in America against Britain in certain Irish quarters, in his opinion the Irish in America did not have enough leverage to influence America against Canada. Furthermore, Bright spoke strongly against any idea that Britain should go to war with America. He argued that this, in any case, would have a disastrous impact on commerce, and that war with America would be a greater crime than war against any other country in the world. None the less, there were those determined on fortifying Canada.

The Government proposed spending £200,000 on defending Quebec, funded partly from the British Treasury and partly by the Government of Canada. Bright was completely against this, not only because he did not believe that America would invade Canada, but if it did, Canada could not be defended given the overwhelming advantage that America would have both geographically and strategically. He was reinforced in his arguments by his belief that it was unacceptable to spend public money on this kind of venture outside Great Britain. He also argued strongly that it was wrong to impose a tax on Canada for the purpose, and that this could lead to an unnecessary separation of Canada from Britain. Bright's arguments against fortification did not prevail, however, and the Government had its way.

Despite his belief that war between Canada (and thus also Britain) and America was unlikely, he did concede that the independence of Canada would remove any such danger, a view shared by Cobden.

It was against this background that the British North America Act was passed at Westminster in 1867. This created a single Parliament with a Senate and a House of Commons, with each province having its own Parliament and Executive. There was a Governor-General for the dominion as a whole and a Lieutenant-Governor for each province. The overall command of naval and military forces remained with Britain. Bright supported the second reading of the Bill, with reservations about the speed with which it had been driven through Parliament. He made clear his objection to a nominated executive council for each province, and insisted that each province should be given the opportunity to decide whether it wished to be part of the federation. While he condemned the idea that the legislative councils should be nominated and not elected, his sense of practicality by this time had led him to believe that Canada, under this new British North America Act, would to all intents and purposes achieve self-government, albeit under the general aegis of a Governor-General and a Federal Parliament. In particular, he supported Nova Scotia in its resistance to being drawn into the federation as a whole, and he presented a petition to Parliament on behalf of its citizens.

The Act created a significant degree of Canadian autonomy, of which Bright approved. As he said on 28 February 1867,

> For my share, I want the population of these Provinces to do that which they believe to be the best for their own interests – remain with this country if they like, in the most friendly manner, or become independent States if they like. If they should prefer to unite themselves with the United States, I should not complain even of that. But whatever be their course, there is no man in this House or in those Provinces who has a more sincere wish for their greatness and their welfare than I have.[46]

This form of devolution survived for 120 years, though the Statute of Westminster in 1931 effectively relinquished direct governmental control over all the dominions, including Canada, so that they then became fully independent, a process that had been evolving for many decades. The British North America Act remained a statute at Westminster until 1982 when, following a court case, legislation was ultimately passed at Westminster repatriating the constitution to Canada, and the last vestiges of British sovereignty were eliminated.

Jamaica and Brutality, 1865–6

Bright's unease at the power of individual governors was highlighted once again in October 1865 following the Morant Bay rebellion in Jamaica. Despite slavery being abolished in 1834, most black inhabitants of Jamaica were effectively excluded from the franchise as they did not meet the financial requirements, in part because of an oppressive taxation system. Indeed, in the 1864 elections, less than 1 per cent of the black population had been eligible to vote. The dissatisfaction this caused was aggravated by a two-year drought that created desperate economic conditions, along with rumours that the white plantation owners intended to restore slavery. To compound matters, when a petition was raised regarding these conditions of inequality, the colonial secretary sent an unsympathetic reply, based largely on the advice of Governor John Eyre, telling the black Jamaicans that hard work was the way out of poverty: 'It is from their own industry and prudence, in availing themselves of the means of prospering that are before them ... that they must look for an improvement in their conditions.'[47]

Matters came to a head in October 1865, when a black Jamaican was imprisoned for trespass on an abandoned plantation. A small protest followed, with one man arrested, but the authorities issued arrest warrants for 28 more. One of these, Paul Bogle, then led about 300 people to the courthouse at Morant Bay. On arrival, they were met with gunfire which killed seven protesters. In the riot that followed, 18 more people, from both sides, were killed. The protesters took control of the town and the unrest spread to the countryside. Governor Eyre proclaimed martial law and sent troops to round up the protesters, which they achieved through indiscriminate violence against the black population. Hundreds of men, women and children were killed and hundreds more executed or flogged, many without a proper trial. The arrest that caused the greatest furore in Britain was that of George Gordon, a preacher and black member of the Jamaican Assembly, who was seen as a spokesman for the poor, but had little involvement in the rebellion. On his arrest in Kingston, an area excluded from the martial law, Governor Eyre ordered Gordon to be moved to Morant Bay for trial. Two days after his trial on 21 October, George Gordon was hanged.

Speaking in Blackburn on 1 December, Bright said, 'I fear that the fame of England has never received a deeper wound or a darker stain ... I say that murder is foul and there is no murder more foul than that which is done by men in authority under pretence of law.' He called for Governor Eyre and his accomplices to 'stand at the bar of justice for the murder of Mr Gordon'.[48] John Stuart Mill shared Bright's views and founded the Jamaica Committee to press for prosecution. Bright joined the Committee, along with other liberals including Charles Darwin, Herbert Spencer, Thomas Bayley Potter, Samuel Morley and Duncan McLaren. Equally vociferous were the supporters of Governor Eyre, who formed their own committee, largely dominated by Tories.

On 9 February 1866 in the House, Bright called again for the Governor to stand trial, describing the atrocity as having 'cast a foul blot upon the character of English Governors'. Subtly bringing to mind the fear of revolution in Britain, and his own ongoing agitation for parliamentary reform, he asked, 'if law be not law to the negro in Jamaica, how long will law be law to the working people or to any of their friends in this country?'[49]

Though an investigative commission did not find Governor Eyre personally responsible, he was recalled to Britain. On his return, his supporters held a banquet in his honour. Charges of murder were brought on two later occasions, which Bright followed closely as a member of the Jamaica Committee, but neither came to trial. Bright must have been mollified to a certain extent, however, by the changes made in Jamaica following Governor Eyre's removal. Under a new Governor, Sir John Peter Grant, the power of the Jamaican Assembly was replaced by a Legislative Assembly and the island became a Crown Colony, a clear move towards self-government, albeit one that would take 150 years to complete.

India, 1860s onwards

Bright's attention to Indian affairs was briefly re-engaged during the American Civil War, with its inevitable consequences for cotton exports. Supported by those opposed to slavery, he repeated his earlier calls for greater security to be given to the Indian cultivators, and for decentralization. However, as James Sturgis argues, while Bright retained his interest in India throughout his career, and 'attained great prominence among Indian reformers between 1870 and 1889', he never really regained the degree of initiative on Indian matters he had previously enjoyed.[50] Indeed, when in December 1868 Gladstone offered him the post of secretary of state for India, Bright declined and, under pressure, took instead the presidency of the Board of Trade. Keith Robbins notes that his resistance to Gladstone's offers was 'a grave step to exchange twenty-five years experience as an independent backbencher for collective responsibility and executive office'.[51]

When it came to the Indian question, Bright could see that his vision for India was some steps removed from what could practicably be achieved as things then stood. Cobden had always disagreed with him over India, calling his vision for Indian self-government 'a self-complacent piece of cant'[52] and preferring a complete withdrawal from India to enable free trade and its benefits to take effect. Though Bright agreed with Cobden on free trade, any idea of withdrawal, or abandonment as he perhaps saw it, went against his moral principles. India would never have the opportunity to develop into a democratic and prosperous nation without support from Britain, which in itself required major reform at home to remove the power of those with a colonial self-interest.

Yet Bright had a firm belief that justice would prevail eventually, with or without his direct involvement. Indeed, in 1885, he wrote in *The Times* that Britain would have to accept that 'the absolute rule in her Asiatic Empire is temporary'.[53] As Sturgis notes, 'Bright thought that the decision to educate the Indians had practically resolved the future course to self-government.'[54] He also probably saw that what was needed was agitation in India on a par with his campaign for parliamentary reform, and he knew that such a vast undertaking was beyond him, given the distance, the size of the country and his other commitments.

Bright continued to seize opportunities as they arose to speak out for the people of India. In 1875, he advocated that the Prince of Wales, when he visited India the following year, should set an example for the improvement of the treatment of the Indian people through the British civil service.

Bright was deeply influenced by the Indian famine in 1877, which reignited his determination to find a solution to India's problems, That year, he again pressed the case for improved irrigation and navigation in India, which he had first raised in the 1850s but which had been sidelined by the building of railways. He still believed that within a decade, at a cost of about £30 million, they would be able to improve the rivers and navigation, and provide canals in India.

In December, he took part in a debate with Sir Arthur Cotton, in which he again pressed the case for decentralization. The five or six separate states he proposed

> would be a thousand times better than our being withdrawn from it now when there is no coherence among those twenty nations, and when we should find the whole country, in all probability, lapse into chaos and anarchy, and into sanguinary and interminable warfare.[55]

Bright certainly understood, and in some ways predicted, the potential chaos in 1948 when Pakistan was created out of India.

But his enthusiasm was dampened by practical considerations. At sixty-seven, he was also beginning to feel his age, as he wrote to J. B. Smith, 'If you & I were younger perhaps we might have been able to do something in this matter.'[56] More importantly, perhaps, he had no sounding board for his ideas: 'I have no one to consult with who knows anything of India, or cares about it,' he wrote to his wife in January 1878.[57] By the following year, however, he appears to have made more Indian contacts and his diaries are peppered with meetings and discussions on India. On 28 February 1879, for example, he records that he was speaking on Indian matters in the House for the first time for 10 or 11 months. Speaking in Birmingham on 16 April, he condemned the Indian empire as being governed by 'a despotism – that is a Government which has no representative institutions, and which by a few men ... the whole government of the Empire is administered'.[58]

Bright's influence regarding Indian affairs also remained through the memory of his earlier, passionate speeches on the issue. For example, Bright's great speech on India in June 1858, described at the time by Russell as 'one of the most remarkable ever delivered in this House',[59] was reiterated in 1881 by William Digby in a pamphlet promoted by the National Liberal Federation. Perhaps most significantly, however, Bright's name and reputation was a byword among Indian reformers because Bright – as in the USA over slavery, at home over parliamentary reform, and in Ireland – was seen as the driving force for change, for equitable treatment of the oppressed and for mutual respect between the government and the governed. One Indian correspondent referred in 1878 to 'what you have done in past times ... which entitles you to the high consideration and gratitude of the population of this vast Indian empire'.[60]

Even today, Bright (affectionately known as 'John Britain') is given pre-eminence over other 'British Friends of India' on the Indian National Congress website, which records:

> So great was his genuine sympathy for India that, when on a certain occasion, a responsible member in the House of Commons made unparliamentary observations regarding the people of India, Bright indignantly observed: 'I would not permit any man in my presence without rebuke to indulge in the calumnies and expression of contempt which I have recently heard poured fourth without measure upon the whole population of India.

The website continues that Bright

> pleaded for 'mercy and justice' to the great Indian people. 'Is it not possible', he said, 'to touch a chord in the hearts of

Englishmen to raise them to a sense of the miseries inflicted on
that unhappy country by the crimes and blunders of our rulers
here? If you have steeled your hearts against the natives, if nothing can stir you to sympathy with their, miseries, at least have
pity upon your own countrymen.'[61]

Once Bright had left the Cabinet in July 1882, he once again found
more time for Indian affairs. That same year, the new Governor-
General of India, Lord Ripon, sought Bright's assistance, and Bright
gave him not only advice but also public encouragement for his
reforms, which included the extension of municipal government,
promoting private enterprise and the abolition of customs duties.

The Indian National Congress met for the first time in Bombay in
1885, and in December of that year Bright hosted a meeting in
Birmingham that was addressed by his friend, Lalmohan Ghosh,
and two other delegates from the Indian Reform Association. In his
speech, Bright reaffirmed his commitment to the idea of self-
government in India, stating that there should be a policy 'that will
enable India to enter tranquilly on the path of self-government
and independence'.[62] This, to say the least, was a bold statement
born out of his deep experience, knowledge and, it has to be said,
disillusionment with the way in which his ideas for decentralization
and for improvements to the infrastructure of India, not to mention
the treatment of Indians themselves, had been slighted. Yet he
believed it would happen. When he met the leading Hindu reformer
and Brahmo religious scholar, Protap Chunder Mozoomdar, in
1883, Bright said, clearly drawing on his experiences of the turbulent times in Britain in the run-up to the Reform Act of 1867,

Never be persuaded to use violence either in speech or act.
Every reform has to be won constitutionally, inch by inch, in this
country. Be not tired to try to obtain your rights ... But never be
violent in anything. All progress has its laws, and laws act slowly.
If you do not get all you want, your children will ...The future
must be allowed to mend the past.[63]

Mahatma Gandhi would have understood.

At the same time, Bright was instrumental in encouraging Indians
to stand for the British Parliament. Ghosh stood twice, unsuccess-
fully, but was later elected president of the Indian National Congress
in 1903. Dadabhai Naoroji was more successful in the British
Parliament and, after meeting Bright in 1886, who promised to find

him a candidature, he subsequently became the Liberal member for
Finsbury Central from 1892 to 1895. Naoroji was also elected president of the Indian National Congress, in 1906.

In July 1887, less than two years before his death, Bright presided
over a meeting of the East India Association in Westminster Town
Hall, where he argued that 'our right to India and the rule of it
at present must depend on the services we render to the millions of
her people'.[64] He called for an altruistic policy and, as he had
throughout his political career, argued that, having acquired India
by conquest in the first place, there was a moral obligation to
govern the country properly. This would have great mutual benefits, but only if Indian interests were put at the forefront of the
policy-making.

In the 1890s, Gandhi himself acknowledged Bright's devotion to
India when he included him in a list of 'eminent Englishmen'
who had shown 'by their writings, speeches and deeds that they
mean to unify the hearts of the two peoples, that they do not believe
in colour distinctions, and that they will raise India with them rather
than rise upon its ruins'.[65]

Africa, 1870s and 1880s

In 1865, Bright, along with Disraeli, had supported an inquiry by a
Select Committee in the House of Commons to look into the future
of British rule in West Africa. Bright, for his part, believed that
absolute withdrawal would be the wisest course for Britain in the
long term. The only reason he could see for Britain's continued presence in Africa was on trade grounds, and he believed that free trade
would be improved if the military presence was removed. The
inquiry, however, concluded that Britain was too deeply embedded
in African affairs to contemplate withdrawal. On its recommenda-
tions, a new streamlined system of government was instituted in the
Gold Coast settlements, overseen by one Governor-in-Chief based
in Sierra Leone. This decision was to cause great unrest, however, as
those tribes that had previously enjoyed close British protection
were alarmed at their abandonment and exposure to aggressive
neighbours.

In 1871, Britain enlarged her West African Gold Coast colony
through the purchase of the settlements of Dutch Guinea. This lit
the fuse for renewed conflict with the Ashanti tribe, who had an
accepted claim over large areas of the coast but whose bellicose
nature and incursions into British-protected Fanti territory had

caused a number of conflicts in the past. When the Ashanti invaded a British fort in 1873, the Government sent in Sir Garnet Wolseley, a distinguished military man with a reputation for quick and efficient action. Bright was appalled. Recently appointed to the Duchy of Lancaster, he attempted in Cabinet meetings to mitigate the war and arrive at a peaceful solution. He admitted that his knowledge of African affairs was limited, but this did not deter him, as his arguments for a peaceful solution were based on moral and democratic principles rather than any strategic or political position. As he wrote to Lord Granville on 26 September 1873, 'I am unhappy about the African question – tho' I know little about it – I cannot vote for war – that is certain.'[66] He had written to Gladstone earlier, saying

> I don't like the system of a war being undertaken ... without special directions and restrictions from the Cabinet. I distrust the soldiers – promotion is so often their object, and revenge and example the pretext for operations and cruelties which are needless and dishonourable.[67]

Resignation over the issue was at the back of his mind, though he could not fully justify such a move.[68]

True to his reputation, Wolseley completed his Gold Coast campaign and subdued the Ashanti within two months of his troops' arrival in January 1874. On his return, in addition to military honours, Wolseley was greeted with adulation from all quarters, including speeches in the Commons and Lords, honorary doctorates from both Oxford and Cambridge, and the Freedom of the City of London. Though Bright was grateful for the swift resolution to the conflict, he appeared unimpressed with Wolseley himself, as his record of a later meeting at Chamberlain's home suggests: 'Sorry to meet there Lord Wolseley. I abhor the profession of the soldier. He is a lively and smart fellow, but does not give the impression of much weight.'[69]

Bright's lack of strategic interest in African affairs did cause him difficulty during the First Boer War, however. This conflict arose largely out of a failure by the new Liberal Government, of which Bright was part, to take any active steps to undo Disraeli's annexation of the Transvaal in 1877, despite Gladstone's censure of the act at the time. The Boers, who had expected some form of self-government to be granted after Gladstone gained power in the spring of 1880, were becoming increasingly restless. But, as Trevelyan notes, 'Bright paid no attention to the question, and failed

to warn his colleagues of their negligence until it was too late.'[70] The
Boers were driven to declare their independence in December 1880
and the war began on 16 December. Bright, however, did not make
any reference to the war in his diary until mid-February, when he
recorded, 'Cabinet. Transvaal War: agreed to propose armistice, and
to send Commissionaire to propose terms of settlement. All most
anxious to prevent further conflict and bloodshed.'[71] During this
Cabinet meeting, both Bright and Chamberlain had called for the
immediate return of the Transvaal to the Boers, but were overruled
by the colonial secretary, Lord Kimberley, who had high hopes for
an African Federation. When news arrived on 1 March of the death
of Sir George Colley, the High Commissioner of South-East Africa
and commander of the British forces there, Bright repeated his call
for peace. As he recorded in his diary on 3 March,

> At 1 o'clock called on Mr. Gladstone; for an hour discussed the
> unhappy Transvaal question. I argued that the recent disaster
> should not interfere with measures for peace, that negotiations
> should go on as if it had not happened ... Mr. Gladstone agreed
> with me. I said it would be impossible for me to consent to any
> measures of a vindictive character, or to the shedding of blood to
> restore the credit of British arms.[72]

With Gladstone and the Cabinet finally convinced, Bright's hopes
for a peaceful outcome were realized through a succession of peace
treaties, culminating in the Pretoria Convention of 3 August 1881,
after which British troops withdrew.

Imperial Federation, 1880s

As the British Empire moved towards its height, Bright's opposition
to the methods of subjugation and expansion became increasingly
vocal. Addressing the Junior Liberal Association of Birmingham on
22 January 1880, Bright drew a vivid picture of the many conflicts in
which Britain was engaged in the name of empire before warning
that,

> No completer ruin has history shown, perhaps, than the great
> ruin of the conquering and sanguinary Roman Empire. Well, I
> believe, whether I read history, sacred or profane, that the punish-
> ment that has fallen upon ancient empires will visit modern
> realms ... if they persist in the pursuit of empire and glory, sacri-
> ficing uncounted and countless multitudes of human lives.

He quoted the poet Dante, saying, 'The sword of heaven is not in haste to smite, Nor yet doth linger.' To much cheering, he added,

> If we, the people of England, tolerate the bloody and the sanguinary crimes which are committed in our name ... we shall have no acquittal at the tribunal by which the actions, not of individuals only, but of nations and peoples, are finally judged.[73]

The increase in British aggression was in large part a result of a desire to shore up Britain's colonies and overseas territories against the growing threat from other European powers, a situation that Bright feared would lead to a frenzied and bloodied competition for territory, not to mention an undesirable increase in areas under imperial control.

At the same time, there was uncertainty about the future of British interests should all colonies eventually adopt self-government, as many had already done. This led to proposals for imperial federation and the idea that the Empire could be transformed into a super state under the democratic government of a central Imperial Parliament at Westminster, allowing Britain to maintain unity and her trade interests while relinquishing some of the financial burden of maintaining and defending an empire. This did not mean the end of colonies, however, as those that had a large 'alien' – that is, non-English speaking – population would still be governed directly by Britain. The Imperial Federation League was formed in London in 1884 to further these aims. It proposed that home affairs would be dealt with by local parliaments throughout the former Empire, including Scotland and Ireland, with each state sending representatives to the central Parliament at Westminster.

Bright was as unimpressed with these ideas as he was with those who promoted them. Speaking alongside Chamberlain in Birmingham on 29 January 1885, Bright asked of the Imperial Federation League, 'What do they propose? That the British Empire – that is the United Kingdom, with all its colonies – should form one country, one interest, one undivided interest for the purposes of defence. The idea, in my opinion, is ludicrous.' He reminded his audience of the ongoing problems in Ireland that had been caused by centuries of inadequate government by, to his mind, the very people now represented by the Imperial Federation League, before adding, 'And now these gentlemen, who do not seem to have any kind of prescription for the case of Ireland, are going all over the world with some notion of binding together all the great colonies of this country.' In the same speech, he condemned a proposal by Lord Grey to create a Colonial Council, likening it to the Indian Council which, he asserted, was widely thought in Government to be 'a great evil'. The correct policy, he said, with which 'to deal with our colonies is to deal with them [as] we do now, to encourage them, to give them freedom as now, to deal justly and fairly with them on all occasions, to cultivate sympathy and good will towards them'. He warned that

> If we bind or attempt to bind them in a closer tie by meddling with them, by allowing them to give counsel, which perhaps we should not follow, we shall find that instead of their being more our friends, they will be less our friends, and that the bond of union will, in all probability, be weakened.

On a practical note, he added, 'I am for friendship and justice to all our colonies and to foreign powers – but I think we have enough on our hands.'[74] Just as one might urge today on the European Union.

In this view, Bright found support from Gladstone, as his diary entry on 5 March 1885 confirms: 'Much interesting conversation on Colonies and Federation. Mr. Gladstone agreed with me that the wisest plan is to leave Colonies much as they are.'[75]

As the debate continued over the years, Bright strengthened his arguments against federation, and his last public speech was on this issue. He objected to the idea of centralized military decision-making, which would inevitably draw reluctant colonies into wars that did not affect them directly. He worried that meddling by a central Imperial Parliament would drive individual states to separate from the federation, which might not be in their best interests. Furthermore, he could foresee problems with parts of the federation that adopted tariff policies at odds with the union as a whole, as Canada had done in 1879. This last point was perhaps closest to his heart. His own vision for the future of the British Empire was that it would become, alongside the USA, a vast free trade area, not unlike the North American Free Trade Agreement (NAFTA), fostering wealth and lasting peace across the globe. As he stated in Birmingham in January 1885, 'Economic facts are much stronger than Imperial federation leagues.'[76] His views would undoubtedly have led him to oppose the notion of anything like a Federal Europe, not least because of the loss of British sovereignty it entails.

CHAPTER 7

Foreign Policy and War

The angel of death has been abroad throughout the land;
you may almost hear the beating of his wings.
(John Bright on the Crimean War, 23 February 1855)

Because of the nature and extent of the British Empire, the question is often asked about which aspects of British intervention overseas were matters of foreign policy and which were matters of Empire. There is, of course, some overlap, but the key questions turn on influence, control and the jurisdiction of the Westminster Parliament, particularly where military force was used for the purpose of maintaining or expanding the colonial – and, later, the imperial – framework. This overlap occurs, for example, in relation to the Afghan Wars and India, and the Transvaal and South Africa in relation to the Boers. Other areas are more clearly defined as matters of foreign policy. In these, British intervention had less to do with colonial or imperial interests and more to do with exercising, or not exercising, the balance of power. The ultimate test was whether the money to engage in these interventions was drawn from imperial funds – from taxation imposed on the indigenous parts of the Empire – or whether it was voted by Parliament for the purpose of engaging in war as a matter of foreign policy. To give some indication of the psychology behind the policy-making, the transition over the past 200 years, and particularly since the Second World War, has been demonstrated by the shift in name from the Ministry of War to the Ministry of Defence.

Underlying Bright's disenchantment with the British Government's approach to foreign affairs were two factors, each of which led back to his firm belief in equality and freedom as expressed through democratic processes. First, the business of waging war was, in fact, very profitable to the ruling classes. At a Birmingham banquet on 29 October 1858, Bright pointed out that 'this foreign policy, this regard for the "liberties of Europe" … this excessive love for the "balance of power", is neither more nor less than a gigantic system of outdoor relief for the aristocracy of Great Britain'.[1]

Second, decisions on matters of foreign policy, being matters of prerogative, lacked the democratic involvement of the people. He launched an attack on the Foreign Office in a speech in Glasgow in December 1858 at the beginning of his great campaign for parliamentary reform:

> When you come to our foreign policy, you are no longer Englishmen; you are no longer free; you are recommended not to inquire. If you do, you are told you cannot understand it; you are snubbed, you are hustled aside. We are told that the matter is too deep for common understandings like ours – that there is a great mystery about it … I have often compared, in my own mind … the Foreign Office of this country with the temples of the Egyptians. We are told by those who pass up and down the Nile that on its banks are grand temples with stately statues and massive lofty columns, statues each one of which would have appeared almost to have exhausted a quarry in its production. You have, further, vast chambers and gloomy passages; and some innermost recess, some holy of holies, in which, when you arrive at it, you find some loathsome reptile which a nation reverenced and revered, and bowed down itself to worship.

While the Foreign Office did not have columns and statues on the same scale, it did have 'a mystery as profound; and in the innermost recesses of it we find some miserable intrigue, in defence of which … the precious blood of our country's children is squandered as though it had no price'. He concluded by calling for the Foreign Office to be 'placed directly under the free control of a Parliament elected by the great body of the people of the United Kingdom'.[2] Bright's views about the Foreign Office are mirrored by the recent constitutional changes bringing much greater control over the prerogative by Parliament.

Because of this lack of democratic accountability, and the great ethical questions which inevitably arose, Bright became deeply engrossed in foreign policy questions whenever they came into his moral sights. By far the most significant foreign policy arena he stepped into was the Crimean War, which drew on all his resources. He took the Crimean issue to the heights of his oratory in the House of Commons but the stress from his conscientious striving for peace broke him physically and led to his being driven out of his parliamentary seat in Manchester. It induced the most bitter personal battle of his political career when he took on the full force of Palmerston and his Government – at the time to no avail – and raised his moral pitch to release his most sublime oratory. Despite his defeat in the Manchester election of 1857 and the great personal cost to himself and his health, it also came full circle, as so often in his life, when later he was proved to have been right.

Palmerston and Bright

Bright was opposed to the Crimean War from the outset. A common assumption, given his Quakerism, is that pacifism was the primary motivation for this opposition. However, as Bright stated on one occasion, 'I have not opposed any war on the ground that all war is unlawful and immoral.'[3] Nevertheless, he was always driven by an attempt to achieve peace and arbitration, if war could be avoided. This was not always possible, as shown in his support of the suppression of the Indian Mutiny and, not least, with the American Civil War, which he regarded as inevitable in the cause of justice for the slave.

Bright set out his case against the Crimean War in a speech in the House on 31 March 1854. Far removed from the pacifism of which he has subsequently been accused, it was based instead on the practical principles he believed the House of Commons would accept – but which the Leader of his Party and his personal enemy, Palmerston, would not. Bright definitively said,

> I shall not discuss this question on the abstract principle of peace at all price, as it is termed, which is held by a small minority of persons in this country, founded on religious opinions which are not generally received ... But I shall discuss it entirely on principles which are held unanimously by all the Members of this House. I shall maintain that when we are deliberating on the question of war, and endeavouring to prove its justice or necessity, it becomes us to show that the interests of the country are clearly involved; that the objects for which the war is undertaken are probable, or, at least, possible of attainment; and, further, that the end proposed to be accomplished is worth the cost and the sacrifices which we are about to incur. I think these are fair principles on which to discuss this question.

And not 'to make this country the knight errant of the human race'.[4] However, this is not how Bright's policy on the Crimean War has subsequently gone down in the pages of history.

The background to the war was that France had claimed it was protecting the holy places on behalf of the Roman Catholic Church, whereas Russia was claiming it was protecting the Greek Orthodox Church. Russia demanded a treaty with Turkey in its desire to protect the adherents of the Greek Orthodox faith living within the Ottoman Empire. In June 1853, the Russians moved into the Danubian Principalities to guarantee the safety of members of the Greek Orthodox community. In July, the British and French sent forces to Besika Bay. By September, the English fleet was making its way to the Bosphorus to protect Constantinople. The Sultan of Turkey called on Russia to evacuate the Principalities, and when Russia refused, declared war. The Turkish fleet was defeated at Sinope.

The Peace Society, led by Cobden and Bright, sent the Quakers, Joseph Sturge, Henry Pease and Robert Charleton, as representatives to St Petersburg to argue for peace. In February 1854, they had a meeting with the Tsar who 'declared to them that he was anxious to maintain cordial relations with England, and that it would not be his fault if it became his foe'.[5] England and France issued an ultimatum to Russia, which was ignored by the Tsar. On 11 March 1854, the English fleet sailed to the Baltic under the command of Sir Charles Napier.

Two days later in the House of Commons, Bright condemned Palmerston, then Home Secretary, and Napier himself, for their belligerent attitude demonstrated at a public dinner that had been held for Napier at the Reform Club. In the debate, Palmerston said of Bright,

> I deem it right to inform the hon. Gentleman that any opinion he
> may entertain either of me personally, or of my conduct, private
> or political, is to me a matter of the most perfect indifference ...
> I therefore treat the censure of the hon. Gentleman with the most
> perfect indifference and contempt.

He was brought to order by the Speaker.[6] The ill-tempered debate led even Thomas Macaulay, who was an enthusiastic supporter of Palmerston, to back Bright. Writing to a friend, he said,

Palmerston's want of temper, judgment and good breeding was almost incredible. He did himself more harm in three minutes than all his enemies and detractors throughout the world had been able to do him in twenty years. I came home quite dispirited.[7]

On 28 March 1854, Britain and France declared war. Bright criticized the weakness and vacillation that had caused England and the other powers to be led by Turkey. He argued that Turkey was beyond resuscitation, was tottering to its fall, and that this could not be averted; nor could Russia's growing power be prevented. England had no interest in the war, he said, and the loss of 'treasure and blood' would not be compensated by any advantages: 'Alliances are dangerous things. It is an alliance with Turkey that has drawn us into this war. I would not advise alliances with any nation, but I would cultivate unity with all nations.'

Palmerston responded that Bright's arguments masked his true objection to the war, which was 'the question of pounds, shillings, and pence ... if he found that, on balancing the account, it would be cheaper to be conquered than to be laid under contribution for defence, he would give his vote against going to war.'[8]

Bright's call for peace, shared by Cobden, was ignored, and both men became intensely unpopular and were verbally abused. In Trevelyan's words,

> They were the 'traitors', they were the 'Russians'; Bright was burnt in effigy; he and his friend were caricatured and vilified in the newspapers that had so often praised them; they were abused in the halls of meeting that had resounded with the thunder of their [Anti-Corn Law] League.[9]

Despite this unpopularity, Bright noted in his diary in August 1854,

> I have withstood the war clamour and am in a small minority apparently, but hope sometimes for better times. My position in the House not worse but better, notwithstanding my opposition to policy of Govt. and House. If permitted to come to another session, hope for a better hearing for, or more concurrence in, what I believe to be sound principles. Have met with many marks of respect and good feeling from men of all parties in the House, and have much reason to be content with what has taken place there so far as I am personally concerned.[10]

By September 1854, the allied armies had landed in the Crimea. The
Battle of Alma took place on 20 September. The siege of Sebastopol
began on the 17 October and the Battle of Balaclava, immortalized
by Tennyson's *The Charge of the Light Brigade*, took place on 25
October. Bright was unmoved. When he was invited to a meeting in
Manchester relating to the war, he chose instead to write a letter
condemning the conflict and attacking the Government for supporting Turkey. The Battle of Inkerman took place on 5 November, by
which time the British army was in great and deepening trouble.

On 22 December, Bright launched a passionate attack on Lord
John Russell and Palmerston. Of Russell, he said that 'he descanted
on the fate of empires, forgetting that there was nothing so likely to
destroy an empire as unnecessary wars'. As for Palmerston, 'In one
short sentence he overturned the New Testament and destroyed the
foundations of the Christian religion.' Bright mentioned members of
the House of Commons who had been killed in the war, and that
hundreds of officers had been lost, but that the Government had
treated the matter lightly. He launched a trenchant personal attack
on Palmerston, stating that he understood the issues as well as did
Palmerston. 'The war cannot be justified,' he said, '...impartial
history will teach this to posterity if we do not now comprehend it.'
He added,

> I am not, nor did I ever pretend to be, a statesman ... I have not
> enjoyed for thirty years, like those noble Lords, the honours and
> emoluments of office. I have not set my sails to every passing
> breeze, I am a plain and simple citizen, sent here by one of the
> foremost constituencies of the empire.

He consoled himself with the thought that 'no word of mine has
tended to promote the squandering of my country's treasure, or the
spilling of one single drop of my country's blood'.[11]

In January 1855, John Roebuck, the MP for Sheffield, moved
for a Select Committee to inquire into the conduct of the war,
which was carried by 157 votes. Lord Aberdeen resigned and
Palmerston became Prime Minister on 6 February. Bright noted in
his diary, 'Palmerston Prime Minister! What a hoax! The aged
charlatan has at length attained the great object of his long and
unscrupulous ambition.'[12]

On the death of Tsar Nicholas, peace negotiations were pursued
and, in Bright's famous words,

I am certain that many homes in England in which there now
exists a fond hope that the distant one may return – many such
homes may be rendered desolate when the next mail shall arrive.
The angel of death has been abroad throughout the land; you
may almost hear the beating of his wings. There is no one, as
when the first-born were slain of old, to sprinkle with blood
the lintel and the two sideposts of our doors, that he may spare
and pass on; he takes his victims from the castle of the noble,
the mansion of the wealthy, and the cottage of the poor and the
lowly, and it is on behalf of all these classes that I make this
solemn appeal.

He repeated his call for peace and added that Palmerston, by adopting this course, could have the satisfaction of knowing that 'at his
word torrents of blood had ceased to flow – that he had restored
tranquillity to Europe, and saved this country from the indescribable
calamities of war'.[13] But it was to no avail.

England and France were determined to humiliate Russia, but
Russia refused to be humiliated. The war continued, with Bright
supporting Russia against his own Government and Prime Minister.
In June, Bright pointed out that Russia would not be prepared to be
treated as if she were a person bound over before a magistrate at
Bow Street:

Russia is a great Power, as England is, and in treating with her
you must consider that the Russian Government has to consult
its own dignity, its own interests, and public opinion, just as
much at least as the Government of this country.[14]

Sebastopol finally fell in September 1855. Bright's campaign
received a belated boost when even the British ambassador in
Constantinople declared that 'John Bright is fully borne out by all
this. If this is a sample of the effects of war, who would not be willing to join his peace party? [Sebastopol] is more like a crater of a
volcano than a ruined city.'[15]

At this time, Disraeli toyed with the idea of an alliance with
Gladstone and Bright.[16] Bright's health, however, was breaking
down. As he wrote later,

About the middle, or near the 20th, of the 1st mo. 1856, I found
myself suffering from an attack of giddiness in the head, which
deprived me almost entirely of the power of mental labour. An

important meeting was fixed for the 28th in Manchester, at
which my colleague, Gibson, and myself were to meet a large
number of our constituents, and I greatly feared that I should
be quite unable to attend it. I consulted my medical adviser
Mr. Holland, and he recommended me to 'take freely of nux
vomica', a medicine of the homoeopathic system. I did so, and
was able to attend the meeting, and spoke for nearly two hours,
with as much force and result as when in my usual health.[17]

However, the effort of speaking for peace at this meeting caused his
health to fail further. It appears that the symptoms might have been
partly psychosomatic. By the time the Treaty of Paris was signed at
the end of March 1856, with both Russia and Turkey giving up the
conquests made during the war, and with the Black Sea prohibited
to naval warfare but open for commerce, Bright's energy was
entirely focused on his health. Cobden also took an interest in his
friend's welfare, believing him to have 'sprained his brain' and
recommending more vegetables and fish and a course of bloodlet-
ting.[18] In March, Bright underwent hydropathic treatment in
Yorkshire, followed by various visits to Scotland and then Algiers
for the winter of 1856/7. There, he gradually recovered and enjoyed
the sights and sounds of North Africa. At the end of December, he
travelled to Nîmes, where, on 29 December, he received a visit from
Eliza Gurney, who had recently met Tsar Nicholas's widow in Nice.
She urged him to visit the Empress, who had inquired after him, but
Bright demurred: 'I told her I always avoided "great people" unless
I had some special object which obliged me to see them.'[19] A few
weeks later, however, he did visit, accompanied by his daughter,
Helen, who had joined him in France. The Empress, curious about
his Quaker background and friends, said to Bright, 'I have wished to
see you, and am glad you are come, for I have observed all you have
said, and I think you speak like a man who speaks from his
conscience, and what you say is true.'[20]

His health restored, Bright developed a renewed interest in the
political situation at home. In February 1857, he supported
Cobden's call for a vote of censure on the Government's Chinese
policy following the Chinese capture of the *Arrow*, a Chinese lorcha
boat flying the British flag, near Hong Kong in October 1856.
Without being given full authority before taking action, the British
resident at Canton, Sir John Bowring, attacked the Chinese in retaliation, and thus started the Second Opium War. Cobden's motion
that 'the Papers which have been laid upon the Table fail to establish

satisfactory grounds for the violent measures resorted to at Canton in the late affair of the Arrow'[21] passed on 3 March with a majority of 16 against the Government. Two days later, Bright received news of this victory by telegraph:

> This rejoiced me greatly for many reasons: that it will serve as a check to the monstrous insolence and guilt of English agents abroad, who so readily have recourse to violence on the smallest pretext; that it will probably overthrow the most unscrupulous and profligate Minister [Palmerston] the country has had in my time; that it will be a blow to the secret gang who manage *The Times* newspaper in the interests of Palmerston; that it shows there is yet a moral sense in England. And I am especially delighted that the blow has been struck by my own greatest political friend, and in accordance with the policy we of the 'Manchester School' have ever professed and defended.[22]

Bright, however, was content to be a doting father as he accompanied his daughter Helen on her first visit to the Continent, touring through France, Switzerland and Italy. When Palmerston called a General Election, it turned on matters of foreign policy. Bright sent an address to the electors of Manchester but did not return from Florence for the election. On 30 March, he was defeated, but the temporarily carefree Bright was unconcerned. He wrote to his wife, 'Thy wish is accomplished, and I am free without having run away from my post! ... Honest men are not in demand just now. Shams are more needed for the foolish notions which are abroad. Perhaps wiser times may come.'[23] In his diary, he wrote,

> It is fitting that, having discarded their faithful representatives, the electors of Manchester should humiliate themselves by returning men wholly incapable of doing them any good or of sustaining the character of their representation in any way ... If I were disposed to be vindictive, I should feel amply avenged on the constituency when I see the men they have delighted to honour. I have done my duty by them, and am free ... private life is infinitely preferable to public honours if unaccompanied by a consciousness of independence and of rectitude of conduct.[24]

As discussed in Chapter 3, Cobden and Milner Gibson also lost their seats. Palmerston was at his height and won with an overall majority of 85, and Bright's star was emphatically dimmed.

The enmity between Palmerston and Bright, over foreign policy, war and the moral conduct of government first came to a head in the Don Pacifico Affair in June 1850, after a Gibraltar-born British subject of Jewish-Portuguese descent, David Pacifico, was attacked by an anti-Semitic mob in Athens. When Pacifico's request to the Greek Government for compensation fell on deaf ears, he appealed for British assistance. Palmerston responded with a blockade of Piraeus by the Royal Navy. In one of the most dramatic debates in the House of Commons, which lasted four days and four nights, John Roebuck moved a resolution supporting Palmerston. Palmerston argued that the British Government should protect British subjects when they could not obtain judgments in foreign law courts, and had been entitled to take the action it had in its naval blockade. He attacked the Greek Government, and argued that 'liberty is compatible with order; that individual freedom is reconcilable with obedience to the law'. He declared,

> Whether, as the Roman, in days of old, held himself free from indignity, when he could say Civis Romanus sum; so also a British subject, in whatever land he may be, shall feel confident that the watchful eye and the strong arm of England, will protect him against injustice and wrong.[25]

Bright, in his diary, said of Palmerston's speech,

> It was a remarkable speech, most able, saying everything that can be said for his policy, but proving conclusively how dangerous that policy is – meddling everywhere, advising, controlling, encouraging, menacing, as he pleases, in every country not of first-class power in Europe. This speech and the debate in general only make it more imperative that this mischievous system should be checked.[26]

Bright and Cobden voted with the Conservatives against the Government, but Palmerston won, with a majority of 46 votes.

This political duel on matters of foreign policy was aggravated in 1861 during an inquiry into the First Afghan War. In the 1830s, Sir Alexander Burns, the ultimate British expert on the history of Afghanistan, had been appointed as the British ambassador to Kabul. The Emir of Afghanistan, Dost Muhammad Khan, persuaded Burns to propose an alliance between India and Afghanistan, under the aegis of the British, to attack the Punjab. In the event, the Indian army supported the Punjab and attacked Afghanistan, removing Dost Muhammad. The British occupied Kabul and installed Shuja Shah Durrani as the new Emir and puppet of the British Government. This action was strongly opposed by the radicals. Palmerston, then foreign secretary, deliberately edited Burns' advice, creating the impression that they had acted along the lines proposed by Burns when in fact they had followed a completely different course. In 1841, the Afghans rebelled and murdered both Shah Shuja and Burns. The British army was surrounded and, in defiance of an agreement for safe conduct, 15,000 soldiers were annihilated in the mountainous regions. Only one survived. Palmerston was criticized vehemently. Britain then sent another army to capture Kabul. Dost Muhammad was released and restored as sovereign in 1842.

This all emerged from correspondence presented to the House of Commons in 1858/9, discrediting Palmerston. There was a call for a committee of inquiry. Bright, by now MP for Birmingham, backed the proposal. Even after 22 years, Palmerston's conduct was still an issue. Bright insisted that the House had the right to establish 'whether there was and is a man in high position in the Government here or in India who had so low a sense of honour and of right that he could offer to this House mutilated, false, forged opinions of a public servant, who lost his life in the public service'.[27] Although the motion for a committee was defeated by 110 votes, Bright's speech cemented the mutual antipathy between himself and Palmerston that had simmered for years.

By this time, however, Bright was again in the ascendant. In June 1859, a need to unite the various liberal factions against the weak Conservative Government gave Bright power, with his crucial influence over the Radical vote. Cobden was in America and, as Trevelyan records, 'everyone told [Bright] that "the fate of the Government was in his hands"'.[28] At the time, the Franco-Austrian War was raging in Italy and, when he met Russell on 3 June to discuss matters, Bright used his strong hand to gain Russell's undertaking that England would remain neutral in the conflict. Russell also suggested that a Reform Bill was on the cards, and that Palmerston might 'go up to the Lords'.[29] With the continued neutrality of Britain agreed, Bright took part in a landmark meeting on 6 June at Willis's Rooms in St James's, where Palmerston and Russell joined forces in the creation of the new Liberal Party. Bright spoke after Palmerston and Russell, promising to work in unity with them, despite his involvement in bringing Palmerston down over the Conspiracy to Murder Bill the previous year (see Chapter 3).

On 16 June, Russell wrote to Bright, saying, 'Till yesterday I could not properly communicate with you.' He mentioned that Palmerston was to be Prime Minister, and that he had been asked to join the Government, but that he was insisting on a 'sound and satisfactory' Reform Bill. If this did not happen, he would resign. Cobden and Milner Gibson were to be offered Cabinet rank, but not Bright himself, because Palmerston 'regretted that the course [Bright] had taken, not with regard to the reform of the House of Commons, but with regard to other institutions, considered essential by the great majority of Englishmen'.[30] Bright did not seek office and was unmoved, though he thought the plan flawed. In his diary on 5 June, when he had first heard of it, he had written,

> Blind fools! – they think Cobden more easy to manage and less dangerous to them than I am. I don't think anything will induce him to join them, nor do I see how I could ... It is pleasant to watch this gang of aristocratic conspirators brought into trouble. We have spoiled their game thoroughly.[31]

Russell became foreign secretary two days later. Cobden would not consider Palmerston's offer to him to join the Government unless Bright was also brought in. Palmerston refused, and at this time, Queen Victoria agreed.

Russell kept to his undertaking that Britain would remain neutral in the Franco-Austrian War. After the Treaty of Villafranca, however, it was felt that the French had abandoned their Italian allies and were now planning to attack Britain. In July, Bright made an impassioned call for a commercial treaty with France as a means of both avoiding any such war and encouraging trade. Michel Chevalier, the French economist, was impressed and took up the call. By the French Commercial Treaty, negotiated personally by Cobden (see Chapter 3), virtually all the tariffs between Britain and France were abolished and the treaty became a template of modern free trade.

Nevertheless, a further threat of war with France emerged in March 1860, when Vittorio Emanuele of Italy signed the Treaty of Turin with Napoleon, ceding Savoy and Nice in exchange for permission to hold a referendum within certain territories in Italy to end their annexation by France. This made up for the shortfalls in the Treaty of Villafranca, which had been agreed between France and Austria, but British sentiment was again firmly against France.

Bright leapt in on 2 March as the treaty negotiations were under way, saying,

> We are not the Parliament of France, we are not the Parliament of Savoy – we are not the Parliament of Europe – but we are the Parliament of England; and, unless it can be shown that there is any direct and obvious interest which this country has in some of these foreign questions which are constantly brought before us, what an absurd spectacle do we offer to Europe and the world with these repeated discussions! ... You cannot prevent the transference of Savoy, but you may, if you like, embroil Europe and bring England into collision with France. I say, perish Savoy – though Savoy, I believe, will not perish and will not suffer – rather than we ... should involve the Government of this country with the people and the Government of France on a matter in which we have really no interest whatever.[32]

Bright's advice was heeded, and war again avoided, despite accusations of his speech being thoroughly 'un-English'.[33]

While Bright and Cobden could not have served happily under Palmerston, given their views on foreign policy, this episode and the French Commercial Treaty showed what these independent-minded backbenchers could achieve. During the negotiations for the Commercial Treaty, even Palmerston had gone so far as to encourage the British ambassador in Paris to make Cobden's path to Napoleon III as easy as possible, and called him 'a good fellow'.[34] But, back from his successful negotiations in France, Cobden refused honours and persisted in attacking Palmerston in the *Morning Star.* As Cobden's business had collapsed, Russell suggested to Palmerston that he should receive a parliamentary pension instead of honours. On the advice of the Chief Whip, Henry Brand, Palmerston refused, on the grounds that – as he explained to Russell – 'Nothing can well be worse, with the single exception of Bright, than the line which Cobden has taken and the language he has held both in and out of Parliament during the last two years.'[35] In 1864, Palmerston again refused to help Cobden, stating that, with respect to Bright and Cobden,

> in public opinion they are inseparably linked together and have run a muck against everything that the British Nation respects and values – Crown, Aristocracy, Established Church, Nobility, Gentry, Landowners. They have laboured incessantly to set class

against class, and the poor against the rich, those who have
nothing against those who have something.[36]

But Bright and Cobden were soon victorious again in their long
battle against Palmerston's foreign policy, when his strategy finally
unwound in the summer of 1864. Palmerston had given an empty
promise of support to Denmark against the intended annexation of
the Duchies of Schleswig-Holstein by Prussia, assuming the threat
would be sufficient to hold off Otto von Bismarck. But when
Bismarck pushed on regardless, Palmerston was forced to withdraw
his offer, and was jeered and laughed out of the House of Lords.
Public opinion was against any British engagement, and the House
of Commons followed suit. Eventually, under pressure from Bright
and Cobden, Palmerston won a vote by a majority of only 18, but
this was a vote for peace – and a victory for Bright and Cobden
within their own party, which undermined the whole of
Palmerston's career. As Bright noted in his diary on 5 July 1864, 'It
is evident that our years of preaching on Foreign Policy and non-
intervention have not been without effect.'[37]

The enmity between Bright and Palmerston lasted until the
latter's death on 18 October 1865. Bright never forgot their differences. Long after Palmerston's death, Bright asked Lord Rosebery,
who had become foreign secretary under Gladstone, whether he had
read about Palmerston's conduct of the Foreign Office. When
Rosebery replied that he had, Bright replied 'Then you know what
to avoid. Do the exact opposite of what he did. His administration at
the Foreign Office was one long crime.'[38]

Aftermath of the Crimea

Palmerston might have died, but the after-effects of his foreign
policy lived on. In 1871, Russia tore up the Treaty of Paris after
France was trampled by Germany in the Franco-Prussian War.
Bright stood firm on the position he had taken in the 1850s,
and wrote to his leader and Prime Minister, Gladstone, warning
against any further involvement in the affairs leading on from the
Crimean War:

> Any interference on our part would fail ... War would destroy your
> Government and ruin your own reputation ... The Crimean War
> is the greatest blot on the reign of the Queen, and what is passing
> now only more demonstrates the folly and uselessness of it.[39]

Gladstone and his foreign secretary, Lord Granville, did indeed avoid war. Britain looked on as the Black Sea once again became the Russian centre for naval warfare, and Sebastopol came back into its own. Bright also encouraged a renewal of the Anglo-French Commercial Treaty, saying to Granville, 'How delightfully "conservative" I am become you will say … I was always "conservative" in feeling and in reality – as those who know me best will freely admit.'[40]

Later, in May 1875, the Eastern Question exploded in the form of rebellion in Bosnia and Herzegovina, followed by the Bulgarian massacres, and Serbia and Montenegro declaring war against the beleaguered Ottoman Empire. With reports of Ottoman atrocities in the newspapers, and Britain's position unclear, Bright was invited to speak at the Manchester Reform Club, which he did on 2 October. His message was clear:

> We regret, the country regrets, the sacrifices of the Crimean war … It is no business of ours to be sending ships and troops nearly three thousand miles to effect territorial changes in which we have no real and no direct interest.

Disraeli had, a few days earlier, given 'a speech of defiance to the people of England, a speech heartless and cruel as respects Serbia and Bulgaria'. Bright reminded his audience of the great changes in Britain since the Reform Act of 1867, and stated that the Prime Minister would be 'swept from his pride of place, and his place of power' by the force of public opinion, which, unlike 1857, could now be expressed through democratic means. He called for a

> solemn and irrevocable decision … that the blood and the treasure of England will never again be wasted on behalf of the Turk, that the vote of our Government, the vote of England in the Parliament of Europe, shall be given in favour of justice and freedom to Christian and Moslem alike – and that the Ottoman power shall be left hereafter to the fate which Providence has decreed to corruption, tyranny, and wrong.[41]

As the conflict escalated, with Russia entering the fray in 1877 on the side of the rebel provinces, Disraeli revived Palmerston's Crimea policy in an opportunistic move to arouse 'the sublime instinct of an ancient people',[42] last seen in Britain during the Crimean War. The meddling that ensued led the nation to the brink of war with Russia.

In the parliamentary debates leading up to this crisis, Bright had spoken, but without his previous vigour, and it had fallen largely to Gladstone to promote non-intervention. This he did, using the very arguments that Bright and Cobden had put forward during the Crimean War. As Bright recorded in his diary on 26 April 1877, 'Gladstone burdened with sense of responsibility in connexion with his share in the Crimean War, and anxious to urge that sense of responsibility on the conscience of the nation.'[43] Bright also received somewhat belated support for his Crimean arguments from Sir Robert Peel, the Liberal son of the former prime minister, who said in the House that the effect on him of Bright's speeches during the Crimean War 'had been such that he had then resolved that he would never do anything to support the Ottoman power in Europe'.[44]

The crisis soon saw Bright back to his old form, supporting Gladstone against Disraeli when other Liberals backed away. After speaking at a meeting in Manchester on 30 April 1878, he recorded a 'disturbance' in his diary, which Trevelyan describes: 'As he came out he was attacked, and his hat was smashed over his head by the Jingoes, who were being set on in all parts of the country to intimidate the advocates of peace.'[45] Bright was truly back in the fray.

Just two weeks later, however, Bright was confronted with a far more personal battle, that of inconsolable grief, when his second wife, Elizabeth, died suddenly in Rochdale when he was away. He withdrew from public life immediately. But his arguments had won the day and war was averted, with Disraeli agreeing to the compromise of the Treaty of Berlin in July 1878.

Bright's moral strength was again proved right, as Gladstone later reminded the House when he delivered his eulogy on Bright's death in 1889, singling out Bright and Cobden's conduct during the Crimean War for particular praise:

> At that time it was – although we had known much of Mr. Bright before – that we learnt something more. We had known the great mental gifts which distinguished him; we had known his courage and his consistency; we had known his splendid eloquence ... But we had not till then known how high the moral tone of those popular leaders had been elevated, what splendid examples they set to the whole of their contemporaries and to coming generations, and with what readiness they could part with popular sympathy and support for the sake of the right and of their conscientious convictions.[46]

The Second Afghan War, 1878–81

After the Treaty of Berlin, Russia set its sights on Afghanistan. Since 1842, when Dost Muhammad had been restored following the First Afghan War, Russia had slowly advanced its territory from Kazakhstan through Uzbekistan and now sat on the border of Afghanistan, a key territory for the stability and protection of Britain's great colony in India. When Russian envoys arrived in Kabul in July 1878, the British Government requested permission to send a diplomatic mission of its own, but the new Emir, Sher Ali Khan, refused. Nevertheless, a mission was dispatched in September 1878. It was turned away when it reached the Khyber Pass. The British forces entered Afghanistan in November. The opening battles of this Second Afghan War were decisive British victories, and British and Indian troops were able to occupy much of the country. But, this success was built on weak foundations.

Sher Ali Khan died in February 1879, and his son, Muhammad Yaqub Khan, sought to stem the British invasion through the Treaty of Gandamak in May of that year, in which he relinquished control of foreign policy to Britain. British representatives were appointed in key locations and the troops withdrew. The peace only lasted until September 1879, however, when the British presence in Kabul was slaughtered in an uprising. Muhammad Yaqub Khan abdicated in October, British troops re-entered the country and the fighting resumed.

Bright denounced Disraeli's policy of seeking to take over Afghanistan. Disraeli had initially expressed an interest in bringing Russia and India together on one boundary, but was now set on annexation. Bright himself was of the view that 'it would be better if the frontiers of the two empires were coterminous'.[47] As he later argued in 1882, it would be more sensible to have people independent and friendly on the Indian frontier 'rather than hostile people in subjection to us'.[48]

The Anglo-Afghan conflict was very close to Bright's heart. He had connected the wellbeing of India with British foreign policy towards Russia years earlier, in 1873. In a speech in Birmingham on 16 April 1879, in which he spoke about Russia, India and Britain, he concluded that Disraeli's Government had shown 'that they are imbecile at home and turbulent and wicked abroad'.[49] That evening, he noted that the speech had '"liberated my mind" on what has often pressed upon it recently and was most kindly received as usual'.[50]

In the General Election of April 1880, the Liberal Party regained power and Bright joined Gladstone's Cabinet as Chancellor of the Duchy of Lancaster. That summer, the invasion of Afghanistan and the march by Sir Frederick Roberts to Kandahar following an uprising by Muhammad Yaqub Khan's brother, Ayub Khan, occupied Bright's thoughts. The effects of the war felt by India were much on his mind. He records meetings in his diary in August 1880 with his friend from Calcutta, Lalmohan Ghosh, alongside anxious comments about Afghanistan: 'There seem only clouds and dangers about us'; 'Future difficult and dark.'[51]

By September, when the garrison at Kandahar was relieved and the army of Ayub Khan broken, the Cabinet was moving towards the decision to evacuate Afghanistan, the Queen having written to Lord Hartington urging that Kandahar should be retained. On 4 September 1880, Bright attended a series of Cabinet meetings at the beginning of the month to discuss the options.[52] His Cabinet colleagues shared his view that the occupation was both a threat to India and an unfair expense for the Indian people, and eventually decided on evacuation for the following year.

Resignation over Egypt

After Gladstone's return to power in April 1880, Bright's hope was that the jingoism that had taken root with Disraeli's Government would disappear. However, whereas previously he had been able to count on the Liberal Party for support against imperialism and all that went with it, by the 1880s this was no longer the case. Once again, Bright found himself on the outside, arguing the case for peace and non-intervention, with only his fellow Manchester School friends for support. For him, this was a moral issue. As he was to say in Birmingham on 29 January 1885, 'If the Manchester policy be dead, then I say let us humiliate ourselves, for morality and Christianity are dead also.'[53]

The height of Bright's battle against the new imperialist and bellicose spirit of the times came in 1882, over Egypt. The opening of the Suez Canal in 1869 had re-invigorated British interest in Egypt, which had been largely dormant since an unsuccessful attempt to occupy the country during the Napoleonic Wars. In 1875, a British inquiry into Egypt's finances had revealed serious problems, caused by excessive borrowing by the Khedive to finance widespread reforms and a war with Ethiopia. When the Khedive's credit finally expired, he was forced to sell his shares in the Suez Canal to Britain, and a system of Anglo-French control of Egypt's government and finances was established. The new regime had an Egyptian prime minister, Nubar Pasha, a British finance minister, Sir Charles Rivers Wilson, and a French minister of public works, the Marquis de Blignières. However, this move caused a nationalist revolt, led by Urabi Pasha, who wished not only to oust the foreign powers but also remove the Khedive. The British, fearful that the nationalists would default on Egypt's debt repayments, and that Britain would lose control of the Suez Canal, took the Khedive's side in this struggle. A fleet of warships, both British and French, was dispatched to Alexandria to put on a display of united power and intimidate Urabi Pasha and his followers. When the ships arrived in Alexandria in mid-May 1882, rumours of an imminent invasion spread and led to renewed unrest in Alexandria. On 11 June, fierce anti-European riots broke out, in which more than 200 Europeans were killed as well as many Egyptians.

Bright, now again a member of Gladstone's Cabinet, looked on in despair. Though he had visited Egypt as a young man on his Grand Tour, Bright did not appear to have a great knowledge of, or even a desire to study, the nuts and bolts of the problems in Egypt. Instead, he focused on the simple point that Egyptian affairs were just that – Egyptian and not British – and was firmly on the side of non-intervention. Yet his poor health and increasing age denied him the energy to fight for the cause of peace as he had done over the Crimean War. Furthermore, he now had a personal and political attachment to the very men, his Cabinet colleagues, whom he needed to challenge, which he had not experienced under Palmerston. It was only as events unfolded that the new Liberal devotion to imperialism became clear. Understandably, therefore, Bright's record of Cabinet meetings in June 1882 shows a mixture of anxiety, vacillating trust – of his friend Gladstone in particular – and an underlying sense of powerlessness. On 19 June, he wrote: 'Egypt. Great difficulty. Past arrangements not wise, and now position almost beyond remedy. French Govt. uncertain and hard to act with.' On 20 June: 'Egypt: warm discussion and great difference of opinion. Very anxious on this question, and doubts as to my position in regard to it.' On 21 June: 'Egypt: discussion less warm, but much difference of opinion. Mr. Gladstone moderate and wise as usual. My anxiety somewhat relieved by more moderate tone.'[54]

By 27 June, Bright was firmer in his position, recording a conversation with Lord Hartington:

I spoke quite frankly: could be no party to invasion or occupation of Egypt. Any mode out of the mess would be better than
occupation and war on or with Turkey, and perhaps quarrel with
France. Time and patience might solve the problem.[55]

However, his difference of opinion with Gladstone was causing him
much trouble, as he recorded on 2 July:

Cabinet at 2 o'clock. Egypt very critical. Opposed strongly
measures which I think tending to force and war. Am nearing
the point when I must decide whether I can retain my place in
the Govt. To leave it may be hurtful to it; to keep with it may be
hurtful to myself.[56]

At this point, he still had some faith in Gladstone to do the right
thing and avoid war – as he wrote on 8 July 1882: 'Egypt. Contended
against eagerness of War and Navy Departments to organize forces
and ships for "operations" – that is war – in Egypt. Mr. Gladstone
firm against extravagant proposals generated in the atmosphere of
the "Services".' But he added, ruefully, 'Painful to observe how
much of the "jingo" or war spirit can be shown by certain members
of a Liberal Cabinet.'[57] He could not equate his view of Liberalism
with these attitudes.

On 11 July, news of the bombardment of Alexandria arrived and
Bright entered a period of tortured self-debate. That evening, he
recorded with some relief that, while sitting next to Gladstone in the
House, there was 'No conversation on the subject which troubled
us both, except his complaint of the way in which everyone seemed
to lose his head: projects of laying telegraph wires all along Suez
Canal, as if various preparations for great war were necessary.' At
home, he drafted three versions of a letter of resignation and wrote
to family members informing them of his intention, but still wrestled
with the question. 'Much troubled all day,' he wrote in his diary:

Great regret at my position. Shall be blamed by many, but
cannot accept the responsibility of War which I deem unjust and
unnecessary. There seems not a single friend of mine with whom
I can consult. Must rely on my own judgement, which I hope will
not mislead me.[58]

On 12 July, he 'felt quite unable' to take his place on the Treasury
Bench during a debate on Egypt. He had written a new resignation

letter that morning, but before he could deliver it, he received a letter from Gladstone, who understood his intention, asking him to take more time to deliberate 'as more favourable news of truce might change view of circumstances'.[59] Bright sent the letter in any case, so that Gladstone might fully understand his position, but agreed to wait a day before making a final decision. The letter read:

> I think in reviewing the doctrines connected with our Foreign policy which I have preached and defended during 40 years of my public life, you will not be surprised at the decision I am now compelled to take. I cannot accept any share of the responsibility for the acts of war which have taken place at Alexandria. I cannot see to what they may lead, and I know not to what greater wrong and mischief they may force the Government. I feel therefore compelled to withdraw from the Administration, and to ask you to place my resignation of the office I hold in the hands of the Queen. I bitterly lament the disappointment of many hopes as I separate myself from your Government. My feelings towards yourself are those of profound esteem and regard, and an overpowering sense of duty has alone forced me to the only course which seems now open to me. To add to your difficulties and to give you trouble is a cause of much unhappiness to me. I can only hope you will be able to judge me rightly and to forgive me.[60]

Besieged with pleas from fellow Liberals to reconsider his resignation, he wrote that evening:

> My perplexity very great. Duty seems to call both ways. Can I help in arresting further mischief, and in hope of this can I remain in office? It is hard that to such a question I should have difficulty in coming at once to a decisive conclusion.[61]

A Cabinet meeting on 13 July made up his mind:

> Took almost no part in the discussion. The case has gone beyond my range, and counsel from me of no avail ... The tone of the conversation at the Cabinet convinced me that I could do nothing more – that with the members of the Cabinet on the Egyptian question I must silently consent to much that I must condemn, or be in constant conflict with them, and that there was nothing for me but to retire.[62]

As Philip Magnus pointed out, 'Bright's words always carried weight with Gladstone. He told his intimates that it was Bright who first made him realise that he might one day be Prime Minister.'[63] Bright's influence came from the fact that, as Roy Jenkins puts it, Gladstone regarded him as 'a great man ... exactly what a Radical ought to be, cloudy and moralising rather than demanding and practical'.[64] But this time, Bright could not convince him. After sending a final letter to Gladstone, in which he confirmed his resignation, the two men met at the corner of the Athenaeum and walked together to Downing Street:

> [Gladstone] then explained his views – to me somewhat strange and unexpected. He urged as if all that has been done in the Egyptian case was right, and even persuaded himself that he is fully justified in the interest of Peace. I made little reply, but gave him no expectation that my view coincided with his or had in any degree changed.

After dining with Gladstone and his daughter, Bright returned home, where he received a note from Gladstone repeating what he had said in their earlier conversation:

> The contents of it much surprised me. He seems to have the power of convincing himself that what to me seems glaringly wrong is evidently right, and tho' he regrets that a crowd of men should be killed, he regards it almost as an occurrence which is not to be condemned ... He even spoke of our being able to justify our conduct in the great day of account.[65]

Such a justification was out of the question for Bright.

On 15 July, he wrote 'what I hope is a final letter to Mr. Gladstone, insisting on my retirement from the Cabinet and my office as Chancellor of the Duchy of Lancaster'.[66] Two days later, Bright received a 'kind note' from Gladstone. Gladstone's biographer, John Morley, gives further details of this note: 'The correspondence closed with a wish from Mr. Gladstone: "Believe in the sore sense of practical loss, and the (I trust) unalterable friendship and regard with which I remain, etc."'[67] The same day, Bright

> spoke shortly on my resignation. House very quiet and friendly, cheering when I rose, and when I sat down. In my old seat 2nd bench below the gangway, the House seems more pleasant to me

this evening than any other this session. Members most friendly, regretting my leaving the Govt. but expressing their sense of my right action.[68]

Bright was critical in his speech of resignation. His reference to the moral law elicited a sharp retort from Gladstone but, in Morley's words, 'still their friendship did appear to remain unalterable, as Mr Gladstone trusted it would'.[69]

Bright left the Duchy of Lancaster on 21 July, and on 25 July he went to the Isle of Wight to return the seals of office to the Queen:

> She was alone. I took the Duchy seals from the box, and said I was sorry to have to give them up. She said, 'And I am very sorry to have to receive them.' I said I thought she would understand my difficulty, and how impossible it was for me to take any other course. She replied that she quite understood it. She hoped I was well, and I thanked her for the kindness she had always shown me. I bowed to her; she returned it; and I left the room. The Queen looked well and young. She was most courteous and kind.[70]

Although there was no bitter rift and, on the surface, things continued as normal between the two statesmen, this episode marked the end of Bright's political relationship with Gladstone and the beginning of his separation from the Liberal Party. His inherent need for independence of action to fulfil his objects and maintain his moral purpose was shown to be inconsistent with collective responsibility, with party and with Cabinet office. He never took office again.

The bombardment of Alexandria also highlighted for Bright his differences of opinion with Joseph Chamberlain, with whom he was moving towards an alliance over Home Rule. As a young man, Chamberlain had canvassed for Thomas Dyke Acland, Bright's Liberal–Conservative opponent in the 1859 General Election, challenging Bright's 'Quaker' approach to foreign policy. Now, as one of Bright's fellow Birmingham MPs, the two men regularly shared a united platform. When it came to Egypt, however, Bright had his reservations. He wrote in December 1882,

> I do not see how I can with advantage take part in a meeting at which it will be impossible to avoid a discussion of the Egyptian question, on which Mr Chamberlain and I are far as the poles

asunder ... He speaks of the 'ignoble doctrine of non-intervention' and the whole tone and argument of his speech in defence of the Government are exactly the stuff on which the foreign policy of Lord Palmerston, and I may almost say of Lord Beaconsfield, was defended. I can have no part in it and shall denounce it when I am forced to speak upon it.

With a public meeting proposed in Birmingham, he found himself once again torn: 'I do not want to assail the Government or to get into open conflict with my colleague, still less to create any difficulty with my friends at Birmingham.'[71] In the event, the meeting was cancelled. 'This is a relief to me,' Bright wrote in his diary. 'Our Birmingham affairs just now are rather "mixed", and the future is not very clearly seen.'[72]

Two years later, when Egypt once again came to the fore with the siege of Khartoum, a Sudanese outpost of the Anglo-Egyptian army, Bright wrote to Chamberlain of the difficult time in 1882:

I told the Cabinet that they had lost their heads. If the reins had not been handed over to the ruffians of the fleet, who were eager for war ... there would have been no war, no bombardment, no city in flames, no thousands of men slaughtered ... The past is past, but it leaves an ugly future ... Let us hope the clouds will lift.[73]

The clouds, however, remained, and the siege of Khartoum continued for nearly 11 months, culminating in the massacre of General Gordon and his troops in January 1885. On 2 March 1885, Bright dined with Gladstone, where they had a 'Long talk on Egypt. He said he had suffered torture during the continuance of the difficulty in that country.' Gladstone wished that Bright was still with him in his Cabinet, but Bright had limited sympathy for him. 'I am very sorry for his troubles,' he wrote that evening. 'I have not made them, and would have saved him from them, if he had been strong enough to have taken my advice.'[74]

Bright was equally unimpressed with Gordon's posthumous position as a national hero. He wrote to a correspondent in March:

Gordon cared little for his own life and apparently less for the lives of others, or he would not have devoted himself to the savagery of war in China and the Soudan ... he accepted the business of war and slaughter in countries many thousands of miles away from his own country, and I suppose thus imagined he was serving God and his country. This would seem to me a sort of madness, which I cannot understand.

In the popular mind, however, Gordon was just the kind of man the British Empire needed. For Bright, this was the crux of his increasing loneliness and isolation as a promoter of peace. He wrote:

> Be the Government Liberal or Tory, much the same thing happens – war with all its horrors and miseries and crimes and cost. Talkers and writers being mostly in favor of it, and the multitude approving or consenting to the wickedness in high places[75]

CHAPTER 8

Oppression in Ireland and British Sovereignty

Force was no remedy.
(John Bright, 1847)[1]

The Irish Question

To those acquainted with Anthony Trollope's perceptive eye into mid-nineteenth-century Anglo-Irish politics in *Phineas Finn*, the character of Turnbull is clearly based on John Bright. As Asa Briggs notes, however, Trollope did not like Bright. He thought that,

> Having nothing to construct, he could always deal with generalities. Being free from responsibility, he was not called upon either to study details or to master even great facts. It was his business to inveigh against evils, and perhaps there is no easier business ... It was his work to cut down forest trees, and he had nothing to do with the subsequent cultivation of the land.[2]

Far from not being not engaged in the cultivation in the land, it was indeed Bright who created the circumstances for modern democracy, ploughing the furrows of England and Ireland from one end to the other in an interminable quest for justice for the working class and their right to engage in the government of the country through their choice of representatives.

The eponymous hero of *Phineas Finn* is equally suggestive of one of Bright's kinsmen, his cousin, Frederick Lucas, a Quaker turned ultramontane Catholic and the founder of the Catholic journal, *The Tablet*. The book turns on the life of Phineas Finn, who makes his way into the House of Commons from the Bar, where before him lies a glittering career. He embroils himself in the issue of tenant

right in Ireland under the influence of an unidentified but extremely
independent-minded Cabinet minister who has taken against his
own Government. Phineas Finn takes up the cause as a matter of
principle and, in a wonderfully woven tale of love and politics, he
ultimately condemns himself to outer darkness, committing political
suicide over his support for the downtrodden Irish peasantry.

All this recalls Frederick Lucas himself, except that Lucas was
truly independent and not attached to any political party. He did,
however, fight unremittingly for the Irish cause as the Member for
County Meath and for the involvement of Irish priests in Irish politics, to the great displeasure of the Primate of Ireland, Archbishop
Cullen. Lucas's friendship with (the now Blessed) John Henry
Newman in the creation of University College Dublin and their
association with the Young Ireland movement was the cause of this
displeasure, although, like John Bright, they were both anxious for
the disestablishment of the Church in Ireland and equally convinced
against the unconstitutional and violent means of some of their
contemporaries.

Frederick Lucas entered the House of Commons in 1852, the
same year as Newman published his *Idea of a University* and
the creation of University College Dublin. When Lucas met Bright
in the Lobby of the House of Commons on 11 November, the
day Lucas took up his seat, Bright, still very much the Quaker
and deeply sympathetic to Lucas's views on tenant rights and the
Irish Church, addressed his Catholic cousin with the question, 'Well,
Fred, and how goes on the old superstition?' Lucas replied,
'Why, John, a great deal better than the new hypocrisy.'[3]

Lucas died prematurely in 1855, but Bright continued his own
and his cousin's commitment to the Irish cause, despite being wary
of Lucas's headlong passion and his Roman Catholicism.

For Bright, Ireland was no casual political engagement. He had
taken a deep personal interest in the welfare of Irish people from an
early age. Indeed, as a young man he had ensured that an Irish
worker in the family business who wanted to return to Ireland was
enabled to do so because he wrote off a fine that the man had
incurred at the works as a result of causing damage.[4] He made
his first trip to Ireland in 1832, aged 21. Accompanied by his
cousin, James Crosland, he sailed from Liverpool to Dublin and
travelled on to Belfast. Bright continues, 'What I most remember
from our journey was the crowd of beggars that gathered round the
coach at every place where we stopped to change horses. Nothing
like it could be seen in England.'[5] This had a powerful influence

on Bright's imagination and remained with him throughout his political life.

This early deep impression of the miseries brought about by the Corn Laws added impetus to Cobden and Bright's campaign for repeal. Indeed, in July 1843, when Bright was engaged in his second bid to win his seat in Durham, following the unseating of Lord Dungannon for bribery (see Chapter 1), he had spoken not only on the Corn Laws, but also on Ireland:

> What is the condition of Ireland? Two millions of her children are paupers; and yet it is a magnificent island, with a soil more fertile than the country in which we live ... with a people ... generous, warm-hearted, intelligent, honest and virtuous and probably, at this moment, more sober than the people of any other country in the world.

He criticized the lack of employment, the Established Church, the administration of the law and lack of impartial justice, and the abuse of the people by landlords who turned them out of their cottages – as many as 70,000 turned out in one year by landlords 'to consolidate their farms, and drive away the miserable people'.[6]

In his maiden speech in the House of Commons, Bright returned to the topic of Ireland, demanding employment, wages and food for her people. He said,

> It is no petty legislation that can do this, no bringing in bills for the recovery of small debts, and making a boast of measures such as that. Land-owners have been our law-makers, and yet everywhere there is suffering, and the landowners are everywhere charged with the mischief ... You have been sowing curses, and you now wonder that curses have grown.[7]

As with America and parliamentary reform, Bright and Disraeli shared an interest and a sympathy for Ireland, with Disraeli describing Irish degradation brought about by 'an absentee aristocracy and an alien church'.[8] It is no coincidence that Disraeli and Bright arrived at similar conclusions, as it was said of Disraeli that he believed it was essential for the Quakers, the Catholics and the Jews as minorities to stick together against the Establishment.

Bright also had a strong bond with Daniel O'Connell – 'the Great Liberator' – who had been elected as a 'repealer' of the Union in 1828 at the famous election in County Clare. Bright greatly admired

O'Connell, and they shared a strong instinct that, however worthy
the cause, change would not come except by agitation. One thing on
which Bright deeply disagreed with O'Connell, however, was the
repeal of the Union. He could accept everything else, but not this.
It is ironic that at the very beginning of his political career and again
at the very end, he should have been faced with political alliances
with two men, O'Connell and Gladstone, who were both committed
to Home Rule.

Maynooth Grant

One of Bright's earliest political battles over Ireland came as early as
1845, when Sir Robert Peel proposed to make a grant to Maynooth
College, a seminary for Irish priests. Bright opposed this as dodging
the necessary radical reforms and seeking, literally, to buy off the
opposition of the Irish Church. Bright said he regretted having to
vote with anti-Catholic members of Parliament, but the remedy was
worse than the cure:

> Did [Irish discontent] arise because the priests of Maynooth are
> now insufficiently clad or fed? I had always thought that it arose
> because one third of the people were paupers ... The object of
> this Bill is to tame down these agitators – it is a sop given to the
> priests. It is hush-money.

He turned on the Established Church as being 'at the root of
the evils' of Ireland. He commiserated with the Irish Catholics that
they had

> everything Protestant – a Protestant clique which has been
> dominant in the country; a Protestant Viceroy to distribute
> places and emoluments amongst that Protestant clique;
> Protestant judges who have polluted the seats of justice;
> Protestant magistrates before whom the Catholic peasant cannot
> hope for justice; they have not only Protestant but exterminating
> landlords, and more than that a Protestant soldiery, who at the
> beck and command of a Protestant priest have butchered and
> killed a Catholic peasant even in the presence of his widowed
> mother.

He was against the Maynooth Grant because 'No priest of the paid
establishment shall ever tell of the wrongs of the people among

whom he is living ... Ireland is suffering, not from the want of another church, but because he has already one church too many.'⁹

Bright's cousin, Frederick Lucas, would have cheered him for this, despite their religious differences. As the Member for County Meath in the 1850s, Lucas himself engaged in just such a campaign, which he carried to Rome, against Archbishop Cullen of Dublin, to ensure that Irish priests could take an active part in Irish politics from the pulpit. In his excoriating speeches, and in the Statement he prepared at the request of the Pope himself, Lucas explained why it was that the bishops in Ireland and the papal representative in Ireland, Monsignore Barnabo, had obstructed his efforts to improve the condition of the Irish people.

Cobden and Bright voted in different directions over Maynooth – the only occasion relating to a major issue in their entire political careers. The Bill passed with a significant majority.

Coercion in Ireland

The Irish famine was desperate. Yet, instead of dealing with the real causes of the unrest that followed, the Government introduced the Crime and Outrage (Ireland) Bill. This was a coercion bill that provided for emergency legislation to be brought in on a local basis to repress agrarian violence. On 13 December 1847, Bright spoke on this Bill:

> I speak as a representative from a county which suffers extremely from the condition of Ireland ...many of the evils which in times past have been attributed to the extension of manufactures in that county have arisen from the enormous immigration from a suffering and pauperised people driven for a sustenance from their own country. As a Lancashire representative I protest most solemnly against a system which drives the Irish population to seek work and wages in this country and in other countries when both might be afforded them at home. Parliament is bound to remedy this state of things.¹⁰

Bright's consistent support, both for Ireland and for the Union with the United Kingdom, was no contradiction. He firmly believed that it was the duty of the British Parliament to legislate through Westminster to ensure the fairness that both countries deserved. He argued that the poverty and misery brought upon the Irish people by the misuse of aristocratic and anti-Catholic rule should be

remedied by fair and proper legislation to remove the causes of
discontent by a humane rule of law uncontaminated by privilege –
and that this law should be passed by the Union at Westminster. For
different reasons, he and Daniel O'Connell, not to mention
Frederick Lucas and others, fought to stabilize the relationship
between Britain and Ireland, the problems of which were growing
ever more dangerous and turbulent precisely because the stubborn,
self-serving legislators and absentee landowners in Westminster
would not reform Irish government in agriculture, tenant rights and
the Poor Law. The consequences of this dominated the domestic
politics of the United Kingdom up to the time of Éamon de Valera
and Michael Collins, and continue to the present day, despite
Bright's advice and campaigns.

The rebellion and agrarian violence of 1848 were put down under
the Crime and Outrage Act, and even Bright, who had previously
petitioned against it, reluctantly felt he had to vote for it. As he
explained later to one of his biographers, R. Barry O'Brien, he did
so on what he regarded as constitutional grounds, namely that
the executive were responsible for law and order and therefore had a
right to pass exceptional legislation for this purpose, despite his view
that 'force was no remedy'.[11]

In the debates on Ireland in 1847 and 1848, Bright argued continuously for the reform of the land laws and the disestablishment of
the Protestant Church. Various experimental land reforms were
attempted, but without success. In one debate, in August 1848,
Bright explained how the Irish diaspora had gained influence in
the USA:

> Driven forth by poverty, Irishmen emigrate in great numbers,
> and in whatsoever quarter of the world an Irishman sets his foot,
> there stands a bitter – an implacable enemy of England ... There
> are hundreds of thousands of the population of the United States
> of America who are Irish by birth, or by immediate descent;
> and be it remembered, Irishmen settled in the United States have
> a large influence in public affairs.

He observed that this influence extended to the election of Congress
and even the presidency. He warned,

> There may come a time when questions of a critical nature will
> be agitated between the Governments of Great Britain and the
> United States, and it is certain that such a time the Irish in that

country will throw their whole weight into the scale against this
country, and against peace with this country.

These would prove to be farsighted remarks.

Having spent 73 days hearing evidence as a member of the
Dublin Election Committee, Bright asserted that the parliamentary
representation of Ireland was 'a fraud'. He continued,

> You have toiled at this Irish difficulty Session after Session, and
> some of you have grown from boyhood to grey headed old men,
> since it first met you in your legislative career, and yet there is
> not in ancient or modern history a picture so humiliating as that
> which Ireland presents to the world at this moment.[12]

Bright was aware that the Irish made a good fist of their
opportunities when they did emigrate, particularly to the USA, so
there was no reason why they should not be able to do so in their
own country.

In April 1849, he blamed the Irish landowners in Ireland and their
representation in Parliament for the lack of reform, arguing that 'the
price paid for it is the ruin and degradation of your country'. He
said, 'I am ashamed, I must say, of the course which we have taken
upon this question.' By contrast, there had been a great subscription
raised in 1846 for Ireland with contributions from the Pope, the
Sultan of the Ottoman Empire, a Native American tribe from
the USA, and even slaves from the Carolinas. He showed that the
distress in Ireland had an impact on England – particularly, as he
was aware, in and around his Manchester constituency. He provided
figures demonstrating that, despite the Irish population being half
that of England, the legacy duty paid on capital in Ireland was only a
fraction of that paid in England – 'the strongest possible proofs of
the poverty of Ireland'.[13]

More recent research has thrown light on the complexities and
class hierarchy in Ireland at this time. As Theodore Hoppen illustrates, the notion that legislation alone would solve the overweening
power of the landlords underestimates the fact that the agricultural
labourers who did not own land were by far the most numerous.
These labourers were gravely exploited by the farmers, even more so
than the farmers were by the landowners. This also emerged from
the Devon Commission, though the tenant right agitation was aimed
at providing the tenant farmers with a sustainable living and way of
life, which in turn would benefit the lower orders. All this led to

massive emigration, with four million people leaving Ireland
between 1850 and 1914.[14]

In an attempt to alleviate the trickle-down problems caused by
debt-ridden, and mainly absentee, landlords, the Encumbered
Estates Act 1849 was brought in to provide for the compulsory sale
of debt-encumbered estates. This led to a shift in ownership, but it
was the Irish landowners who benefited and became richer still.
From Bright's point of view, this had merely compounded the problems of the lower orders. Whatever the continuing degradation of
the agricultural labourer, the Irish farmers themselves became
profoundly disaffected, leading to serious rural disturbances. In
Bright's view, the Irish question would be settled if Irish tenant
farmers were given the opportunity to buy their land, and if the
peasants were encouraged to make improvements to their holdings
and become efficient, which they would only do if they had a proper
interest in the land itself. A combination of the disestablishment of
the Irish Church and land reform, in Bright's view, would produce
the right results and eliminate poverty and rebellion, while at the
same time bringing England and Ireland together.

Visits to Ireland, 1849 and 1852

So concerned was Bright about the state of Ireland that he returned
there to see for himself. Between 10 August and 8 September 1849, he
went from Dublin to Wicklow, down to Wexford, to Cork and Kerry,
then travelled north to Limerick, Tipperary and Connaught before
returning to Dublin, building up a formidable array of facts and
evidence from personal interviews. He had been influenced deeply
by the report of the Devon Commission in 1845, which showed that
landlords piled rent increases on to tenants who made improvements
to their land, effectively confiscating the value of the improvements.
The Devon Commission concluded that this injustice had been the
cause of crime and disorder, leading Peel to bring in a Bill in 1845 to
protect the tenants against their landlords. But the proprietors flatly
refused the reforms and the Government abandoned the Bill.

Bright, armed with the Devon Report, found increasing evidence
that the situation was deteriorating, with poverty, hovels and workhouses everywhere, and landlords refusing leases to Roman
Catholics. He noted that the Skibbereen workhouses held thousands
of men, women and children. He found similar situations in Bantry
and Tralee, and that average wages in Ireland were ninepence per
day. By contrast, where the tenants were allowed to buy their farms,

they prospered. A week after arriving in Ireland, Bright recorded that the late Lord Mountmorris had 'received £16,000 a year and never expended a shilling on improvements'.[15] The tenants had gone to America. The following day, he saw an air of prosperity in small farms at Kilmore where leases had been granted and some had bought their farms.[16]

On 29 August, Bright stayed in Tipperary with Charles Bianconi, an Italian who had settled in Ireland and created a public conveyance system in 1815. He owned 1,000 acres of land.[17] In Bright's words, Bianconi

> never forgives the man who tells a lie, or who takes anything clandestinely or dishonestly. Gives his men, if they retire, their full wages 5/- to 7/- per week as pension ... they never retire unless wholly unable to work, as their perquisites or fees are so much more than the wages. Governs his men not so much by surveillance as by moral principles.

He described Bianconi's home, Longfield, as having bulletproof windows and doors, with a yard with high walls and large, bullet-proof doors.[18] Even the enlightened employers remained at risk.

Travelling from Scariff to Tuam, Bright found a Catholic arch-bishop with an income of £700 a year living opposite a Protestant bishop with an income of over £5,000. Bright was convinced that it was the Protestants who were at the root of the trouble, not the Catholics. Everywhere, he observed evictions with 'whole villages of houses unroofed ... A few rafters reared against the wall with sods over it and straw for a temporary hovel.'[19]

On his return from Ireland, Bright drew up his own Tenant Rights Bill based on his researches and spoke about it to Lord John Russell. In Bright's words, 'He was evidently anxious on the question, but, not understanding it, he seems hardly to know how to deal with it. I mentioned my having drawn a short Bill and wishing to show it to him, and he expressed a desire to see it.'[20] But nothing came of this for decades, other than a half-baked Irish Reform Bill in 1850, which Bright denounced when the Lords raised the rating franchise to £15 and Russell accepted £12, which achieved no real change. The Bill passed, but the Church was not disestablished, there was no land reform and the Irish were effectively disenfranchised. Bright would have to wait until 1880 before he could drive through the Land Act with Gladstone to make significant changes to the system of tenure.

The question nevertheless continued to vex Bright. In January 1851, he wrote to Cobden that he attributed the murders in the north of Ireland to bad relations between landlord and tenant. The same month, he wrote to Charles Villiers, arguing that Ireland had no rulers, and that those who did rule were agents for the aristocracy of the United Kingdom. As he later asked in a Tenants Right Debate in February 1852, 'Can the cats wisely and judiciously legislate for the mice?'[21]

Bright went back to Ireland in 1852 and, writing to Cobden, pointed out that all that was heard about Ireland came from the English press. 'I find the Irish as individuals, or collected as a meeting, just about as reasonable as the English and as willing to accept what is just in settlement of their claims,' he wrote.[22] He also urged against the establishment of the Protestant Church ruling over the Irish Catholics. That year, Bright put forward his proposals for the disestablishment of the Irish Church, which he had first raised in 1849.

Disestablishment of the Irish Church, 1860s

For the next 15 years, however, the Irish question remained stagnant. Bright's attention turned first to the Crimea and then to the great causes of parliamentary reform and the American Civil War. He believed that there would be no change in the Irish situation unless power was denied to the aristocracy by granting household suffrage to the man in the street.

The situation in Ireland was by no means calm, however. On 28 January 1860, around the time of the difficulties with France and the French Commercial Treaty, Bright recorded that, at dinner with Gladstone at Downing Street, Henry Herbert, the MP for Kerry and former Chief Secretary for Ireland, thought 'a French landing in Bantry Bay would be welcomed by Irish people in the south generally, so ill is the feeling against England'.[23] By 1865 the situation in Ireland had become so dire and the Fenians so active that civil disorder and agitation during the Irish State Trials erupted into an organized movement to throw the English out of Ireland. The Fenians' activities extended to England, Canada and, as the Civil War was ending, America.

Bright reaffirmed his policy of land reform and the disestablishment of the Irish Church in the knowledge that coercion, whether driven by the Tories or the Whigs, and the crushing of the violent Fenians would not solve the problem. Only peaceful, constitutional reform and the removal of grievances could ease the situation. Fortunately, at that stage, Bright and Gladstone saw eye to eye on both the disestablishment of the Irish Church and land reform. By contrast, though Disraeli did seem to understand the Irish question, the bulk of the Conservative Party were only interested in their land and in coercion, not reform.

In 1866, there was a new Irish Coercion Bill to suspend habeas corpus, which stirred Bright on 17 February to one of his greatest speeches in the House of Commons. Never had his predictions over the past decades been more justified. Bright praised the Irish as 'a people of cheerful and joyous temperament' who had been embittered against the United Kingdom Government. He contended that the majority of the Irish people 'would unmoor the island from its fastenings in the deep, and move it at least 2,000 miles to the West' – in other words, to the USA – if only they could do so. This statement was based on his belief that the Irish diaspora in the USA was, 20 years on from the Great Famine and without any improvement in the conditions of those left at home, more than ever committed to support insurrection against England. He asked Gladstone, then Chancellor of the Exchequer, 'Whether this Irish question is above the stature of himself and of his colleagues?' If so, he suggested they 'come down from the high places which they occupy, and try to learn the art of legislation and government before they practise it'. He urged that the issue be divorced from party in the national interest, praising first Gladstone for understanding the issue and then Disraeli for his genius, before adding,

> But suppose it were possible for these men, with their intellects, with their far-reaching vision, to examine this question thoroughly, and to say for once, whether this leads to office and to the miserable notoriety that men call fame which springs from office, or not, 'If it be possible, we will act with loyalty to the Sovereign and justice to the people, and if it be possible, we will make Ireland a strength and not a weakness to the British Empire.'[24]

No one was spared his reproach.

Bright returned to Dublin later that year, where he gave a speech at the Rotunda on 30 October, arguing again for the disestablishment of the Church and the setting up of a 'parliamentary commission empowered to buy up the large estates in Ireland belonging to the Irish nobility, for the purpose of selling them on easy terms to the occupiers of the farms and to the tenantry of Ireland'.[25] Profoundly moved by social justice, his sense of morality and the deprivation of the Irish people led Bright to adopt a policy of ultra-radical measures, even the appropriation of Irish land. He quoted a Dubliner who had told him that the Irish 'are rather in the country than of it, and that they are looking more to America than they are looking to England'.[26]

In 1867, the army was called into Ireland on a significant scale to deal with the growing discontent. Among others, Frederick Harrison and Professor Beasley, both intimates of Karl Marx, proposed a petition urging that the rebellious Fenians be given 'as much leniency as was consistent with the preservation of order'. The petitioners, having asked Gladstone to present the petition to the Commons and being met with a refusal, asked Bright. Consenting, Bright broke the normal conventions and read out the entire petition, punctuated by interruptions from the floor. Bright concluded with the words, 'In the general spirit of that petition, I entirely agree.'[27]

His call for a parliamentary commission frightened the aristocracy. In June, Thomas Anson, the Earl of Lichfield, moved the discharge of the petition. Yet, in Bright's absence from the debate that followed, Disraeli took the high ground as Chancellor of the Exchequer, stating that 'We shall not appear to sanction the idea that we are endeavouring to suppress opinions of which we do not approve.'[28] Anson's motion was rejected.

In September, two Fenians, Thomas Kelly and Timothy Deasy, escaped from police custody in Manchester, and a police sergeant was killed in the process. The three Fenians who had organized the escape, William Philip Allen, Michael Larkin and Michael O'Brien, were arrested and faced execution. Bright met the 19-year-old Allen's uncle and aunt and reviewed the evidence, which he regarded as unreliable. Because of this, and his repugnance at the idea of capital punishment, he made strong representations on behalf of the three men and urged Justin McCarthy (editor of the *Morning Star* after Samuel Lucas's death, and later an MP and one of Charles Stewart Parnell's right-hand men) to oppose any suggestion that the accused should be hanged. He argued that desperate men were coming to the fore, desperate deeds being done, as he had predicted, and that men were becoming reckless while British statesmanship was helpless. 'The Tory Government is reaping the results of Tory principles,' he said.[29] Despite Bright's representations, however, the three men were hanged on 23 November 1867.

On 4 February 1868, Bright returned to the Irish question in Birmingham. He argued for the common interests of England and Ireland, and that 'the Irish people never consented to that legislative union, and that their right to protest against it, and their right to ask for the restoration of their Parliament ... has not and cannot be destroyed'. He raised the question of whether it was possible to create a union with Ireland, and called for 'the most perfect harmony in the two countries'. The great controversies, he argued, were to do with the Church and the land. The Irish people were

> the same people as ourselves; we all speak, with a little difference of accent, the same language; we read the same books; and Irishmen write a great many of the books which we read in England. Our interests are the same; our family connections are wonderfully interlaced.

Expressing his belief in the sovereignty of the British Parliament, he argued that

> There is nothing that a Parliament in Ireland could do that the Imperial Parliament could not do if it tried to do it. There is nothing with regard to the true interests of the people that an independent Republic could do which a Parliament in London could not do.[30]

On 9 March 1868, Bright noted in his diary Derby's recent retirement:

> Benjamin Disraeli reigns in his stead! A great triumph of intellect and courage and patience and unscrupulousness, employed in the service of a party full of prejudices and selfishness and wanting in brains. The Tories have hired Disraeli, and he has his reward from them.[31]

On the same day, Bright discussed the Irish Church issue with Lord Russell and the next day discussed it again with Gladstone. On 11 March, Bright recorded in his diary that the Church Rates Regulation Bill, as it was called, passed through Committee:

> It is the Bill I recommended to the House several years ago.'[32]

The following day, he went to see Gladstone. They 'agreed that a specific motion should be brought forward after the present debate

is over in such form as to pledge the House to the abolition of the
Irish Church.[33] He put it to the House on 13 March that

> I am in favour of more proprietors ... I believe that you can
> establish a steady class of moderate proprietors, who will form a
> class intermediate between the great owners of land and those
> who are absolutely landless, which will be of immense service in
> giving steadiness, loyalty, and peace to the whole population of
> the island.

– a position latterly summarized as the 'Farming Propriety'. He
referred to an anecdote of Addison's about a man who made a
living by cheating the country people: 'The man was not a Cabinet
Minister, he was only a mountebank —but he set up a stall, and
offered to the country people to sell them pills that were very good
against earthquake.' This was met with roars of laughter in the
House, as he went on, 'Well, that is about the state of things that
we are in now. There is an earthquake in Ireland. Does anybody
doubt it?' He referred, with a prescient ecumenicism, to the
proposal for a Royal Charter for a new Catholic university, which
had been promoted by Newman with the involvement of his cousin,
Frederick Lucas:

> We are after all, I believe, of one religion. I imagine that there
> will come a time in the history of the world when men will be
> astonished that Catholics and Protestants, Churchmen and
> Nonconformists, have entertained such suspicion of and
> animosity against each other.[34]

The following evening, Bright noted in his diary,

> Last night and to-day almost overwhelmed with compliments on
> my speech, but hope my head is not turned or weakened by so
> much praise. Lord Dufferin wrote me a very kind note – thinks
> the speech will do 'incalculable good' in Ireland.[35]

Gladstone then took up the issue. He asserted that the Established
Church must be undone and religious equality established. He put
down resolutions to this effect on the Established Church (Ireland)
Bill, strongly supported by Bright. Gladstone's resolutions were
carried in the House on 22 May 1868, but the Bill faltered in the
House of Lords.

Over the ensuing months, the Irish question continued to create turbulence. Disraeli began to play politics but, given his U-turn on the Reform Act the previous year, the Tories were not of a mind to allow him any latitude over Ireland. They were determined that ownership of the soil would remain in the hands of their landowning friends and relations.

The situation culminated in Disraeli resigning and advising the Queen to dissolve Parliament on 4 May. The Queen declined to accept his resignation, but said she would dissolve Parliament when public business permitted. When Disraeli claimed that he had special influence with the Queen regarding the dissolution of Parliament, Bright condemned him – no doubt aggravated by the way Disraeli was claiming exclusive credit for the Reform Act the previous year when he had owed so much to Bright for its passage. Bright also condemned some on his own side for keeping Disraeli's Government alive.

On 5 May, Bright met Gladstone in Regent Street, where they discussed the Irish question under a street lamp. On 7 May, at Gladstone's house, further consultations were held with Bright and others, including Lowe ('Strange to meet Lowe in consultation with Gladstone after what occurred two years ago on the Reform question,' Bright noted).[36]

That evening, Bright recorded 'a night of stormy debate' in the House:

> I attacked Disraeli with great severity at the close of the discussion – compelled to do it by his insolence. The House rang with the cheers of our party. His reply showed how hard I had hit him; but the punishment was just, and I spoke the truth as I believed it. There was extraordinary excitement throughout the House.[37]

The Irish question now coincided with the end of Disraeli's Government. Bright had launched a bitter attack on Disraeli for talking at large 'with a mixture of pompousness and sometimes of servility' in relation to his interviews with the Queen, and for putting the Queen in the forefront of a struggle. For this, Bright concluded that Disraeli was

> guilty of a very high crime and a great misdemeanour against his Sovereign and against his country. And there is no honour, and there is no reputation, there is no glory, there is no future name that any Minister can gain by conduct like this that will acquit

him to posterity of one of the most grievous offences against his
country which a Prime Minister can possibly commit.[38]

Bright's onslaught drove Disraeli into a fury, which brought their
previously mutual friendly relations, at any rate up to the Reform
Act of 1867, finally to an end.

On 3 June, Bright spoke in Liverpool in favour of the disestablishment of the Church, pointing out that, of the Irish population,
4.5 million were Roman Catholic and only 700,000 were Protestant.
He added that, in Ireland, the Catholics 'own scarcely any of the
land'[39] and he argued strongly for the continuing unity of Ireland
within the United Kingdom as a matter of justice.

Parliament was dissolved in November. In the ensuing General
Election, the Liberals won by a majority of 116. Gladstone offered
Bright a seat in the Cabinet as secretary of state for India. Bright
refused, explaining that he had proposed his views in 1858 as to
what was needed for reform in the government of India but public
opinion had not yet advanced sufficiently to adopt his policies. He
had thought this might be coming for some time. In his diary on 20
May, he had noted, 'I am already half-appointed "Secretary of State
for India"! My friends little know how little I wish for office, or how
insuperable are the difficulties in the way of my accepting it, if
offered to me!'[40] Gladstone continued to press him and eventually,
after much inner turmoil and, aware that Gladstone needed him
until the Irish Church question was settled ('I am not sure that he
was not the inventor of the word "disestablish"' Gladstone had
remarked of Bright),[41] to Gladstone's relief, he consented to join the
Cabinet but only as president of the Board of Trade. As he put it, 'In
that office, perhaps, I may do a little good, and perhaps I may
prevent some harm.'[42]

On 1 March 1869, Gladstone introduced his Bill for the disestablishment of the Irish Church. Speaking on 19 March in support of
this Bill, Bright argued that he regarded it as 'tending to a more true
and solid union between Ireland and Great Britain; I see it giving
tranquillity to our people.'[43] The second reading was carried by a
majority of 18 and the Bill went to the Lords where it passed, after
some controversy, on 20 July 1869.

Ireland in the 1870s

Despite this victory over the Church, before long Bright had to
confront other members of the Gladstonian Government, including

Gladstone himself, over the fatal issue of Irish land tenure. In pressing the case for tenants to be able to buy their land on reasonable terms, Bright displayed a strong sense of Jeffersonian ownership, a philosophy of a stake in the land. He had the highest regard for Thomas Jefferson and read his works closely, making annotations. As Herman Ausubel notes, in making his case for land reform, Bright drew attention specifically to what was happening in America under the Homestead Act as an indication of what could be done in Ireland.[44] His Cabinet colleagues, however, preferred to improve the lot of the tenant farmers rather than empower them through land ownership.

Addressing his constituents in Birmingham on 11 January 1870, Bright turned his attention to the land issue. He pointed out that he had found this a very difficult question for over 20 years, the land in Ireland being in the hands of very few proprietors who 'have done nothing for the cultivation of the soil'. Agriculture was the greatest industry in Ireland, with the occupier being almost entirely at the mercy of the proprietor, 'And thus have grown up suspicion and hatred and wrong, and a social war.' He argued for legislation, urging that

> this is not a question for party ... it is not a question for class or party contest. It is a question for conscientious patriotism, and every man should consider it as if the prosperity and the peace of the United Empire depended upon its wise solution.

He linked the Reform Act of 1867 with justice in Ireland – both were means to achieving lasting peace and a lasting union – and said, 'I hope before long we shall give to Irish men free land and a free vote ... Not that Ireland is to be made a paradise, but that Ireland should be greatly improved.'[45]

Gladstone introduced his Irish Land Bill on 15 February, under which it was presumed that all improvements were the property of the tenant and it was up to the landlord to prove the contrary. Despite his difference of opinion with Gladstone over the land question, Bright decided not to be curmudgeonly about the improvement of the Irish tenant farmers during the passage of the Bill. He did not renege on his principle objective of land purchase, however. He also urged the Government to be aware of the need to show clemency to the Fenian prisoners lest they become martyrs. Regarding this, the analogy with recent Irish experience of the peace process would have appealed to Bright's sense of justice and practicality.

The Bill was enacted on 1 August, with an amendment by Bright for land purchase. However, these so-called 'Bright Clauses' were undermined by the Irish Executive, which prevented the purchase arrangements from having their full effect.

During the passage of the Bill, however, Bright's health failed him, as it had in 1857/8. In a state of complete exhaustion, but short of a nervous breakdown, he stepped back from public life in February 1870. By the summer, he was seriously ill and had withdrawn to Llandudno, where he stayed until October. As his daughter, Mary, reported, 'He was hardly able to walk without assistance, unable to read or even to sign his name for a long time, although his brain remained perfectly clear and unharmed.'[46] On 3 August 1870, he resigned his office and seat in the Cabinet: 'I feel more quiet and less burdened now it is done.'[47] He then suspended his resignation, but confirmed it on 17 November on his return to Rochdale. It was announced in the newspapers on 20 December. In May 1871, he went to Scotland to fish, and the Queen invited him to stay at Balmoral, but he did not feel well enough.

On 14 November 1871, Gladstone pressed Bright to rejoin the Cabinet and offered him the chancellorship of the Duchy of Lancaster without much in the way of ministerial duties. Bright was not expected to make a decision until he returned to the House of Commons.

During early 1872, he spent his time in Rochdale and kept out of London almost entirely until late July. He did, however, engage in one very public disagreement in January, a precursor, as it turned out, to his great falling out with Gladstone in the following decade. Bright wrote to Daniel O'Donoghue, MP for Tralee, utterly repudiating the suggestion that he was in favour of Home Rule in Ireland, and with it any question of undermining the sovereignty of Parliament. In a letter widely published both at home and in America, he stated

> I hope no one has ventured to say anything so absurd and untrue ... To have two representative legislative assemblies or Parliaments in the United Kingdom would, in my opinion, be an intolerable mischief; and I think no sensible man can wish for two within the limits of the present United Kingdom who does not wish the United Kingdom to become two or more nations, entirely separated from each other.[48]

That summer, Gladstone pressed him again to rejoin the Government. The two men met on 27 July 1872 and discussed the Irish question. Three days later, Bright declined Gladstone's offer. September to October included family visits to the Clarks at Street and the Priestmans at Bristol, and then on to Scotland to stay at Inveraray with his friend, the Duke of Argyll, before travelling to York, where he met up with his old friend, Charles Sumner. Winter was spent at One Ash in Rochdale. He eventually returned to the House of Commons in February 1873 though, with his health still in a delicate state, his attendance was sporadic over the next few months.

In the meantime, Gladstone was in difficulty. The Government, having torn through an energetic reform programme, which included not only the Irish question but issues such as national education and the ballot, was in terminal decline, dismissed by Disraeli the previous year as 'a range of exhausted volcanoes'.[49] Gladstone announced the Government's resignation on 13 March 1873, but had to remain in office because Disraeli would not take over.

By August, the Government was in deep trouble, and Gladstone, needing his support and counsel, urged Bright once again to return to the Cabinet as chancellor of the Duchy of Lancaster. This time, driven by sympathy for Gladstone's predicament and gratitude for the Prime Minister's support over the Irish Church and land issues, Bright consented. As he wrote to one correspondent, 'I never made a greater sacrifice, but I could not desert Gladstone. Don't blame me; I am, perhaps, more deserving of pity.'[50]

Having agreed to rejoin the Cabinet, Bright went to Scotland in September 1873 without much enthusiasm for the work ahead. He was upset when his break was interrupted by a letter from Lord Granville instructing him to go to Balmoral. 'Cabinet meeting next week – disgusting!' he wrote in his diary.[51] On 30 September at Balmoral, he kissed hands and received the seals of the Duchy of Lancaster and returned to London two days later. There, he found himself involved in discussions on the Ashanti War. He felt deeply unhappy at being involved in a Government at war. It also kept him out of the Irish question for the next 18 months.

By 17 January 1874, Gladstone's administration was finished and the dissolution of Parliament was announced on 26 January. During the General Election, Bright was returned for Birmingham without opposition. With Disraeli now prime minister, the Irish question was largely off the agenda for the present. Bright immediately took off again for Scotland, returning to London in the middle of April, before going back for July and August, and again in October.

On 3 February 1875, Gladstone retired from the leadership of the Liberal Party. Bright, despite deeply regretting this step, supported Lord Hartington, who took over. The issues in Ireland, however, remained unresolved and simmering.

Bright regarded Home Rule as a deliberate policy of creating an independent Ireland. He objected to this on constitutional grounds and saw it as being completely unnecessary, if only the British Parliament would give justice to the Irish people. He regarded Parnell and his followers with extreme distaste, not only because they were resolute for an independent Ireland but also because they undermined the procedure of the House of Commons. Bright himself had fought the Irish battle for the Irish people over decades with the aim of justice and a constitutional settlement. He deeply resented Parnell's rebellious and revolutionary approach, as he had of the Fenians in the 1850s and 1860s.

On 25 March 1876, a motion was introduced relating to parliamentary reform in Ireland, proposing the assimilation of the borough franchise in both countries. Bright supported it strongly, on the grounds that it would invite the Irish people to co-operate with Parliament so that there would be no need for them to have their own Parliament. It was defeated, but there was a mere majority of 13 against.

Land Act and Coercion Bill, 1880–2

Parliament was dissolved on 8 March 1880, and in April Bright was returned with Philip Muntz and Joseph Chamberlain as Members for Birmingham. Overall, 349 Liberals were returned, with 243 Conservatives and 60 Home Rulers. Gladstone was again prime minister and Bright again became chancellor of the Duchy of Lancaster.

A new Irish Land Bill was announced in the Queen's Speech. The new Parliament also saw a Compensation for Disturbance Bill to give security to tenants against unfair eviction, which passed on 26 July in the House of Commons, but was thrown out on 4 August by the intransigent Lords by a massive majority of 331 to 51.

In August, during a debate on law and justice in Ireland, Bright returned to 'the necessity of a large and fundamental change with regard to the ownership and tenure of land'.[52] To this he added the issue of the Irish constabulary, which he regretted had, of necessity, to be harsher than in England. He also condemned the lack of proper justice that Catholic offenders received from Protestant jurors. The debate was long and, as on so many other occasions, Bright referred in his diary to the obstruction of Irish members. The House sat all night until 1 o'clock the following afternoon, though Bright himself left at 2 a.m. 'and left the House to its labours'.[53]

On 10 November 1880, Bright recorded a Cabinet discussion on coercion and the Land Bill followed by a discussion with Chamberlain on the Irish question.[54] As the situation in Ireland worsened, there had been calls for the suspension of habeas corpus and harsh legislation to deal with disturbances. Parnell, along with the Land League Chiefs, was prosecuted. Bright, firmly against coercion, was deeply concerned and critical of Government policy.

Bright's dilemma on Ireland was similar to that he faced over both the American Civil War and India, which was how to restore constitutional order. As Travis Mills demonstrates, Bright's conservatism was very much in line with a Quaker sense of justice and stability. His faith in the Westminster 'mother of Parliaments' extended to the belief that it was for Westminster itself to remedy past mistakes – whether in Ireland, the Empire or even, perhaps, in the USA. In line with this, and with the situation in Ireland deteriorating rapidly, during a Cabinet meeting on 13 December Bright offered 'no objection to measures of repression' if the condition of the country did not improve.[55]

The Cabinet discussions on the issue were long and intense. On 17 December, Bright noted that he had written 'a Memorandum on Commission for Purchase of Farms in Ireland, for circulation among members of the Cabinet'.[56] In this paper, Bright urged that his so-called 'Bright Clauses', the machinery of which had not worked as he had hoped, be improved and enlarged. On 30 December, he records 'Cabinet Council: long discussion on Habeas Corpus suspension – most unpleasant matter for discussion. I wish I could escape from official responsibilities. Am made very unhappy by the difficulties which surround the Govt. in connexion with Irish affairs.'[57] The following day there was a further Cabinet discussion on the Irish Land Bill that went on for three hours, in respect of which Bright recorded 'nearer approach to agreement and to mode of dealing with the question'.[58] These proposals enabled differences between landlord and tenant to be adjudicated by a tribunal, and to fix fair rents. Though Bright's view was that this was not the sole issue by any means, and that the real question was enabling the farmers to acquire the land and thereby to improve the lot of all those in the lower agricultural sector, he welcomed the proposed bill with its commitment to free sale, fixity of tenure and fair rent, together with land purchase.

Bright had, however, underestimated the extent of Parnell's and his followers' intransigence, not to mention their involvement with anti-British Irish-American activities. Irish obstructionism had become rife, and 1881 brought with it an upsurge in Parnellite agitation in the House of Commons itself. On 14 January 1881, Bright visited Gladstone, who was at home, suffering from a cold. They discussed ways of overcoming obstruction by the 'rebels', but to no avail.

A new Coercion Bill was introduced in January 1881. Bright was extremely concerned that coercion would not succeed. He even went so far as to advise Gladstone not to make an example of Parnell, which in Bright's view would only make him more popular. Sir Charles Dilke, the parliamentary under-secretary of state for foreign affairs, was against the idea of coercion, but he notes in his own diary that, despite trying to persuade Bright against coercion, Bright had been converted 'to the view that things had grown to be very bad, and that by locking up a small number of the chiefs the rule of law might be restored. I did not agree, but his opinion showed me how completely I was isolated.'[59]

The Irish issue was debated again on 17 and 18 January, with Gladstone speaking, according to Bright, 'with much force and oppressiveness on the Irish question and obstruction in the House.'[60] On 24 January, Bright noted, 'Irish Suspension of Habeas Corpus Act proposed by W. E. Forster in a powerful speech.'[61] The following day there was further obstruction in the debate and the House sat continuously for 22 hours. On 1 February, the debate again continued throughout the night and Bright spoke, as he put it, 'about 1 o'clock, briefly but satisfactorily to our friends'.[62]

A historic moment in the procedure of the House occurred at 9 o'clock the following morning, 2 February, when the Speaker closed the debate and insisted on a division. The House had been sitting continuously for 41 hours, discussing whether Mr Forster's Coercion Bill should even be brought in, as it would be subjected to continuous obstruction by the Irish members. This procedure, known today as 'the closure', had been obtained by a majority of 164 to 19 to introduce the Bill itself. Speaker Henry Brand (a former Chief Whip), when asked by Henry Labouchere under what Standing Order he had acted, replied that he had acted on his own responsibility out of his sense of duty to the House.

Though Bright notes that he 'was not present at this curious and unexpected scene', the following day, he witnessed the dramatic exclusion of the Irish Party from the House.[63] He recorded:

> House: strange scene. Irish Party, obstructing, objected to Mr. Gladstone speaking and defied the Chair. Speaker 'named' the member obstructing, and finally Irish Members, 30 or more, were suspended during sitting by vote of the House, and were removed by the Serjeant-at-Arms – a strange and humiliating spectacle. House, cleared of disturbing element, becomes calm. Mr. Gladstone, in a speech of great force and beauty, moved resolutions to amend mode of procedure which, after debate, were carried at 2 o'clock with great cheering. The House seemed relieved after the removal of Irish obstructives.[64]

This may have been cheered at the time, but the consequences of it in modern times have been profound and the procedure has embedded itself in a way that has greatly undermined the independence of Parliament.[65] It has now become an instrument of undemocratic oppression, accompanied as it is by programme motions, the reduction of debate, and unacceptable whipping to the point of farce.

On 18 February 1881, the Coercion Bill was again considered and the debate became stormy. In his diary, Bright notes Parnell's presence, and that the Irish members were unruly and almost beyond control. He left the House before 1 a.m. 'wearied with the disorder which it seemed impossible to suppress. We must be approaching some crisis or catastrophe.'[66] Despite Bright saying, in a speech on the proposals on 27 January, that the offences, crimes and vices which Irish people had committed 'arise rather from the condition into which those who should be those superiors have brought them than from their own hearts', he found himself, with the deepest misgivings, voting for a Coercion Bill.[67]

As O'Brien points out, Bright's support for Forster's Coercion Bill dismayed many Irish nationalists. Yet Bright's long record of support for Ireland mitigated any anger that might have been felt:

> For over twenty years [Bright] has been striking out from the shoulder in our favour. Are we to throw him over because he now strikes out against us? ... he thinks that his wretched Coercion Bill is necessary to satisfy English public opinion in order to get through a real strong Land Bill.[68]

O'Brien later discussed Bright's speech with Bright himself, saying that he had not liked it, to which Bright (with a smile and stroking his chin with his finger) replied,

> I dare say you didn't. What would you have? Remember, I voted for coercion before. The position I have always taken has been that you cannot resist the demand of the Minister who is responsible for the administration in Ireland, though you may say, as I have certainly said, that other remedies must be applied.

Bright then went on,

> The suspension of the Habeas Corpus Act had been successful in the case of the Fenians; we supposed it would be successful in the case of the Land League; that was the mistake ... The conspiracy was more widespread and more deeply rooted than we were led to suppose. It was not a case for a suspension of the Habeas Corpus Act.

Bright admitted he had been wrong, but he knew he had been right in calling for greater land reform, and it was the failure by Government to deliver this that had led to the creation of the Land League. He also reminded O'Brien that 'if we had not passed a Coercion Act we could not have got a good Land Bill through'.[69]

On 22 February 1881, Bright expressed in Cabinet his concerns about the proposed Land Bill, stating that it was too complicated and that it needed more amendment on the issue of land tenure. On 25 February, the Coercion Bill was read for a third time.

Meanwhile, the unrest continued. On 17 March, there was an attempt to blow up the Mansion House, the official residence of the Lord Mayor of the City of London which, according to Bright, was said to have been done by an 'Irishman from America, whose name is known to the police, and whose coming and objects have been telegraphed from the States.'[70] The obstructionism also continued in the House, with intermittent outbursts from the Irish Members. Bright described the Parnellites as 'violent and their conduct disgraceful'.[71]

Gladstone brought in the Irish Land Bill on 7 April 1881, a bill that insisted on the 'three Fs' – fixity of tenure, fair rent and free sale. The Duke of Argyll, to Bright's regret, resigned from the Cabinet over this issue, influenced as he was by a professor from Oxford who took the view that the Bill transgressed the laws of political economy and who, according to Gladstone, 'applied the principles of political economy, in all their unmitigated authority, to the people and circumstances of Ireland "exactly as if he had been proposing to legislate for the inhabitants of Saturn or Jupiter"'.[72]

Later that month, Disraeli died. As Bright recorded in his diary on 17 April,

> Heard of the death of Disraeli – Lord Beaconsfield – which took place at 1/2 past 4 this morning. He has been ill for about a month, and with little belief in his recovery on the part of his doctors. His death will create a great interest in this country and elsewhere, but I do not think it will make any sensible difference in public affairs. His life has been devoted to the pursuit of his own personal ambition, and political principles and his Party have been made subservient to that end. His success shows what may be done by unworthy means, and to offer him as an example is to encourage other men to do evil. In his private life and character, I think he has been kind and generous where his main pursuit was not interfered with. I have had many friendly conversations with him, but not for some years past, and I have not spoken to him since he left the House of Commons.[73]

All this carries with it a great baggage of history, for Bright certainly co-operated closely with Disraeli on many matters, in particular over the Reform Act. Bright, after recording in his diary the funeral of Disraeli at Hughenden on 26 April, which he did not attend, he referred to Millais' portrait of Disraeli as being 'not good and not pleasant to look at".[74] And that was not all. On 9 May, the House debated a motion to establish a monument to Disraeli in Westminster Abbey, and Bright was careful to note that he was not present: 'Could not vote for monument, and did not go to the House till the question was disposed of. Mr. Gladstone's magnanimity led him into the mistake of proposing the monument: the Party much against it.'[75]

On 29 July 1881, the Land Bill had its third reading. The Tory Party leaders could not bring themselves to participate in the final vote and almost all were absent. After a massive majority of 220 for and 14 against, Bright noted that there was 'enthusiastic cheering for Mr Gladstone'.[76] Inevitably, however, there was difficulty in the House of Lords. On 6 August, the Cabinet decided to resist the Lords' amendments and on 10 August Bright records that, on consideration of these, there was an 'unpleasant night – Irishmen violent and offensive'.[77] The week that followed saw a great deal of furious activity by the Parnellites, but at last the Lords gave in and the Land Bill passed into law. By October, however, the obstruction had become so severe that the Cabinet decided to arrest Parnell, of which Bright records, 'No other course possible.'[78]

In his annual New Year speech to his constituents on 3 January 1882, with Chamberlain by his side, Bright again tackled the Irish issue: 'The question is whether you are to allow terror to be master in a considerable portion of Ireland, or whether you should attempt some remedy?' He referred to the undeniable reality of a conspiracy, which was treason to the Crown and 'whose object is the breaking up of the United Kingdom. It is not love of the tenantry of Ireland, but it is the hatred of England.' He mentioned in particular the raising of money from the Irish diaspora in America, but while condemning the conspirators and the Irish emigrants, he reminded his audience that 'the Irish people have a right to complain'.[79]

In the House of Commons on 30 March 1882, he tackled the question of Irish obstructionism and the issue of parliamentary procedure. The Chamber and the galleries were full, as Members and strangers alike gathered to hear him speak. He outlined the prime minister's resolution 'with regard to what is called the closure or shutting up of the debate', explaining that when fewer than forty members 'continue to speak without any moderation or limit of time, and there is a general weariness in the House, and a sense that the debate may reasonably come to close' then it may be closed if over 100 members agreed. The other proposition the Government put forward was if there were more than 40 members engaged in obstruction, then 200 would be needed to close the debate. He argued that there was a greater purpose in Parliament to be achieved if these procedures were brought in.[80] For him, it was a matter of proportionate balance to be used exceptionally in the national interest. He did not forsee, but perhaps should have, that this precedent would lead to the abuse of such procedures. The motion was received with great enthusiasm in the House and was carried by a majority of 39. Outside the House of Commons, the measures taken to address the difficulties in Ireland were less effective, and it had become clear that the Land Act of 1881 would not produce the results that Bright had hoped. Then, on 6 May 1882, Thomas Burke, the permanent under-secretary for Ireland, and Lord Frederick Cavendish, who had replaced Forster as chief secretary of Ireland after Parnell had been released from gaol in April, were murdered in Dublin. The 'Phoenix Park murders', as they were known, gave a clear indication that the Irish conspirators would stop at nothing, and that their hatred of the British and coercion had deeper roots than the Land Act would resolve. When Bright learnt of the murders, he wrote: 'Heard this morning of the dreadful murder last evening in Dublin of Lord F. Cavendish and Mr. Burke – a crime scarcely equalled in our modern years,'[81] and noted that only the previous Friday he had sat next to Cavendish and, on parting, had wished him a pleasant voyage across the Irish Sea.

The atmosphere in the House was very tense. On 11 May, Bright noted that he was deeply concerned that Harcourt's Prevention of Crime Bill for Ireland was too severe without any conciliation.[82] As this Bill progressed through the House, it was peppered with obstruction by the Irish members and, over the following months, some were suspended and others left the House on a regular basis. In addition to the difficult atmosphere in Westminster, Bright also had to contend with a growing distance between himself and Gladstone over the Egyptian question. Matters came to a head in early July, when news arrived of the bombardment of Alexandria, and by the end of the month Bright had resigned the Duchy of Lancaster and left the Government (see Chapter 6). Though he continued to attend the House, Bright stepped back from public life and much of the remainder of the year was spent visiting friends in Scotland, Leamington, Llandudno and elsewhere.

CHAPTER 9

Home Rule, Party Splits and the End

To leave Parliament now would be an immense relief,
but I care for the Party and for its objects and for the country.
(Bright, writing to Joseph Chamberlain, 1 June 1886)

Bright and Chamberlain

Those who have claimed that Bright disappeared from the forefront of public life following his great triumph over parliamentary reform – a view shared even by his biographer, G. M. Trevelyan – seem to have a historical blind-spot. As to his impact, as Enoch Powell said of Joseph Chamberlain, 'All political lives, unless they are cut off in mid-stream at a happy juncture, end in failure, because that is the nature of politics and of human affairs.'[1] Bright, however, in his struggle for justice and freedom, was successful as a catalyst in changing the politics of his time. Even in the 1880s, Bright was changing the terms of political trade, slaying his political opponents, making his mark definitively against Home Rule and on the Irish question, and even splitting his own party on an issue of principle and national interest. Moreover, not only did many of the causes championed by Bright, such as free trade and parliamentary reform, outlive him but, as Roland Quinault has suggested, many subsequent events, including the 1903 Irish Land Purchase Act, the 1906 Liberal landslide, the 1911 Parliament Act and the ensuing Irish Home Rule crisis, can all be ascribed to Bright's 'prescience'.[2]

Of this continuing legacy, arguably the most important relationship of Bright's later life was that with Joseph Chamberlain. Though in parliamentary terms it only became truly significant from the mid-1880s, Bright had been instrumental in fostering Chamberlain's political career for many years. Chamberlain had

lived in Birmingham from 1854, when he had been sent to the city
to work in the family's screw-making firm at the age of 18. Living
and working in the heart of Birmingham's industrial community,
Chamberlain was drawn into the city's strong tradition of Radical
Liberal politics. He had followed Bright's career actively from
the time Bright took his seat as the Member for Birmingham in
1858. In his eulogy of Bright in the House of Commons on Bright's
death in 1889, he recalled with admiration Bright's first speech
as the Member for Birmingham, in which Bright had stated that
'the attractions of power had not turned me aside; that I had
not changed my course from any view of courting a fleeting popularity', and that 'a man whose political career is on a line with his
conscientious convictions can never be unfaithful to his constituents
or to his country'.[3]

In 1867, Chamberlain joined Birmingham Town Council and, in
the wake of Bright's great reform campaign, set about realizing his
own ideas for social reform within the city. He founded the
Birmingham Education League, with George Dixon MP and Jesse
Collings among others, to promote universal and non-sectarian
elementary education. Bright was not involved directly in this movement but, as J. Travis Mills points out, contrary to some assertions,
'the subject of national education made a strong appeal to Bright
from the very beginning, and even before the beginning, of his
public work'.[4] Indeed, he had first met Cobden through a shared
interest in educational reform. Bright had continuously proposed
better provision for elementary education and, in 1866, had advocated the state school system in use in the USA. In 1873, Bright
assured Chamberlain of his opposition to the denominational
system, which discriminated against Nonconformism. This was a
position he had held for some time, and had condemned the
Education Act of 1870 as being 'the worst passed by a Liberal
Parliament since 1832'.[5] Bright did not, however, support
Chamberlain on the question of excluding the Bible from schools,
nor did he follow Chamberlain in campaigning for the disestablishment of the Church of England in the late 1870s.

Bright and Chamberlain became firm allies, though not always in
complete agreement. Their paths had inevitably crossed since Bright
first took up his seat in Birmingham, but the two men only really
came to know one another when Chamberlain became the city's
mayor in 1873. Thereafter, they met regularly in private when Bright
visited his constituency. In 1876, Chamberlain became Bright's
partner as Member for Birmingham – until 1885, despite being one

constituency, it returned two MPs – with Bright introducing his disciple to the House on the day Chamberlain took up his seat. That the relationship was close is clearly reflected in the tone of their correspondence, and their condolences over one another's bereavements around this time – Chamberlain's second wife dying in 1875, and Bright losing his second wife in 1878.

Chamberlain greatly admired Bright's style of conviction politics. As he said of Bright on the issue of parliamentary reform and commitment to the working class, 'Let the Party follow the example of its most earnest, most honest and most popular member, and it will not have cause to complain of the ingratitude or of the indifference of the country.'[6] Chamberlain also followed Bright's support of the agricultural labouring class, which had played a significant role in prompting Joseph Arch to found the National Agricultural Labourers' Union in 1872. A year later, during the course of a speech in Birmingham, Bright called for household suffrage in the counties, beginning a new campaign for the enfranchisement of the agricultural vote, which was realized in 1884. Chamberlain himself adopted Arch's policy in 1885, building on Bright's original inspiration a decade before.

Both men were trenchantly opposed to the use of the powers of the Lords to frustrate the Commons. As Chamberlain said in 1883, in reply to Gladstone, 'I agree with Mr Bright that a hereditary legislature cannot be a permanent institution in a free country and if ever it sets itself against the will of the people, it must bend or break.'[7] In August 1884, Bright himself went even further, stating in *The Times* with great prescience that the Lords' veto should be limited to two parliamentary sessions. This was later realized in the passing of the Parliament Act in 1911, which is still on the statute book today.

Chamberlain stated in his political memoir that Bright ensured Gladstone made Chamberlain president of the Board of Trade in April 1880[8] – by all accounts, because Bright was convinced that Chamberlain was a true free trader. Indeed, in 1881, Bright and Chamberlain both resisted proposals in Birmingham to support duty on foreign sugar. Chamberlain even went so far as to claim in 1896 that his Imperial Customs Union was in line with Cobden's principles of free trade.

On foreign policy and the Empire, both Bright and Chamberlain, though differing on the engagement by the military in matters of Empire, shared an interest in the economic and political development of British possessions. However, when Bright resigned from Gladstone's Government in 1882 over Egypt, Chamberlain initially fell out with him. However, he wrote to Bright a few months later, admitting that in retrospect Bright might have been be right and that he was profoundly unhappy 'that we should differ almost for the first time on questions of so much importance'.[9] Later, he would go so far as to say, 'It has been very painful to me to find myself separated from you even for a short time and I rejoice that there is still so much on which I share all your sentiments and am prepared humbly to follow in your footsteps.'[10] Cordial relations were restored, with Chamberlain declaring in 1883 that Bright had obtained 'a larger measure of success than has attended the efforts of any other statesman'.[11] The following year, Chamberlain was happy to concede that, with regard to Egypt 'you were right and we were wrong'.[12]

Bright, however, did not share Chamberlain's commitment to Imperial Federation, and in 1888, in his last public speech in Birmingham, he repudiated the whole idea. Yet, the distance between them on this subject came gradually, both Chamberlain and Bright having resisted the creation of the Imperial Federation League by W. E. Forster in 1884. Had he still been alive, Bright would not have supported Chamberlain's intransigent and belligerent attitude towards the Boers in 1900. Jan Christian Smuts himself seems to have thought Bright would have supported him when he said, 'If there were only another John Bright.'[13]

As Roland Quinault states,

> Chamberlain spent much of his career following in Bright's footsteps. However, Chamberlain had a mind of his own and there were occasions when he insisted on going his own way in opposition to Bright. But even then, Chamberlain often returned, like the prodigal son, to Bright's line of policy ... Bright was in many ways a father figure to Chamberlain. Bright helped to mould Chamberlain's policies; he assisted his rise and he provided him with a model of what a Birmingham based reformer could achieve.[14]

Irish Storm Clouds Return

The primary issue of the day when Bright returned to Westminster at the beginning of 1883 was Ireland. The situation had not improved. On 16 March 1883, Bright heard an explosion at Government offices in Parliament Street – 'dynamite; supposed Fenian outrage', he recorded in his diary[15] – an incident that led to the Explosive Substance Bill, with severe penalties for dynamite conspirators, being carried through both Houses in one day.

In June 1883, Birmingham hosted a week of banquets and festivities to celebrate the 25th anniversary of Bright's first election to the city. On 13 June, Bright was presented with a portrait of himself by Frank Holl, for whom he had sat reluctantly, and an engraved silver dessert service that cost 600 guineas. He noted in his diary that evening that there were as many as 20,000 people at the meeting, and that he was 'alarmed at the cost and beauty of presents'.[16] He was also presented with 120 addresses from every part of the land celebrating his political career and his achievements. Among these was a eulogy by Earl Granville, who was one of Bright's few remaining political contemporaries, having entered public life at about the same time.

That same week in Birmingham, both Bright and Chamberlain launched attacks on the Conservatives in Parliament, not only for obstructionism but also for allying themselves with the Irish members, whom Bright described as 'rebels', who had broken their oath of allegiance by associating with enemies of the country. Sir Stafford Northcote, the Conservative leader of the opposition in the Commons, raised this as a matter of privilege. It was debated on 18 June and successfully rebutted by Bright. As he noted in his diary, 'The charge was ridiculous, but he made it, and I had to reply. The charge was absurd, and failed. It was childish, and was thought so by men of his own party.'[17] Chamberlain also got into trouble because he had attacked the Queen for not sending representatives to Bright's festivities, though, as Bright said, 'they were not missed!' Salisbury regarded this as 'a new, a sinister, a most terrible feature in our constitutional history' and the Queen deeply resented Chamberlain's remarks.[18] On being asked to modify his language, Chamberlain did the reverse, saying that he would not be bribed into silence.

On 26 January 1884, the Fenians caused an explosion at Victoria Station, but no one was killed. On 30 January, Bright returned at Birmingham Town Hall to the issue of the Irish land question, reiterating the reforms he had advocated as far back as 1849. He distanced himself from any suggestion of nationalization of land in Ireland or elsewhere, condemning the idea of nationalization, but reaffirming the need for a fair system of land tenure.

During March 1884, during a debate on the Representation of the People Bill, Bright argued for greater enfranchisement in Ireland. Bright argued that, just as they had removed the grievance of the

Established Church in Ireland, so now they should give a proper franchise and representation to the Irish people. 'I am determined to stand by the Act of Union,' he said. 'There are two paths open to us – the Union by force and on the old lines, and the Union with justice ... prosperity and peace.'[19]

The rest of the year saw wrangles over this issue between the House of Commons and the House of Lords, and between the Conservatives, the Liberals and the Irish. By the time the Franchise Bill received its second reading on 4 December 1884, the Liberal Government reigned supreme and the Conservatives were in deep despair. In March 1885, Sir Robert Peel, son of the former prime minister, told Bright he thought the Conservative Party was almost destroyed.

Home Rule, however, was about to destroy the Liberal Party itself. Bright, in February 1885, was feeling uneasy about his role in Parliament:

> After many years of labour in the public cause I often feel humbled that I have done so little. Yet it is pleasant to know that this little is or has been appreciated by those who can judge of what has been attempted. I am shy of going up to the House, for I have not been very well, and Parliament offers me nothing of service to tempt me to spend much time within its walls.[20]

The next few years were to lead him into renewed and final trials of conscience and political will.

The spiral of violence in Ireland, intensified by the execution of Fenians, demonstrated to Bright that the British were not prepared to foster harmony, but the pivot point of Home Rule now became an obsession for Gladstone. In April 1885, Bright proposed to Lord Dalhousie that there should be a central council in Dublin with 64 representatives, two from each of the 32 county boards, to represent 32 counties. This council would have functions of education and local taxation, but exclude foreign affairs, defence, the police and import duties.[21] Chamberlain held similar views. Yet, while Bright insisted on sovereignty for the Westminster Parliament in critical areas of government, within a year Bright had agreed with Gladstone's idea of eliminating Irish members at Westminster, if such a scheme could be made workable.[22]

By June 1885, Gladstone had been defeated. The thunderbolt struck on 8 June. Formally on the issue of the Budget, but essentially over the fate of General Gordon in Khartoum and over Ireland, the

Government was suddenly defeated by a majority of 12, with a sudden convergence of Conservatives and Parnellites and the absence of 70 Liberal MPs. The dissolution was postponed until the redistribution of parliamentary seats following the previous year's Reform Act, and a Conservative Cabinet, led by Lord Salisbury, was formed until the General Election took place in November.

The 1885 General Election

Lord Randolph Churchill had been preparing for a coup d'état in the Conservative Party since 1880. The Home Rule crisis gave him the opportunity; the means and the objective were through the bid for the working-class vote in Birmingham – Bright's own territory. Birmingham had been divided into single-member constituencies for the General Election of 1885 and, as will be seen later, this settlement was crucial to the future development of all the parties. The Conservative Party leader, the Marquess of Salisbury (formerly Viscount Cranborne), had been bitterly opposed to all that Bright stood for in seeking the vote for the working class in the 1860s, and was equally opposed to Disraeli's conversion to Bright's cause in 1867. Randolph Churchill, however, understood better than Salisbury that this was where the future of the Conservative Party lay. By this time, Bright was the undisputed advocate of the working-class vote. Nothing could better illustrate the opportunistic means by which Churchill sought to satisfy his overwhelming ambition to lead the Conservative Party than to pitch his tent on the very territory that Bright had nurtured for the purpose of giving democratic rights to the working class.

The means that Churchill employed in seeking to remove Bright from his seat had been turning in the mind of the so-called Fourth Party since 1880, in his alliance with Sir Henry Drummond-Wolff, Sir John Gorst and, to a lesser extent, Salisbury's nephew, Arthur Balfour. In 1883, Churchill openly attacked Stafford Northcote in the letters column of *The Times*. On 19 April of that year, after a ceremony in which the statue of Disraeli was unveiled in Parliament Square on the second anniversary of his death, Drummond-Wolff and Churchill conceived the idea of creating an organization to promote the memory of Disraeli and create a new middle- and working-class bastion at the grass roots level to support Lord Randolph's bid for power. Thus, the Primrose League was created as an unlikely, but highly effective, weapon employed from outside the walls of Westminster by Churchill to supplant Stafford

Northcote in the Commons, outflank Salisbury in the Lords and acquire for himself the prize of the leadership of the Conservative Party. The Primrose League was spectacularly successful, but today is almost completely forgotten, though it has been recently brought back to life by Alistair Cooke, now Baron Lexden, the historian of the Conservative Party, in his book, *A Gift from the Churchills: The Primrose League, 1883–2004.*

Lord Randolph's aim in the General Election of 1885 was to destroy the bastion of Joseph Chamberlain and the Liberal Party by leading an assault on the very heart of the Liberal Radical cause – the Birmingham Central Division. Far from Bright being a declining force in British politics after 1867, as has been suggested, a highly significant decision – and a forgotten move of great strategic importance at the time – was made by the Birmingham Liberals when they determined that Bright himself would take the full force of Churchill's bid in this seat, leaving Chamberlain in safer and less turbulent waters to the west.

The mainstay of Churchill's Birmingham campaign was the Primrose League, and the driving force of the League was Churchill's mother, the Duchess of Marlborough, and his wife, Jennie Jerome. March 1885 saw the Duchess become President of the Ladies' Grand Council to further her desire that the League should 'show the nation that the Conservatives are interested in the wellbeing and comfort of the people'.[23] Thus they set out, with Jennie and a contingent of Dames from the Primrose League canvassing door-to-door and factory-to-factory in the depths of Birmingham. In Winston Churchill's own words,

> Lord Randolph was helped from morn till night by his wife and mother, at the head of their Primrose Dames. These ladies canvassed the whole of the Central Division street by street and house by house; and the Duchess of Marlborough ... visited the factories and addressed the workmen effectively on her son's behalf.[24]

All this despite the fact that Jennie Churchill and Randolph had separated. What was particularly significant was the method they employed – canvassing by women on a massive scale. Thousands of women were put to work, organized through the Ladies' Grand Council of the Primrose League. It can only be supposed that Bright's constituents were astonished by the sight, though Bright made no mention of it in his diary. Indeed, it is said that no fewer than 10,000 non-resident voters from the Primrose League were brought in to canvass in the campaign. Precisely how many were deployed in the Central Division of Birmingham is not known.

Curiously, Churchill lost interest in the Primrose League, though it became the bulwark of Conservative election victories for the next 30 years, while the Constituency Associations withered on the vine. This was one of the main reasons why Salisbury was able to gain and retain the very vote that Bright had given to the working class. The Primrose League reached 200,000 members by early 1886, and a million by the time of Bright's death. By 1918, it had two million members.[25]

Bright retained his seat, but Lord Randolph's wife, Jennie, subsequently stated that 'to have brought down the great Mr Bright's majority to 400' – in fact, it was 773 – 'was a virtual triumph. The Radical Caucus and Mr Chamberlain's stronghold were shaken to their foundation.'[26] Nothing could be more ironic than that a scion of the house of Marlborough, the very epitome of aristocracy, should have come so close to destroying Bright in his own lair.

Winston Churchill, in his history of his father's life, related the saga of Lord Randolph's failed attack on Bright's bastion of Birmingham, with Bright notably unmoved by the event. This included his election speech, which tactfully paid tribute to Bright while seeking to unseat him.

Lord Randolph was regarded by Queen Victoria as 'so mad and odd', and Conservative MPs who were known to disapprove of him regarded him as 'an unprincipled adventurer copying Dizzy'.[27] Lord Randolph's mask fell, however, when he admitted that his appeal for Tory democracy (and for the votes of the working class) was 'chiefly opportunism'.[28] This was not an accusation that could be levelled at his opponent in the Central Division of Birmingham.

While Lord Randolph had employed the massed ranks of the Primrose League for reasons of opportunism and political expediency, Bright and Chamberlain were moving inexorably towards Liberal Unionism on the issue of Westminster sovereignty and on conviction and principle. Winston Churchill, in his biography of his father, described John Bright as being 'by himself a tower' in his opposition to Gladstone on the issue of Home Rule.[29] Ironically, this issue would become the basis of the new Conservative Party, which Lord Randolph Churchill's aspirations to lead were only thwarted by his premature death.

The 1885 General Election and the issues surrounding the settlement regarding single-member constituencies also highlighted another long-standing matter of principle for Bright. As Quinault points out, 'It was Bright who inspired the reorganisation of the Birmingham Liberal Party by his strenuous opposition to the minority clause of the Second Reform Act.'[30] Bright had consistently repudiated proportional representation for decades, and continued to do so now even though its adoption, or even that of the alternative vote, would have benefited the Liberal Unionists and minority views. The real principle for him was the freedom of choice by the individual voter to make a personal decision at the ballot box and then for that choice to determine the government of the country through Parliament. Bright would have rejoiced in the annihilation of the Liberal Democrat policy on the alternative vote (AV) in the referendum of 2011. As Vernon Bogdanor points out, in respect of the limited vote that was enacted in 1867, it was 'opposed by the three leading parliamentarians of the day – Bright, Gladstone and Disraeli'.[31] All of these understood thoroughly that politics consists of fighting for the soul of one's own party and its identity, and persuading the electorate accordingly, and not relying on false contrivances or devices to deliver unmerited power – or even the keys to Number 10 Downing Street.

The subsequent evolution of the arguments for proportional representation and the alternative vote were consistently opposed, not only by John Bright, but also by Gladstone and Salisbury. The old cynic, David Lloyd George, was against it in 1918, but in favour in 1931, when it suited him. Austen Chamberlain, after the first Speaker's Conference on Electoral Reform in 1917, stated he was against it for his Conservative Party:

> I was brought up as a Radical. I sat at the feet of John Bright, and the whole of the Liberal party with the exception of a few theoretical philosophers regarded this proposal or anything like it as anathema, denounced it up and down the country as a Tory doctrine to defeat the democracy, and resisted it consistently and persistently.[32]

Liberal Unionism and the New Conservatism

The Conservative Government was defeated in the General Election of 1885. Ireland returned 85 utterly intransigent Home Rulers to Parliament with massive majorities behind them. Parliament was now poised for even more serious disruption, with the Irish getting close to the balance of power in a Parliament consisting of 333 Liberals and 233 Conservatives. Theoretically, Gladstone had a majority of 100, but Parnell's 85 were trenchantly independent. Indeed, taking into consideration the Home Rulers within the Liberal Party, the Liberal majority on Irish issues was itself 85. The Liberal and Parnellite votes on Ireland thereby cancelled each other out.

Bright remained at Rochdale for the first few weeks of the new Parliament and did not return to London until March 1886. Meanwhile, there were indications of impending disaster for Gladstone and the Liberal Party. Chamberlain had joined Gladstone's Cabinet but, as he wrote to Bright, with Gladstone intent on Home Rule, he feared he would 'not be able to sail with him for long'.[33] Bright wrote to Chamberlain in mid-December 1885, saying that it would be 'a blessed thing' for the English Parliament to dispense with Ireland, on the basis that the Irish would be excluded from English and Scottish internal matters[34] – not unlike the current West Lothian question on Scottish devolution.

In March 1886, Bright spoke to the Marquess of Hartington and Gladstone in a succession of meetings. On 12 March, in a long discussion with Gladstone, Bright elicited that Gladstone's policy was to settle the land question and to remove Irish representation at Westminster. Bright stated, 'I entirely agree with him, if it is possible.'[35] Bright had become deeply disaffected by the Irish agitation, the Parnellites and their complete lack of constitutional propriety. It is a remarkable admission by Bright that the obstructionism and attitude of Parnell and his followers had driven him to believe that the United Kingdom Parliament and Government could continue to rule in Ireland without Irish members participating at Westminster – particularly as he had vigorously advocated proper representation for Ireland during the passage of the Third Reform Act in 1884. It demonstrates the extent to which he regarded the Parnellites as rebels, unfit to sit and legislate for their fellow countrymen.

On 13 March 1886, Chamberlain specifically demanded a statement from Gladstone repudiating an independent legislature for Ireland. Bright supported his demand. Bright also took issue with Gladstone over his Land Bill, which proposed to buy out the landlords en masse, and which Bright construed as a surrender to the Parnellites.

Appropriately on St Patrick's Day, 17 March, Bright spoke to Chamberlain, who was poised to resign from the Cabinet but, aware that he was the junior partner, was delaying his departure until he had Bright's support. Three days later, on 20 March, Bright had a two-hour discussion with Gladstone, at Gladstone's request, on the Irish question. Bright noted in his diary,

> He gave me a long memorandum, historical in character, on the past Irish story, which seemed to be somewhat one-sided, leaving out of view the important minority and the views and feelings of the Protestant and loyal portion of the people. He explained much of his policy as to a Dublin Parlt. and as to Land purchase.

Bright argued that the 1881 Act had done all that was reasonable for the tenants, and that it would be wrong to adopt the policy of the Parnellites 'and get rid of landholders, and thus evict the English garrison, as the rebels call them'. In his furious rejection of their unconstitutional and rebellious behaviour, Bright was even prepared to modify his policy regarding the landlords. He continued,

> Mr. G. is in favour of excluding all Irish representation from the Imperial Parlt. Thinks Irish members in Dublin and at Westminster not possible. Irish members think they could not supply representatives for both Houses. I told him I thought to get rid of the Irishmen from Westminster, such as we have known them for 5 or 6 years past, would do something to make his propositions less offensive and distasteful in Gt. Britain, tho' it tends to more complete separation.

Bright warned Gladstone how concerned many of his friends were about his policy on Ireland before addressing the failings of the Land Bill:

> I thought he placed far too much confidence in the leaders of the Rebel Party. I could place none in them, and the general feeling was and is that any terms made with them would not be kept, and that, thro' them, I could not hope for reconciliation with discontented and disloyal Ireland.

Bright had been firm, but noted that Gladstone 'was very friendly, and said how much he relied on such assistance as I could render him'.[36] Bright, however, was not confident that his advice would be heeded.

On 3 April, Bright had a conversation with Childers: 'He is miserable and the Govt. in a very unpleasant and unsafe condition.'

That same day, he recorded an invitation to dine with the Gladstones. He wrote:

> In my present position as to the Irish question, would rather not. It is difficult to oppose a Minister on a critical question and to associate with him and frequent his table. This morning I told him I thought he could not carry his Bill, but I do not see how he is to escape the danger he has placed himself in. I am grieved to see the peril to himself, and to the Party, and to Ireland. There is a certain wilfulness in all this not usual with him, and it does not promise any good.[37]

Gladstone brought his Home Rule Bill forward in the House of Commons on 8 April, speaking for three hours on the Irish government proposals. There was provision for an Irish executive responsible to an Irish legislature, but the Westminster Parliament would retain control over foreign policy, customs and excise, trade and navigation, the issue of currency and the post office. In other words, there would be continuing representation at Westminster, but considerable devolution.

Four days later, on 12 April, Bright did dine with Gladstone, whom he recorded as being 'very cheerful and well'.[38] On 16 April, Gladstone put forward his Irish land scheme, but to Bright's utter and complete dismay, he had decided to grant Home Rule.

However much he sympathized with the causes of Irish discontent, Bright simply could not accept the idea that there should be an effectively independent Parliament in Ireland, an outpost of anti-British Irish-Americanism driven by the policies of Parnell. An Irish Parliament on Parnellite terms would simply be a Trojan horse in the British Empire and would mean the end of union between the two countries.

To get Bright on side, Gladstone and his followers devised an entire campaign to appeal to his loyalty to the Party, and specifically to flatter him that he had immense influence and power. They recalled his victories – over the Corn Laws, the Paper Duties Bill and the Reform Act of 1867 – and that he had led the campaign to disestablish the Irish Church. But Bright would not play ball. He stood by his principle that the unity of the United Kingdom under one Parliament had to be preserved at all costs. This would not be achieved by coercion or by capitulation, but by employing the motto to which he returned throughout his life: 'Be just and fear not'.

Out of respect for a friendship developed over the decades, Bright refused to agitate openly against Gladstone. He had kept away when the Bill was read for the first time without division, and resisted Chamberlain's and Hartington's overtures to take a pre-eminent public role in their attack on Home Rule, Chamberlain having by then left the Government. He did, however, write a lengthy warning letter to Gladstone on 13 May from Rochdale.

'I feel outside all the contending sections of the Liberal party – for I am not in favour of home rule, or the creation of a Dublin parliament,' he wrote. Despite his sense of justice for the Irish people, for the tenant farmers, and for the Roman Catholics, all of whom he passionately believed deserved protection, his argument was primarily in defence of the constitutional rights of those on the other side of the equation:

> I cannot consent to a measure which is so offensive to the whole Protestant population of Ireland, and to the whole sentiment of the province of Ulster so far as its loyal and Protestant people are concerned ... I cannot agree to exclude them from the protection of the Imperial Parliament ...
>
> It may be that my hostility to the rebel party, looking at their conduct since your Government was formed six years ago, disables me from taking an impartial view of this great question ...If I could believe them loyal – if they were honourable and truthful men, I could yield much – but I suspect that your policy of surrender to them will only place more power in their hands to war with greater effect against the unity of the 3 Kingdoms with no increase of good to the Irish people.

He clearly believed that the Parnellites had forfeited any right to representation of any kind.

Bright's letter demonstrated an intrinsic and instinctive moral force in response to the political manoeuvrings of the Conservatives, the Parnellites, the Liberal Party and Gladstone:

> if a majority supports you, it will be one composed in effect of the men who for six years past have insulted the Queen, have torn down the national flag, have declared your lord lieutenant guilty of deliberate murder, and have made the Imperial Parliament an assembly totally unable to manage the legislative business for which it annually assembles at Westminster.[39]

Gladstone had requested that Bright return to London to discuss matters. When he arrived on 14 May, he found a letter from Gladstone waiting for him at the Reform Club. He would not be meeting Gladstone, but Samuel Whitbread, whom Gladstone had deputed for the purpose. Bright met Whitbread, but to no effect. In a letter to Whitbread on 17 May, Bright urged Gladstone to withdraw the Bill, saying he was heading for defeat and that 'He would be responsible for the greatest wound the Party has received since it was a Party.' He added that he was 'urged by several men in the House to say in the House what I am now writing. I fear to speak – lest I should say too much'.[40]

This situation, however, despite Bright's refusal to attack Gladstone openly, was unsustainable. Indeed, Bright's participation in the process of the subsequent defeat of Gladstone's Bill caused the final rupture between the two statesmen. From his letters to Chamberlain and others at this time, it is clear that Bright saw Gladstone as having destroyed the Liberal Party. They had maintained close relations for so many years, and Bright had forgiven Gladstone's support of the Crimean War and of the South in the American Civil War, but he could not now forgive him for abandoning the sovereignty of the Westminster Parliament, his country and his party by not merely giving in, but by capitulating to Parnell and Irish nationalism.

On 31 May 1886, there was a historic meeting in Committee Room 15. With the Liberal Party splitting, Chamberlain invited those Liberals to the meeting 'who, being in favour of some sort of autonomy for Ireland, disapproved of the Government Bills in their present shape'.[41] Bright objected to any kind of autonomy of the kind that either the Parnellites or the Home Rulers regarded as autonomous, but Chamberlain desperately appealed to Bright:

> The meeting tomorrow will be one of the most important ever held – for on its decision will depend the fate of the Government and of the Party. I do most earnestly beg of you to be present and to give us the benefit of your experience and judgement. I know that you have an instinct in these things which is always right.[42]

Out of regard for Gladstone, Bright did not attend the meeting, but he wrote his famous letter to Chamberlain that was decisive in turning the meeting into a split in the Liberal Party:

My dear Chamberlain,

My present intention is to vote against the Second Reading, not
having spoken in the debate. I am not willing to have my view of
the Bill or Bills in any doubt. But I am not willing to take the
responsibility of advising others as to their course. If they can
content themselves with abstaining from the division, I shall be
glad. They will render a greater service by preventing the threatened dissolution than by compelling it, if Mr. Gladstone is
unwise enough to venture upon it. You will see from this exactly
where I am. A small majority for the Bill may be almost as good
as its defeat and may save the country from the heavy sacrifice
of a General Election. I wish I could join you, but I cannot
now change the path I have taken from the beginning of this
unhappy discussion. Believe me always, Sincerely yours, John
Bright.

P.S. If you think it of any use you may read this note to your
friends.[43]

Later, in 1899, Chamberlain wrote to John Bright's son, J. A. Bright,
sending him this famous letter and several other letters on the same
issue. 'Your father's announcement,' Chamberlain noted, 'affected
the decision which I have no doubt now was the correct one.'[44]
However, the day after Bright had sent his letter to Chamberlain,
Bright wrote again, appearing to have second thoughts about the
influence of his letter:

I was surprised when Mr. Gaine told me last night of your decision and that my proposed vote had much influenced it – for my
note was intended to make it more easy for you and your friends
to abstain from voting in the coming division. If I had thought
I should do harm I should have said something *more* or *less*. Even
now if it is not too late I could join you in abstaining if we could
save the House and the country from a dissolution which may
for the Liberal Party turn out a catastrophe the magnitude of
which cannot be measured. For myself I have no anxiety, for to
leave Parliament now would be an immense relief, but I care for
the Party and for its objects and for the country.

To dissolve will be an act of grievous wrong on the part of the
Minister, the question does not require it, the country does not
demand it, and only the pride of the chief who is disappointed at
his failure can make it in any way necessary.

I am very much grieved at the crisis at which we have arrived and wish I could discover any way of escape. If there is no way we must submit, but the prospect is very gloomy for the Party and for the two countries.

Lord Hartington meets his friends this afternoon. Having moved the amendment, to withdraw is almost, perhaps quite, impossible with him and them.

You are to speak this evening and will have to declare your course. So that I fear there is not time for any reconsideration of the position unless you make some reservation which will enable you to change front before Thursday. I will do anything I can to meet your views. Yours sincerely, John Bright.

I shall be at the Reform Club if you have anything to write.[45]

On 5 June, he wrote again to Chamberlain:

I see nothing more that can be done. Mr. G. is very obstinate and I suspect cannot now yield. I see some of the Government party ask for my letter to you. I am unwilling to put any weapon into their hands, although in that letter I see nothing that can be of use to them. I am not sure we shall have a dissolution if the Bill is rejected, for I suspect the Government people are less confident as to the future Parliament ... I am not sure that the fear of dissolution will not after all carry the second reading. I shall regret it, but the discussions between now and October or February will I hope more effectually kill the Bill. But I believe no [Irish] Parliament is needed and I shall not support one.

Bright added as a postscript, 'I thought your speech admirable.'[46]

On 7 June 1886, in the company of 92 other Liberal members, including Chamberlain, Bright went into the Opposition Lobby and voted against Gladstone and the Government. The Home Rule Bill was defeated by 341 votes to 311.

It is by no means impossible that in the deeper recesses of Bright's mind and thoughts, having campaigned for his entire life for fair and just treatment for the Irish people, that he believed that the Irish, having given the Parnellites a massive 'Irish' majority, had taken for granted the benefit of his reforms. Instead of showing loyalty to Great Britain, they had thrown it back in his face and voted for Parnell and national independence.

In the words of Parnell, on his statue in O'Connell Street in Dublin, 'No man has a right to fix the boundary to the march of a nation.' Yet by voting against Gladstone and the Government on 7 June, Bright did just that. In the last resort, Bright regarded treason and rebellion against the established authority of the Crown as more heinous than anything else and undermined the Westminster democracy for which he had worked.

Bright explained himself further on 9 June 1886, in a letter to Chamberlain regarding a draft address that was being circulated between the Liberal Unionist leaders. Chamberlain had proposed a Canadian-style Dublin assembly, to which Bright objected strongly:

> I am against anything in the shape of taking the name of a Parliament in Dublin, and I will not go to the Colonies for an example for us. The Canadian Confederation is even now show-ing symptoms of breaking down, and I wish to maintain the unity of our Government. Our business seems to me to be to show that the Bills are bad, rather than to suggest something better … The strife seems even now beginning in Ireland, and it may spread and the future is dark. It is sad that this has been promoted by the unwise action of our great Minister … I waver from day to day as to the wisdom or the duty of remaining in Parliament. I see no prospect of further usefulness. And quiet, after long years of work, is both needful and pleasant.
>
> Perhaps the storm may blow over, but some wrecks may strew the shore.[47]

Chamberlain wrote back the same day, saying 'I expect you are right – you generally are – and I shall alter my address cutting out the allusions to Canada.'[48]

By his actions, Bright was assumed to be the elder statesman of the Liberal Unionists. For his part, however, he preferred to try to maintain the unity of the Liberal Government, despite having voted against Home Rule. He was naturally concerned about what would happen in the case of a dissolution. If there was a General Election, he could be opposed by a Liberal candidate. With that in mind, he wondered whether he wanted to stand at all.

On 10 June 1886, a dissolution was announced. Two days later, Bright consented yet again to be the candidate for the Central Division of Birmingham – at this stage as a Liberal and not specifi-cally as a Liberal Unionist, reflecting the political fluidity that existed at that time. He still hoped to maintain the coherence of the Liberal Party. At the same time, he complained about Liberals standing against sitting Liberal Unionists, but fell short of calling for a Liberal Unionist Association. Bright, Chamberlain and Hartington agreed they would not have a joint manifesto.[49]

On 28 June, Bright received a message from the Queen about 'how much satisfaction she had in what I had said in connexion with the Irish question, and desired that I should know it. The Queen is much against what is proposed.'[50] Queen Victoria understood very well that disunity with Ireland, part of her kingdom, would have a direct effect on the monarchy. Two days later, Bright was made a Doctor of Civil Law at Oxford, an honour he had previously stated he 'would rather decline'.[51] He noted the Vice-Chancellor's complimentary treatment of him, however: 'he introduced into the usual formal address of admission the words "patria et libertatis", which was thought remarkable, and which I thought very kind'.[52]

The General Election of July 1886 was fought over Home Rule, with Birmingham as its main battleground. The Gladstonian resistance was led by Francis Schnadhorst, the Liberal administrative supremo who was secretary of both the Birmingham Liberal Association and the National Liberal Federation. He had led the fight against Chamberlain following his resignation from Government and his subsequent open attack on Gladstone, but, following Gladstone's lead, Schnadhorst clearly intended to remain on good terms with Bright. The result was that Gladstonian candidates were put up to oppose all the Birmingham Liberal Unionists apart from, as Peter Marsh describes him, 'the revered Bright'.[53] For his part, despite being clearly on the side of the Unionists, Bright stood as a plain Liberal, in line with his desire to maintain unity.

On 1 July, Bright spoke at a meeting in Birmingham Town Hall, reiterating his view that the underlying cause of the troubles in Ireland were economic, not political. As James Sturgis notes,

> His most telling blow against the two bills [Home Rule and the proposed Land Bill] was that the Home Rule Bill did not entrust to the Dublin parliament the control over land. This failure to hand over the first duty of government – i.e. the preservation of property – was in his eyes an admission of failure.[54]

On 5 July, the results of the election were coming in. Bright noted, 'Results so far against the Government – that is Mr Gladstone and his Bills.'[55] The final results were Gladstonian Liberals 191, Liberal Unionists 78, Conservatives 315 and Parnellites 86. Bright was counted among the Liberal Unionists.

In one of the most historic events of the nineteenth century, Bright and Chamberlain had ended their political association with Gladstone. The Liberal Unionist Party was born, and would subsequently unite with the Conservative Party.

On 7 December 1886, Bright records in his diary a 'Meeting and banquet of "Unionist" Party in London. A letter from me to Lord Hartington read at the meeting.'[56] Though Bright had effectively become a Liberal Unionist, he was still sitting on the Liberal Benches but voting on occasion with the Conservatives. It was noted by Lord George Hamilton that Bright did not speak at all in the three-day debate on Irish matters in March 1887 regarding the Criminal Law Amendment (Ireland) Bill. As Hamilton pointed out,

> a great deal depended upon the action which he personally took. If he abstained from voting or voted against the Government, the Unionist Coalition would have been practically broken up. On the other hand if he, in order to avert Home Rule, voted for a procedure which was so contrary to his previous professions, the Coalition would receive a fresh source of strength and cohesion. When the Division Bell rang, Mr. Bright, who was sitting close by Gladstone, without a moment's hesitation walked straight into the Government lobby

and voted against the Coalition he despised.[57]

As Bright himself recorded, 'Mr. Gladstone and Opposition and their Irish allies rose and left the House, beaten and disgusted.'[58]

Though Bright had parted ways politically with Gladstone, the tumultuous events of 1886 did not end the personal affection these two great statesmen held for each other. Personal friendship remained important, and when Bright had bumped into Gladstone in Piccadilly in February 1887, he recorded in his diary:

> Had not seen him since the defeat of his Irish Bill last year. We stopped and shook hands. I remarked we had been far apart for some time. He said, 'I hope we may before long be nearer together again, which I doubted, or feared, we might not be...'[59]

As Trevelyan comments, 'The careful entry in the journal, with the hour and the spot noted... shows that to Bright the occasion was full of emotions which he does not attempt to define.'[60] On 14 June 1887, Bright wrote to Gladstone in reply to a letter about a statement Bright had made regarding Ulster. After dealing with the matter at hand, Bright ended by saying, 'I grieve that I cannot act with you as in years past, but my judgment and my conscience forbid it. If I have said a word that seems harsh or unfriendly, I will ask you to forgive it.'[61]

They remained opposed, however, on the great political issue of the day. On 17 June, Bright voted in a division in the Crimes Bill Committee and 'Irishmen left the House disgusted at their failure.' In the same journal entry, Bright also referred to a conversation with Mr Wilson, who had 'done much to expose, and I hope to break down, the criminal gang in Parlt. and in Ireland'.[62] Indeed, on 10 June, the Conservative Government had successfully voted through the famous 'guillotine resolution' which ensured that, if the Bill was not through the committee within seven days, the chairman must put the remaining clauses without amendment or debate. This again, like the closure motion, was a procedural innovation supported by Bright but which, one has to say, sowed the seeds of the present sham in Parliament, where these procedures are used as a matter of course, actively preventing discussion in the House and thereby undermining the very democratic system for which Bright had fought.

On 14 July, the Parnellites were so defeated that they did not dare, as Bright put it, to vote against the Irish Land Bill. On 26 August, Bright went to London 'for division on proclamation of Irish Rebel League'.[63] Gladstone had challenged the proclamation that the Irish National League be declared 'a dangerous Association' under the recent Criminal Law and Procedure (Ireland) Act.[64] Bright voted with the majority against Gladstone's motion. This was the last political entry that he made in his diary.

One of his last political statements was in a letter to a correspondent in November 1887, in which he wrote:

> Mr. Gladstone stops the way .... His followers still have faith in him and are anxious to return him to power. They are furious because the Conservatives are in office, and blame me and others for keeping them there. They seem blind to the fact that Mr. Gladstone put them in office ... We cannot allow Mr. Gladstone to go back to office with his Irish policy ... I prefer to join hands with Lord Salisbury and his colleagues than with Mr. Parnell and his friends the leaders of Irish rebellion.[65]

Bright put patriotism and the sovereignty of Westminster ahead of his party. What is truly ironic about this statement was that there had been no more bitter enemy of democracy than Salisbury when, as Lord Cranborne, he launched a violent onslaught on the very principle of democracy on which Bright fought his campaign for household suffrage. With the opportunism of Disraeli, Bright had delivered to the Conservative Party and the country the Reform Act of 1867. Now, Bright had become with Chamberlain part of a new Conservatism, as it were, fulfilling his words of 1859 – ('I profess to be in intention as Conservative as you are')[66] and 1867 – ('I begin to be an authority with the Tory Party!').[67]

Any suggestion that Bright had lost his political mettle by the 1880s, let alone the late 1860s as even Trevelyan asserts,[68] is clearly wrong. Though Bright had not spoken in the House of Commons since January 1886, this was largely out of his 'personal regard' for Gladstone, and he had continued to exert his influence in the Chamber through his attendance and participation in divisions. His diaries demonstrate that, towards the end of his life, particularly after the loss of his second wife in 1878, he certainly began to feel somewhat lonely and weary, but his willpower and conviction kept him going. Although he retained affection for the Liberal Party and for Gladstone, he had lost faith in the soul of the Party and in his last years found himself, in all conscience, in alignment with the Liberal Unionists. He published 40 letters in the press supporting the Liberal Unionist Cause, and proposed in 1888 that a pamphlet containing these letters should go to every voter in Birmingham – fighting his cause for Westminster to the end.

In the second half of 1887, however, his health declined and he withdrew from public life. Following a severe cold in May 1888, he became seriously ill with kidney disease and diabetes and, after rallying briefly during the summer, by November his health was failing. Everyone feared the end was coming.

The End

From his sickbed at One Ash, Bright asked his eldest son, Albert, to write Gladstone a final letter. Albert wrote:

> He wished me to write to you and tell you that 'he could not forget your unvarying kindness to him and the many services you have rendered to the country'. He was very weak and did not seem able to say any more, and I saw the tears running down his cheeks. He is quite conscious and calm, and suffers no pain. He is just slipping away from us.[69]

Gladstone wrote back that Bright had been little absent from his thoughts of late:

> I can assure you ... that my feelings towards him are entirely unaltered by any of the occurrences of the last three years, and that I have never felt separated from him in spirit. I heartily pray that he may enjoy the peace of God on this side of the grave and on the other. His many noble acts and words will live in the memory of his countrymen, and in my own they will always be associated with a thankful sense of the singularly harmonious relations which during many years it was permitted me to hold with him as friend and as colleague ... I should much prize his knowing that all his kindly sentiments are returned now when his hour draws near and mine can hardly be far distant.[70]

Bright's strength continued to ebb away over the following months. He was nursed by his daughters, with regular visits by his small granddaughters, and his dog, Fly, for company. Finally, on the morning of 27 March 1889, 'after some hours of unconsciousness, he sank peacefully to rest'.[71]

Under Bright's pillow was a letter from the Queen. R. A. J. Walling records that, when it became clear that Bright was dying, 'the Queen's message to him was among the earliest and the most sympathetic of the hundreds that poured into "One Ash" from every part of the world'.[72] Bright, the great scourge of the aristocracy, had always been a great monarchist, and while Victoria had initially had serious doubts about him, once she had discovered his true allegiance both to the Crown and to the country – and to the working class, the great mass of her subjects – she came to admire and respect him. She had once declined to accept him as a member of the Cabinet and a Privy Councillor in 1859, but that was a long time before. In 1868, when he became president of the Board of Trade, he noted in his diary, 'The Queen was very considerate and kind to me...'. She had not required him to kneel on taking office in appreciation of his religious convictions.[73]

There had also been a number of invitations to Balmoral, and by the time Bright had visited Windsor with a deputation of Quakers in May 1887, the depth of their regard for one other – and the ease with which they conversed – was clear. On that occasion, the Queen asked to see Bright alone. He recorded,

> I was recd. with a pleasant greeting and smile ... The Queen told me she was pleased with my course on the Irish question ... She

spoke sorrowfully of the course of Mr. Gladstone and thought his mind strangely diverted in the line he has taken on Irish affairs. She said she was going down to Scotland for a rest, when I remarked that I was afraid she suffered from the duties and anxieties of the time.[74]

Bright was buried in the graveyard of the Friends Meeting House in Rochdale, where he had worshipped since he was a child. It is a simple grave with a plain, horizontal stone slab bearing only the words, 'John Bright/Died March 27 1889/Aged 77 Years' – without so much as a mention of his being an MP. The day before the funeral on 30 March, his open coffin was placed in the drawing room of One Ash. 'He looked exquisite,' one of his daughters wrote, 'His face refined and pure, with a look of majesty on it and perfect peace.'[75] The mill workers came to pay their respects – the *New York Times* reporting that 3,000 people viewed the body in that single day.[76] Bright's daughter continued,

> It was a strange and touching sight, … They came straight from the Mill in their working clothes – the women with their shawls over their heads, and many brought their children. It was curious to watch their faces as they came, a constant stream, walking gently in single file round the coffin and out again, in perfect silence, many quietly weeping, especially the older people who had been at the Mill all their lives.[77]

Walling describes how, at the funeral,

> [an] immense concourse of people saw him pass for the last time through the streets of Rochdale. The multitude was silent; only the clatter of the horses' hoofs on the paved streets broke the stillness; but the mourning family were conscious of a universal sorrow, intensely felt in this his home, coming to them in great waves from every corner of the world where men spoke the language he had spoken. The affection of the English people for John Bright transcended the bitterness of the time.[78]

The number of people attending the funeral threatened to overwhelm Rochdale. To accommodate all the mourners, tickets were issued, the burial ground was boarded over to protect the other graves, platforms were erected and a wall was pulled down so that the crowd could spill over into the churchyard of the adjacent

Methodist chapel. But still there was not enough room and many had to attend instead a memorial service in the Rochdale Public Hall.[79]

The funeral procession included deputations from Liberal, Liberal Unionist and Conservative associations, as well as those from local societies and institutions, with two hundred mill workers flanking the hearse as Bright's coffin made its way to the burial ground. The pallbearers were eight men from the Mill. Chamberlain was among the many MPs present. Though Gladstone was himself unable to attend, the secretary of the Gladstonian National Liberal Federation was there, as was Gladstone's son, Henry. The Queen, who was abroad, arranged for a special equerry to be present on her behalf. When the coffin was lowered into the grave, the *New York Times* reported, there remained four wreaths:

> One was sent from Biarritz by Queen Victoria. Attached to it was her Majesty's autograph. Another was from the Prince and Princess of Wales, with a card bearing the words 'As a mark of respect'. The third was from Mr Bright's workpeople, and the fourth from Miss Cobden. Attached to Miss Cobden's wreath was a card inscribed, 'In loving memory of my father's best friend'.[80]

This simple burial, among his people and without fanfare, was typical of Bright's modesty. There had been a 'loud demand' that Bright be buried at Westminster Abbey,[81] but instead, a memorial service was held in the Abbey on the same day as Bright's funeral. This was attended by members of both the Commons and the Lords, including Lord Hartington, and representatives of the Royal Family, as well as crowds of people from all classes wishing to pay their respects.

'O death, where is thy sting? O grave, where is thy victory?'

Bright had gone, yet one final victory shortly after his death demonstrated that his influence, even from the grave, was still as strong as ever. With Bright's seat in Birmingham vacant, Randolph Churchill was mooted again as the Tory candidate. In a new alliance, however, Chamberlain and Salisbury combined to reject Churchill and instead to accept Bright's eldest son, John Albert Bright, as the Liberal Unionist candidate, much to Churchill's distress. While the Gladstonians initially decided not to fight the seat, they later changed their minds. The outcome of the 1889 election was that John Albert Bright, benefiting from his late father's legacy and the

Tory vote, defeated Gladstone's candidate by over 3,000 votes, giving the Liberal Unionists their first great victory.[82]

John Albert Bright's Liberal Unionist successor in Birmingham, Sir Ebenezer Parkes, later assumed the official label 'Unionist' in 1910 and formally became 'Conservative' when the new Conservative and Unionist Party was created in 1912. This new Conservative party spread from Birmingham across the country in the General Election of 1912 and preserves its original name even today.

As the Conservative historian Robert Blake asserts, the birth of the Conservative Party 'can be indisputably traced' to 1846 from the repeal of the Corn Laws and the delivery of Bright's 'great principle'.[83] How ironic and yet appropriate, therefore, that Bright's final endowment – of his own Birmingham seat to the Liberal Unionists – should within but a few years have been consolidated into a bastion of the Conservative and Unionist Party.

Thus John Bright's innate conservatism – described by Walter Bagehot as 'The Conservative vein in Mr Bright'[84] – and his loyalty and commitment to the sovereignty of the Westminster Parliament lived on. As Chamberlain declaimed, 'The great tribune of the people is dead but his voice yet speaketh and you will hear it and respond.'[85]

Notes

Preface

1 For a discussion of the current state of Parliament, see Riddell, Peter, *In Defence of Politicians (In Spite of Themselves)* (London, 2011).
2 Ausubel, Herman, *John Bright: Victorian Reformer* (New York, 1966) p. 239.

Introduction

1 Briggs, Asa, *The Age of Improvement* (2nd edn) (London, 2000) p. 271.
2 Hahn, Thomas, 'John Bright's letters to America at Rush Rhees Library', *University of Rochester Library Bulletin* 30/1/Autumn (1977), p. 72.
3 Ibid., pp. 296–7.
4 McCarthy, Justin, *Reminiscences*, Vol. I (London, 1899), pp. 66–7.
5 Ausubel: *John Bright*, p. 219.
6 Trevelyan, G. M., *An Autobiography and Other Essays* (London, 1949), p. 34
7 Morley, John, *The Life of Richard Cobden*, Vol. II (London, 1908), pp. 184–5.
8 Roberts, Andrew, *Salisbury: Victorian Titan* (London, 1999), pp. 57–8.
9 Marx, Karl, and Engels, Frederick, *Collected Works*, Vol. 15 (London, 1975–2004), pp. 238–42.
10 Marx and Engels: *Collected Works*, Vol. 16, pp. 87–90.
11 Hahn: 'Bright's letters to America', fn 17.
12 Ridley, Jasper, *Lord Palmerston* (London, 1970), p. 736.
13 Marx and Engels: *Collected Works*, Vol. 37, pp. 625–6.
14 McLellan, David, *The Thought of Karl Marx* (London, 1995), pp. 55–6.
15 Briggs, Asa, *Victorian People: A Reassessment of Persons and Themes 1851–67* (revd edn) (Chicago, 1972), p. 200.
16 Marx and Engels: *Collected Works*, Vol. 49, pp. 459–60.

17 See Bill Cash, 'John Bright: homage to a liberal', *The Economist*, 25 March 1989.
18 Carnegie, Andrew, *The Autobiography of Andrew Carnegie and the Gospel of Wealth* (New York, 2006), pp. 243–4.
19 Pillai, P. N. Raman, 'John Bright and India', *Indian Review* XII/8/August (1911), p. 609.
20 Underhill, F. H., *In Search of Canadian Liberalism* (Toronto, 1960), quoted in James L. Sturgis, *John Bright and the Empire* (London, 1969), p. 185.
21 Sturgis: *Bright and the Empire*, p. 185.
22 Ibid., p. 188.
23 http://www.congress.org.in/new/british-friends-of-india.php. Accessed 4 March 2011.
24 O'Brien, R. Barry, *John Bright: A Monograph* (London, 1910), p. 1.
25 HC Deb, 29 March 1889, vol. 334, cc1175–6.
26 O'Brien: *John Bright*, p. 264.
27 Dale, A. W. W., *The Life of R. W. Dale of Birmingham* (London, 1898), p. 437.

Chapter 1: The Unquiet Quaker

1   Trevelyan, G. M., *The Life of John Bright* (London, 1913), p. 4.
2   Ibid., pp. 1–2.
3   O'Brien, R. Barry, *John Bright: A Monograph* (London, 1910), p. 78.
4   Briggs, Asa, *Victorian People: A Reassessment of Persons and Themes: 1851–67* (revd edn) (Chicago, 1972), p. 198.
5   Walling, R. A. J. (ed.), *The Diaries of John Bright* (London, 1930), p. 17.
6   Robbins, Keith, *John Bright* (London, 1979), p. 66.
7   Woodward, Llewellyn, *The Age of Reform* (2nd edn) (Oxford, 1962), p. 121.
8   HC Deb, 12 May 1851, vol. 116, c928.
9   Walling: *Diaries of John Bright*, p. xi.
10 Ibid., p. xii.
11 Robbins: *John Bright*, p. 16.
12 Ibid., p. 227.
13 Ibid., p. 201, nt 2.
14 Smiles, Samuel, *Self Help with Illustrations of Character and Conduct* (New York, 1860), pp. 236–7.
15 Walling: *Diaries of John Bright*, p. 504.
16 Ibid., pp. 558–9.
17 Ibid., p. 372.
18 Ibid., p. 504.
19 Ibid., p. 508.
20 HC Deb, 29 March 1889, vol. 334, c1178.

21 Trevelyan: *John Bright*, pp. 13–14.
22 Briggs: *Victorian People*, p. 210.
23 Trevelyan: *John Bright*, p. 18.
24 Travis Mills, J., *John Bright and the Quakers*, Vol. II (London, 1935), p. 173.
25 Trevelyan: *John Bright*, p. 19.
26 Ibid., p. 24.
27 Ibid., p. 18.
28 Ibid., p. 18.
29 Walling: *Diaries of John Bright*, p. 13.
30 Trevelyan: *John Bright*, p. 24.
31 Ibid., p. 55.
32 Walling: *Diaries of John Bright*, p. 17.
33 Robbins, Keith, *John Bright* (London, 1979), pp. 20–1.
34 Villiers' tenacity on the issue of the Corn Laws was matched only by his longevity, surviving as MP for Wolverhampton until 1898, where he died in harness at the age of 96.
35 Davis, John, *Richard Cobden's German Diaries* (Munich, 2007), p. 27. For a discussion of Bright's relationship with the Manchester Chamber of Commerce and its rival, the Manchester Commercial Association, see Silver, Arthur, *Manchester Men and Indian Cotton, 1847–1872* (Manchester, 1966).
36 Robertson, W., *Life and Times of the Right Hon. John Bright*, Vol. I (London, 1884), p. 90.
37 Prentice, Archibald, *The History of the Anti-Corn Law League*, Vol. I (London, 1853), pp. 160–1.
38 HL Deb, 14 March 1839, vol. 46, c610.
39 Trevelyan: *John Bright*, p. 143.
40 All equivalent figures have been estimated based on the 2009 Retail Price Index using the calculator at www.measuringworth.com.
41 Robertson: *John Bright*, Vol I, p. 94.
42 Frederick Lucas was the brother of Samuel Lucas (Bright's brother-in-law and editor of the *Morning Star*) and nephew of William Cash. He founded the Catholic periodical, *The Tablet*, in London in May 1840. The publishing offices were moved to Dublin in 1849, and Lucas became the MP for County Meath in 1852. He was a close friend of Daniel O'Connell and John Henry Newman, whom he helped with the establishment of the Catholic University College of Dublin.
43 Longmate, Norman, *The Breadstealers: The Fight Against the Corn Laws, 1838–1846* (London, 1984), p. 88.
44 Ibid., p. 84.
45 Ibid., p. 86.
46 Francis Place to Richard Cobden, 29 September 1840, quoted in Longmate: *The Breadstealers*, pp. 89–90.

47   Robertson: *John Bright*, Vol. I, p. 120.
48   Ibid., p. 124.
49   Ibid.
50   Bright to Cobden, 10 September 1841, quoted in Trevelyan, p. 43.
51   Bright's speech on the unveiling of Cobden's statue, Bradford, 25 July 1877, quoted in Trevelyan: *John Bright*, p. 43.
52   Robertson: *John Bright*, Vol. I, p. 130.
53   Ibid., p. 133.
54   Prentice: *Anti-Corn Law League*, Vol. I, pp. 303–11.
55   Barnett Smith, George, *The Life and Speeches of the Right Hon. John Bright, MP*, Vol. I (London, 1881), p. 92.
56   Bright to Cobden, March 1842, quoted in Robbins: *John Bright*, p. 34.
57   Tallack, William, *Howard Letters and Memories* (London, 1905), p. 211.
58   Robertson: *John Bright*, Vol. I, p. 135.
59   Longmate: *The Breadstealers*, p. 66.
60   Ibid., p. 78.
61   Ibid., p. 66.
62   For the same reason, Smiles was then transferred as secretary to the National Providence Institution in London, founded by William Cash and his family in 1835.
63   Longmate: *The Breadstealers*, p. 88.
64   Ibid., p. 94.
65   Robertson: *John Bright*, Vol. I, pp. 139–40.
66   Bright to Cobden, 3 May 1842, quoted in Trevelyan: *John Bright*, p. 78.
67   Ausubel, Herman, *John Bright: Victorian Reformer* (New York, 1966), p. 33.
68   Trevelyan: *John Bright*, p. 82.
69   Robertson: *John Bright*, Vol. I, p. 151.
70   Longmate: *The Breadstealers*, pp. 139–40.
71   Longmate: *The Breadstealers*, p. 140.
72   Ibid., p. 140.
73   Wyke, Terry, *A Hall for All Seasons: A History of the Free Trade Hall* (Manchester, 1996), pp. 9–15. Later, in the 1850s, yet another, truly magnificent, hall was built, designed to be as permanent as the political reforms that inspired its construction. Terry Wyke's book was published to coincide with its refurbishment in 1996.
74   Robertson: *John Bright*, Vol. I, p. 152.
75   HC Deb, 17 February 1843, vol. 66, c838.
76   HC Deb, 17 February 1843, vol. 66, c839.
77   Robertson: *John Bright*, Vol. I, p. 157.
78   Ibid., Vol. I, p. 166.

79 See Southall, Humphrey, 'Agitate! Agitate! Organize! Political travellers and the construction of a national politics, 1839–1880', *Transactions of the Institute of British Geographers*, New Series 21/1 (1996), pp. 177–93.

80 Barnett Smith, Vol. I, p. 48.

81 Robertson: *John Bright*, Vol. I, p. 174.

82 Ibid., p. 173.

83 Barnett Smith: *Life and Speeches*, Vol. I, p. 41.

84 Robertson: *John Bright*, Vol. I, p. 175–6.

85 Ibid.

86 Robertson: *John Bright*, Vol. I, p. 179.

87 Ibid.

88 Ibid.

89 Longmate: *The Breadstealers*, p. 176.

90 Grant, James, *The British Senate: Random Recollections*, Vol. II (London, 1838), p. 210.

91 Robertson: *John Bright*, Vol. I, p. 183.

92 Ibid., p. 179.

93 HC Deb, 7 August 1843, vol. 71, cc341–2.

94 'The National Protest on Manchester's Rejection of John Bright', quoted in Vincent, John, *The Formation of the Liberal Party 1857–1868* (London, 1972), p. 197.

Chapter 2: The Corn Laws in Parliament

1 Robertson, W., *Life and Times of the Right Hon. John Bright*, Vol. I (London, 1884), p. 185.

2 Ibid., p. 190.

3 Travis Mills, J., *John Bright and the Quakers*, Vol. II (London, 1935), pp. 161–86.

4 Robbins, Keith, *John Bright* (London, 1979), p. 18.

5 Longmate, Norman, *The Breadstealers: The Fight Against the Corn Laws, 1838–1846* (London, 1984), p. 178.

6 Ibid., p. 179.

7 Robertson: *John Bright*, Vol. I, p. 205.

8 HC Deb, 1 February 1844, vol. 72, c102.

9 Robertson: *John Bright*, Vol. I, pp. 205–6.

10 Longmate: *The Breadstealers*, p. 206.

11 Robertson: *John Bright*, Vol. I, p. 210.

12 HC Deb, 19 July 1844, vol. 76, cc1103–4.

13 Robertson: *John Bright*, Vol. I, p. 219.

14 Ibid., p. 221.

15 Barnett Smith, George, *The Life and Speeches of the Right Hon. John Bright, MP*, Vol. I (London, 1881), p. 113.

16 Robertson: *John Bright*, Vol. I, p. 224.

17 Trevelyan, G. M., *The Life of John Bright* (London, 1913), p. 130.
18 Ibid., p. 131.
19 Robertson: *John Bright*, Vol. I, p. 245.
20 Read, Donald, *Cobden and Bright: A Victorian Political Partnership* (London, 1967).
21 Robbins: *John Bright*, p. 78.
22 Travis Mills: *Bright and the Quakers*, Vol. I, p. 266.
23 Robertson: *John Bright*, Vol. II, p. 247.
24 Ibid.
25 Ibid., p. 252.
26 Longmate: *The Breadstealers*, p. 210.
27 Ibid., p. 212.
28 Robertson: *John Bright*, Vol. I, p. 262.
29 Ibid., p. 263.
30 Longmate: *The Breadstealers*, p. 213.
31 Robertson: *John Bright*, Vol. I, pp. 273–4.
32 Ibid., p. 299.
33 Robertson: *John Bright*, Vol. I, p. 300.
34 Ibid., p. 305.
35 Ibid., p. 307.
36 Ibid., p. 306.
37 HC Deb, 22 January 1846, vol. 83, c69.
38 Ibid., cc94–5.
39 HC Deb, 16 February 1846, vol. 83, c1043.
40 Trevelyan: *John Bright*, p. 147.
41 Robertson: *John Bright*, Vol. I, p. 319.
42 HC Deb, 17 February 1846, vol. 83, cc1129–30.
43 Robertson: *John Bright*, Vol. I, pp. 319–20.
44 HC Deb, 20 February 1846, vol. 83, cc1346–7.
45 HC Deb, 27 February 1846, vol. 84, c292.
46 HC Deb, 15 May 1846, vol. 86, c675.
47 Ibid., cc694–706.
48 Disraeli, Benjamin, *Coningsby, or The New Generation*, Bk II (London, 1844), ch. V.
49 Walling, R. A. J. (ed.), *The Diaries of John Bright* (London, 1930), p. 153.
50 Ibid., p. 167.
51 Ibid., p. 172.
52 Ausubel, Herman, *John Bright: Victorian Reformer* (New York, 1966), p. 15.
53 Longmate: *The Breadstealers*, p. 224.
54 Ibid., pp. 223–4.
55 HC Deb, 29 June 1846, vol. 87, c1055.
56 Walling: *Diaries of John Bright*, pp. 80–1.
57 Ibid., p. 111.

58 Ibid., p. 112.
59 Ibid.
60 Trevelyan: *John Bright*, p. 150–1.
61 Hawkins, Angus, *The Forgotten Prime Minister: The 14th Earl of Derby*, Vol. I (Oxford, 2008), p. 318.
62 Trevelyan: *John Bright*, p. 145.
63 Leech, H. J., *The Public Letters of John Bright* (London, 1885), p. 222.

Chapter 3: Parliamentary Reform

1 Barnett Smith, George, *The Life and Speeches of the Right Hon. John Bright, MP*, Vol. I (London, 1881), p. 300. Philip Muntz was the brother of the Radical MP, George Muntz, and a leading Liberal in Birmingham.
2 Robbins, Keith, *John Bright* (London, 1979), p. 72.
3 Walling, R. A. J. (ed.), *The Diaries of John Bright* (London, 1930), p. 83.
4 Ibid., p. 83.
5 Trevelyan, G. M., *The Life of John Bright* (London, 1913), p. 183.
6 HC Deb, 18 April 1848, vol. 98, c472.
7 Trevelyan: *John Bright*, p. 183.
8 Ibid.
9 Ibid., p. 184.
10 Walling: *Diaries of John Bright*, p. 301, nt 1.
11 Trevelyan: *John Bright*, p. 184.
12 Cobden to Bright, 2 March 1842, quoted in Trevelyan: *John Bright*, p. 76.
13 Bright to Cobden, 21 December 1848, quoted in Ausubel, Herman, *John Bright: Victorian Reformer* (New York, 1966), p. 34.
14 Bright to Villiers, 21 December 1848, quoted in Trevelyan: *John Bright*, p. 184.
15 HC Deb, 5 June 1849, vol. 105, c1198.
16 Robertson, W., *Life and Times of the Right Hon. John Bright*, Vol. II (London, 1884), p. 149.
17 Ausubel: *John Bright*, p. 48.
18 Trevelyan: *John Bright*, p. 185.
19 Ibid., p. 185.
20 Robertson: *John Bright*, Vol. II, p. 10.
21 HC Deb, 23 November 1852, vol. 123, c351.
22 HC Deb, 25 November 1852, vol. 123, c504.
23 HC Deb, 16 December 1852, vol. 123, c1666.
24 Walling: *Diaries of John Bright*, p. 130.
25 Ibid., p. 130.
26 Ibid., p. 462.
27 Ibid., pp. 130–1.

28 Ibid., p. 131.
29 Hawkins, Angus, *The Forgotten Prime Minister: The 14th Earl of Derby*, Vol. II (Oxford, 2008), p. 67.
30 Trevelyan: *John Bright*, pp. 209–10.
31 Bright to Cobden, 14 January 1853, quoted in Trevelyan: *John Bright*, pp. 210–11.
32 HC Deb, 11 April 1854, vol. 132, c851.
33 Ridley, Jasper, *Lord Palmerston* (London, 1970), p. 577.
34 Bright to Villiers, 12 January 1854, quoted in Trevelyan: *John Bright*, p. 212.
35 Bright to Cobden, November 1853, quoted in Trevelyan: *John Bright*, p. 212.
36 Walling: *Diaries of John Bright*, p. 186.
37 Ibid., p. 218.
38 Ibid., pp. 224–5.
39 Bradford, Sarah, *Disraeli* (London, 1982), p. 235.
40 Robertson: *John Bright*, Vol. II, p. 92.
41 Ibid., p. 85.
42 Ibid., pp. 93–4.
43 Taylor, A. J. P., *Essays in English History* (London, 1976), p. 110.
44 Trevelyan: *John Bright*, p. 260.
45 Robertson: *John Bright*, Vol. II, p. 103.
46 Ibid., p. 106.
47 Walling: *Diaries of John Bright*, p. 230.
48 Robertson: *John Bright*, Vol. II, pp. 112–3.
49 Trevelyan: *John Bright*, p. 263.
50 Walling: *Diaries of John Bright*, p. 233.
51 Ridley: *Palmerston*, p. 648.
52 Robertson: *John Bright*, Vol. II, p. 119.
53 Ibid., p. 134.
54 HC Deb, 13 June 1854, vol. 134, c85.
55 Ibid., c84.
56 Walling: *Diaries of John Bright*, p. 132.
57 Robertson: *John Bright*, Vol. II, p. 108.
58 Walling: *Diaries of John Bright*, p. 234.
59 Trevelyan: *John Bright*, p. 269.
60 Ibid.
61 Ibid., p. 270.
62 Robertson: *John Bright*, Vol. II, p. 156.
63 Walling: *Diaries of John Bright*, p. 235.
64 Ibid., p. 235.
65 Robertson: *John Bright*, Vol. II, p. 168.
66 Ibid., pp. 173–4.
67 HC Deb, 24 March 1859, vol. 153, cc773–792.
68 Walling: *Diaries of John Bright*, p. 236.

69   HC Deb, 28 February 1859, vol. 152, c1025.
70   HC Deb, 19 March 1860, vol. 157, c845.
71   HC Deb, 24 March 1859, vol. 153, cc791–2.
72   Briggs, Asa, *Victorian People: A Reassessment of Persons and Themes: 1851–67* (revd edn) (Chicago, 1972), p. 200.
73   John Bright to Samuel Morley, 9 April 1859, quoted in Leech, H. J., *The Public Letters of John Bright* (London, 1885), pp. 71–4.
74   Barnett Smith: *Life and Speeches*, Vol. I, p. 300.
75   Ibid., p. 303.
76   Walling: *Diaries of John Bright*, p. 241.
77   Ibid.
78   Ibid., p. 242.
79   Ibid.
80   Ridley: *Palmerston*, p. 659.
81   Walling: *Diaries of John Bright*, p. 243.
82   Trevelyan: *John Bright*, p. 283.
83   Robertson: *John Bright*, Vol. II, p. 197.
84   Ibid., p. 198.
85   HC Deb, 21 July 1859, vol. 155, c190.
86   Ibid., cc191–8.
87   Ausubel: *John Bright*, p. 59.
88   HC Deb, 21 July 1859, vol. 155, c201.
89   Morley, John, *The Life of William Ewart Gladstone*, Vol. II (London, 1903), p. 20.
90   Walling: *Diaries of John Bright*, p. 244.
91   Trevelyan: *John Bright*, p. 284, fn 1.
92   Robertson: *John Bright*, Vol. II, p. 208.
93   Samuel Lucas (1811–65), was the founder of the Emancipation Society, which promoted anti-slavery in the USA, the brother of Frederick Lucas and a nephew of William Cash, the author's great-grandfather. Lucas's wife, Margaret Bright Lucas, John Bright's sister, was the chief founder and President of the British Women's Temper-ance Association and a vigorous campaigner for women's suffrage.
94   Vincent, John, *The Formation of the Liberal Party 1857–1868* (London, 1972), p. 96.
95   Donaldson Jordan, H., 'The reports of parliamentary debates, 1803–1908', *Economica* 34/November (1931), p. 443.
96   Joseph Sturge (1793–1859) founded the British and Foreign Anti-Slavery Society. One of the first members of the Anti-Corn Law League, he also campaigned for 'complete suffrage'. He was a leader of the 'People Diplomacy' movement, seeking arbitration for the avoidance of war and worked closely with Richard Cobden and others for a series of peace congresses throughout Europe.
97   Hawkins: *Derby*, Vol. II, p. 257.

98   Briggs, Asa, *The Age of Improvement* (2nd edn) (London, 2000), p. 372.

99   Monypenny, William Flavelle, and Buckle, George Earle, *The Life of Benjamin Disraeli, Earl of Beaconsfield,* Vol. IV (London, 1916), p. 274.

100 Report by Palmerston to Queen Victoria, 27 January 1861, quoted in Monypenny and Buckle: *Disraeli,* Vol. IV, p. 293–4.

101 HC Deb, 5 February 1861, vol. 161, cc108–9.

102 Walling: *Diaries of John Bright*, p. 253.

103 Prest, John M., *Lord John Russell* (London, 1972), p. 298.

104 Walling: *Diaries of John Bright*, p. 270.

105 Ibid., p. 285.

106 Robbins: *John Bright*, p. 153.

107 Briggs: *Age of Improvement*, p. 429.

108 Hawkins: *Derby,* Vol. II, p. 254.

109 Ausubel: *John Bright*, p. 125.

110 Ibid., p. 136.

111 Robertson: *John Bright,* Vol. II, p. 326.

112 Robbins: *John Bright*, p. 172.

113 Walling: *Diaries of John Bright*, pp. 275–6.

114 Ibid.

115 Trevelyan: *John Bright*, p. 332.

116 Walling: *Diaries of John Bright*, p. 278.

117 Trevelyan: *John Bright*, p. 332.

118 Ibid., p. 333.

119 Ibid., p. 332.

120 Walling: *Diaries of John Bright*, p. 279.

121 Robertson: *John Bright,* Vol. II, pp. 344–6.

122 Walling: *Diaries of John Bright*, p. 284.

123 Ibid.

124 Ibid., p. 285.

125 Ibid.

126 Ibid., p. 286.

127 Robertson: *John Bright,* Vol. II, p. 358.

128 Walling: *Diaries of John Bright*, p. 286.

129 Ibid., p. 287.

130 Robertson: *John Bright,* Vol. II, p. 366.

131 Ibid., p. 363.

132 Walling: *Diaries of John Bright*, p. 287.

133 Ibid., p. 289.

134 See McCarthy, Justin, *Reminiscences*, Vol. I (London, 1899), pp. 142–65 for an account of McCarthy's time at the *Morning Star*.

135 Robertson: *John Bright,* Vol. II, p. 374.

136 Ibid., pp. 374–5.

137 Trevelyan: *John Bright*, p. 344.

138 Ibid.

139 Robbins: *John Bright*, p. 176.
140 Trevelyan: *John Bright*, p. 344.
141 'The Political Wall-flower', *Punch, or the London Charivari*, 25 November 1863.
142 Bright to S. Fox, 24 October 1865, quoted in Robbins: *John Bright*, p. 176.
143 Bright to Charles Sturge, 21 December 1865, quoted in Trevelyan: *John Bright*, p. 345.
144 Robertson: *John Bright*, Vol. II, p. 381.
145 Trevelyan: *John Bright*, p. 346.
146 Bright to Villiers, January 1866, quoted in Robbins: *John Bright*, p. 179.
147 Bright to Gladstone, 10 February 1866, quoted in Smith, F. B., *The Making of the Second Reform Bill* (Cambridge University Press, 1966), p. 65.
148 HC Deb, 17 February 1866, vol. 181, c688.
149 Trevelyan: *John Bright*, p. 353.
150 Ibid., p. 351.
151 Watt, Francis, *Life and Opinions of the Right Hon. John Bright* (London, 1886), p. 241.
152 Trevelyan: *John Bright*, p. 351.
153 Smith: *The Second Reform Bill*, p. 72.
154 HC Deb, 13 March 1866, vol. 182, cc147–8.
155 HC Deb, 18 March 1867, vol. 186, c62.
156 Trevelyan: *John Bright*, p. 353.
157 HC Deb, 13 March 1866, vol. 182, cc219–220.
158 Robertson: *John Bright*, Vol. III, p. 5.
159 Gladstone to Russell, 20 June 1866, quoted in Smith: *The Second Reform Bill*, p. 114.
160 Robbins: *John Bright*, p. 182.
161 Trevelyan: *John Bright*, p. 357.
162 Disraeli to Derby, 25 June 1866, quoted in Monypenny and Buckle: *Disraeli*, Vol. IV, p. 440.
163 HC Deb, 17 March 1845, vol. 78, c1028.

Chapter 4: The New Democracy

1 Bright to T. B. Potter, 30 June 1866, quoted in Robbins, Keith, *John Bright* (London, 1979), p. 17.
2 Trevelyan, G. M., *The Life of John Bright* (London, 1913), p. 360.
3 Roberts, Stephen, *The Chartist Prisoners: The Radical Lives of Thomas Cooper (1805–1892) & Arthur O'Neill (1819–1896)* (Oxford, 2008), p. 133.
4 Ibid., p. 135.
5 Bright to Thomas Lloyd, 25 March 1866, quoted in Leech, H. J., *The Public Letters of John Bright* (London, 1885), pp. 106–9.

6 Documents of the First Internationale I, p. 289, quoted in Leventhal, F. M., *Respectable Radical: George Howell and Victorian Working Class Politics* (London, 1971), p. 53.

7 Robbins, Keith, *John Bright* (London, 1979), p. 221.

8 George Howell to Walter Morrison, 23 April 1872, quoted in Leventhal: *Respectable Radical*, p. 53.

9 Leventhal: *Respectable Radical*, p. 64.

10 Ausubel, Herman, *John Bright: Victorian Reformer* (New York, 1966), p. 151.

11 Bright to Howell, 19 July 1866, Bishopsgate Institute George Howell Collection, Howell 1/3.

12 Bishopsgate Institute George Howell Collection, Howell 1/3.

13 Bright to Richard Congreve, 24 November 1866, quoted in Robbins: *John Bright*, p. 190.

14 Briggs, Asa, *Victorian People: A Reassessment of Persons and Themes: 1851–67* (revd edn) (Chicago, 1972), p. 194.

15 Ibid., p. 230.

16 Roberts: *The Chartist Prisoners*, p. 134.

17 Hawkins, Angus, *The Forgotten Prime Minister: The 14th Earl of Derby*, (Oxford, 2008), Vol. II, p. 319.

18 Trevelyan, p. 365.

19 Robertson, W., *Life and Times of The Right Hon. John Bright*, Vol. III (London, 1884), p. 25.

20 Ibid., p. 362.

21 Trevelyan: *John Bright*, pp. 363–4.

22 Walling, R. A. J. (ed.), *The Diaries of John Bright* (London, 1930), p. 295.

23 Thorold Rogers, James E., *Speeches on Questions of Public Policy by the Right Honourable John Bright MP* (London, 1898), p. 398.

24 Disraeli to Cranborne, 26 December 1866, quoted in Monypenny, William Flavelle, and Buckle, George Earle, *The Life of Benjamin Disraeli, Earl of Beaconsfield*, Vol. IV (London, 1916), p. 463.

25 Hawkins: *Derby*, Vol. II, p. 320.

26 Disraeli to Derby, 18 November 1866, quoted in Monypenny and Buckle: *Disraeli*, Vol. IV, p. 459.

27 Hawkins: *Derby*, Vol. II, p. 319.

28 Morley, John, *The Life of William Ewart Gladstone*, Vol. II (London, 1903), p. 223.

29 Ibid., p. 225.

30 Robbins: *John Bright*, p. 190.

31 Trevelyan: *John Bright*, p. 370.

32 Vincent, John, *The Formation of the Liberal Party 1857–1868* (London, 1972), p. 196.

33 Monypenny and Buckle: *Disraeli*, Vol. IV, p. 486.

34 Walling: *Diaries of John Bright*, p. 294.

35 Ibid., p. 295.

36 Ibid.
37 Monypenny and Buckle: *Disraeli*, Vol. IV, pp. 498–500.
38 Walling: *Diaries of John Bright*, p. 255.
39 HC Deb, 25 February 1867, vol. 185, cc968–70.
40 Walling: *Diaries of John Bright*, pp. 295–6.
41 Banks Stanhope to Taylor, 13 March 1867, quoted in Smith, F. B., *The Making of the Second Reform Bill* (Cambridge University Press, 1966), p. 160.
42 Walling: *Diaries of John Bright*, pp. 296–7.
43 Smith: *The Second Reform Bill*, p. 161.
44 Cecil, Lord Robert Gascoyne, 'The Theories of Parliamentary Reform', *Oxford Essays* (London, 1855–8), pp. 52–79.
45 Walling: *Diaries of John Bright*, p. 298.
46 Ibid.
47 Blake, Robert, *Disraeli* (London, 1966), p. 461.
48 Trevelyan: *John Bright*, p. 380.
49 Walling: *Diaries of John Bright*, p. 298.
50 Ibid., p. 552.
51 Monypenny and Buckle: *Disraeli*, Vol. IV, p. 510, nt 1.
52 The archive of the Clark shoe manufacturing family, C & J Clark Ltd, is held by the Alfred Gillett Trust in Street, Somerset.
53 Speech to the National Union of Conservative and Constitutional Associations, 24 June 1872, quoted in *The Times*, 25 June 1872, p. 7, col. f.
54 Edward James Saunderson to his wife, 18 March 1867, quoted in Smith: *The Second Reform Bill*, pp. 172–3.
55 Walling: *Diaries of John Bright*, p. 298.
56 Ibid., p. 299.
57 Ibid., p. 299.
58 Ibid., p. 300.
59 Ibid., p. 301.
60 Ibid., p. 302.
61 Ibid.
62 Morley: *Gladstone*, Vol. II, p. 233.
63 Monypenny and Buckle: *Disraeli*, Vol. IV, p. 533.
64 Robertson: *John Bright*, Vol. III, pp. 49–50.
65 Ibid.
66 George Howell to Thomas Hughes, 5 May 1867, quoted in Leventhal: *Respectable Radical*, p. 90.
67 Walling: *Diaries of John Bright*, p. 304.
68 Smith: *The Second Reform Bill*, pp. 196–7.
69 Penman, John Simpson, *The Irresistible Movement of Democracy* (New York, 1923), p. 669.
70 Smith: *The Second Reform Bill*, p. 197.
71 HC Deb, 17 May 1867, vol. 187, cc708–11.

72   Morley: *Gladstone*, Vol. II, pp. 225–6.
73   *Daily Telegraph*, 12 June 1867.
74   HC Deb, 17 May 1867, vol. 187, cc712–9.
75   Ibid., cc720–6.
76   HC Deb, 17 May 1867, vol. 187, c756.
77   Disraeli to Gathorne Hardy, 18 May 1867, quoted in Monypenny and Buckle: *Disraeli*, Vol. IV, pp. 540–1.
78   Monypenny and Buckle: *Disraeli*, Vol. IV, pp. 555–6.
79   HC Deb, 20 May 1867, vol. 187, c800.
80   Walling: *Diaries of John Bright*, p. 307.
81   Ibid., p. 310.
82   HC Deb, 15 July 1867, vol. 188, cc1528–9.
83   Cox, Homersham, *The Reform Bills of 1866 and 1867* (London, 1868), p. 201.
84   Smith: *The Second Reform Bill*, p. 236.
85   Briggs: *Victorian People*, p. 231.
86   Bright to Beales, 18 August 1867, quoted in Leech: *Public Letters*, pp. 135–6.
87   Trevelyan: *John Bright*, p. 380.
88   Phillips, Melanie, *The Ascent of Woman: A History of the Suffragette Movement* (London, 2003), p. 132.
89   Ibid.
90   Walling: *Diaries of John Bright*, p. 379.
91   Ibid.
92   Ibid., p. 509.
93   HC Deb, 24 March 1884, vol. 286, c637.
94   Walling: *Diaries of John Bright*, p. 513.
95   Ibid., p. 514.
96   Bright to John Bigelow, March 1863, quoted in O'Brien, R. Barry, *John Bright: A Monograph* (London, 1910), pp. 177–8.
97   Robertson: *John Bright*, Vol. III, p. 319.
98   Trevelyan: *John Bright*, p. 440.
99   Walling: *Diaries of John Bright*, p. 514–5.
100 Ibid., p. 521.

Chapter 5: Lincoln and Bright

1   Horace Greeley (1811–72) was editor of the *New York Tribune*.
2   Walling, R. A. J. (ed.), *The Diaries of John Bright* (London, 1930), p. 290.
3   Travis Mills, J., *John Bright and the Quakers*, Vol. II (London, 1935), p. 242.
4   Ibid.
5   Dudley, Thomas H., 'Three critical periods in our diplomatic relations with England during the late war' *Pennsylvania Magazine of History and Biography*, vol. 17 (1893), p. 43.

6 Letter from P. M. Hamer (National Archives) to J. G. Randall, quoted in Randall, J. G., *Lincoln the Liberal Statesman* (New York, 1947), p. 237.

7 Seward to Sumner, 11 October 1861, quoted in Travis Mills: *Bright and the Quakers*, Vol. II, p. 240.

8 Trevelyan, G. M., *The Life of John Bright* (London, 1913), p. 296.

9 Washington, Booker T., *Frederick Douglass* (London, 1906), p. 115.

10 Dudley: 'Three critical periods', p. 42.

11 Bigelow, John, *Retrospections of an Active Life* (New York, 1909–13), Vol. I, p. 413.

12 Hahn, Thomas, 'John Bright's letters to America at Rush Rhees Library', *University of Rochester Library Bulletin*, 30/1/Autumn (1977).

13 Ibid., fn 17.

14 Bigelow: *Retrospections*, Vol. IV, p. 332.

15 Bright to Seward, 21 October 1865, quoted in Hahn: 'Bright's letters to America'.

16 Ibid.

17 Bright to Francis Jackson Garrison, 17 February 1886, quoted in Hahn: 'Bright's letters to America'.

18 Moore, Frank, *Speeches of John Bright MP on the American Question* (Boston, 1865), pp. x–xi.

19 Trueblood, David Elton, *Abraham Lincoln: Theologian of American Anguish* (New York, 1973), p. 120.

20 Travis Mills: *Bright and the Quakers*, Vol. II, p. 217.

21 Sandburg, Carl, *Abraham Lincoln: The Prairie Years and The War Years* (New York, 1982), p. 212.

22 Trevelyan: *John Bright*, p. 304.

23 Read, Donald, *Cobden and Bright: A Victorian Political Partnership* (London, 1967), p. 218.

24 Robbins, Keith, *John Bright* (London, 1979), p. 157.

25 Trevelyan: *John Bright*, p. 302.

26 Robertson, W., *Life and Times of the Right Hon. John Bright*, Vol. II (London, 1884), p. 284.

27 HC Deb, 13 March 1865, vol. 177, c1619 – this was before they fell out in 1867.

28 Russell, William Howard, *My Diary North and South* (Boston, 1863), p. 39,

29 Trevelyan: *John Bright*, p. 304,

30 Robertson: *John Bright*, Vol. II, p. 273,

31 Ibid.

32 Robbins: *John Bright*, p. 160,

33 Trevelyan: *John Bright*, p. 302,

34 Bright to James Henderson, 4 September 1861, quoted in Robbins: *John Bright*, p. 158

35 Travis Mills: *Bright and the Quakers*, Vol. II, p. 240.
36 Sandburg: *Abraham Lincoln*, p. 267.
37 Foreman, Amanda, *A World on Fire: An Epic History of Two Nations Divided* (London, 2010), p. 183.
38 Robertson: *John Bright*, Vol. II, pp. 281–8.
39 Travis Mills: *Bright and the Quakers*, Vol. II, p. 230.
40 O'Brien, R. Barry, *John Bright: A Monograph* (London, 1910), p. 138.
41 Pierce, Edward L., *Memoir and Letters of Charles Sumner*, Vol. II (Boston, 1877–93), p. 141.
42 Travis Mills: *Bright and the Quakers*, Vol. II, p. 236, fn 2.
43 Cobden to Sumner, 12 February 1862, quoted in Pierce: *Charles Sumner*, Vol. IV, p. 147.
44 Bright to Sumner, 5 December 1861, quoted in Trevelyan: *John Bright*, p. 314.
45 Bright to Sumner, 7 December 1861, quoted in Trevelyan: *John Bright*, p. 315.
46 Bright to Sumner, 14 December 1861, quoted in Trevelyan: *John Bright*, pp. 315–6.
47 Sandburg: *Abraham Lincoln*, p. 269.
48 O'Brien: *John Bright*, p. 141.
49 Sandburg: *Abraham Lincoln*, p. 269.
50 Bright to Cobden, 9 December 1861, quoted in Trevelyan: *John Bright*, p. 315.
51 Cobden to Bright, 6 December 1861, quoted in O'Brien: *John Bright*, p. 143.
52 HC Deb, 17 February 1862, vol. 165, c381.
53 Walling: *Diaries of John Bright*, p. 257.
54 Sandburg: *Abraham Lincoln*, p. 314.
55 Sumner to Bright, 5 August 1862, quoted in Pierce: *Charles Sumner*, Vol. IV, p. 83.
56 Sandburg: *Abraham Lincoln*, p. 319.
57 Morley, John, *The Life of William Ewart Gladstone*, Vol. II (London, 1903), p. 79.
58 Bright to Sumner, 10 October 1862, quoted in Trevelyan: *John Bright*, p. 320.
59 Morley: *Gladstone*, Vol. II, p. 81.
60 Robert E. Lee's Royalist ancestors came from Langley in Shropshire, but left England during the English Civil War in the 1640s.
61 Travis Mills: *Bright and the Quakers*, Vol. II, p. 225.
62 Robertson: *John Bright*, Vol. II, p. 304.
63 Sumner to Bright, 28 October 1862, quoted in Pierce: *Charles Sumner*, Vol. IV, p. 106.
64 *Morning Star*, 17 January 1863.

Notes **301**

65 Travis Mills: *Bright and the Quakers*, Vol. II, p. 190.
66 Trevelyan: *John Bright*, p. 309.
67 Bright to his wife, 19 July 1862, quoted in Trevelyan: *John Bright*, p. 317.
68 Bright to Sumner, 6 December 1862, quoted in Trevelyan: *John Bright*, p. 309.
69 Trevelyan: *John Bright*, p. 327.
70 Bright to Sumner, 6 December 1862, quoted in Trevelyan: *John Bright*, pp. 320–1.
71 Bright to Sumner, 30 January 1863, quoted in Ausubel, Herman, *John Bright: Victorian Reformer* (New York, 1966), p. 130.
72 Trevelyan: *John Bright*, pp. 307–8.
73 Sumner to Bright, 17 April 1863, quoted in O'Brien: *John Bright*, p. 152.
74 O'Brien: *John Bright*, p. 152.
75 Robertson: *John Bright*, Vol. II, pp. 302–3.
76 Pierce: *Charles Sumner*, Vol. IV, p. 130.
77 HC Deb, 27 March 1863, vol. 170, cc71–2.
78 Trevelyan: *John Bright*, p. 319.
79 O'Brien: *John Bright*, pp. 151–2.
80 Sandburg: *Abraham Lincoln*, p. 445.
81 Trevelyan: *John Bright*, p. 322.
82 HC Deb, 30 June 1863, vol. 171, cc1834–5.
83 Bright to Sumner, 31 July 1863, quoted in Trevelyan: *John Bright*, p. 323.
84 Bright to Villiers, 5 August 1863, quoted in Trevelyan: *John Bright*, p. 319.
85 Charles Francis Adams to Lord Russell, 5 September 1863, quoted in O'Brien: *John Bright*, p. 158.
86 Bright to Sumner, 11 September 1863, quoted in Trevelyan: *John Bright*, pp. 319, 323.
87 Bright to Sumner, 18 February 1864, quoted in Trevelyan: *John Bright*, pp. 323–4.
88 Walling: *Diaries of John Bright*, p. 281.
89 Bright to Sumner, September 1864, quoted in Trevelyan: *John Bright*, p. 324.
90 Trevelyan: *John Bright*, p. 325.
91 Walling: *Diaries of John Bright*, pp. 289–90.
92 Bright to his wife, 23 April 1865, quoted in Ausubel: *John Bright*, p. 141.
93 Walling: *Diaries of John Bright*, p. 290.
94 Bright to Sumner, 29 April 1865, quoted in Trevelyan: *John Bright*, p. 326.
95 Travis Mills: *Bright and the Quakers*, Vol. II, p. 242.
96 Ibid., pp. 242–3.

97 Walling: *Diaries of John Bright*, p. 340.
98 Travis Mills: *Bright and the Quakers*, Vol. II, p. 234.
99 Bright to Sumner, 26 October 1867, quoted in Travis Mills: *Bright and the Quakers*, Vol. II, pp. 234–5.
100 Bright to Lord Granville, 25 September 1872, quoted in Travis Mills: *Bright and the Quakers*, Vol. II, p. 236.
101 Walling: *Diaries of John Bright*, p. 309, fn 1.
102 Ibid., p. 351.
103 Travis Mills: *Bright and the Quakers*, Vol. II, p. 242.
104 O'Brien: *John Bright*, p. 160.
105 Letter to John Bright dated 12 April 1867, Rochdale Local Studies Library.
106 Walling: *Diaries of John Bright*, p. 297
107 Trevelyan: *John Bright*, p. 327.
108 Bright to Mr Forbes, 31 July 1863, quoted in Trevelyan: *John Bright*, p. 327.
109 Barnett Smith, George, *The Life and Speeches of the Right Hon. John Bright, MP*, Vol. II (London, 1881), pp. 299–300.
110 Walling: *Diaries of John Bright*, p. 428.
111 Barnett Smith: *Life and Speeches*, Vol. II, pp. 300–1.
112 Walling: *Diaries of John Bright*, p. 559.

Chapter 6: A Just Foreign Policy

1 Dutt, Romesh Chunder, *India in the Victorian Age: An Economic History of the People* (London, 1904), p. 129. Romesh Chunder Dutt, C.I.E. (1848–1909) was at University College London (UCL) and a barrister at Middle Temple. He returned to India and was the first Indian to attain an executive post. After retiring as Commissioner of Orissa, he returned to UCL to lecture in Indian History. He was President of the Indian National Congress and a member of the Bengal Legislative Council.
2 HC Deb, 30 June 1848, vol. 99, cc1414–68.
3 H. T. Manning, *British Colonial Government after the American Revolution 1782–1820*, discussed in Sturgis, James L., *John Bright and the Empire* (London, 1969), p. 80.
4 Stephen was Permanent Under-Secretary of State for the Colonies 1836–47.
5 Sturgis: *Bright and the Empire*, p. 81.
6 HC Deb, 31 March 1848, vol. 97, c1185.
7 Sturgis: *Bright and the Empire*, p. 90.
8 Bright to Sturge, 24 September 1857, quoted in Sturgis: *Bright and the Empire*, p. 92.
9 *Manchester Examiner and Times*, 23 March 1853, quoted in Sturgis: *Bright and the Empire*, p. 37.

10 Bright to Cobden, 12 October 1850, quoted in Sturgis: *Bright and the Empire*, p. 39.

11 Sturgis: *Bright and the Empire*, p. 16.

12 Dutt: *India in the Victorian Age*, p. 132.

13 Ibid., p. 142.

14 HC Deb, 27 June 1853, vol. 128, c883.

15 HC Deb, 3 June 1853, vol. 127, c1176.

16 *The Times*, 31 January 1850, p. 6, cols d–e.

17 HC Deb, 20 March 1855, vol. 137, c887.

18 HC Deb, 3 August 1854, vol. 135, c1249.

19 HC Deb, 13 June 1851, vol. 117, c765–6.

20 HC Deb, 22 February 1848, vol. 96, cc1077–8.

21 Sturgis: *Bright and the Empire*, p. 26.

22 Bright to Sturge, 27 March 1853, quoted in Sturgis: *Bright and the Empire*, p. 18.

23 HC Deb, 11 July 1854, vol. 135, c81.

24 HC Deb, 25 July 1853, vol. 129, cc781–2.

25 HC Deb, 3 June 1853, vol. 127, c1185. The Government of India Act 1833 also created Crown Agents, who were subsequently accused of milking the Empire.

26 Ibid., c1186.

27 Ibid., cc1187–94.

28 HC Deb, 11 July 1854, vol. 135, c80.

29 *The Times*, 10 June 1853, p. 4, col. e.

30 *Manchester Examiner and Times*, 2 February 1853, p. 6, col. c.

31 Bright to Cobden, 16 April 1857, quoted in Morley, John, *The Life of Richard Cobden*, Vol. II (London, 1908), p. 173.

32 Bright to Sturge, 16 August 1858, quoted in Sturgis: *Bright and the Empire*, p. 45.

33 HC Deb, 20 May 1858, vol. 150, cc951–62.

34 HC Deb, 24 June 1858, vol. 151, c351.

35 Hoppen, Theodore, *New Oxford History of England: The Mid-Victorian Generation 1846–1886* (London, 1998), p. 105.

36 HC Deb, 24 June 1858, vol. 151, cc346–53.

37 Robertson, W., *Life and Times of the Right Hon. John Bright*, Vol. II (London, 1884), p. 133–4.

38 HC Deb, 1 August 1859, vol. 155, cc812–3.

39 HC Deb, 19 July 1859, vol. 155, cc49–50.

40 Walling, R. A. J. (ed.), *The Diaries of John Bright* (London, 1930), p. 185.

41 HC Deb, 20 March 1855, vol. 137, c887.

42 Sturgis: *Bright and the Empire*, p. 88.

43 *The Times*, 9 October 1866, p. 7, col. e.

44 Ibid., 30 October 1858, p. 9, col. d.

45 Robertson, Vol. II, p. 284.

46 HC Deb, 28 February 1867, vol. 185, c1185.
47 Rose, J. H., Newton, A. P. and Benians, E. A. (eds), *The Cambridge History of the British Empire, Volume Two: The Growth of the New Empire, 1783–1870* (Cambridge University Press, 1940), p. 736.
48 *The Times*, 1 December 1865, p. 7, col. e.
49 HC Deb, 09 February 1866, vol. 181, c323.
50 Sturgis: *Bright and the Empire*, p. 68.
51 Robbins, Keith, *John Bright* (London, 1979), p. 205.
52 Ibid., p. 57.
53 *The Times*, 8 December 1885, p. 7, col. d.
54 Sturgis: *Bright and the Empire*, p. 71, nt 9.
55 Trevelyan, G. M., *The Life of John Bright* (London, 1913), p. 266.
56 Bright to J. B. Smith, 8 September 1877, quoted in Sturgis: *Bright and the Empire*, pp. 73–4.
57 Bright to his wife, 20 January 1878, quoted in Sturgis: *Bright and the Empire*, p. 73.
58 *The Times*, 17 April 1879, p. 11, col. b.
59 HC Deb, 8 July 1858, vol. 151, c1095.
60 Sturgis: *Bright and the Empire*, p. 77.
61 www.congress.org.in/new/british-friends-of-india.php. Accessed 4 March 2011.
62 *The Times*, 8 December 1885, p. 7, col. d.
63 Pillai, P. N. Raman, 'John Bright and India', *Indian Review*, XII/8 /August (1911), pp. 608–16.
64 *The Times*, 9 July 1887, p. 9, col. d.
65 Gandhi, Mohandas Karamchand, *The Collected Works of Mahatma Gandhi* (Delhi, 1958), Vol. I, p. 163.
66 Bright to Granville, 26 September 1873, National Archives, PRO 30/29/52.
67 Bright to Gladstone 17 September 1873, quoted in Sturgis: *Bright and the Empire*, p. 109.
68 Walling, R. A. J. (ed.), *The Diaries of John Bright* (London, 1930), p. 358.
69 Walling: *Diaries of John Bright*, p. 510.
70 Trevelyan: *John Bright*, p. 430.
71 Walling: *Diaries of John Bright*, p. 456.
72 Ibid., p. 458.
73 *The Times*, 23 January 1880, p. 11, col. c.
74 *The Times*, 30 January 1885, p. 6, col. c.
75 Walling: *Diaries of John Bright*, – 5 March 1885, p. 524.76 *The Times*, 30 January 1885, p. 6, col. c.
76 *The Times*, 30 January 1885, p. 6 col. c.

Chapter 7: Foreign Policy and War

1   Robertson: *John Bright*, Vol. II, p. 142.
2   Trevelyan: *John Bright*, pp. 278–8.
3   Quoted in Briggs, Asa, *Victorian People: A Reassessment of Persons and Themes: 1851–67* (revd edn) (Chicago, 1972), p. 213.
4   HC Deb, 31 March 1854, vol. 132, cc244–62.
5   Robertson: *John Bright*, Vol. III, pp. 32–3.
6   HC Deb, 13 March 1854, vol. 131, c680.
7   Robertson: *John Bright*, Vol. III, p. 35.
8   HC Deb, 31 March 1854, vol. 132, cc265–80.
9   Trevelyan: *John Bright*, pp. 215–6.
10 Walling: *Diaries of John Bright*, pp. 176–7.
11 HC Deb, 22 December 1854. vol. 136, cc890–3.
12 Walling: *Diaries of John Bright*, p. 184.
13 HC Deb, 23 February 1855, vol. 136, cc1761–2.
14 HC Deb, 7 June 1855, vol. 138, c1611.
15 Briggs: *Victorian People*, p. 217.
16 Hawkins, Angus, *The Forgotten Prime Minister: The 14th Earl of Derby*, Vol. II (Oxford, 2008), pp. 118–19.
17 Walling: *Diaries of John Bright*, p. 203.
18 Robbins: *John Bright*, p. 115.
19 Ibid., p. 210.
20 Ibid., p. 216.
21 HC Deb, 26 February 1857, vol. 144, c1485.
22 Walling: *Diaries of John Bright*, p. 223.
23 Ibid., p. 211.
24 Ibid., pp. 225–6.
25 HC Deb, 25 June 1850, vol. 112, cc380–444.
26 Walling: *Diaries of John Bright*, p. 111.
27 HC Deb, 19 March 1861, vol. 162, c74.
28 Trevelyan: *John Bright*, p. 280.
29 Ibid., p. 281.
30 Ibid., p. 282.
31 Walling: *Diaries of John Bright*, p. 239.
32 HC Deb, 2 March 1860, vol. 156, cc2168–70.
33 Trevelyan: *John Bright*, p. 288.
34 Ridley, Jasper, *Lord Palmerston* (London, 1970), p. 706.
35 Ibid., p. 707.
36 Ibid.
37 Walling: *Diaries of John Bright*, p. 282.
38 Ridley: *Palmerston*, p. 793.
39 Trevelyan: *John Bright*, p. 417.
40 Robbins: *John Bright*, p. 211.
41 Robertson: *John Bright*, Vol. III, p. 148.

42 Trevelyan: *John Bright*, p. 419.
43 Walling: *Diaries of John Bright*, p. 390.
44 Ibid., p. 403.
45 Trevelyan: *John Bright*, p. 422.
46 HC Deb, 29 March 1889, vol. 334, cc1170–1.
47 Barnett Smith, George, *The Life and Speeches of the Right Hon. John Bright, MP,* Vol II (London, 1881), p. 288.
48 Sturgis: *Bright and the Empire*, p. 78.
49 Barnett Smith: *Life and Speeches,* Vol. II, p. 288.
50 Walling: *Diaries of John Bright*, p. 421.
51 Ibid., p. 446.
52 Ibid., pp. 448–9.
53 *The Times*, 30 January 1885, p. 6, col. b.
54 Walling: *Diaries of John Bright*, p. 482.
55 Ibid., p. 483.
56 Ibid., p. 484.
57 Ibid., p. 485.
58 Ibid., p. 486.
59 Ibid., p. 486.
60 Trevelyan: *John Bright*, p. 433.
61 Walling: *Diaries of John Bright*, p. 486.
62 Ibid., p. 487.
63 Magnus, Philip, *Gladstone: A Biography* (corrected edn) (London, 1960), pp. 144–5.
64 Jenkins, Roy, *Gladstone* (London, 1995), p. 440.
65 Walling: *Diaries of John Bright*, pp. 487–8.
66 Ibid., p. 488.
67 Morley, John, *The Life of William Ewart Gladstone,* Vol III (London, 1903), p. 85.
68 Walling: *Diaries of John Bright*, pp. 488–9.
69 Morley: *Gladstone,* Vol. III, p. 85.
70 Walling: *Diaries of John Bright*, p. 490.
71 Trevelyan: *John Bright*, p. 435.
72 Walling: *Diaries of John Bright*, p. 492.
73 Trevelyan: *John Bright*, pp. 435–6.
74 Walling: *Diaries of John Bright*, p. 524.
75 Trevelyan: *John Bright*, p. 437.

Chapter 8: Oppression in Ireland and British Sovereignty

1 O'Brien, R., *John Bright: A Monograph* (London, 1910), p. 57.
2 Briggs, Asa, *Victorian People: A Reassessment of Persons and Themes: 1851–67* (revd edn) (Chicago, 1972), p. 198.
3 Lucas, Edward, *The Life of Frederick Lucas MP*, Vol. II (London, 1886), p. 4.

4   Robertson, W., *Life and Times of the Right Hon. John Bright*, Vol. I (London, 1884), p. 70.
5   Walling, R. A. J. (ed.), *The Diaries of John Bright* (London, 1930), p. 15.
6   Barnett Smith, George, *The Life and Speeches of the Right Hon. John Bright, MP*, Vol. I (London, 1881), pp. 46–7.
7   HC Deb, 7 August 1843, vol. 71, c341.
8   HC Deb, 16 February 1844, vol. 72, c1016.
9   HC Deb, 16 April 1845, vol. 79, cc819–21.
10 HC Deb, 13 December 1847, vol. 95, c988.
11 O'Brien: *John Bright*, p. 57.
12 HC Deb, 25 August 1848, vol. 101, cc534–8.
13 HC Deb, 2 April 1849, vol. 104, cc165–79.
14 Hoppen, Theodore, *New Oxford History of England: The Mid-Victorian Generation 1846–1886* (London, 1998), pp. 572–3.
15 Walling: *Diaries of John Bright*, p. 101.
16 Ibid., p. 102.
17 See Bianconi, M. O'C. and Watson, S. J., *Bianconi: King of the Irish Roads* (Dublin, 1962).
18 Walling: *Diaries of John Bright*, p. 103.
19 Ibid., p. 105.
20 Ibid., pp. 106–7.
21 HC Deb, 10 February 1852, vol. 119, c367.
22 Trevelyan, G. M., *The Life of John Bright* (London, 1913), p. 167.
23 Walling: *Diaries of John Bright*, p. 245.
24 HC Deb, 17 February 1866, vol. 181, c686–90.
25 Trevelyan: *John Bright*, p. 350.
26 Thorold Rogers, James E., *Speeches on Questions of Public Policy by the Right Honourable John Bright MP* (London, 1898), p. 184.
27 O'Brien: *John Bright*, pp. 67–8.
28 HC Deb, 14 June 1867, vol. 187, c1904.
29 O'Brien: *John Bright*, pp. 70–1.
30 Robertson: *John Bright*, Vol. III, pp. 69–70.
31 Walling: *Diaries of John Bright*, p. 314.
32 Ibid., p. 315.
33 Ibid.
34 HC Deb, 13 March 1868, vol. 190, cc1647–62.
35 Walling: *Diaries of John Bright*, p. 315.
36 Ibid., p. 323.
37 Ibid., p. 323.
38 HC Deb, 7 May 1868, vol. 191, c1943.
39 Robertson: *John Bright*, Vol. III, p. 79.
40 Walling: *Diaries of John Bright*, p. 326.
41 Robertson: *John Bright*, Vol. III, p. 87.
42 Ibid., pp. 88–9.
43 HC Deb, 19 March 1869, vol. 194, c1894.

44 Ausubel, Herman, *John Bright: Victorian Reformer* (New York, 1966), p. 173.
45 Robertson: *John Bright*, Vol. III, pp. 101–3.
46 Trevelyan: *John Bright*, p. 411.
47 Walling: *Diaries of John Bright*, p. 344.
48 Bright to The O'Donoghue, 20 January 1872, quoted in Robertson: *John Bright*, Vol. III, p. 107.
49 Speech by Disraeli, Manchester, 3 April 1872, quoted in Walling: *Diaries of John Bright*, p. 354.
50 Trevelyan: *John Bright*, p. 413.
51 Walling: *Diaries of John Bright*, p. 356.
52 HC Deb, 26 August 1880, vol. 256, c182.
53 Walling: *Diaries of John Bright*, p. 448.
54 Ibid., p. 450.
55 Walling: *Diaries of John Bright*, p. 451.
56 Ibid., p. 452.
57 Ibid., p. 453.
58 Ibid.
59 Life of Sir Charles Dilke, Vol. I, p. 362, quoted in Walling: *Diaries of John Bright*, p. 453.
60 Walling: *Diaries of John Bright*, p. 454.
61 Ibid.
62 Ibid., p. 455.
63 Ibid.
64 Ibid., p. 456.
65 See the essay by the former Clerk of the House of Commons, Sir Edward Fellowes, entitled 'The Commons in Transition', ed. A. Harry Hanson and Bernard Crick (London, 1970)
66 Walling: *Diaries of John Bright*, p. 457.
67 Robertson: *John Bright*, Vol. III, p. 242.
68 O'Brien: *John Bright*, p. 78.
69 Ibid., pp. 78–80.
70 Walling: *Diaries of John Bright*, p. 460.
71 Ibid., p. 465.
72 Ibid., p. 461, fn 4.
73 Ibid., p. 462.
74 Ibid., p. 463.
75 Ibid.
76 Ibid., p. 468.
77 Ibid., p. 469.
78 Ibid., p. 470.
79 Robertson: *John Bright*, Vol. III, pp. 253–5.
80 HC Deb, 30 March 1882, vol. 268, cc314–27.
81 Walling: *Diaries of John Bright*, p. 478.
82 Ibid., p. 479.

Chapter 9: Home Rule, Party Splits and the End

1   Powell, Enoch, *Joseph Chamberlain* (London, 1977), p. 151.
2   Quinault, R., 'John Bright and Joseph Chamberlain', *The Historical Journal* 28/3/September (1985), pp. 623–46, 645.
3   HC Deb, 29 March 1889, vol. 334, c1177.
4   Travis Mills, J., *John Bright and the Quakers*, Vol. II (London, 1935), p. 100.
5   Ibid.,Vol. II, p. 114.
6   Chamberlain, Joseph, 'The Next Page of the Liberal Programme' (1874), p. 417, quoted in Quinault: 'Bright and Chamberlain', p. 261.
7   Chamberlain to Gladstone, 21 December 1883, quoted in Quinault: 'Bright and Chamberlain', p. 633.
8   Chamberlain, Joseph, *A Political Memoir 1880–92*, ed. from the original manuscript by C. H. D. Howard (London, 1953), pp. 2–3.
9   Chamberlain to Bright, 15 July 1882, quoted in Quinault: 'Bright and Chamberlain', p. 637.
10 Chamberlain to Bright, 5 January 1883, quoted in Quinault: 'Bright and Chamberlain', p. 638.
11 *The Times*, 14 June 1883.
12 Chamberlain to Bright, 14 January 1884, quoted in Quinault: 'Bright and Chamberlain', p. 638.
13 Hancock, W. K., *Smuts: The Sanguine Years, 1870–1919* (Cambridge, 1962), quoted in Sturgis, James L. *John Bright and the Empire* (London, 1969), p. 189.
14 Quinault: 'Bright and Chamberlain', p. 645.
15 Walling, R. A. J. (ed.), *The Diaries of John Bright* (London, 1930), p. 495.
16 Ibid., p. 501.
17 Ibid., p. 502.
18 Ibid., p. 501.
19 HC Deb, 24 March, 1884, vol. 286, cc640–8.
20 Bright to Rupert Potter, 21 February 1885, quoted in the *Pall Mall Gazette*, 2 April 1889, p. 1, col. c.
21 Walling: *Diaries of John Bright*, p. 525.
22 Ibid., p. 535.
23 The Duchess of Marlborough to Jennie Churchill, 3 November 1885, quoted in Cooke, Alistair, *A Gift from the Churchills: The Primrose League, 1883–2004* (London, 2010), p. 34.
24 Churchill, Winston Spencer, *Lord Randolph Churchill* (London, 1906), Vol. I, pp. 467–8.
25 The League was dissolved in 2004.
26 Cornwallis-West, Mrs, *Reminiscences of Lady Randolph Churchill*, p. 129, quoted in Cooke: *Gift from the Churchills*, pp. 34–5.

27 Cooke: *Gift from the Churchills*, p. 38.
28 Ibid.
29 Churchill: *Lord Randolph Churchill*, Vol. II, p. 116.
30 Quinault: 'Bright and Chamberlain', p. 628.
31 Bogdanor, Vernon, *The People and the Party System: The Referendum and Electoral Reform in British Politics* (Cambridge, 1981), pp. 102–3.
32 HC Deb, 4 July 1917, vol. 95, c1186.
33 Chamberlain to Bright, 5 February 1886, quoted in Quinault: 'Bright and Chamberlain', p. 640.
34 Robbins, Keith, *John Bright* (London, 1979), p. 253.
35 Walling: *Diaries of John Bright*, p. 535.
36 Ibid., pp. 536–7.
37 Ibid., p. 539.
38 Ibid., p. 540.
39 Bright to Gladstone, 13 May 1886, quoted in Morley, John, *The Life of William Ewart Gladstone*, Vol. III (London, 1903), pp. 327–9.
40 Bright to Whitbread, 17 May 1886, quoted in Trevelyan, G. M., *The Life of John Bright* (London, 1913), pp. 452–4.
41 Walling: *Diaries of John Bright*, p. 543.
42 Chamberlain to Bright, 30 May 1886, quoted in Quinault: 'Bright and Chamberlain', p. 642.
43 Bright to Chamberlain, 31 May 1886, quoted in Trevelyan: *John Bright*, p. 454–5.
44 Chamberlain to J. A. Bright, 16 January 1899, quoted in Trevelyan: *John Bright*, pp. 455–6.
45 Bright to Chamberlain, 1 June 1886, quoted in Trevelyan: *John Bright*, p. 456.
46 Bright to Chamberlain, 5 June 1886, quoted in Trevelyan: *John Bright*, pp. 456–7.
47 Bright to Chamberlain, 9 June 1886, quoted in Trevelyan: *John Bright*, pp. 457–8.
48 Chamberlain to Bright, 9 June 1886, quoted in Quinault: 'Bright and Chamberlain', p. 642.
49 Robbins: *John Bright*, p. 258.
50 Walling: *Diaries of John Bright*, p. 545.
51 Ibid., p. 544.
52 Ibid., p. 545. 'Patria et libertatis' translates as 'country and freedom'
53 Marsh, Peter T., *Joseph Chamberlain: Entrepreneur in Politics* (New Haven, 1994), p. 251.
54 Sturgis: *Bright and the Empire*, p. 165.
55 Walling: *Diaries of John Bright*, p. 546.
56 Ibid., p. 548.
57 Trevelyan: *John Bright*, p. 459.
58 Walling: *Diaries of John Bright*, p. 553.

59 Ibid.

60 Trevelyan: *John Bright*, p. 460.

61 Bright to Gladstone, 14 June 1887, quoted in Trevelyan: *John Bright*, pp. 460–1.

62 Walling: *Diaries of John Bright*, p. 557.

63 Ibid., p. 560.

64 HC Deb, 26 August 1887, vol. 320, cc33–152.

65 Walling: *Diaries of John Bright*, p. 551.

66 HC Deb, 24 March 1859, vol. 153, c791.

67 Walling: *Diaries of John Bright*, p. 298.

68 Trevelyan, G. M., *British History in the Nineteenth Century* (London, 1922), p. 349.

69 Albert Bright to Gladstone, 27 November 1887, quoted in Trevelyan: *John Bright*, p. 462.

70 Gladstone to Albert Bright, 27 November 1887, quoted in Trevelyan: *John Bright*, p. 463.

71 Trevelyan: *John Bright*, p. 464.

72 Walling: *Diaries of John Bright*, p. 549.

73 Ibid., p. 323.

74 Ibid., pp. 555–6.

75 Trevelyan: *John Bright*, p. 464.

76 *The New York Times*, 30 March 1889.

77 Trevelyan: *John Bright*, p. 464.

78 Walling: *Diaries of John Bright*, p. 561.

79 *The Times*, 30 Mar 1889, p. 11, col. f.

80 *The New York Times*, 31 March 1889.

81 Ibid., 29 March 1889.

82 See Marsh: *Chamberlain*, pp. 314–6.

83 Blake, Robert, *The Conservative Party from Peel to Churchill* (London, 1970), p. 59.

84 Robbins: *John Bright*, p. 262.

85 *The Times*, 22 June 1892, quoted in Quinault: 'Bright and Chamberlain', p. 644.

Bibliography

Ausubel, Herman, *John Bright: Victorian Reformer* (New York, 1966).

Barnett Smith, George, *The Life and Speeches of the Right Hon. John Bright, MP* (London, 1881).

Bianconi, M. O'C., and Watson, S. J, (Translated into Italian by P. del Bigio, 1993) *Bianconi: King of the Irish Roads* (Dublin, 1962).

Bigelow, John, *Retrospections of an Active Life* (New York, 1909–13).

Blake, Robert, *Disraeli* (London, 1966).

——, *The Conservative Party from Peel to Churchill* (London, 1970).

Bradford, Sarah, *Disraeli* (London, 1982).

Briggs, Asa, *The Age of Improvement* (2nd edn) (London, 2000).

——, *Victorian People: A Reassessment of Persons and Themes: 1851–67* (revd edn) (Chicago, 1972).

Bogdanor, Vernon, *The People and the Party System: The Referendum and Electoral Reform in British Politics* (Cambridge, 1981).

Brown, David, *Palmerston: A Biography* (Yale University Press 2010).

Carnegie, Andrew, *The Autobiography of Andrew Carnegie and the Gospel of Wealth*, (New York, 2006).

Cecil, Lord Robert Gascoyne, 'The Theories of Parliamentary Reform', *Oxford Essays* (London, 1858), pp. 52–79.

Chamberlain, Joseph, *A Political Memoir 1880–92*, ed. from the original manuscript by C. H. D. Howard (London, 1953).

Churchill, Winston Spencer, *Lord Randolph Churchill* (London, 1906).

Cooke, Alistair, *A Gift from the Churchills: The Primrose League, 1883–2004* (London, 2010).

Cox, Homersham, *The Reform Bills of 1866 and 1867* (London, 1868).

Dale, A. W. W., *The Life of R. W. Dale of Birmingham* (London, 1898).

Davis, John, *Richard Cobden's German Diaries* (Munich, 2007).

Disraeli, Benjamin, *Coningsby, or The New Generation* (London, 1844).

Donaldson Jordan, H., 'The reports of parliamentary debates, 1803–1908', *Economica* 34/November (1931), pp. 437–49.

Dudley, Thomas H., 'Three critical periods in our diplomatic relations with England during the late war', *Pennsylvania Magazine of History and Biography* 17 (1893), pp. 34–54.

Dutt, Romesh Chunder, *India in the Victorian Age: An Economic History of the People* (London, 1904).

Ferguson, Niall, *Civilization: The West and the Rest* (London, 2011).

Foreman, Amanda, *A World on Fire: An Epic History of Two Nations Divided* (London, 2010).

Gandhi, Mohandas Karamchand, *The Collected Works of Mahatma Gandhi* (Delhi, 1958).

Grant, James, *The British Senate: Random Recollections* (London, 1838).

Greeley, Horace, *The American Conflict: A History of the Great Rebellion in the United States of America* (Hartford, 1860–64).

Hahn, Thomas, 'John Bright's letters to America at Rush Rhees Library', *University of Rochester Library Bulletin* 30/1/Autumn (1977), pp. 72–91.

Hawkins, Angus, *The Forgotten Prime Minister: The 14th Earl of Derby* (Oxford, 2008).

Hoppen, Theodore, *New Oxford History of England: The Mid-Victorian Generation 1846–1886* (London, 1998).

Jenkins, Roy, *Gladstone* (London, 1995).

Leventhal, F. M., *Respectable Radical: George Howell and Victorian Working Class Politics* (London, 1971).

Leech, H. J., *The Public Letters of John Bright* (London, 1885).

Longmate, Norman, *The Breadstealers: The Fight Against the Corn Laws, 1838–1846* (London, 1984).

Lucas, Edward, *The Life of Frederick Lucas MP* (London, 1886).

Magnus, Philip, *Gladstone: A Biography* (corrected edn) (London, 1960).

McCarthy, Justin, *Reminiscences* (London, 1899).

McLellan, David, *The Thought of Marx* (London, 1995).

Marsh, Peter T., *Joseph Chamberlain: Entrepreneur in Politics* (New Haven, 1994).

Marx, Karl and Engels, Frederick, *Collected Works* (London, 1975–2004).

Monypenny, William Flavelle and Buckle, George Earle, *The Life of Benjamin Disraeli, Earl of Beaconsfield* (London, 1916).

Moore, Frank, *Speeches of John Bright MP on the American Question* (Boston, 1865).

Morley, John, *The Life of William Ewart Gladstone* (London, 1903).

———, *The Life of Richard Cobden* (London, 1908).

Nye, John Vincent, 'The myth of free-trade Britain and fortress France: tariffs and trade in the nineteenth century', *The Journal of Economic History* 51/1/March (1991), pp. 23–46.

O'Brien, R. Barry, *John Bright: A Monograph* (London, 1910).

Penman, John Simpson, *The Irresistible Movement of Democracy* (New York, 1923).

Phillips, Melanie, *The Ascent of Woman: A History of the Suffragette Movement* (London, 2003).

Pierce, Edward L., *Memoir and Letters of Charles Sumner* (Boston, 1877–93).

Pillai, P. N. Raman, 'John Bright and India', *Indian Review* XII/8/August (1911), pp. 608–16.

Powell, Enoch, *Joseph Chamberlain* (London, 1977).

Prentice, Archibald, *The History of the Anti-Corn Law League* (London, 1853).

Prest, John M., *Lord John Russell* (London, 1972).

Quinault, R., 'John Bright and Joseph Chamberlain', *The Historical Journal* 28/3/September (1985), pp. 623–46.

Randall, J. G., *Lincoln the Liberal Statesman* (New York, 1947).

Read, Donald, *Cobden and Bright: A Victorian Political Partnership* (London, 1967).

Riddell, Peter, *In Defence of Politicians (In Spite of Themselves)* (London, 2011).

Ridley, Jasper, *Lord Palmerston* (London, 1970).

Robbins, Keith, *John Bright* (London, 1979).

Roberts, Andrew, *Salisbury: Victorian Titan* (London, 1999).

Roberts, Stephen, *The Chartist Prisoners: The Radical Lives of Thomas Cooper (1805–1892) & Arthur O'Neill (1819–1896)* (Oxford, 2008).

Robertson, W., *Life and Times of the Right Hon. John Bright* (London, 1884).

Rose, J. H., Newton, A. P. and Benians, E. A. (eds), *The Cambridge History of the British Empire, Volume Two: The Growth of the New Empire, 1783–1870* (Cambridge University Press, 1940).

Russell, William Howard, *My Diary North and South* (Boston, 1863).

Sandburg, Carl, *Abraham Lincoln: The Prairie Years and The War Years* (New York, 1982).

Saunders, Robert, *Democracy and the Vote in British Politics, 1848-1867: The Making of the Second Reform Act* (Ashgate 2011).

Silver, Arthur, *Manchester Men and Indian Cotton, 1847–1872* (Manchester, 1966).

Smiles, Samuel, *Self Help with Illustrations of Character and Conduct* (New York, 1860).

Smith, F. B., *The Making of the Second Reform Bill* (Cambridge University Press, 1966).

Southall, Humphrey, 'Agitate! Agitate! Organise! Political travellers and the construction of a national politics, 1839–1880', *Transactions of the Institute of British Geographers*, New Series 21/1 (1996), pp. 177–93.

Sturgis, James L., *John Bright and the Empire* (London, 1969).

Tallack, William, *Howard Letters and Memories* (London, 1905).

Taylor, A. J. P., *Essays in English History* (London, 1976).

Thorold Rogers, James E., *Speeches On Questions of Public Policy by the Right Honourable John Bright MP* (London, 1898).

Travis Mills, J., *John Bright and the Quakers* (London, 1935).

Trevelyan, G. M., *The Life of John Bright* (London, 1913).

———, *British History in the Nineteenth Century, 1782-1901* (London, 1922).

———, *An Autobiography and Other Essays* (London, 1949).

Trueblood, David Elton, *Abraham Lincoln: Theologian of American Anguish* (New York, 1973).

Vincent, John, *The Formation of the Liberal Party 1857–1868* (London, 1972).

Walling, R. A. J. (ed.), *The Diaries of John Bright* (London, 1930).

Washington, Booker T., *Frederick Douglass* (London, 1906).

Watt, Francis, *Life and Opinions of the Right Hon. John Bright* (London, 1886).

Woodward, Llewellyn, *The Age of Reform* (2nd edn) (Oxford, 1962).

Wyke, Terry, *A Hall For All Seasons: A History of the Free Trade Hall* (Manchester, 1996).

Index